Nietzsche and Epicurus

Also Available from Bloomsbury

Nietzsche and Friendship, Willow Verkerk
Understanding Nietzsche, Understanding Modernism, ed. Brian Pines and Douglas Burnham
Nietzsche and The Antichrist: Religion, Politics, and Culture in Late Modernity, ed. Daniel Conway
Conflict and Contest in Nietzsche's Philosophy, ed. Herman Siemens and James Pearson
Nietzsche's Search for Philosophy: On the Middle Writings, Keith Ansell-Pearson
Epicurus and the Singularity of Death: Defending Radical Epicureanism, David B. Suits
Health and Hedonism in Plato and Epicurus, Kelly Arenson

Nietzsche and Epicurus

Nature, Health and Ethics

Edited by
Vinod Acharya and Ryan J. Johnson

BLOOMSBURY ACADEMIC
LONDON • NEW YORK • OXFORD • NEW DELHI • SYDNEY

BLOOMSBURY ACADEMIC
Bloomsbury Publishing Plc
50 Bedford Square, London, WC1B 3DP, UK
1385 Broadway, New York, NY 10018, USA
29 Earlsfort Terrace, Dublin 2, Ireland

BLOOMSBURY, BLOOMSBURY ACADEMIC and the Diana logo are trademarks of
Bloomsbury Publishing Plc

First published in Great Britain 2020
This paperback edition published in 2021

Copyright © Vinod Acharya, Ryan J. Johnson, and Contributors 2020

Vinod Acharya and Ryan J. Johnson have asserted their right under the Copyright, Designs and Patents Act, 1988, to be identified as Editors of this work.

For legal purposes the Acknowledgements on p. vii constitute an extension of this copyright page.

Cover design by Charlotte Daniels
Cover image © Dr_Microbe / Getty Images

All rights reserved. No part of this publication may be reproduced or transmitted in any form or by any means, electronic or mechanical, including photocopying, recording, or any information storage or retrieval system, without prior permission in writing from the publishers.

Bloomsbury Publishing Plc does not have any control over, or responsibility for, any third-party websites referred to or in this book. All internet addresses given in this book were correct at the time of going to press. The author and publisher regret any inconvenience caused if addresses have changed or sites have ceased to exist, but can accept no responsibility for any such changes.

A catalogue record for this book is available from the British Library.

A catalog record for this book is available from the Library of Congress.

ISBN: HB: 978-1-3500-8630-2
PB: 978-1-3502-7916-2
ePDF: 978-1-3500-8631-9
eBook: 978-1-3500-8632-6

Typeset by Deanta Global Publishing Services, Chennai, India

To find out more about our authors and books visit www.bloomsbury.com and sign up for our newsletters.

Contents

Acknowledgements	vii
Notes on contributors	viii
Abbreviations	x

Introduction *Vinod Acharya and Ryan J. Johnson*   1

Part One Encounters: Body, mood, geography and the aesthetic

1 The philosophical literature after Plato: literary prose and philosophical style – The case of Epicurus *Carlotta Santini*   11

2 The Gastrosophists! A seven-course meal with Epicurus and Nietzsche *Ryan J. Johnson*   26

3 'Wisdom that walks in bodily form': Nietzsche's travels with Epicurus *Jill Marsden*   38

4 Epicurean gardens and Nietzsche's white seas *Babette Babich*   52

5 What reason is there in the body?: Bodily suffering and happiness *Céline Leboeuf*   68

Part Two Comparative studies

6 Eternal recurrence: Epicurean oblivion, Stoic consolation, Nietzschean cultivation *Michael Ure and Thomas Ryan*   81

7 Nietzsche and Guyau on the temporality of Epicurean pleasure *Federico Testa* 96

8 Nietzsche, Hobbes and the tradition of political Epicureanism: Morality, religion and the social contract *Paul Bishop*   110

9 Passionate individuation: Epicurean self-cultivation in Mill and Nietzsche *Matthew James Dennis*   125

Part Three Appropriations and ambivalences

10 'And Epicurus triumphs anew': On Nietzsche's *Daybreak* *Vinod Acharya* 143

11 Enjoying riddles: Epicurus as a forerunner of the idea of gay science? *Patrick Wotling* 159

12 Great politics and the unnoticed life: Nietzsche and Epicurus on the boundaries of cultivation *Peter S. Groff* 172

Part Four Critical assessments

13 Nietzsche con/tra Epicurus: The necessity of noble suffering for intoxication with life *Michael J. McNeal* 189

14 'The milieu in which he moved as a foreign figure': Nietzsche's revaluation of Epicurus *Daniel Conway* 205

Bibliography 221
Index 241

Acknowledgements

First and foremost, we acknowledge the free spirit who set this project in motion: Keith Ansell-Pearson. Keith has been an inspiration for us personally, as he is probably the most original voice in Nietzsche studies today. Keith generated the momentum for this book, and we are honoured to bring to completion the book he started. We also express gratitude to all our contributors. Each of them worked with us through our often-tedious requests, and we hope that the final product is well worth their efforts. We are grateful to the anonymous reviewer for Bloomsbury Press for their helpful comments. Thanks also to Liza Thompson, Frankie Mace and Lucy Russell at Bloomsbury for trusting us as we assumed control of the volume, and for their help seeing it to publication. We thank Jonathan Shaw and Pierce Johnson, and Madison Aycock philosophy students at Elon University, for their tireless efforts formatting and indexing this text. Most of all, we thank our partners and families – Saya and Summer Acharya, and Erin Rutherford. It is their daily love, support and tolerance that give us a *why* to live, which allows us to bear any and every *how*.

Parts of Jill Marsden's paper have been published as 'In Proximity to Epicurus: Nietzsche's Discovery of the Past Within', *The Agonist*, X (II): 11–24.

A version of Peter Groff's essay was published as 'Great Politics and the Unnoticed Life: Nietzsche and Epicurus on the Boundaries of Cultivation', *The Agonist*, X (II): 59–74.

Contributors

Vinod Acharya is Senior Instructor in the Philosophy Department at Seattle University, USA. He teaches and writes on Nietzsche, various topics in the history of philosophy, contemporary philosophy and the philosophy of science and technology. He is the author of *Nietzsche's Meta-Existentialism* (De Gruyter, 2014).

Babette Babich is Professor of Philosophy at Fordham University in New York City. Among her books are *The Hallelujah Effect* (2016), *Words in Blood, Like Flowers* (2006), and the edited collection, *Reading David Hume's 'Of the Standard of Taste'* (2019).

Paul Bishop is William Jacks Chair of Modern Languages at the University of Glasgow. He is the author of *German Political Thought and the Discourse of Platonism* (Palgrave Macmillan, 2019), *On the Blissful Islands with Nietzsche & Jung* (Routledge 2017) and *Ludwig Klages and the Philosophy of Life* (Routledge 2017), and editor of *A Companion to Friedrich Nietzsche, Life and Works* (Camden House 2012).

Daniel Conway is Professor of Philosophy and Humanities and Affiliate Professor of Religious Studies, Film Studies and Law at Texas A&M University (USA).

Matthew James Dennis is a Marie Skłodowska-Curie Research Fellow at TU Delft in the Netherlands. He works on how emerging technologies affect our practical lives, especially their potential for character development and personal transformation. He has previously published articles on Foucault, Deleuze, Nietzsche and Spinoza, and was the winner of the ASCP's Postgraduate Essay Prize in 2017.

Peter S. Groff is Associate Professor of Philosophy at Bucknell University. He has written on Nietzsche, Islamic philosophy and comparative questions across traditions. His most recent scholarship focuses on cultivating an intercultural dialogue of sorts between Nietzsche, select classical Islamic philosophers and certain Greek and Hellenistic sources regarding philosophy as a way of life.

Ryan J. Johnson is Assistant Professor of Philosophy at Elon University in North Carolina. He is the author of *The Deleuze-Lucretius Encounter* (Edinburgh 2017), *Deleuze, A Stoic* (Edinburgh 2020), contributing co-editor of *The Movement of Nothingness* (Davies Group 2012) and of *Contemporary Encounters with Ancient Metaphysics* (Edinburgh 2017).

Céline Leboeuf is Assistant Professor of Philosophy at Florida International University. Her research on embodiment lies at the intersection of the critical philosophy of race, feminist philosophy and phenomenology.

Jill Marsden is Senior Lecturer in the School of the Arts at the University of Bolton, United Kingdom. She is the author of *After Nietzsche: Notes Towards a Philosophy of Ecstasy* (Palgrave Macmillan, 2002) and an assortment of essays on Nietzsche. She is currently working on the concept of 'literary thinking'.

Michael J. McNeal is a native of Colorado and an independent scholar who teaches as an adjunct instructor at various universities on its Front Range. He publishes on Nietzsche's thought, international affairs and education. His current research examines nihilism, reactionary populism and the exacerbation of both by environmental degradation and globalization.

Thomas Ryan completed a PhD in Philosophy at Monash University and the University of Warwick in 2018 with a thesis titled *The Affirmation of Eros: Passion and Eternity in Friedrich Nietzsche's The Gay Science*.

Carlotta Santini (1984) is tenured researcher (*Chargé de recherche*) at the CNRS and at the École Normale Supérieure in Paris. She is editor of the philological Nachlass of Friedrich Nietzsche in Italy (Adelphi) and France (*Les Belles Lettres*). Her field of research is nineteenth-century German culture and Reception of Antiquity.

Federico Testa is Early Career Fellow at the Institute of Advanced Study at the University of Warwick, where he currently teaches in the departments of philosophy and sociology. His main interests are post-Kantian philosophy, ethics and political and social theory. His research also explores the modern and contemporary receptions of ancient philosophy. He has published pieces on Foucault, Nietzsche, Canguilhem, Guyau, Hadot and others.

Michael Ure is Senior Lecturer in the School of Social Sciences, Monash University. He is the author of *Nietzsche's Therapy* (Lexington 2008), *Nietzsche's The Gay Science* (Cambridge University Press 2019) and many essays in the history of philosophy and political theory.

Patrick Wotling graduated from the Paris École Normale Supérieure, and currently is Professor of Contemporary Philosophy at Reims University. He is the author of *Nietzsche et le problème de la civilisation* (1995, 2012), *La philosophie de l'esprit libre* (2008, 2019), *Dictionnaire Nietzsche* (in cooperation with Céline Denat, 2013) and *'Oui, l'homme fut un essai'. La philosophie de l'avenir selon Nietzsche* (2016).

Abbreviations

Nietzsche

A	*The Anti-Christ*
AOM	*Assorted Opinions and Maxims/ Mixed Opinions and Maxims*
BAW	*Werke und Briefe: Historisch-kritische Gesamtausgabe* (references include the volume number and page)
BGE	*Beyond Good and Evil*
BT	*The Birth of Tragedy* (references to the 1886 Preface ('An Attempt at Self-Criticism') is indicated with the abbreviation AS followed by the relevant section number).
CW	*The Case of Wagner*
D	*Daybreak/Dawn*
DS	*David Strauss*
EH	*Ecce Homo* (references include an abbreviated section name)
FEI	*On the Future of our Educational Institutions*
GM	*On the Genealogy of Morality/Morals*
GS	*The Gay Science*
HH	*Human, All Too Human* (Vol. I)
HL	*On the Use and Disadvantage of History for Life*
KGW	*Werke: Kritische Gesamtausgabe* (references include the division and volume numbers, followed by the page number)
KSA	*Sämtliche Werke: Kritische Studienausgabe* (references include the volume number, followed by the fragment number, and any relevant aphorism; or simply, the volume and page number)
KSB	*Sämtliche Briefe: Kritische Studienausgabe* (references include the volume, followed by the letter number)
NCW	*Nietzsche Contra Wagner* (References include the relevant chapter title)
PTAG	*Philosophy in the Tragic Age of the Greeks*
RWB	*Richard Wagner in Bayreuth*
SE	*Schopenhauer as Educator*

TI	*Twilight of the Idols* (references include an abbreviated chapter title, followed by the section or the aphorism number, if any)
TL	'On Truth and Lies in an Extra-Moral Sense'
UM	*Untimely Meditations*
WP	*The Will to Power*
WS	*The Wanderer and His Shadow*
Z	*Thus Spoke Zarathustra* (references to Z list the part number, followed by an abbreviated chapter title and the relevant section number when applicable)

Note: References to Nietzsche's texts are to sections or aphorisms, not page numbers, unless stated otherwise. For some texts, page numbers are provided in addition to section numbers for greater specificity. Where Nietzsche's prefaces are cited, the letter *P* is used followed by any relevant section number.

Epicurus

LH	Letter to Herodotus
LP	Letter to Pythocles
LM	Letter to Menocoeus
PD	Principal Doctrines
VC	Vatican Collection

Introduction

Vinod Acharya and Ryan J. Johnson

Why Nietzsche and Epicurus?

Why Nietzsche *and* Epicurus? Why devote an entire book to the connection between the German philosopher of the will to power and the hedonist from Samos who practised the tranquil life? Indeed, it appears that the two philosophers hold views that are fundamentally at odds with one another. While Epicurus advocates for the elimination of pain and the disciplining of desires, Nietzsche affirms the excesses of Dionysian joy and the inevitability of great suffering for the creation of values. While Epicurean science appears to make metaphysical pronouncements about the structure of the cosmos, Nietzsche attacks metaphysical truths and emphasizes that science, too, inevitably relies on fictions and falsifications. And while Epicurus endorses a modest life and withdrawal from politics, Nietzsche's thought anticipates a 'great politics'. A thinker of Heidegger's stature says this about the Epicurus–Nietzsche connection:

> In truth, of course, the world is no garden, and for Zarathustra it dare not be one, especially if by 'garden' we mean an enchanting haven for the flight from being. Nietzsche's conception of the world does not provide the thinker with a sedate residence in which he can putter about unperturbed, like the philosopher of old, Epicurus, in his 'garden'. (1991: v.2, 52)

We contend that such dismissals are misleading. Not only do they ignore Nietzsche's lifelong fascination with and admiration for Epicurean thought and its historical significance but also, more importantly, they neglect key Epicurean impulses behind Nietzsche's philosophical development and practice. Epicurus's influence is particularly evident on Nietzsche's so-called middle-period writings, spanning roughly from the publication of the first volume of *Human, All Too Human* in 1878 to *The Gay Science* in 1882. And since, as Keith Ansell-Pearson has noted, 'the middle writings have been sorely neglected ... and key questions concerning their character and the role they occupy in Nietzsche's thinking as a whole are often marginalized',[1] there has also been a general disregard for the Nietzsche–Epicurus relationship, at least until quite recently.[2]

One side effect of this disregard is the tendency to exaggerate the excesses of Nietzsche's thought; another consequence is to discount the relevance of

Epicureanism for diagnosing modern discontent and for developing ways to combat it, something Nietzsche well recognized. This is not to deny that Nietzsche became increasingly critical of Epicurus, particularly in his post-Zarathustra works, but simply to emphasize that Nietzsche's attack must be situated in the context of his admiration for the Hellenistic philosopher, which did not entirely vanish even in his later writings.[3]

The chapters collected in this volume seek to rectify these shortcomings in Nietzsche and Epicurus scholarship. By examining Nietzsche's evolving relationship to Epicurean thought, from his earliest lectures to his published writings to his final appraisals, this volume reveals an essential and inspiring link between two seemingly incompatible thinkers. In doing so, the current volume also calls into question any rigid periodization of Nietzsche's philosophy into early, middle and late period by revealing deep and fascinating continuities in his thought. Periodization is taken to be an issue, which is addressed in several fruitful ways through the focus on Nietzsche's evaluation of Epicurus, rather than a settled matter.

We isolate two interconnected themes that determine Nietzsche's interest in Epicurus: a novel conception of nature in contrast to modernity's science of mathematized nature, and an ethics of self-cultivation, which opposes the moral bankruptcy and decadence of contemporary subjectivity.

Epicurus and modern malaise

Even during the supposed 'enlightened' middle period of Nietzsche's thought,[4] where Nietzsche defends science, reason and the will to knowledge in his battle against religion, morality and metaphysics, he cautions against the pursuit of truth for its own sake (see HH 31–4; D 535; GS 110). Although Nietzsche's later genealogical account traces modern 'will to truth' back to Christianity and Platonism (GS 344, 357; GM III: 24–5, 27), one of its original expressions in the history of science is to be found in Francis Bacon. It is demonstrated in Bacon's declaration of the majestic power of experimental science to establish absolute dominion over nature, which became modernity's epistemological imperative.[5]

The mechanization of nature exemplified in Descartes's reduction of animals to machines, the interpretation of nature as a 'mathematical manifold'[6] in Galileo and Newton and the ensuing revolutions of industry and modern technology increasingly alienated humans from nature and vice versa. As modern humans found themselves stuck with mere representations of nature (now reduced to a quantifiable object) rather than nature itself, scepticism became the greatest threat. Not directly and immediately, but only through conceptual and socio-moral abstraction, could one experience the world, as Nietzsche's critique of our lack of regard for the 'closest things' (*nächste Dinge*) emphasizes (WS 5, 6).[7]

Consider what Nietzsche writes in an aphorism entitled, 'Forgotten nature': 'We speak of nature and forget to include ourselves: we ourselves are nature, *quand même*. It follows that nature is something different from what we think of when we speak its name' (WS 327). Failing to see ourselves as part of nature, not only do we misconceive nature but we also become alienated *from ourselves*. A symptom of this self-alienation is the fragmentation of the subject, betrayed, for example, by the division of Kant's three *Critiques* – on truth, goodness and beauty – which implies three different and irreconcilable modes of thinking and being in the world.

Nietzsche analyses the fragmentation of the subject in terms of contemporary valuelessness. While in prehistoric and pre-modern societies, humans resorted to otherworldly constructs (which entailed, among other things, a spiritualizing of nature, and therefore, a different kind of 'prejudice' than the modern one (D 31)) – out of ignorance, fear and the exigencies of self-preservation – these metaphysical fictions, nevertheless, generated, for the most part, coherent systems of practices, which secured the stability and unity of subjectivity in the context of a given community. For Nietzsche, Christianity's intervention, in particular, deeply undermines any genuine possibility for humans to continue to rely on moral–metaphysical fictionalizing in order to guide their earthly lives. Nevertheless, the contemporary subject remains an incoherent mishmash of transformed and attenuated values inherited from a long tradition, which no longer make possible true greatness or the elevation of the human animal. Nihilism poses a serious threat.

In the era of individualism, when the 'individual' becomes a universal category, individuality becomes impossible. As Walter Benjamin puts it, 'a person of the greatest individuality would turn out to be the exemplar of a type' (1999: 22). For Nietzsche, the way out of this paradox, out of life-denying weariness, is to affirm precisely that possibility of modernity, which signals its moral bankruptcy: its 'passion for knowledge' (D 429). Not only can we now inquire into things, the knowledge of which was previously forbidden or tainted by morality, but we can also experiment with different ways of being and evaluating. The key is to develop a new non-moral and anti-metaphysical conception of nature, which neither divinizes nature nor drives a chasm between it and humans (see GS 109). Here Epicurus is one of Nietzsche's great inspirations.

While technological developments may allow us to read more and more of the substantial fragments of Epicurus's *On Nature* (*Peri phuseôs*), a major treatise containing thirty-seven papyrus rolls, which was found among the charred papyrus fragments at the Villa of the Papyri at Herculaneum, we may provide a general sketch of Epicurus's view from currently available materials.[8] The Greek word for nature, *phusis* (φύσις), denotes the physical stuff out of which things emerge and the organizing principle of this making, but its primary sense is growth or genesis. *Phusis* does not name a fixed and static thing, which may be subjected to quantitative domination and mathematical exhaustion, but, rather, the immeasurable power of matter that the Greeks regularly witnessed in the terrible storms and volcanic eruptions occurring around the Mediterranean. Seeking to contain these natural forces, Plato and Aristotle depicted nature as determinable through formal principles. Arguably, this drive to subdue nature eventually spawned modern science's will for domination.

While Epicurus sought to develop a coherent and convincing account of nature, he did not reach for immaterial, transcendent forms but, instead, cultivated a bodily appreciation for *phusis* using only the material principles of Democritus's atomism. Nature, for Epicurus, is an infinite swarm of atoms and void; however, he deviates from

Democritus in insisting on the phenomenon of the swerve or the 'clinamen', which has fascinated and irritated philosophers ever since. The clinamen is the infinitesimally slight indeterminate swerve of atoms that marks the production of the infinite variety of natural forms. Locating the swerve at the heart of matter, Epicurus formulated an account of *phusis* as productive indeterminacy. While nature follows distinct patterns of production, the swerve inherent to matter entails an indeterminacy of knowledge, which precludes mathematical or conceptual exhaustion (see LP 86–8).[9] Further, the swerve also entails or enables freedom, in both humans and animals.[10]

Since natural kinds are not perfectly determinable through transcendent principles, Epicurus offers a different account of individuation: limits. A major part of Epicurean science is determining the genesis of individuals by locating the limits of nature.[11] The way to do this is not through formal principles, either Platonic forms or mathematical idealization, but through sensation. Epicurean science is an art of sensation. We know nature not through formalization or quantification but through affects.[12] Truths are in sensation (see LH 38–40, 50–2). Science is thus a matter of sensuous encounters, of sculpting one's engagement with the world according to the limits nature sanctions, not the quantities we impose on it. Epicurean physics, in short, is a bodily, not a cognitive, science. The Epicurean physicist does not dominate or divinize nature but cultivates sensory practices in the garden. Rather than alienated and fragmented, an Epicurean sees herself as part of nature, as conditioned by nature's limits, a being generated by the same material processes that produce earth, air, animals, towers and all things.

For Epicurus, this implies that the knowledge of nature is not unconnected to or alienated from the human quest to live a good life. On the contrary, it is necessary for the pursuit of tranquillity (PD XII); it endorses an ethical orientation, a certain care of the self with itself, an exercise of freedom, a practice of living, which is an 'art', since it issues no absolutely set guidelines for living well. Nietzsche was inspired by this Epicurean link between knowledge and self-cultivation, especially in his middle-period writings, in his quest to revitalize modern subjectivity.

Contributions

The present volume, which is divided into four parts, features chapters that explore different aspects of the themes of nature and/or ethics in problematizing the Epicurus–Nietzsche connection. Part I addresses the question of what draws Nietzsche to Epicurus by focusing on the affinities in the bodily, material, environmental and aesthetic dimensions of their respective thought. Chapters here explore Nietzsche's interpretation of Epicurean style, the practices of eating and thinking in both philosophers, the Epicurean inspiration behind Nietzsche's physical style of thought, themes of travel, geography and constitution, the importance of Nietzsche's hermeneutic philology, his interpretation of Epicurean sensual pleasures, and the relationship between health, suffering and philosophy in both philosophers. Chapters in Part II draw comparisons between Nietzsche's view of Epicurus and those of other philosophers, such as Jean-Marie Guyau, Thomas Hobbes and John Stuart Mill, and schools of thought such as Stoicism. Topics discussed here include eternal recurrence and its ethical significance, the temporality of Epicurean pleasure, the social contract, passionate individuation and human flourishing. Chapters in Part III examine substantial Epicurean themes in Nietzsche's middle-period writings such as the ethics of self-cultivation and the embodiment of Epicurean virtues, Nietzsche's Epicurean passion for knowledge and his non-dogmatic pursuit of truth, and Nietzsche's practice of the Epicurean, apolitical, hidden way of life. Some of these chapters also highlight key tensions and ambivalences in Nietzsche's attitude to the philosopher from Samos, anticipating discussions in the concluding Part IV. The final two chapters assess Nietzsche's critique of Epicurus, particularly in the post-Zarathustra works, and examine how he attempts to move beyond his Greek predecessor, despite his continuing admiration for him.

Part I Encounters: Body, mood, geography and the aesthetic

Focusing on Nietzsche's early lectures on ancient Greek literature, **Carlotta Santini's** contribution examines Nietzsche's evaluation of Epicurus, the writer and his style, in the context of the literary landscape of antiquity. Santini demonstrates that, for Nietzsche, the Epicurean style – clarity and precision in prose, stripped of rhetoric embellishments and poetic artifices – corresponded to a particularly advanced stage in the evolution of the Greek scientific spirit and the thirst for knowledge. Further, Santini emphasizes that the simplicity and 'naturalness' of Epicurus's style is a product of elaborate finesse, care and effort, and it serves as an inspiration for Nietzsche's own philosophical practice.

Taking up Epicurus's joyous affirmation of the manifold materiality of eating pleasures and Nietzsche's interrogation of the moral effects of food, **Ryan J. Johnson** offers an Epicurean–Nietzschean philosophical way of eating and thinking called *gastrosophia*, the joyful wisdom of the belly, in Chapter 2. Organized as a seven-course philosophical meal, this chapter shows how Epicurus and Nietzsche are gastrosophist thinkers because they demonstrate how eating is a veritable way of *doing* philosophy. Baking Nietzsche's food metaphorics with a tradition of materialist thinking that Epicureanism inaugurates, Johnson sketches an ethics based on the 'laws of the stomach'.

In Chapter 3, **Jill Marsden** shows how the beginning of Nietzsche's aphoristic style of writing characterizing his middle period aligns with a material practice of thinking outside wherein walking becomes thinking. With a sensitivity to material conditions in which philosophy emerges, Marsden shows how Epicurus and Nietzsche are both attuned to the material practice of thinking outside. After discussing how Nietzsche's travels with Epicurus orient his thinking of body and earth, especially his philosophy of the 'nearest things', Marsden charts a thought path linking Epicurus to Nietzsche's reflections on the affirmation of life: *amor fati* as the affective precondition for Nietzsche's eternal return.

Nietzsche assesses the 'sensual pleasures of Epicurus' as his 'opulence': a 'tiny garden, figs, small cheeses, and three or four friends'. **Babette Babich**, in Chapter 4 begins by reviewing Nietzsche's hermeneutic philology and continues to explore the notion of Epicurus's recipe for happiness and certain ambiguities especially with respect to Epicurus's garden, including a reflection on constitution, geographic loci and the difference Nietzsche's own classical formation can make for us. Babich includes a reference to monumental history, between garden and sea.

In Chapter 5, **Céline Leboeuf** examines Nietzsche's remark that Epicurean philosophy is born out of continual suffering. Leboeuf elucidates Nietzsche's own view of philosophy as arising out of the sufferer's overcoming of their suffering, and therefore requiring the ability to switch between the perspectives of suffering and health, which is essential to his project of the revaluation of values. Leboeuf argues that the Epicurean cultivation of modest pleasures similarly signifies not only a negation of pain but also health and a particular way of life, which makes Epicurus a philosopher after Nietzsche's own heart.

Part II Comparative studies

In Chapter 6, **Michael Ure** and **Thomas Ryan** examine Epicurean, Stoic and Nietzschean accounts of the eternal recurrence and their ethical significance. Ure and Ryan show how the three accounts view recurrence from a therapeutic and ethical perspective but attribute to it different outcomes: Lucretius derives pleasure from the prospect of eternal oblivion, Seneca cultivates tranquil contemplation of fate and Nietzsche incites a craving for ourselves as artworks worthy of eternity. In all the three cases, eternal recurrence is deployed as a 'spiritual exercise' to suit their distinct therapeutic or transformative ends.

In Chapter 7, **Federico Testa** uses the figure of Epicurus as a lens through which to compare Jean-Marie Guyau and Nietzsche. Understanding Epicureanism as an intellectual force that re-emerges every time religious enthusiasm waxes and intellectual servitude wanes, Guyau emphasizes the Epicurean sage as an 'artist of happiness'. The middle-period Nietzsche finds in Epicurus a fellow traveller in the sea of suffering and the creator of a 'heroic-idyllic' model of philosophizing. Testa articulates the notions of time underlying Nietzsche's and Guyau's interpretations, tracking divergences and convergences in their reading of the temporality of pleasure in Epicurus.

Paul Bishop, in Chapter 8, addresses Nietzsche's ambiguous attitude towards Epicurus by triangulating these two thinkers with Hobbes. By focusing on their respective interpretations of politics, morality and the social contract, Bishop's study discerns various continuities between Epicurean philosophy and those of Hobbes and Nietzsche, while also emphasizing key specificities of each thinker's thought. Bishop maintains that ultimately it is the liberating characteristic of Epicureanism that makes Epicurus attractive to both Hobbes and Nietzsche, despite the glaring differences.

In contrast to contemporary accounts, which understand human flourishing in terms of exercising moral virtues, in Chapter 9 **Matthew James Dennis** explores how the kind of individuality that is most meaningfully expressed in the context of our passionate attachments is essential for flourishing. Dennis bases his analysis on key texts by Mill and Nietzsche, which were most influenced by Epicurus. Thus, in contrast to the dominant trend in modern virtue ethics that is decisively influenced by Socrates and Aristotle, Dennis grounds his alternate approach to human flourishing in an Epicurean-inspired tradition.

Part III Appropriations and ambivalences

In Chapter 10, **Vinod Acharya** suggests that *Daybreak* is the most Epicurean of Nietzsche's works. Acharya shows that in *Daybreak* Nietzsche employs key Epicurean concepts and strategies in his diagnosis of and resistance to the ongoing moral decay of contemporary subjectivity. In his attempt to revive the latter, Acharya argues, Nietzsche creatively cultivates in the modern context important Epicurean virtues such as *phronēsis*, self-sufficiency, magnanimity, honesty, courage and gratitude. Epicureanism, in contrast to the moral tradition, represents for Nietzsche a unique path to individuation involving nature, knowledge and pleasure.

In Chapter 11, **Patrick Wotling** distinguishes between the different senses of 'Epicurus' from those of 'Epicurean' in Nietzsche's text. While 'Epicurus' is celebrated for his passion for knowledge, he is also reproached for his negative conception of pleasure. The term 'Epicurean' for Nietzsche, argues Wotling, represents a champion of the 'gay science', a riddle lover who takes delight in thinking, but who also enjoys life's seductive inventiveness, and who, therefore, avoids a dogmatic worship of truth. From Nietzsche's perspective, therefore, Epicurus and his school were ultimately not 'Epicurean' enough.

In Chapter 12, **Peter S. Groff** focuses on Nietzsche's attitude towards an underacknowledged aspect of Epicurus's teachings: the controversial advice to 'live unnoticed'. While Nietzsche was familiar with this credo and took it to heart, Groff shows how it ultimately stood at odds with, and lost out to, his irresistible temptation to engage in great politics. Groff tracks and illuminates Nietzsche's conflicted appreciation for the virtues of the Epicurean unnoticed way of life.

Part IV Critical assessments

In Chapter 13, **Michael J. McNeal** attempts to explain how the resonance of Epicurus's way of life with Nietzsche's middle works are prima facie at odds with aspects of his mature thought. Synthesizing the breadth of recent scholarship on this issue, McNeal tracks Nietzsche's changing relationship with the Hellenistic hedonist. McNeal shows that although Nietzsche eventually replaces Epicurus's ethics of self-care as *ataraxia* with noble struggle and the agonistic striving for distinction, Nietzsche's fondness for Epicureanism persisted through his late works.

Daniel Conway explains Nietzsche's volte-face evaluation of Epicurus in Chapter 14. Realizing that his earlier enthusiasm was tinctured by illness, which prompted him to seek the relief of an idyllic life of modest pleasures, Nietzsche, upon recovering from illness, marshals the insights from his experience with decadence to solve the 'riddle of Epicurus'. Nietzsche's alternative history (absent the Apostle Paul) postulates how combining Jesus's pacific love and Epicurus's modest pleasures would have afforded an occidental version of Buddhism.

Notes

1. Ansell-Pearson (2018: 2).
2. Keith Ansell-Pearson leads the way here. See especially, Ansell-Pearson (2013, 2014b, 2015c, 2018).
3. See, for instance, GS 375 and A 58.
4. Recent studies on the middle works include Franco (2011), Cohen (2009), Abbey (2000) and more recently Ansell-Pearson (2018).
5. See Bacon (2000: Book. I, aphorisms 98 and 129).
6. Husserl (1970: 23).
7. In this introduction, we have used R. J. Hollingdale's translations of WS and D for Cambridge University Press.
8. Nietzsche knew of and was excited by the discovery at Herculaneum. In an August 1883 letter to Heinrich Köselitz, he writes, 'On Democritea and Epicurea – a world of research that is still not exhausted. … You know the Herculaneum library, whose papyri are being slowly and laboriously made to talk, is the library of an Epicurean; so there *are* hopes for the discovery of authentic writings by Epicurus!' See Letter 119 in Nietzsche (1996b) or KSB 6:460.
9. Refer to Vincenzo (1994: 390–1), Deleuze (2017) and Nail (2018: 195–201).
10. Consult Sedley (1983) and Purinton (1999). Also see, Michel Serres (2018) and Nail (2018: 201–5).
11. Morel (2010: 199); Johnson (2017: 237–9).
12. Morel (2000: 77).

Part One

Encounters: Body, mood, geography and the aesthetic

1

The philosophical literature after Plato: literary prose and philosophical style

The case of Epicurus

Carlotta Santini

Introduction[1]

The question of Nietzsche's relationship with Greek philosophy, or rather with specific figures and personalities of ancient philosophy, constitutes a complex field of study that has yet to be exhausted. Nietzsche engaged directly with many philosophers: Socrates and Plato in particular, Aristotle and the debate on the *Poetics* and even pre-Platonic philosophers such as Heraclitus. Within this panorama, the figure of Epicurus is perhaps not one of the most apparent. In fact, he received much less attention than the aforementioned ancient authors, and Nietzsche's attitude towards the philosopher from Samos can often be said to be ambiguous.

Nevertheless, Nietzsche's treatment of Epicurus can be considered in many ways exemplary. In a brief series of texts and excerpts, Nietzsche's reading of Epicurus reveals the same criticisms levelled towards ancient philosophy in general, which always manifest themselves on different levels: from metaphysical–theoretical to ethical–moral, social–historical to existential, through to stylistic and literary. In this chapter I will adopt this latter approach, focusing in particular on Nietzsche's criticism of Epicurus the 'writer' and his style, and reconstructing his role within the literary landscape of antiquity. I will base my analysis in particular on 1) Nietzsche's *Lessons on the History of Greek Literature*, given in Basel between 1874 and 1876; 2) some letters he exchanged with the musician Heinrich Köselitz (better known as Peter Gast) concerning Epicurus; and 3) on a group of *Posthumous Fragments* from 1874 (group 35), particularly significant for treating the question of style in relation to Epicurus. As we will see, this kind of historical–literary observation has important implications for the philosophical evaluation of the author.

Epicurus polygraphus

Among the few well-circumscribed textual passages concerning the figure of Epicurus, Nietzsche's letters to Heinrich Köselitz offer perhaps the best-known and most coherent context.[2] The first mention of the philosopher from Samos in his correspondence with the musician dates back to 1879, reaching its peak in 1883. In particular, in a letter dating from the end of August 1883 (KSB 6:460), Nietzsche comments with great enthusiasm on the 'news' (not especially up-to-the-minute if truth be told) of an archaeological discovery in the city of Herculaneum, which had brought to light an entire archive once belonging to a patrician of Epicurean sympathies.[3] Nietzsche's enthusiasm stemmed from his hope that the site would provide access, sooner or later, to fragments or even entire scrolls of Epicurean works.

What interested Nietzsche, therefore, was the possibility of having direct access to Epicurus's texts, to the *ipsissima verba*. This interest in the original (or the occasional Roman copy) had a double philological motive. The first and most obvious one was to draw directly from the source of Epicurean thought without having to go through 'Epicureans' or anti-Epicurean detractors (which always implies an interpretation or manipulation). Even today, in fact, our knowledge of Epicurean doctrine mostly passes through the simultaneously 'turbid and refined lens' of Lucretius (D 72) or that of the historical contenders to the Epicurean school, the Stoics – notably, as Nietzsche reminds us, through Seneca (KSB 6:446).[4] It is not only the idea of gaining access to Epicurus's thought that interests Nietzsche, however, but also the availability of his writings tout court; that is, the possibility of being able to read works written 'by the hand' of Epicurus. Nietzsche's primary interest in Epicurus is, in fact, an eminently literary one.

The 'irony of fame' (KSB 6:446) and the inscrutable *fatum libellorum* (KSA 1: 811) made that few testimonies and no complete works by one of the most prolific authors of antiquity have survived, despite the fact that Epicurus was best known for his writings. In his *Lessons on the History of Greek Literature*, Epicurus is mentioned in a list of the most famous 'polygraphs' of history, alongside others including the grammarian and poet Callimachus and the philosophers Chrysippus, Aristotle and Theophrastus. In Raphael's famous fresco *The School of Athens*, Epicurus is depicted surrounded by wine leaves (a Dionysian attribute) with his head bowed over a book, in the act of writing. Tradition recognizes him as the father of 300 books.[5]

In the wake of Diogenes Laertius, whose *Lives of Eminent Philosophers* represents the most important source for the life of Epicurus, Nietzsche reports that the philosopher's followers were particularly proud of their master, who was always original despite writing a lot. The ancient confrontation or even clash between Epicurus and the philosopher Chrysippus also focused on this particular aspect of polygraphy.

> Apollodorus of Athens in his Collection of Doctrines, wishing to show that what Epicurus wrote with force and originality unaided by quotations was far greater in amount than the books of Chrysippus, says, to quote his exact words, 'If one were to strip the books of Chrysippus of all extraneous quotations, his pages would be left bare.' So much for Apollodorus. Of Chrysippus the old woman who sat

beside him used to say, according to Diocles, that he wrote 500 lines a day. Hecato says that he came to the study of philosophy, because the property which he had inherited from his father had been confiscated to the king's treasury. (Diogenes Laertius 7.181)

In his text Diogenes Laertius warns us that many of the testimonies concerning Epicurus have been distorted by his detractors.[6] The news reported at the end of the quotation by Diocles and Hecato, for example, conceals two very precise criticisms that were levelled at Epicurus, and which can be summarized as follows: writing too much and writing tout court.

Let us start with the latter. Criticism of the practice of writing in the Greek world is a very complex issue, on which ancient authors expressed themselves on several occasions. Writing has been accused variously of being detrimental to memory, of providing an illusion of knowledge,[7] of weakening reasoning and of prejudicing philosophy,[8] which should only be carried out in the true dialectic. The Socratic Diktat, according to which philosophy is exercised only in free speech, was also one of the traditional elements used to distinguish the true philosophers from the false masters, the Sophists. Hecato's allusion to the economic hardships endured by Epicurus after the confiscation of his patrimony is a clear insinuation that risks placing him on an equal footing with the Sophists and those who, like them, commercialized knowledge through public teaching. The very act of writing can be compromising, according to Nietzsche, who once again quotes Plato in support of this thesis: 'You know yourself that the most influential and important men in our cities are ashamed to write speeches and leave writings behind them, through fear of being called sophists by posterity' (Plato 1913: 257d; KGW II/5, 31).[9]

But Epicurus himself would not have been insensitive to this anathema towards writing. One of the dictates of the 'Epicurean wise man', mentioned by Nietzsche in his *Lessons on the History of Greek Literature*, was, in fact, 'to leave written words behind him, but not to publish them'.[10] For example, a dialogue's transcription was intended to spread and facilitate its reception among the students of the Epicurean School, as well as to hand down to posterity a sort of portrait of the teacher; it could not and should not, however, go beyond its circle of sympathizers to become widespread in the public domain or, even worse, to become a business tool. Now, the extraordinary editorial fortune of Epicurean writing tells a different story. In fact, the unsatisfactory formulation of this ambiguous precept is proof in itself of the conflicting attitude of Epicurus – one of the most famous polygraphs of antiquity – towards writing. In a not dissimilar way, recalls Nietzsche, another famous opponent of writing in philosophy, Plato, 'wrote a lot for someone who considers writing only a beautiful παγκάλη πα|διά'.[11]

If Hecato insinuates that Epicurus, just like the Sophists, became a writer for venal reasons, even the information reported by Diocles, according to which the philosopher wrote up to 500 lines a day, conceals latent criticism: not only did Epicurus feel the reprehensible need to write but he also wrote a great deal, and wrote quickly. Throughout his lifetime Nietzsche repeatedly accused the contemporary publishing industry of being compulsive and bulimic. He is well known for his reserved attitude towards journalism, which swamped the world with books of dubious interest, devaluing literature and demeaning style.[12]

In his *Lessons on the History of Greek Literature* Nietzsche provides many examples in favour of parsimony in the art of writing, careful balance in the choice of vocabulary and ongoing honing of style. That prolificity (and prolixity) were rare and unwelcome in antiquity can be proven by an anecdote concerning the tragedian Euripides:

> Euripides once told a tragic poet that he had finished three verses in three days with great effort, to which the poet replied that he had instead composed a hundred verses. In response to these words Euripides replied: 'But here is the difference: your verses will only last three days, mine will last forever.' (KGW II/5, 123)[13]

But even the modern age offers Nietzsche some good examples of economy in writing: Goethe speaks of how, when writing the second part of *Faust*, he transcribed, in one good day, as many lines as his hand could cover (KGW II/5, 317).

Writing a lot and writing rapidly means writing badly, that is, without care, re-reading or leaving time for the language to settle down and the style to develop. The damage is first and foremost aesthetic, but it could easily become ethical since the absence of 'rumination' harms not only the language in question but also the thought processes developed and expressed through it. But Nietzsche's position towards Epicurus seems to suspend the judgement on this point. Epicurus wrote a lot, therefore he wrote badly? His detractors would certainly seem to think so. The grammarian Aristophanes judges Epicurus's way of writing as uncultivated (ἰδιωτικωτάτῃ) and Cicero, in *Brutus*, defines the Epicurean education as very unsuited to eloquence.[14]

Nietzsche is less strict on this point. This is not just a case of excessive writing or journalistic superficiality. Among the aforementioned duties attributed to the Epicurean sage, enumerated in Nietzsche's *Lessons on the History of Greek literature*, the second one warns against speaking well:

> οὔτε ῥητορεύειν καλῶς [Don't speak well]: so states another precept. Of course, the Epicurean sage is accused not only of being pure in expression, but also of being ἀμαθής [uncultivated]. The Epicurean wise man challenged the education of the time precisely in relation to linguistics and polyhistory.[15] Athen, XIII, 588 states: 'Knowing everything does not mean being an initiate.' Epicurus himself in his letter to Pythocles says: 'Raise your sails, my friend, and escape all kinds of culture.'[16]

A specific method lies behind the choice to write a great amount in a short space of time: 'The Stoics did not write well on purpose, the Epicureans did not write well out of principle' (KGW II/5, 31). Put in a slightly different way in the same lesson, we find:

> In this respect, the Stoics and the Epicureans followed the same path, with the Stoics employing a non-artistic style spontaneously and the Epicureans adopting the same style intentionally. Dion. Hal., *comp.*, 30, reports: 'No one has developed dialectics as much as Chrysippus and no one has written in a worse way. Epicurus followed the principle that the speaker should aim for clarity only: when the

inconstant artistic judgement is not taken into account it is not difficult to write.'
(KGW II/5, 216)

Epicurus therefore chose to deliberately ignore aesthetic needs and to concentrate only on achieving clarity in his writing.

Struggle for prose, struggle for science?

Since Epicurus wrote a lot, does this mean he was a bad writer? Nietzsche was not so sure of the validity of this particular axiom and, for this reason he claims, like in the letter to Köselitz, the possibility of 'reading' Epicurus. Three letters, 'extraordinarily beautiful and rich in content' (KGW II/5, 218), documented by Diogenes Laertius and attributed to Epicurus, invite Nietzsche to be cautious. Additionally, the philologist Valentin Rose recalls among the titles attributed to this author a dialogue tellingly entitled *Symposium*.[17] The clear references of this title to the tradition of Platonic dialogues, and to the genre of symposium dialogue that developed from them, invite us to think of the text as a philosophical one written in a particularly precise manner according to the dictates of rhetorical art and, therefore, with both philosophical and literary intentions in mind.

Epicurus therefore did not write badly; instead, he deliberately wrote poorly using little rhetoric. Nietzsche, following a principle that he established in 1868 and that he applied to his entire analysis of the history of Greek literature, was convinced that the evaluation of a particular style or author must take into account the reasons behind the author's choice of style:

> Style in philosophical writing. The assessment of the stylistic problem depends on what is required of the philosopher i.e. whether the goal is the attainment of pure scientific knowledge or the dissemination of philosophical knowledge; whether the aim is teaching or education. (BAW IV, 213)

This refers clearly to the two great models of ancient philosophy who, for Nietzsche, also represent two kinds of 'writer': Plato and Aristotle. Tradition presents them to us as two opposite examples. Plato is the ideal writer, composing his dialogues as perfect rhetorical machines designed to educate the students of his school and to train them in philosophical discourse. From Aristotle, on the other hand, were only preserved transcriptions of the courses held at his school, documents that were not intended for wider circulation but that more or less directly testified to the type of scientific work that took place there. 'Sometimes – if we judge from what he left behind – one sees too many of the bare bones in Aristotle' (KSA 7:37[4]; trans. Richard T. Grey).

Yet, ancient tradition also tells of dialogues written by Aristotle (Rose 1863), which, as Nietzsche recalls (KGW II/5, 187), equalled for Dionysius of Halicarnassus (Dion. Hal. comp., c. 24) only those of the divine Plato. This shows that when the philosopher's aims shift, and the conditions of his writing change, even the most arid, dry style of a thinker like Aristotle (in whom you can see the bare bones) can metamorphose into – surpass even – the elevated and elegant style of a writer like Plato. How does the figure of Epicurus fit into this context, and what role does his prolific and deliberately rapid production – freed from any aesthetic pretensions – play in the economy of the history of ancient philosophy? To try to understand this, it is useful to take a step back and retrace, alongside Nietzsche, what we might define as the literary history of ancient philosophy or, rather, the history of ancient philosophical literature.

To speak of the history of philosophy and the history of philosophical literature is not the same thing. For Nietzsche in particular, there are various types of philosophy, only some of which can properly be defined as 'literary'. There was, for instance, a kind of philosophy that was practised and transmitted orally, which survives, for example, in the maxims of the Seven Wise Men and the Orphic testimonies. There was also a tradition of philosophical writing, some of which has survived, which originated with Anaximander. Then we can observe the flourishing season of Platonic literature, with the development of the genre of philosophical dialogue. Finally, beginning with Aristotle and lasting throughout the Hellenistic period, we can note the spread of a veritable scientific philosophical literature in the form of treatises. A summary of this tradition, inevitably trivializing Nietzsche's refined reflections on the early philosophers and Greek wisdom, is beyond the scope of this contribution, as is the much-discussed question of the definition of pre-Platonic philosophers.[18] What is of most interest for the present discussion is one particular aspect of Nietzsche's reconstruction of the history of ancient philosophy: that of the expressive medium.

We have already seen an important distinction, noted by Nietzsche on several occasions, between those philosophers who wrote and those who did not (such as Thales and Socrates), between those who chose the literary medium and those who were faithful to the practice of dialectical discourse and education. This distinction between writing and orality is certainly an important one for Nietzsche, but it is not the decisive one. In fact, he makes another more fundamental, though more sophisticated, distinction, which also constitutes the basis on which the orality/writing distinction is justified: I am referring here to the difference between prose and poetry, between the use of a poetic language subject to the laws of rhythm and metrics and a language closer to everyday common use, stripped of artistic superstructures.

Philosophy originated in Greece at a time when the eminently oral poetic tradition dominated. Contrary to claims regarding orality set out in recent studies,[19] Nietzsche was convinced that the major paradigmatic shift in antiquity – writing supplanting the medium of orality – arose out of the decadence of the poetic medium and the adoption of the prose, which enabled and fostered this transition from orality to writing. If poetry contained sufficient rhythmic and metric structures to communicate ideas without the help of further mnemonic means or material support, it was prose, stripped of such structures, that necessarily made use of the written medium. Nietzsche believed that the Greek philosophical tradition was wholly responsible for the estrangement from poetry and consequently for the eradication of the artistic and artificial aspects (*künstlerisch* and *kunstlich*) of literary production.

Officially, Greek philosophy arose among those wise men active in the area of Miletus, in the Ionian region of Asia. The first 'philosopher', Thales, did not produce books. He was among those who did not write (οἱ μηδὲν γράφουτες).[20] The first true philosophical literary tradition dates back to Anaximander, who was active in the same area. The fact that philosophy, understood as a literary genre, emerged in the Asiatic Ionian region had an impact upon the development of its character and the literary form it would adopt. In this region, the dialect used in the poetic tradition was, in fact, neo-Ionic, derived from the ancient Ionic one employed by Homer, but from which it differed considerably. Many authors composed their work using this dialect: Mimnermus, Archilochus and Herodotus, through to Hippocrates, Democritus and all the first philosophers. This dialect favoured the development of expression in prose and, before Gorgian rhetoric determined the hegemony of the Attic dialect, it was the dialect of the prose par excellence. Even poetry produced in the neo-Ionic dialect – iambic and elegiac – was closer in character to the spoken language and was very similar rhythmically to the prose. An elegy, for example, was not sung per se but recited over a musical accompaniment. The iambic verse, in turn, had rhythmic affinity with the spoken language, hence the reason it became incorporated into the dialogue of tragedy.

This development of a scientific and philosophical prose, which, originating in the Ionian area, then became Panhellenic, contrasts with another written tradition that favoured the metric form as the worthiest expression of the highest truths:

> The context of philosophical prose writing was opposed by several philosophers who made use of the metron i.e. they continued to employ it. In such cases, the prejudice against prose remained; on the other hand, the poet within these philosophers was not completely suppressed. Indeed, some of them, like Empedocles and Parmenides, had something visionary about them. (KGW II/5, 188)

This poetic–philosophical current recognized the Orphic and Dionysian traditions as precursors, and it has been linked as well to Pythagoras. It, nonetheless, remained marginal despite its longevity when compared to the advancement of a philosophical and scientific discourse that was better suited to the precision of prose. The development and affirmation of this literary, scientific and philosophical prose was a constant yet controversial process.

The reasons behind the Greeks' distrust of a phenomenon that was produced in its very own bosom were essentially threefold and related to 1) the extraordinary prestige of the poetic medium, which was held in high esteem in Greece; 2) the consequent distrust of writing; and 3) a general misunderstanding of science. This last point is particularly interesting. Nietzsche observes in *The Pre-Platonic Philosophers* (KGW II/4, 233) that, although the tradition concerning the ancient philosophers tended to treat them with the respect they deserved, they were, nonetheless, considered as foreigners – literally rather than merely figuratively. Indeed, they were supposed to be Thracians, Phoenicians, Egyptians or, at the very least, Sicilians; philosophers, in other words, were attributed every possible lineage other than Greek in order to demonstrate that philosophy was not born in Greece but was something imported, barbaric even or, in any case, derived from foreign teaching.[21]

> The aversion of classical Hellenism to the rigors of science (as opposed to the rigors of life) in favour of good deeds is best demonstrated in the Athenian (φιλόλογος)

> Socrates: the philosophers before him (a small number!) have done a tremendous job in mathematics, astronomy and physics. Since now, of course, Thales is a real Phoenician, Pythagoras a disciple of the Egyptians, and Democritus, a real scientific type, is perhaps a Thracian, as was the case for the scientific historian Thucydides. Socrates made fun of these scientific people, saying that astronomy was something for night guards and sailors and one should not want to know what the gods have kept in store for them ... Of course, science then became honourable again thanks to a half-Macedonian (like Aristotle) and many half- and pure Egyptians and Semites, so that the Alexandrian heyday of science could finally appear as a product of the Greek spirit. (KGW II/5, 311–12)

As for the second point, that of writing, its use was not unknown in ancient Greece, but it was limited to inscriptions or commercial practices.

> What of the manner in which writing was later held in high esteem, to the extent that education became solely a literary one? Scientific-minded individuals – mathematicians, astronomers, doctors and natural scientists – promoted this widespread respect for writing. Writing allowed them to present their ideas as purely as possible, leaving emotion aside. Now, this is precisely why writing in general can be so difficult to understand: sentiment and emotion are not easy to express using signs. Question marks, exclamation marks and so on are very poor aids in this respect. But if one wants to express thoughts as purely as possible, as, for example, in the fields of mathematics, physics and logic, then writing is sufficient because it seeks to avoid affect. (KGW II/5, 282–3)

Gradually, through dialects like the neo-Ionic one, flat and devoid of the ornaments of poetic language, and through writing that stabilized linguistic processes, the thought that made use of such instruments came to be fixed and specified, caught up in a virtuous circle of mutual determination:

> The greater the desire for the logic and what is scientific, the more writing gains respect, as the instrument for them. Now, this could be called one of the Greeks' greatest achievements: to gradually prepare their language for the task of communicating thoughts and knowledge; all sorts of clever ways of avoiding the difficulties of this task are invented. ... The extraordinary pride felt by the Greeks upon rendering their language sober, flexible and logical filtered through to the people; the masses recognized this phenomenon in Euripides and by the philosophers. This in turn increased the value of writing. Euripides was the first great reader among the poets (indeed, he owned a library); Aristotle, the first logician, was given the nickname ἀναγνώστης [reader] by Plato. (KGW II/5, 283)

In the process of rendering the Greek language 'scientific' and a medium for philosophy, writing has only an auxiliary value with respect to prose. Prose is the real medium of philosophical language, which opposes the artifices of poetry and pursues the objective of stripping language of all that is superfluous, enabling reason and that which is essential to speech to emerge. The struggle for prose (KSA 7:37[4]) over poetry is at the same time a struggle for science, for accuracy, for the precision of expression that corresponds to thought. And it is within this 'scientific' current, at a particularly advanced stage, that the figure of Epicurus can be located, and the value of his prose understood.

In his letter to Köselitz of the end of August 1883, cited at the beginning of this discussion, Nietzsche recalls his past philological studies: 'I worked on *Democritea* and *Epicurea* zealously enough' (KSB 6:460). For those of us who have an in-depth knowledge of the scientific production of the philologist Nietzsche, this statement cannot help but be surprising. In fact, if the works that Nietzsche refers to as his *Democritea* are more or less well known,[22] the same cannot be said of *Epicurea*. In the philological notes, Epicurus is always mentioned alongside the theoretician of atomism, appearing as his subordinate. In this game of cross-reference between two authors – about whom we have little information and of whose work only a few traces remain – Epicurus plays the role of the epigone. He is the one who shares the spirit of the great Democritus, adopting and propagating his theories.

At this stage in Nietzsche's reflection, the statement about the identity – of philosophical contents and aspiration – between Democritus and Epicurus is especially important. It allows us, in fact, to recognize a characterization of Epicurus as a 'scientific' spirit, following the more closely delineated description of Democritus by Nietzsche. Democritus is, in fact, defined by Nietzsche as

> a confident rationalist who believes in the redemptive action of his system and considers everything bad and unfinished outside of it. In this way he attains, the first among the Greeks, a scientific character. This consists in the attempt to explain a quantity of phenomena in a unitary way without calling for help at the most critical moments, a *deus ex machina*. This new scientific type made a great impression on the Greeks. ... Democritus himself perceived this as a new principle of life; a scientific discovery was more precious to him than the whole Persian kingdom. (BAW III, 348)

The scientific character as a distinctive marker – this time explicit – of the philosopher Epicurus clearly emerges in a fragment from 1878 (KSA 8:33[9]) in which Nietzsche questions the idea of Europe and the spirit of modernity that informs it. This important fragment can only really be understood once we have dealt with the rather ambitious historical–philosophical and literary scenario I have been outlining since the beginning of this contribution. According to the Nietzschean reconstruction contained in this fragment, the Greek culture that generated the philosophical tradition was nurtured from the outset by 'Thracian and Phoenician elements ... that constituted its first ... scientific cores (*wissenschaftliche keime*)' (KSA 8:33[9]). Once more we find the 'foreign' elements that constituted the first components of ancient scientific thought, of which Nietzsche speaks in the Lessons.

Epicurus plays a central role in the historical–cultural reconstruction of fragment 33[9]. For Nietzsche, he is, in fact, the most evolved interpreter of the scientific spirit and thirst for knowledge, the apex of what we could define as the *esprit géométrique* of antiquity. The modern age, continues the fragment, could not outdo Epicurus. Thus, for Nietzsche who, at that time, was engaged in writing his most 'Enlightened' book (*Human, All too Human*), Epicurus's genius and scientific spirit have never been surpassed, let alone matched. As an exponent of the 'scientific' current within Greek thought, Epicurus wrote in prose. He produced large quantities of text rather rapidly, that is, without much consideration, since his prose had to be stripped of all artifice in order to achieve its goal without unnecessary hindrance. If Plato wrote during a period that was still greatly influenced by orality, in which the laws of rhetoric supplanted those of metrics in giving rhythm to the philosophical style, Epicurus, belonging to the generation that followed Aristotle, already lived in the age of the reader (ἀναγνωστικοι) and despised the artifices of Platonic language.[23] Epicurus did not write badly, 'but recognized only the stylistic principle of clarity; it is thus not even difficult to write, if one does not care about the inconstant artistic judgment' (KGW II/5, 31).

The war he waged against the beautiful form [*Kampf gegen die schöne Form*] (KGW II/5, 216) was the same one waged against the poetic residues and frills of Isocratic prose, which constituted the rhetorical evolution of the world of poetic orality, up to that point dominant in Greece and never completely overcome. What this battle against beautiful writing sought was the achievement of clarity, the *Deutlichkeit* as Nietzsche defined it, adopting a Leibnizian term, which was indispensable to scientific writing. Following the example of Epicurus, and in order to free himself from the fetters of the modern style, Nietzsche sought the application of an ancient precept: just as it took the adepts five years of silence before they could access the rudiments of initiatory knowledge, so Nietzsche wished his contemporaries well:

> Five-year Pythagorean prohibition on reading ... 'Beautiful style' is an invention of the flashy orators. Why should one take such pains with language! Clarity is enough, as Epicurus believed. (KSA 7:37[5]; trans. Richard T. Gray)

Conclusion: A difficult facility

As Epicurus says, why take so much care over language if clarity is enough? This question should be addressed to Nietzsche himself, who devoted some of his most beautiful pages throughout his career – not only in these philological texts but also in the famous 'New Prefaces' to his philosophical writings – to his obsession with style, his search for his own style and his study of the style of other authors. *Epicurus and Style* is the title of an important fragment from the years 1876–77, produced either at the same time as or shortly after the *Lessons on the History of Greek Literature* cited so far: fragment 23[7]. This fragment explains precisely what kind of 'clarity' Epicurus aspired to, and how his quick and careless style actually masked an effective kind of working upon the language:

> Epicurus's position on style is typical in many respects. He believed he could return to nature because he wrote as he liked. In reality, so much concern for expression was inherited and raised in him that he only let himself go a little bit and yet was

not completely free and unconstrained. The 'nature' he achieved was the instinct for style which was drawn by habit. This is called naturalism: one stretches the bow a little more slackly, e.g. Wagner in his behaviour towards music and the art of singing. The Stoics and Rousseau are naturalists in the same sense: mythology of nature! (KSA 8:23[7])

In this important fragment many key words from Nietzschean philosophy can be noted. Let us look at some of them. The naturalness (*Naturalisiren*) of the Epicurean style is, for Nietzsche, the very opposite of *laisser aller* (*sich gehen lassen*) or of a style lacking in care. If Epicurus aims to achieve the clarity and immediacy of a style that imitates nature, the result he achieves is something other, indeed. His 'Nature' is a nature in quotations, which is only attainable after a long period of practice (*Gewohnheit*). It is not the uncultivated Rousseauvian nature of man that precedes all forms of education; rather, it is a product of education itself, it is a habit. It is therefore an example of that 'Second Nature' (*Zweite Natur*) of which Nietzsche speaks in the second *Untimely Meditation*[24] that overlaps with the First Nature and which, through effort and care, becomes so well assimilated that it seems (and definitively is) more natural than nature itself. This nature that contradicts nature (GS 80), and thus surpasses it, is the fruit of labour, of rules and of a style that has been acquired. In contrast to the 'Mythology of Nature' of Rousseau or the Stoics (the latter of whom wrote badly spontaneously or on purpose!), the naturalness of Epicurus's sober style is actually the artistic product of elaborate finesse.

In the group of aphorisms 37 of 1874, quoted earlier on several occasions, together with the numerous mentions of Epicurus, Nietzsche lists a series of observations on the style of the ancient philosophers, the practice of writing well and the stylistic strategies to be adopted. Among these notes, one in particular, 'The simple comes last and is most difficult,'[25] recalls the famous definition of Great Style from the *Lessons on the History of Greek Rhetoric*:

> The great 'style' is difficult to grasp: it is strange how the liberating and perfection-seeking geniuses of an art, because they remove the constraints and explicit characteristics [*Maniere*] of the genres and take possession of their means, easily give their contemporaries the impression of being naturalists or virtuosos or even amateurs. (KGW II/4, 394)

The simplicity to which Epicurus aspires is the final and most difficult element, achieved only after much work has been performed upon the language. This difficult simplicity is the purest feature of an author's style; it represents the most personal and spontaneous form of expression he can reach, without being the most primitive and crude. Again, in fragment 37[4]: 'When effective, a good text will cause one to forget that it is a literary work; it is effective in the same way as the words and actions of a friend' (KSA, 7, 37[4]; translation Richard T. Gray).

Why, then, should so much effort be put into language? Here we unmask the rhetorical question posed by Nietzsche to Epicurus.[26] *Deutlichkeit* is enough, according to Epicurus, but it is also the hardest thing to achieve. Of all the ancient philosophers,

Epicurus thus became a model for Nietzsche. 'It is time to begin a life-long work on language' (KSA 7: 37[4]; trans. Richard T. Gray). Owing to Nietzsche's constant search for his own style, a style capable of conveying his philosophical message, he is perhaps one of the few authors to have sought so ambitiously to thematize the question of style. For Nietzsche, the question of literary style is an all-embracing one. It concerns primarily literature or writing, which, in modern times, has become an indispensable medium for communicating a philosophical message. Moreover, the writing style speaks to us of the human being in his totality: it reveals to us the character, experience and feelings of a thinker – of a people or nation even – which the style of national literature inevitably discloses.

This is the reason for Nietzsche's enthusiasm and his hope of being able to 'read' Epicurus after the (not new) discovery of the Villa of the Papyri. The 'hand' of the writer Epicurus would allow Nietzsche to 'feel the character of Epicurus' (GS 45) in order to fully understand his thoughts and spirituality.[27] As his correspondence with Köselitz reveals,[28] Nietzsche had repeatedly been compared to Epicurus and this was, for him, a particularly welcome comparison.[29] As other contributions in this collection will certainly highlight, Nietzsche recognizes himself in many aspects of Epicurus's philosophy: his tragic pessimism; his understanding of pain;[30] his heroic attitude, at the same time, titanic and enlightened, towards death (KSA 8:28[15]); and, last but not least, in his Dionysian response to existence, which decreed ostracism on the part of the later philosophical traditions, including the Christian one.[31]

Epicurus can also be considered, in many respects, quasi an alter ego for Nietzsche. Regardless of the validity (or not) of this comparison, there is at least one element that allows us to affirm that Nietzsche somehow recognized himself in Epicurus, an element that is once again closely linked to the kind of literary and stylistic reflection I have been outlining throughout this contribution. 'Einige werden posthum geboren' is the famous motto according to which Nietzsche delivers his work to posterity in *Anti-Christ* and *Ecce Homo*.[32] We find almost no major philosophical work in which Nietzsche does not declare himself a member of that group of posthumous men who were misunderstood or misinterpreted by their contemporaries, only to be understood by future generations. 'Posthumous men are misunderstood, but better heard than the actual men. Or, more strictly: they are never understood: and therefore their authority (comprendre c'est égaler)' (KSA 12:9[76]). Among these posthumous men, Epicurus is one of the few to be explicitly mentioned.

> *The eternal Epicurus.* Epicurus has lived in all ages and still lives on, unknown to those who called and call themselves Epicureans, and without any reputation among the philosophers. He himself forgot his own name, too: it was the heaviest burden that he ever cast off. (WS 227)

Now, being posthumous is a typical characteristic of literary works. The posthumous existence of an author like Epicurus or Nietzsche is determined by his writing as well as by his philosophy. In Nietzsche's case, the adoption of – or search for – a particular style essentially prevented his contemporaries from understanding his work. If an individual cannot read a text, it stands to reason that he cannot understand it.

Nietzsche, like Epicurus, wrote with posterity in mind; his writing paved the way for his posterity. In this sense, the work of both Epicurus and Nietzsche can be considered as a formative pathway or philosophical school that educates thought, rendering it capable of autonomously attaining those goals that traditional philosophies claim to be readily available and explained to the intellect.

Notes

1. Note: All quotations from Nietzsche's published works, KGW, BAW, KSB, KSA as well as some posthumous fragments are my translations. The only exceptions are Richard T. Gray's translation of some of the unpublished notes from KSA, which are duly noted, and Gary Handwerk's translation for WS (both translations for Stanford University Press).
2. See in particular the following letters to Köselitz; 22 January 1879 (KSB 5:799), 8 December 1881 (KSB 6:177), 1 July 1883 (KSB 6:428), 3 August 1883 (KSB 6:446) and a letter of the end of August 1883 (KSB 6:460).
3. I am referring to the famous Villa of the Papyri, probably owned by Lucio Calpurnio Pisone Cesonino, patron of the Epicurean philosopher Philodemus of Gadara. The discovery of the villa and its papyrus scrolls was not really 'news'. In fact, it was discovered in the eighteenth century, with the papyrus being found as early as 1752. Attempts to unroll the charred papyrus to read its contents had already begun in the eighteenth century and one of the last attempts during Nietzsche's time was made at the Louvre in Paris in 1877. The enthusiasm and novelty expressed by Nietzsche can perhaps be explained as a kind of concession vis-à-vis the recipient of his letter, Heinrich Köselitz, who had little or no knowledge of the 'state of the art' regarding Epicurean papyrology.
4. 'It is one of the ironies of fate, that we have to believe a Seneca in favour of Epicurean manliness and loftiness of soul – Seneca, a man to whom one should, on the whole, always lend an ear, but never give one's faith and trust. In Corsica people say: Seneca è un birbone [Seneca is a rascal]' (Translation by Anthony M. Ludovici). The source for this motto is Ferdinand Gregorovius, *Corsica* (Stuttgart: Cotta 1869), 252.
5. The term 'book' (*biblos*) here does not correspond to today's meaning, which identifies a single independent work, but to a unit measuring the material on which it was written (the papyrus scroll). Each work in the modern sense, therefore, was made up of several 'books'. Nietzsche confuses the number of 'books' to be attributed to Epicurus. He speaks in his *Lessons* of 600 books (KGW II/5, 187), while Diogenes Laertius mentions 300 books. Three hundred books are correctly mentioned in BGE 7.
6. In his writings on Diogenes Laertius's sources (KGW II/1, 75–167,191–245), Nietzsche offers a convincing reason for the biographer's sympathy towards Epicurus. One of the main sources for the *Lives* was, in fact, Diocles of Magnesia, author of a *Life of the Philosophers* and a *Compendium of Philosophers*. His work was substantially copied by Diogenes, who admits to being an ardent defender of Epicurean thought.
7. See the famous Myth of Theuth in Plato's *Phaedrus*: 'The story goes that Thamus said many things to Theuth in praise or blame of the various arts, which it would take too long to repeat; but when they came to the letters, "This invention, O king," said Theuth, "will make the Egyptians wiser and will improve their memories; for

it is an elixir of memory and wisdom that I have discovered." But Thamus replied, "Most ingenious Theuth, one man has the ability to beget arts, but the ability to judge of their usefulness or harmfulness to their users belongs to another; and now you, who are the father of letters, have been led by your affection to ascribe to them a power the opposite of that which they really possess. For this invention will produce forgetfulness in the minds of those who learn to use it, because they will not practice their memory. Their trust in writing, produced by external characters which are no part of themselves, will discourage the use of their own memory within them. You have invented an elixir not of memory, but of reminding; and you offer your pupils the appearance of wisdom, not true wisdom, for they will read many things without instruction and will therefore seem to know many things, when they are for the most part ignorant and hard to get along with, since they are not wise, but only appear wise' (Plato 1913: 274e–5b).

8 See the letter to Pherecydes that Diogenes Laertius reports as being attributed to the 'non-writer' Thales, and which Nietzsche recalls several times: 'I hear that you intend to be the first Ionian to expound theology to the Greeks. And perhaps it was a wise decision to make the book common property without taking advice, instead of entrusting it to any particular persons whatsoever, a course which has no advantages. However, if it would give you any pleasure, I am quite willing to discuss the subject of your book with you; and if you bid me come to Syros I will do so. For surely Solon of Athens and I would scarcely be sane if, after having sailed to Crete to pursue our inquiries there, and to Egypt to confer with the priests and astronomers, we hesitated to come to you. For Solon too will come, with your permission. You, however, are so fond of home that you seldom visit Ionia and have no longing to see strangers, but, as I hope, apply yourself to one thing, namely writing, while we, who never write anything, travel all over Hellas and Asia' (Diogenes Laertius I, 43–4). The irony of this letter – written by someone who criticizes a man who spends all his time writing and doing little else – is that it contains a summary of all the ancient controversies surrounding the use of writing in the philosophical sphere.
9 The reference is to Plato's *Phaedrus* (Harold North Flower translation).
10 KGW II/5, 217. In reality Diogenes Laertius X.120 says, 'He will leave written words behind him, but will not compose panegyric.'
11 KGW II/5, 321. The reference is to Plato's *Phaedrus* (1913: 276e).
12 A criticism of journalism can also be found in a fragment from 1874 (KSA 7:37[5]), which I will return to shortly in a context that once again references Epicurus.
13 The source is Val. Max., III, 7.
14 'perfectus Epicureus evaserat, minime aptum ad dicendum genus' (Cicero, 131).
15 In Hellenistic times, polyhistory or polymatia meant the encyclopaedic knowledge that men of letters, polygraphs in particular, demonstrated. 'Writing a lot' and 'knowing a lot' are two different phenomena that, even today, rightly or wrongly, are considered to be closely linked.
16 KGW II/5, 218. The last quotation is Diogenes Laertius X.6.
17 Rose (1863: 121). Nietzsche was very familiar with this work and its author, as evidenced by the numerous mentions in the Nachlass 1867–8. He reviewed, indeed, another work by the same author, Rose (1868).
18 I would instead encourage you to refer to the many studies, including recent ones, that have tackled this issue. To quote some main references: Laks (2018) and Ghedini (1999).
19 Havelock (1981), Havelock (1986), Ong (1982) and Lord (1960).

20 See note 8.
21 Herodotus, who probably travelled to Egypt, claimed that the Greeks had learned science from the Egyptians and that he himself had discovered how even sacred elements had been imported from Egypt to Greece.
22 A series of unpublished notes on the tradition of the constitution of the *corpus democriteum*: BAW III, 245–79, 332–5, 344–50, 362–8; BAW IV, 36–106. This project of Nietzsche was set aside once the thesis that fuelled its conception collapsed. According to Nietzsche's hypothesis, the *corpus democriteum* – of which only a few fragments and mentions of some titles remain – was the result of an erudite falsification made in Roman times by the publisher Thrasil of Mende, a grammarian active in Emperor Tiberius's circle.
23 See Epicurus's famous criticism of the Platonists as being *Dionysokolax* (BGE 7), which was a term used to describe actors (Diognes Laertius X.8). This was because of the particular mise en scène of their philosophy, language and all practices within the academy. Plato himself was called a great Cagliostro by Nietzsche (KSA 13:14[116]), precisely in relation to Epicurus's aforementioned critique. Nietzsche deployed this term when describing another great 'magician' and 'necromancer', the musician Wagner, who used artistic reform as a weapon of seduction.
24 HL 3. Also see KSA 1: 684.
25 KSA 7:37[3]; translation Richard T. Gray.
26 See KSA 7:37[5].
27 See the letter to Köselitz, 1 July 1883 (KSB 6:428) on the bust of Epicurus and its expressiveness that betrays will power and spirituality, both conceived as intellectual gifts.
28 See note 1.
29 To Köselitz, 8 December 1881, KSB 6:177.
30 To Köselitz, 22 January 1879, KSB 5:799.
31 'Dionysian' and 'Epicurean' are commonly (and wrongly) considered as synonyms in the everyday use of these terms.
32 A 'Foreword'; EH 'Books' 1.

2

The Gastrosophists!

A seven-course meal with Epicurus and Nietzsche

Ryan J. Johnson

Amuse-bouche: Why food and eating?

Remember the opening line of Aristotle's *Metaphysics* – 'All humans by nature desire to know' (980a20)? The reason, he argues, is that humans delight in their senses, especially vision, the most discerning sense. With sight ranked highest, Aristotle constructed a hierarchy of faculties that rendered subsequent philosophy oculocentric. At the bottom was taste, the basest, most bodily sense. This is the standard story of philosophy, following like footnotes, à la Whitehead, from Plato and Aristotle to today. Yet if we look to a different ancient philosopher, forty years Aristotle's younger, we can tell a different story: Epicurus's garden.

Epicureanism was the first 'counter tradition' in the history of Western philosophy. The clearest marker of this contrariety is the dynamic materialism with which Epicurus flattened the ocularcentric hierarchy of the senses. For him, taste is the primary human power. Eating, the stomach – these are the defining elements of an Epicurean life. As the seventeenth-century Mexican nun Sor Juana Inés de la Cruz describes in her own 'kitchen philosophy': 'If Aristotle had cooked stews, he would have written a lot more' (2009: 35). Ignorant of stomach wisdom, it is unsurprising that Aristotle died of stomach ailments (Chroust 1973: 181).[1] Epicurus, however, does not denigrate food and eating but, instead, sparks a tradition that leads, we argue, directly to Nietzsche. Following Epicurus' joyous affirmation of the manifold materiality of bodily pleasures, especially eating, and Nietzsche's interrogation of the moral effects of food, this chapter offers an Epicurean–Nietzschean philosophical way of eating and thinking called *gastrosophia*. We call these two food philosophers 'The Gastrosophists!' because they take seriously the wisdom of the stomach.

This chapter is organized as seven courses – a philosophical *service à la Russe*. 1st: Amuse-bouche; 2nd: Potage; 3rd: Hors d'oeuvre; 4th: Entrée; 5th: Plat Principal; 6th: Dessert; 7th: Digestif.[2] At the end, while enjoying coffee, we see that gastrosophia is more than simply the philosophy *of* food; it is eating as a way of doing philosophy. To get there, let us finish this amuse-bouche by rewriting Aristotle's opening line: 'All humans by nature desire to *eat*.'

Potage: Metaphor or truth (or neither)

Nietzsche's writings are stuffed with culinary metaphors. For example, 'spirit (*Geist*) is a stomach' appears in *Beyond Good and Evil* (230), 'incorporation' (*Einverleibung*) as experiment of 'incorporating truth' is in *Gay Science* (110) and many more.[3] We will focus on two others: (1) Modernity and its abuse of history as digestion, and (2) interpretation as rumination.

(1) Much of Nietzsche's early and middle writings use the language of digestion to express Modernity's unhealthy use of history.

'Modern man', writes Nietzsche, 'drags around with him a huge quantity of indigestible stones of knowledge, which ... can sometimes be heard rumbling about inside him' (UM 78). Hegel is the paradigmatic modern thinker of indigestion given that, for him, the 'mightiest and most all-embracing' form of the *Absolute Idea* 'embraces and holds everything within itself' (1976: 841). This insatiable hunger to consume everything is indicative of Modernity's knowledge constipation. Yet, given the radical sweep of dialectical sublation, maybe it is better to say that the Hegelian system concludes not with a universal omnivorism but with total expulsion. As Zizek puts it: '"First you eat, then you shit." Shitting is the *conclusion* of the entire process: without it, we would be dealing with the "spurious infinity" of an endless process of sublation' (2011: 223). Either way, Nietzsche diagnoses that this modern epistemological eating disorder was 'unknown to the peoples of earlier times' (UM 78). Contrary to an Epicurean taxonomy of desires, Modernity's appetite is ravenous, which is why it would not be surprising 'if such a culture should not perish from indigestion' (UM 79).

(2) Contrary to Modernity's constipated or bulimic epistemology, Nietzsche speaks of a certain art of reading as 'rumination' in *Genealogy of Morality*: 'One thing is necessary above all if one is to practice reason as an *art* in this way ... something for which one has almost need to be a cow, and in any case *not* a "modern man": *rumination*' (GM 23).[4] A ruminant (like a cow or goat) does not simply chew and swallow because of its digestive process including a multi-compartment stomach. Cows thus chew and swallow many times. More precisely, cows first take plant material into the first stomach chamber, where bacteria breaks it down, before the cow regurgitates and reprocesses the particulate matter. This is 'chewing the cud'. More finely processed food is re-swallowed, now going into a second chamber for further mechanical processing, before the mass is passed to the true stomach – the Abomassum – where digestive enzymes break down the bacteria and release nutrients. As the cow repeatedly chews, swallows, regurgitates, so should one read aphorisms. Deleuze appreciates this art of reading as rumination:

> I would like to do philosophy in the manner of cows: rumination. ... There is only one author who knew how to ruminate, and is great among the great: Nietzsche. This is why Nietzsche has the sacred animal: the cow. He said that cows were cows of the sky [citing the Egyptian myth], but that for him rumination consisted in throwing out an aphorism and reading it twice. (1983)[5]

However, Sarah Kofman argues, the direction of these culinary metaphorics can be inverted. For Nietzsche (and Epicurus), it is wrong to see eating and bodily activity as secondary, merely meant to serve and help explain what is primary: thinking. Nietzsche often inverts the order of metaphor so that eating and the body are primary, thinking and the mind secondary. Nietzsche, Kofman argues, 'consider[s] the metaphors which take consciousness as their model as *inferior to those which take the body as their model*' (1972: 44).[6] Nietzsche himself suggests this: 'We must assume there is a *master*; but it is *not* in consciousness, for consciousness is an organ, like the stomach' (GOA XIII: 588 in Kofman 1994: 26). We view the language of digestion and ruminations not merely as metaphors but more literally, physically and existentially. If anything, thinking and mental activities are metaphors *for the body*.

Yet, this is not right either. The metaphoric relation is *two-way*. Neither the body nor the mind is subordinated. The effect of bi-directional thinking and eating metaphorics – thinking is like eating and eating is like thinking – transforms the difference between metaphor and truth by intensifying the analogy until the difference between them becomes indiscernible. 'By means of this reciprocal (yet not equivalent) metaphorical expression of the body by consciousness and of consciousness by the body', writes Kofman, 'Nietzsche deletes the metaphysical opposition between the soul and the body and establishes between the two an *original relation of symbolic* expressivity' (1994: 26). Dissolving truth into a 'movable host of metaphors, metonymies, and anthropomorphisms' is only half of the operation if metaphor remains opposed to truth and illusion to reality (Nietzsche 2006: 117).[7] If it is not enough to render truth metaphorical, for the other operation happens simultaneously, metaphor resolves into truth. Just as Epicurus flattened the Aristotelian hierarchy of the senses, Nietzsche flattens the hierarchy of truth and metaphor. The best way to see this is to turn to historical parallels.

Hors d'oeuvre: Historical parallels

While Hegel dominated the first half of nineteenth-century German philosophy, by the time Nietzsche was at university, intellectual circles were filled with critics of Hegel's absolute idealism. Strongest among these critics were the German Materialists, including Ludwig Feuerbach and Karl Marx, who led passionate returns to matter. Before Hegel, materialism was basically outlawed in Germany. Catholic and Protestant prosecutions of prior materialists forced materialist ideas into anonymity and secrecy (Bayertz 2017). Post-Hegel, however, the intellectual climate of Germany was more receptive to materialist answers to philosophical queries, though it was still difficult for materialists to work in universities. Since every rise in materialist thinking invokes a return to the ancient materialists, we can draw a parallel between, on the one hand, the German Materialists' reaction to the dominance of the idealism of Hegel, and on the other, Hellenistic responses to the idealisms of Plato and Aristotle: (1) Stoics and Feuerbach, (2) Cynics and Marx, (3) Epicureans and Nietzsche.

(1) While Stoics were thoroughgoing materialists, they still posited a rationally organized cosmos. This cosmological conception led them to scorn pleasure and promote the virtuous life. This virtuous life is distinctly human; the human is a citizen of the cosmos. Feuerbach's anthropological materialism is akin to the Stoics' insofar as

they both placed the human being near the centre of the cosmos (1989). We thus group Stoicism and Feuerbach as anthropological materialists insofar as their conceptions of natural order entails prioritizing humans.[8] (2) Cynics rejected civilization tout court, including the cooking fire Prometheus gifted humankind. Rather than living like civilized humans, Cynics lived like dogs. They craved *raw* nature, uncooked meat, hence Diogenes' experiments with cannibalism (1958: VII.73).[9] Similarly, we see in Marx the drive to cultivate ways of life beyond the economic, social and political formations that normalized people through material processes of capitalism. Living free of capitalist valuation, Marxism echoes the way the Cynics' raw wildness opposes civilization. We thus group Cynics and Marxists in a kind of post-humanist/post-capitalist materialism. (3) Epicureans cultivated a third variety, one which ended neither in anthropocentricism nor in bestialism. We might call it a materialism that is human but *not too* human. To see how, consider a third kind of materialism in nineteenth-century Germany: metaphysical materialism.

Metaphysical materialism flourished in the second half of nineteenth-century Germany. 'Few individuals', Frederick Gregory claims, 'influenced public opinion in nineteenth-century Germany more than these men' (1977: ix, 177). Foremost among these was Jacob Moleschott. As a physiologist and medical doctor, he modelled a 'metaphysical materialism' on natural science's practices of experimentation and observation (Gregory 1977: xi). A clear example of such metaphysical materialism is Moleschott's insistence on the materiality of force. Force, for him, is a way of describing the motion of matter. Viewing force as immaterial, by contrast, is like 'ascribing immortal spirit (*Geist*) to steel or amber' (Gregory 1977: 89; Moleschott 1850: 242). Electricity, heat and light are merely movements of matter. 'Life', writes Moleschott, 'is not the emanation of a very special force ... [but] a condition [*Züstand*] of matter, grounded in its inalienable qualities, governed by characteristic phenomenal movements which call forth to matter heat and light, water and air, electricity and mechanical vibration' (1852: 373 in Gregory 1977: 95). Hence his emphasis on cycles, such as *Blutbildung* (hemopoiesis or the formation of blood cells) and *rückbildung* (retrogression or remission), as constitutive of individuality (Gregory 1977: 93). Plants, animals and humans are individuated by cycles of material flux.

This insistence on the material basis for life made Moleschott increasingly interested in food. His *Die Lehre der Nahrungsmittel*, for example, assumes the tone of a nutritionist, prescribing 'housewives with inside information on what to give their families and how to cook it' (Gregory 1977: 89).[10] Diet is central to living well, for 'it was an error to believe that mental activity did not require the consumption of matter' (Moleschott 1850: 242 in Gregory 1977: 89). While different types of lives – expectant mother, artist, thinker – required different diets, Moleschott claimed that the effects of certain types of foods, such as spices, 'could lead to restless passion and insidious jealousy' (Hymers 2006: 3; Gregory 1977: 89). Echoing Socrates' identification of the cause of war in the *Republic*, Moleschott claimed that a spice-free Europe would have fewer wars (Plato 2005: 373e; Moleschott 1850: 189 in Gregory 1977: 89).[11] Echoing Pythagoras' denunciations of beans, Moleschott saw 'beans [*Erbsenstoff*]' 'as the food of the revolution' (Hymers 2006: 3). Without acknowledging his potential racism, Moleschott explained the differences between ethnicities through diet:

Italians were idle because of the oil, pasta and vino they consumed; Hindus were inclined to mysticism because of their rice and spices; Irish were sluggish because of their 'sluggish potato blood' (1850: 132 in Gregory 1977: 89). While Nietzsche did not openly embrace Moleschott's metaphysical materialism, as it reeks of the 'naïve scientism', he appreciated the connections that Moleschott noticed between eating and living (Hymers 2006: 3). In particular, Nietzsche seems fascinated by the ways in which diet shapes morality.[12]

Entrée: Food and morals

Near the beginning of *The Gay Science*, Nietzsche poses an intriguing, though seemingly impossible, task, which must be inspired by Moleschott's materialism.[13] He suggests that some sedulous soul should undertake a 'study of moral matters' that considers the precise ways in which materiality influences moral tastes, behaviour, judgements, imperatives and so on (GS I:7). This study would open 'an immense field for work', including a study of the influence on morality of work schedules, sleep, marriage, friendship, punishment, a 'comparative history of law' and other seemingly extra-moral things (GS I:7). Nietzsche was especially interested in the moral effects of food: 'What is known of the *moral effects of different foods*? Is there any *philosophy of nutrition*? ... There is so much in them to think about' (GS I:7).[14] With Epicurus as our guide, let's think about these things right now.

Ecce Homo includes a Moleschottian assessment of the influence of cultural cuisine on character. German cuisine, he writes, lacks 'conscience because it puts soup before the meal, and because it overcooks meat, vegetables, and pastries, not to forget the "bestial prandial drinking habits"' (EH 'Clever' 1). Hence the 'German spirit' is one of 'distressed intestines' and 'indigestion' (EH 'Clever' 1). The English diet, a modern kind of 'cannibalism' compared to German cuisine, gives the English 'spirit *heavy* feet' (EH 'Clever' 1). Hence the hefty preoccupation with consequentialism and imperialism in England. The 'best cuisine', Nietzsche claims, 'is that of *Piedmont*', the northwest region of Italy bordering France and Switzerland surrounding Turin, where Nietzsche lived prior to his collapse.

However provocative this is, Nietzsche is not claiming that foods will always and only have some distinct moral effect. He is simply showing that moral sentiments (indignation, admiration, censure) are connected to diet because what we eat affects, in oft-mysterious ways, how we think and act, including our moral pronouncements. Hence *Daybreak* claims, 'all the products of his thinking are bound to reflect the condition he is in', especially diet (D 29).

While many ridicule the suggestion that diet shapes moral reasoning, personal experiences with shifts in mood and disposition in a single day suggest otherwise. For example, irritability is common when one is suffering from acid reflux or indigestion, and this might, according to social science, make us more likely to condemn or judge. A study of the effects of satiety and hunger on patterns of sentencing in court found that judges were more likely to find defendants guilty before lunch, when they were hungry, and more likely to be merciful after eating (Danzinger 2011).[15] Nietzsche already smelled this: 'When you are physically tired you will bestow on things a pale and tired coloration, when you are feverish you will turn them into monsters!' (D 539). Nietzsche is attuned to the ways in which what is excluded from morality affects moral judgements and evaluations. We often misidentify what drives us, especially when it is a matter of food. Notice how Nietzsche phrases this observation in terms of nutrition:

> We can scarcely name even the cruder [drives]: their number and strength, their ebb and flood, their play and counterplay among one another, and above all the laws of their *nutriment* remain wholly unknown to him. ... The nutritional requirements of the totality of the drives ... all according to the nutriment which the moment does or does not bear with it ... starvation ... overfeeding ... but the nourishment is scattered ... the hungry ... thirst ... taste every condition ... as in *hunger*, which is not content with *dream food*. (D 74–5)

He is very clear: 'Our moral judgments and evaluations too are only images and fantasies based on a *physiological process unknown to us*' (D 72, 76).[16] Showing us that we are 'unknown to ourselves', especially insofar as what drives action, Nietzsche attunes us to the force of food (GM 15). Thus, when describing the torture of deliberating the possible consequences of an action, 'quite incalculable physical influences come into play' (D 79), such as what we have eaten or how food is affecting us in imperceptible ways.

Returning to his proposal for a vast study of moral matters, Nietzsche knows that even if the most industrious people took on such a study, they 'will find that it involves too much work simply to observe how differently men's instincts have grown and might yet grow' further (GS I: 7). No one person's efforts would suffice because it 'would require whole generations, and generations of scholars who would collaborate systematically, to exhaust the points of view and the material' (GS I:7) Even if success were possible, what Nietzsche calls 'the most insidious question of all' would arise: 'Whether science can furnish goals of action' (GS I:7). Even if some global research project could exhaustively study all moral matters, this does not mean that science can make moral recommendations. Still, there is perhaps one giant step between science and a new morality, one that includes 'centuries of experimentation' (GS I:7). The 'time for that', Nietzsche suggests, 'too, will come' (GS I:7).

Now for the obvious question: Has that time now come? Are we, in the twenty-first century, ready for new experiments in living? It is nearing two centuries since the physiological discoveries that inspired Moleschott, and over 2,000 years since Epicurus offered a philosophy centred on eating and bodily pleasures. We have collected data and performed bodily experiments throughout the world, and we have decades of vast, multinational, rigorous studies of nutrition, diet, agronomy, composting, addiction and more. Have we performed the industrious study Nietzsche imagined? Is it now time for new experiments in living? Though we cannot say for sure, we can offer a meagre proposal, one that involves that part of the science of moral matters that focuses on food and eating. We call it *gastrosophia*.

Plat principal: Gastronomy, or the laws of the stomach

In *Ecce Homo*, Nietzsche says that he is 'much more interested in a question on which the salvation of humanity depends' than on any question concerning '"God", "immortality of the soul", "redemption": "the *question of nutrition*"' (EH 'Clever' 1). The most important question is: 'How do *you*, among all people, have to eat to attain your maximum strength?' (EH 'Clever' 1). To answer this, we harness the force of this Epicurus–Nietzsche encounter in order to sketch the first values of gastrosophia.

The term 'gastrosophia' is my neologism.[17] It is related to the French *gastronomie*, the title of Joseph de Berchoux' 1814 poem on the good life, which is a play on *Gastrologia*, common translation of the title of Athenaeus' ancient lost poem: *Deipnosophistaí* (Δειπνοσοφισταί) (see Berchoux 1819). Gastronomia (γαστρονομία) combines the Greek *gastro*(γαστήρ) and *nomos* (νόμος). *Nomos* means 'law, rule, custom', and philosophy is fascinated by it. But not *autonomy gasto*. *Gastro* means 'belly' or 'stomach', referring to anything that is stuffed, such as a womb. Except Nietzsche and Epicurus, philosophy has largely ignored consideration of the *nomos* of the *gastros*. Gastronomy takes the stomach as the *kanōn* (κᾰνών), the measure or rule for living. We, however, are talking about gastrosophia.

With the belly out front, gastrosophia ferments common moral dualisms: heteronomy/autonomy, contingency/necessity. If autonomy conveys the laws given by and to self, and heteronomy conveys the laws given from another, gastrosophia is somewhere between autonomy and heteronomy. Gastrosophia includes laws from the self and the other, the self as other, the other within; it folds both self and other, inside and outside, together in a single act or in a set of habits. Gastrosophia also distorts another moral dualism: necessity and contingency. The stomach communicates both simultaneously: it is necessary to eat, but what is eaten, to some degree, is contingent. Eating brings need and choice together into a single bite. Yet even this necessity, especially in an original sense, carries a sense of creativity that is not simply implied in autonomy. Consider, for example, how humans learned that the foods we take for granted are not only safe to eat, but nutritious, often delicious. It should dumbfound us whenever we think about how we learned to make certain kinds of cheeses, or how we learned to grow corn.[18] The point is that food bakes together categories that much of philosophy keeps apart: necessity, contingency, choice, creativity. As such, we are not simply interested in blind rule-following but in cultivating new values, which requires wisdom – *sophia* (σοφία). Here are the first three values of gastrosophia.

First Value: *Waste as symptom of sickness*. Consider a basic principle of atomic physics: nothing comes from nothing and nothing returns from nothing. And its correlate: something only becomes something. Parmenides' prohibition holds for atomism: no creation ex nihilo. The difference is that Parmenides responds to this prohibition with the One, atoms with multiplicity. While this is primarily a physico-metaphysical principle, given Epicurus' insistence that laws of nature apply both to smallest (atoms) and to largest things (infinite multiverse), we ask what such a principle means for the human diet. The gastrosophic answer: Waste is a symptom of sickness.

To say that nothing is completely created or destroyed in nature is to say that nothing is wasted in nature. Beyond humans, there is no such thing as waste. Only humans have trash. Epicurus advocated retreat from politics into the Garden because he thought humanity has lost its connection with nature, and the Garden was a space where they might shed their humanity and relearn the lessons of nature. The best way to understand this is to frame the difference between human civilization and nature as a difference in type of *limits*. Humans impose unnatural limits on nature, thereby creating waste. Waste is the byproduct of the misalignment of human limits and natural limits. As Epicurus' diagnosis of human ills is directed at this misalignment, we gastrosophists offer a modern diagnosis: waste is a sign of a life misaligned with nature. Gastrosophia offers an Epicurean-inspired metaphysical value: eliminate ways of living that produce waste by seeking out natural limits.

Second Value: Pleasure as indicator of health. Dan Barber, a contemporary Epicurean chef, says that the pleasurable thing and the ethical thing run along parallel lines: 'Good farming and delicious food are inseparable' (2014: 8). He is speaking about a certain class of pleasures – pleasures of delicious food – which we classify according to Epicurus' taxonomy: natural and necessary pleasures (Epicurus 1994: 34). Barber calls this parallel a 'serendipity' that emerges when we locate natural limits and live accordingly. Given the webs of causal interactions that spread out from the swerve (*clinamen*) to the eating of a delicious carrot, it is serendipitously true that culinary pleasures and ethics map onto each other. Most interesting is the justification for this mapping. The pursuit of great flavour, for Barber, entails ecological and ethical practices. A delicious carrot embodies a series of decisions made by farmers and growers that were intensely ethical. For Barber, it is impossible to unethically raise carrots or unthoughtfully grow raspberries that are delicious. He considers this connection so obvious he calls it 'axiomatic'. Here is his Epicurean logic.

Take two carrots: one delicious, one tasteless. While it is possible to get decent carrots at grocery stores, they are much more common at farmers' markets. The reason is that small farmers raise diversities of vegetables and often diversities of carrots. On small farms, biodiversity organizes its ecology, and when an ecology is biodiverse, land improves. Compare this to monocultural farming, where a single crop is the only thing grown over hundreds of acres. While monocultures seem more efficient, they require constant human intervention. Like a drug addiction, monoculture farming is like taking an opiate to curb pain, then taking another drug to cut the craving to the opiate; then that other drug has negative side-effects on the kidneys, and so another drug is required to save the kidneys, and so on. By contrast, with biodiverse, sustainable farming practices, we can turn to the wisdom of nature (i.e., farm according to nature's limits) to maintain a healthy ecology. While this biodiverse farming might, in some ways, be less efficient, it produces tastier, more sustainable, more *ecologically responsible* and *ethically responsive* ways of growing food. Materially speaking, the two strikingly different carrots tell two different stories about how to live. A more delicious carrot embodies an entire approach to the world, one that connects the pleasure of the tongue and stomach to the composition of nature.

Third Value: Nature determines pleasure's limits. To see how to cultivate a life reflective of natural limits, consider Epicurus' taxonomy. For Epicurus, there are two kinds of pleasures: *kinetic* and *katastematic*, which Cicero terms *voluptas movens* (moving pleasure) and *voluptas stans* (stable pleasure).[19] Epicurus considers the latter – katastematic or stable – more desirable pleasures. Still, since absolute rest is impossible in atomic theory, the ground of the kinetic–katastematic distinction is situated in movement itself. Katastematic pleasure is a kind of motion, it is just an accordant, composed and harmonious movement, which Plutarch describes as 'light and gentle movement' (1967: 1122e). Kinetic pleasure is then more chaotic and volatile movement, and pain is very chaotic, disorganized and unrestrained movement.

Now for some nuance of Epicurus' taxonomy. When Epicurus defines katastematic pleasure negatively – *not* being thirsty, *not* being hungry – what he is doing is removing any reference to pain from his account of the ideal pleasure. To say that katastematic pleasure is the absence of pain, anxiety, sadness and fear, is to say that they are totally absent from such pleasure. Epicurean pleasure thus escapes the whole pleasure–pain, positive–negative, distinction, swerving away from, rather than opposing itself to, the lack-and-fulfilment cycle of empty desires Epicurus identified as the sickness affecting the Greeks. This distinction is hard to notice and easy to confuse, as Nietzsche also saw: people are deceived by the pleasure of civilization because they

> are always *seeking* a deceiver: that is to say, a wine to stimulate the senses. If only they can have *that,* they are quite content with bad bread. Intoxication means more to them than nourishment – this is the bait they will always take! ... this mob taste, which *prefers intoxication to food* ... takes its origin in the highest intellects and has flourished in them for millennia. (D 188)

By contrast, Epicurean katestamatic pleasures are stable because they are forms of harmonious movement that aligns with natural limits, rather than unstable and chaotic limits of the human world. Gastrosophia cultivates pleasures that follow the limits of the natural world.

What Nietzsche admires most about Epicurus is the transformation of hedonic concepts into morsels of bodily wisdom. In *Human, All Too Human*, a passage entitled 'The philosopher of luxuriance', Nietzsche points directly to that Garden thinker: 'A tiny garden, figs, a bit of cheese, and three or four friends besides – this was luxuriance for Epicurus' (HH 192). To render luxury simple or simplicity luxurious, that is the gastrosophic art of Epicureanism that Nietzsche admires, the clearest example of which is the transformation of pleasure from an erratic indulgence into a balanced sense of health and peaceful sensuality. Sensing in Epicurus what he calls 'the happiness of the afternoon of antiquity', Nietzsche tastes the elegance of this ancient philosopher: 'Never before has sensuality been so modest' (GS 45).

Fourth Value: Eating as philosophy. Let us be bold: Gastrosophia is not simply the philosophy *of* food but the cultivation of a way of eating that is itself philosophical. Gastrosophia erases the distance between philosophy and food such that philosophy is no longer an external tool applied to a problematized object but becomes a re-conception of food itself as a philosophy object, while philosophy becomes something grown, harvested, eaten and expelled. For gastrosophists, food holds as much philosophical value as any canonical object of philosophical study – such as truth or justice that we find in classical works like Kant's *Critique of Pure Reason* or Plato's *Republic*. Just as not every book is a philosophy book, only some; just as not every discussion is a philosophical discussion, only some; there are some meals, but not all, that are *forms of philosophizing*. It is one thing to philosophize *about* food, to do the philosophy *of* food, but it is something altogether different to value *eating as a philosophical act* and *philosophy as a kind of eating*. If philosophy truly is a way of living, then eating, an undeniable part of life, must itself be philosophical. We gastrosophists claim that it is not a matter of doing a philosophy *of* food but of actualizing the philosophical potential in our ordinary lives.

These are the first fours values of gastrosophia, emerging out of the Nietzsche–Epicurus encounter: (1) *Waste as symptom of sickness*, (2) *Pleasure as indicator of health*, (3) *Nature as determinant of pleasure's limits*, (4) *Eating as philosophy*. The task of future gastrosophists is to take these and to cook up new values. Epicurus' is offering what Nietzsche calls a 'slow cure' (D 462). Epicurus' cure sparks a re-evaluation of our values by returning the body to the earth so that it is reconstructed by means of natural limits. In doing this, gastrosophists – such as Nietzsche and Epicurus – offer up glimpses of the 'virtues of the future' (D 551).

Dessert: Savouring philosophy

With these four values in hand and our bellies almost full, we now discern how eating and thinking with Epicurus and Nietzsche reorients the history of philosophy.

The term '*Philosophia*', Nietzsche notices, has been misunderstood. It does not merely mean 'love of wisdom' because the *sophia* that is loved (*philia*) or the *sage* that loves wisdom is fundamentally gastrosophic. 'The Greek word "sage", writes Nietzsche, 'is related to *sapio*, I taste, *sapiens*, he who tastes, *sisyphos*, the man of keenest taste. A sharp savoring and selecting or a meaningful discriminating, makes out the peculiar art of philosophy' (PTAG 43). His point is that prior to and undergirding philosophical knowing and judging, we taste and we eat. In this sense, the mouth and belly become the origin of normativity. Similar to Kant's aesthetic judgement, while the 'should' of the mouth and the belly does not (and cannot) point to an objective determination in the world that would demonstrably justify its normative force, there is still a drive to articulate a 'should' when one tastes something wonderful or something terrible: 'You *must* try this asparagus', we might say. There is a connection between orality and morality, if *m-orality* can be traced back to 'mouth' + 'oral'. Might this be a genealogy of orals?

Recalling the role of taste at the origins of philosophizing recasts a distinction that has often put philosophy in a bad light: theory and practice.[20] Gastrosophia brings together theory and practice insofar as philosophical eating cannot be reduced to *either* theory *or* practice. This logic is located in the inability to turn philosophical eating into mere theory or practice, perhaps a sort of *negative* inference. Since gastrosophia *cannot* fall purely into either category, it becomes something beyond both. To play with hyphens, it becomes: practice-theory or theory-practice; or maybe: practical theory or theoretical practice. In an act of philosophical eating, thinking and doing collide. Mind and body uncomfortably unite; spirit becomes matter and matter spirit. Eating makes the *outer inner* and the *inner outer*. To eat is to bring the outside inside such that the inside is no longer simply inside but now (and has always) contains an element of the outside. Eating is the outside becoming inside and the inside becoming outside. Eating is the corporeal act of turning *inside out* or *outside in*. Failing to take food and eating seriously, to pretend like one can survive and thrive on the idea of food, what Nietzsche calls '*dream food*', rather than actual food is what he identifies as 'the most characteristic quality of modern man because it fails to strike the proper balance between interiority and exteriority' (D 74–5).

Digestif: Eating Nietzsche

Quite a luxurious meal we have had. A seven-course meal seems decadent, and given Epicurus and Nietzsche's respective critiques of decadence, we might feel uneasy about it. After all, we want to avoid what Nietzsche calls 'the after dinner nausea' (BGE 282). Risking this, there is one last task, one last thing to taste, this company of eaters. See this quote? Don't read it yet.

Tear it out. Seriously, rip it right out of this book!

> In the midst of the ocean of becoming we awake on a little island no bigger than a boat, we adventurers and birds of passage, and look around us for a few moments: as sharply and as inquisitively as possible, for how soon may a wind not blow us away or a wave not sweep across the little island, so that nothing more is left of us! But here, on this little space, we find other birds of passage and hear of others still who have been here before – and thus we live a precarious minute of knowing and divining, amid joyful beating of wings and chirping with one another, and in spirit we adventure out over the ocean, no less proud than the ocean itself. (D 314)

Did you do it? I hope so. Now put it in front of you, preferably on a plate. Is it there? Once it is, read it several times. First read it quickly, then more and more slowly. On the last, the slowest, read it aloud. Try to taste the words as you speak them, one by one. What do they taste like – a bitter consonant or a smooth vowel? What do you taste when Nietzsche's words are in your mouth? Now pick up that paper, crumble it into a ball, put it in your mouth, and eat it. Chew it slowly, grinding like a cow. Once it is soft enough, swallow it. Then turn the page and start the next chapter.

Notes

1 But we should not forget that Epicurus is said to have died of kidney stones, caused usually due to dehydration.
2 For other ways to order a meal/essay, recall the cannibalistic titles of the three seasons of the TV show *Hannibal*. The first season follows the French *service à la Russe*, the

second and third season, respectively, follow the Japanese or Kaiseki style (Sakizuke, Hassun, Takiawase, Mukōzuke etc.) and Italian (Antipasto, Primavera, Secondo, Aperitivo, etc.) haute cuisine.
3   Another good one: 'Conscience is an organ like a stomach' (WP II: 276).
4   For another take on this, see Allen (1991).
5   '*La Cours de Gilles Deleuze*', 11 February 1983, http://www2.univ-paris8.fr/deleuze/article.php3?id_article=124
6   My translation, with emphasis added.
7   TL 117.
8   Notice that as the Stoics identified Socrates as the best example of the Stoic sage and Feuerbach was a devoted Hegelian for years, both of them retained sympathies for their idealist masters.
9   Diogenes Laertius (1958: VII.73).
10 Referring to Moleschott (1850: 45–67).
11 We should not forget the desire for spices played in ugliness of European colonization of India (see Roy 2010).
12 Bayertz agrees that 'Nietzsche is a difficult case. He picked up many of the findings of the natural sciences and sided on this with the scientific materialists who sought to destroy all kinds of traditional beliefs, e.g. in free will or in God. But he parted company with the scientific materialists when it came to their positive goals: democracy, for example' (Bayertz 2017).
13 For evidence of Nietzsche's reading of the German Materialists, see Stack (1983).
14 Emphases added.
15 While there has been some debate as to the accuracy of this study (Lakens 2017), the disagreement seems to concern the *amount* of the difference in sentencing (sentencing while hungry or while full) and to include other factors in shifts in sentencing. Nothing seems to disprove the effect of hunger on judgement and sentencing.
16 Emphasis added.
17 I invented it to teach a Senior Seminar class at Elon University in Fall 2016.
18 See Pollan (2007) for speculations about the origin and spread of corn.
19 While most commentators agree that Epicurus himself held this distinction, Boris Nikolsky argues that this tradition was imposed on Epicurus by subsequent doxography. See Nikolsky (2001).
20 Carolyn Korsmeyer notices this: 'The very idea of a division between theory and practice is hard to conceive' (2002: 29).

3

'Wisdom that walks in bodily form'
Nietzsche's travels with Epicurus

Jill Marsden

Wisdom has not taken a step beyond Epicurus – and often it is many thousands of paces behind him (KSA 8:23[56]).[1]

It is winter 1876 in Sorrento, the air bright and taut. Nietzsche's pen is poised for a new direction in his philosophy but first he pauses 'like a wanderer pauses, to take in the vast and dangerous land through which [his] mind [has] hitherto travelled' (GM P: 2). This 'pause' on the path marks the beginning of the aphoristic style of writing that will characterize Nietzsche's 'middle period'; from this point on, thought-as-travel will be less a metaphor than the material practice of thinking outside. As Nietzsche's connection to university philosophy atrophies, *walking becomes thinking*. Writing from Sorrento to Reinhart von Seydlitz, Nietzsche imbues his strolling with allegorical significance.

> There are such good walks on sheltered paths between the orange trees, where one is continually calmed by the stillness and it is only in the violent movement in the pines *above* that one *sees* how outside, in the world, a storm is raging. (Reality and simile of our local life – *true* in both senses). (KSB 5:599)

This nascent philosophical insight finds its way into *Human, All Too Human*,[2] but now Nietzsche's footsteps through the orange grove are retraced by 'the Epicurean' enjoying a precious serenity in the grip of a coming storm:

> The Epicurean, then, makes use of his higher culture to make himself independent of prevailing opinions; he lifts himself above them, while the Cynic remains at the stage of negation. He walks, as it were, along windless, sheltered twilight pathways, while above him the tops of the trees roar in the wind and disclose to him how fiercely agitated the world outside is. (HH 275)

The haven of his tranquil path suggests to Nietzsche a contrast, which he proceeds to embellish, between the cool composure of the Epicurean wanderer and the resilience of the Cynic, the latter charging 'naked into the rushing wind', hardening himself to the point of insensibility (HH 275). The contrast is revisited in a similar form in *The Gay Science*, where the 'extreme sensitivity' of the Epicurean intellectual constitution – which 'seeks out the situation, the persons, and even the events' – is generally commended above the flintiness of the Stoic who cultivates the kind of iron stomach that is capable of absorbing anything (GS 306). When Nietzsche traces new thought paths, along the Italian coast, up the hills of Genoa or through Alpine valleys, it is this Epicurean voyage in fine discriminations that marks his journey: a sensitivity to the place, climate and material conditions in which philosophy comes to be.

Nietzsche claims that Epicurus is one of the thinkers to whom he has listened and with whom he has had 'to come to terms' with when he has 'wandered long alone' (AOM 408). That Nietzsche's discovery of Epicurus should unfold in his movement through the landscapes of Italy and Switzerland, suggests that ideas have their own climate and optimum conditions for growth (his 'Sils Maria revelation' of eternal return being a notable example). In two striking passages in which Nietzsche writes most fulsomely about Epicurus, he conjures up beautifully serene, sun-lit settings (WS 295, GS 295), both of which locate an 'experience' of Epicurean happiness rather than describing a philosophical 'stance'. In what follows, I explore how Nietzsche's encounter with Epicurus informs the directions that his 'very physical style of thinking'[3] takes through his middle-period writings. The first part of the chapter discusses how Nietzsche's travels with Epicurus's help to orient his thinking of the body and the earth, most specifically his philosophy of the 'nearest things'. The second part charts a new thought path that links Epicurus to Nietzsche's own reflections on affirmation of life, in particular, the experience of *amor fati* as the affective precondition for Nietzsche's eternal return.

The earth, the garden and the 'Nearest Things'

Writing from the Italian Riviera in 1881, Nietzsche claims to experience the character of Epicurus differently than perhaps anyone else. Envisioning the ancient philosopher in rapt contemplation at the edge of the sea he partakes in the joy of the imagined scene:

> *Epicurus.* Yes, I am proud of the fact that I experience the character of Epicurus differently to perhaps anyone else, and enjoy in all that I read and hear of him the happiness of the afternoon of antiquity: I see his eye gazing out on a vast, white sea, over the rocks along the shoreline where the sun lies, whilst big and small animals play in its light, secure and serene like this light and that eye itself. Such happiness could only have been invented by one who is suffering continually, the happiness of an eye looking out on a becalmed sea of existence and which can now no longer tire of its surface, and the colourful, tender, quivering skin of the sea. Never before has sensuality been so modest. (GS 45)

Attuned to the character of 'Epicurus', Nietzsche feels an affinity of disposition, something more physical than intellectual empathy or philosophical debt. It is as if the ancient philosopher 'lives on' in his own thinking, confirming the assertion that he makes in the aphorism '*The eternal Epicurus*': 'Epicurus has lived at all times and is living still, unbeknown to those who have called and call themselves Epicurean, and without reputation amongst philosophers' (WS 227). When Nietzsche proudly declares an accord with the philosopher who sought to 'live unknown', he may be alluding to his capacity to feel joy in spite of suffering. However, he may also be suggesting a more profound connection, a presentiment within himself of sensibilities from the past. To explore what it might mean to 'feel' powers of the past 'within oneself' (GS 10), it is necessary to travel with the idea in Nietzsche's writing. Here the specificity of the location of the experience seems to offer a first clue.

Much of the writing from Nietzsche's 'middle period', including *Dawn* (1881) and *The Gay Science* (1882), was produced during his time in the radiant Liguria region of the Italian Riviera. Nietzsche spent many hours walking in the Mediterranean hills, resting in the hottest part of the day to absorb the warmth of the sun. In *Ecce Homo* he likens both the text of *Dawn* and its author to a basking sea beast, sunbathing among the rocks near to Genoa where 'almost every sentence of that book was thought, *hatched* [*erschlüpft*]' (EH 'Dawn' 1). Alone and sharing 'secrets with the sea' (EH 'Dawn' 1), the thinker's ideas mature; concepts proliferate, sentences swell and branch out. Praising this work site, Nietzsche writes to Franz Overbeck:

> I think so often about you, especially in the afternoon when almost every day I sit or lie in my secluded cliffs along the coast, resting like a lizard in the sun, while my thoughts embark on some adventure of the spirit. My diet and the division of the day should eventually do me good! Sea air and clear skies: now I see that these are indispensable to me! (KSB 6:76)

Nietzsche writes to Peter Gast and to his mother and his sister on the same day, repeating the lizard image and enthusing about the beneficial effects of the sea and clear sky on his health (KSB 6:74, 75). As is immediately apparent from these remarks, Nietzsche's description of himself sequestered among the rocks in the afternoon sun calls to mind his representation of the contemplative, ocean-gazing Epicurus. Writing to friends about the Genovese coast, he likens its solitude to that of 'an island of the Greek archipelago' (KSB 7:757): 'No doubt about it, there is something *Greek* about this place' (KSB 7:759). In such a setting it is possible that lines of Epicurean verse lap at the edge of his consciousness, as Nietzsche takes pleasure in watching the sea.[4] However, beyond these possible associations and resemblances, a more fundamental material kinship with Epicurus is discernible. When Nietzsche extols the blessings of the climate (sea air and clear skies), marrying them with more domestic matters (diet, division of the day), he reinforces his commitment to the ancient conception of philosophy as the 'art of living'. In further correspondence to Overbeck from St. Moritz, Nietzsche likens his fastidious attention to small details to a *classical* style of living:

> The air is almost better than Sorrento, and is full of fragrances, the way I like it. The way I divide my day, my life-style, my diet – these things would not have dishonoured a wise man of old: everything *very simple* and yet a system of fifty sometimes very delicate considerations. (KSB 5:864)

As is well known, Epicurus commends the virtues of the simple life, particularly the wisdom of liberation from profligate desires and 'turmoil of the mind'.[5] However, as Nietzsche makes clear, simplicity is compatible with a high degree of specificity; indeed, his conception of the 'extremely sensitive' Epicurean constitution is consonant with this. In *Dawn*, he suggests that his philosophy might be seen as a 'translation' into reason of the 'circuitous paths' of his drives: drives for 'gentle sunlight, bright and buoyant air, southerly vegetation, the breath of the sea, fleeting meals of meat, eggs and fruit, hot water to drink, daylong silent wanderings' (D 553). In this sense, the 'content' of Nietzsche's philosophical reflections is inseparable from its 'location'. The possibilities and directions of his deliberations depend to a high degree upon the material conditions of their genesis. Beyond what might appear both rhetorical and polemical flourish, Nietzsche professes an intrinsic relation between weather and ideas. For example, sunlight is accorded a high priority because it is claimed that a lack of light has a retardant effect upon 'our perception of the nearest things' (WS 8). Indeed, according to Nietzsche we have been schooled to despise 'the present and neighbourhood and life' because we have dwelt too long in fog and gloomy weather, gazing wanly at worlds beyond. Even the few who have dwelt in the '*brighter* fields of nature and spirit' have inherited in their blood some of this 'poison of contempt for the nearest things' (WS 16).

The importance of these meteorological conditions and parochial concerns is formulated most explicitly in *The Wanderer and His Shadow*, where Nietzsche claims that the most immediate 'nearest things' [*nächste Dinge*] such as the division of the day, eating, sleeping and other 'small and everyday' matters have been ill-considered in the discipline of philosophy, which has been wrongly oriented towards the 'farthest things' such as metaphysical questions of immortality, god and the soul (WS 6). At no point does Nietzsche explicitly identify Epicurus as an inspiration for the philosophy of the nearest things but the connections are everywhere implicit. For example, the two sections of *The Wanderer and His Shadow* (WS 5 & 6) that introduce the doctrine of the nearest things are directly succeeded by a lengthy passage on the consolations of Epicurean teaching. The 'wonderful insight' that Nietzsche attributes to Epicurus is the realization that to quell the tempests of the soul 'it is absolutely not necessary to have resolved the ultimate and outermost theoretical questions' (WS 7). Faith in the notion of ultimate truth is undermined by Epicurus's embrace of a 'multiplicity of hypotheses' and by his insistence on the gods' disregard for the affairs of mortals (WS 7).[6] Further evidence for the Epicurean influence on Nietzsche's 'nearest things' is to be found in his private notes. Under the title 'The Doctrine of the Nearest Things' he adds the phrase 'retreat from politics' to the familiar litany (division of the day, nourishment, solitude, etc.). The injunction to 'retreat from politics' has a distinctly Epicurean resonance, as do the closing lines of the note, which outline the 'trinity of joy': elevation, illumination, tranquillity. When he elaborates on these lines in *The Wanderer and His Shadow* (332), Nietzsche declares that 'tranquillity' [*Ruhe*], 'greatness' and 'sunlight' are the three good things that 'a thinker desires and demands of himself'. Here the flows between different kinds of forces are united by joy rather than divided according to ontological kind: hopes and duties, elevating intellectual ideas and even the way a thinker 'lives day by day and the landscape in which he dwells' participate collectively in thoughts in which 'all things earthly are transfigured'.[7]

Epicurean philosophy and the nearest things are developed by Nietzsche as elements of a broader philosophical relationship to 'the earth'. Keith Ansell-Pearson proposes that 'Nietzsche is attracted to the Epicurean emphasis on the modesty of a human existence' (2014b: 3), exemplified by simple pleasures and philosophizing in a garden, away from public view: 'A small garden, figs, little cheeses and in addition, three or four good friends – that was the opulence of Epicurus' (WS 192). In his letters to Peter Gast during the 1880s, Nietzsche makes frequent reference to the idea of Epicurus's garden, reflecting repeatedly on the environment in which Epicurus thinks: '*Where* are we going to revive the garden of Epicurus?' (KSB 5:826); 'What I envy in Epicurus are the disciples in his garden' (KSB 6:457). He even compliments Gast for 'everything redolent of the air and fragrance of Epicurus's garden' that has emanated from his recent letters (KSB 6:452). Epicurus's garden seems to represent for Nietzsche, the essential practice of thinking 'outside', both in the sense of being deeply involved with the flows of earthly things and in the sense of being independent of prevailing orthodoxy. In a *Nachlass* fragment, Nietzsche describes the 'lapping of waves on the shore on a quiet summer day' as 'Epicurus's garden happiness' (KSA 8:30[31]). Recalling the 'happiness of the afternoon of antiquity', this is a savouring of the sea at its most soothing, its gentle lull and rush. Away from the academy and the Lyceum, both of which were subject to the scrutiny of the city, the Epicurean garden was a place in which disciples became attuned to the natural world. For the disciples who ate the fruit and vegetables that were grown there, gardening activity was not just an education in the cycles of nature, but an immersion in the elemental: 'Here, in the convergence of vital forces in the garden's microcosm, the cosmos manifested its greatest harmonies; here the human soul rediscovered its essential connection to matter' (Harrison 2008: 73). For Robert Harrison, the most important lesson that the Epicurean garden imparted to those who tended it was that life, in all its variations, 'is intrinsically mortal' and that 'the human soul shares the fate of whatever grows and perishes on and in the earth' (74). Such wisdom calls to mind Nietzsche's old philosopher in *On the Future of our Educational Institutions*, who counsels that if you want to lead a young person on the right educational path, you must ensure that everything is done to preserve the youth's direct and personal relationship with nature:

> Forest and stone, storm and vulture, the single flower, the butterfly, the meadow and the mountainside must speak to him in their own tongues; at the same time he must be able to recognise himself in them as though in countless dispersed reflexes and reflections, in a colourful whirlpool of changing appearances. (FEI 4, KSA 1: 716)

Harrison points out that tending the garden not only served to reinforce the essential imbrication of the human in nature, it also was a potent reminder about the need to tame its wilder forces. Epicurean serenity or *ataraxia* requires continued maintenance if anxiety is to be kept at bay: 'Indeed, a distinct tension pervades the state of *ataraxia*, albeit in a quiet and mastered form, much like the mastered tension that pervades the serene appearance of human gardens' (Harrison 2008: 75).[8]

In *Dawn* Nietzsche reconfigures the Epicurean maxim to 'live unnoticed' to issue the warning that it is lack of continued attention to the smallest of things that leads to our ruin.

> *Do not perish unnoticed*. Not all at once but continually our aptitude and greatness crumble away. It is the scraps of vegetation that grow up, in and around everything and understand how to cling everywhere, that ruin what is great in us – the daily, hourly, wretchedness of our environment which we disregard, the thousand rootlets of this or that small, fainthearted sensation, which grows out of our neighbourhood, out of our duties, our sociality, the way we divide up the day. Should we fail to notice this little weed, we shall ourselves perish of it unnoticed! (D 435)

According to Nietzsche, '*almost all the physical and psychical frailties* of the individual' stem from the failure to attend to the 'nearest things' (WS 6). This is a far-reaching claim because if suffering, both physical and psychological, is attributed to neglect of the nearest things, an Epicurean discernment is required to 'weed out' the forces inimical to life. Moreover, the possibility of 'health' and life affirmation is intimately connected to knowing what is for good or ill in the present moment. Lack of knowledge and poor regard for the nearest things is the baneful legacy of Platonic–Christian values. From the perspective of the latter, the 'nearest' and 'farthest things' are fundamentally different in kind, the latter having been prized as ideal forms, ungrounded in matter and removed from active processes of materialization ('culture'). Because these realms have been regarded as mutually discontinuous, the world is perceived as a mass of isolated beings, unitary souls and brute material forms. However, for Nietzsche, the 'nearest things' are flows, forces and drives: paths between realms the Platonic–Christian world view characterizes as essentially separate. The nearest things do not adhere to the membrane of the self. They constitute the self. They *are* the paths.

Nietzsche's own catalogue of the 'nearest things' include personal preferences and some eccentric proclivities (hot water to drink, daylong silent wandering) but attention to these things is not about knowing 'who' you are; it is about valuing the formative forces that progressively 'make' you. Long after the 'positive' estimation of Epicurus in Nietzsche's middle-period writings, the doctrine of the nearest things endures in his philosophy. For example, in *Ecce Homo*, Nietzsche identifies the impact of the nearest things in terms of the task of 'becoming what one is': 'little things' like nutriment, place, climate and recreation 'are more important than anything that has been considered of importance hitherto' (EH 'Clever' 10). In case this seems a simple, pre-critical determinism it is essential to add the caveat that the physical environment in which writing and thought are possible is reciprocally conditioned by prevailing beliefs. Material forces influence thought, but ideas also have physical effects on the body. Nietzsche integrates this idea into a notebook draft for the most well-known section of *The Gay Science*: the moment in which the thought of the eternal return is first announced by a 'demon'. To the anticipated question 'But if everything is necessary, how can I be in charge of my own actions?' (KSA 9:11[143]). Nietzsche gives the following response: 'You say that food, place, air, society shape and determine you?

Well, your opinions do still more for these determine you to this food, place, air, society' (KSA 9:11[143]). Formed within a 'culture', like cells in solution, perceptions and beliefs have a shaping power on how the nearest things are experienced. Nietzsche goes on to say that 'if you incorporate [*einverleibst*] the thought of thoughts it will change you': 'you' will come to embody the thought; it will become part of your landscape.

Thoughts in which 'all earthly things are transfigured' are fuelled and sustained by the microclimate of the body, which they, in turn, influence through ingrained habits and incorporated beliefs. 'Nature', be it exemplified by a garden, a shoreline or a philosopher, is not dead matter requiring the impress of human reason before achieving any measure of significance or sense. The philosophy of the nearest things helps us to cultivate sensitivity to 'non-human forces acting both outside and inside the human body' (Bennett 2010: xiv). Vast amounts of our bodies are composed of non-human elements, a point not easily grasped because we tend to isolate nature anthropomorphically, according to eye, according to form. As Nietzsche remarks, we speak of nature 'and forget to include ourselves' (WS 327).

> How foreign and superior is our behaviour concerning what is dead, the anorganic, and in the meantime we are three quarters water, and have anorganic minerals in us that perhaps do more for our well and ill being than the whole of living society! (KSA 9:11[207])

Walking with Epicurus, Nietzsche is able to feel forces that have not been translated into the vocabulary of human emotion. The nearest things are thought paths that do not meet at a node of subjectivity. On the contrary, they create a landscape of vital materiality, a 'body' from which consciousness has already withdrawn.

It is to be recalled that at the close of *The Wanderer and the Shadow*, the 'shadow' says to the 'wanderer' that nothing has pleased him more than the promise that has been made in the text to become a 'good neighbour to the nearest things' (WS 16). The proximity of Epicurus is also felt in the closing section of *The Wanderer and the Shadow*:

> Only to *the enobled man will the freedom of spirit* be granted; to him alone does the *alleviation of life* approach and salve his wounds; he first must say that he lives for *joy* and for the sake of no further goal; and in any other mouth his motto would be dangerous: *Peace around me and goodwill to all nearest things*. (WS 350)

To live for joy and for the sake of no other goal is to make a profound affirmation. The state of serene calmness (*ataraxia*) so highly valued by Epicurus is achieved through a grateful embrace of life and particularly an embrace of the nearest things, the gifts of the earth.

2 Paths to affirmation

Epicurus is a fellow traveller with Nietzsche throughout the middle-period writings and a tacit interlocutor on his journey towards affirmation of life. His presence is strongly felt in *The Gay Science*, particularly in Book Four which opens with an affirmation made for the New Year and which closes with the revelation of eternal return and the advent of Zarathustra. In addition to the passages that mention Epicurus or address distinctively Epicurean themes (friendship, happiness, gratitude, suffering), there are many sections dedicated to the nearest things: place, weather, lifestyle and habit. As we have seen, being a good neighbour to the nearest things is fundamental to the serenity and joy at the heart of Epicurean wisdom. Reflecting on *The Gay Science* in *Ecce Homo*, Nietzsche declares that it shows a 'hundred signs of the proximity of something incomparable' (EH 'Zarathustra' 2). His allusion is to the revelation of eternal return, but we might add that *The Gay Science* also shows a hundred signs of the proximity of Epicurus.

Section 276 of *The Gay Science*, which opens Book Four, asserts the resolution to see beauty in necessity, a position that might seem 'strongly reminiscent of Stoicism':[9] '*Amor fati*: let that be my love from now on!' (GS 276) Vowing to love fate, Nietzsche speaks about wanting only to be a 'Yes-Sayer' and not an 'accuser' (GS 276). While this could be read as reconciliation to a radical lack of freedom, such an interpretation hinges upon seeing the self and world as fundamentally separate. From the perspective of the philosophy of the nearest things, this division is no longer tenable. Loving fate is itself part of that fate and not a position external to what 'is'. It is an exercise in modesty, a new way of understanding what might mean to 'live unknown'. Fields of forces in interaction co-produce specific thoughts, some of which manifest in human languages, some of which do not. As the old philosopher in Nietzsche's education lectures reminds us, 'we' are dispersed among the 'colourful whirlpool of changing appearances' and it is forest and stone, meadow and mountainside that must 'speak' to us in 'their tongues' (FEI 4). Once again, the proximity of Epicurus is felt in Nietzsche's writings, for this section is directly followed by a passage entitled 'Personal providence' which affirms the beauty of chance and commends the 'gods of Epicurus' to the extent that these 'carefree and unknown ones' have no involvement with the petty concerns of mortals (GS 277).

In *Philosophy as a Way of Life*, Pierre Hadot alludes to E. Hoffman's claim that 'it is precisely because the Epicurean considered existence to be the result of pure chance that he greeted each moment with immense gratitude, like a kind of divine miracle' (1995a: 252). Indeed, to feel goodwill to all nearest things is to mark a decisive break with the forces that 'accuse life' and to affirm a this-worldly love of the here and now. This bears on the relation of thought to its 'physical' context because Epicurean philosophy cannot thrive in the big cities, which lack quiet and expansive places for reflection and which are dominated by ostentatious monuments to 'other-worldly' discourse (GS 280). In 'Architecture for those who wish to pursue knowledge', Nietzsche writes that the abandoned churches will not meet the needs of the secular thinker: 'We godless ones could not think *our thoughts* in such surroundings' (GS 280). The environment for godless philosophy must be conducive to its this-worldly flourishing: 'We want to see *ourselves* translated into stone and plants, we want to take walks *in ourselves* when we wander around these buildings and gardens' (GS 280).

To see ourselves translated into stones and plants, to take circuitous paths 'in ourselves' as we stroll around buildings and gardens, is to refuse the basic Platonic–

Christian presumption of the 'inner' sanctum of thought. Even supposing it could be isolated, locating 'a thought' inside a human skull seems as futile as Descartes grasping for the pineal gland. Being a good neighbour to the nearest things entails rejecting the boundary between the brain and somatic forces – which are themselves constrained by a prior thinking of the body as a physical entity and property of the self. If it is the case that fractions of a landscape can be conscious and self-conscious and privilege themselves as human through the miracle of primate psychology, might not larger fractions, which are almost certainly more complex, be credited with a will and a consciousness of a kind? In section 291 of *The Gay Science* entitled 'Genoa', Nietzsche says that he has studied the buildings and landscapes of this city for a long time and declares that he can see the 'faces' of past generations.

> Genoa. I have looked upon this city for a good while, its villas and pleasure gardens and the wide circuits of its inhabited heights and slopes. Finally I must say this: I see *faces* of past generations. This district is strewn with the images of bold and autocratic men. They have *lived* and have wanted to live on – they say so with their houses, built and decorated for centuries, and not for the fleeting hour: they were well disposed to life [*sie waren dem Leben gut*], however ill-disposed they may often have been towards themselves. (GS 291)

To become 'well-disposed to life' manifests itself as a desire to live on. This is not a desire for immortality but for the externalization of desire, its manifestation in things. For Nietzsche, thought is 'of' the world, not 'in' the thinker. All the default settings of language militate against taking this idea as far as it will go. To think of the soul or self as an internal entity is a Christian prejudice. For Nietzsche, souls are not unitary, immaterial, ghosts of another world. On the contrary, rare human beings of an age are best thought of as 'the suddenly emerging after-shoots [*plötzlich auftauchende Nachschösslinge*] of past cultures and their powers: as atavisms of a people and its ethos' (GS 10). In a wonderful passage, 'Why we have to travel' (AOM 223), Nietzsche claims that 'the past continues to flow within us in a hundred waves; we ourselves are, indeed, nothing but that which at every moment we sense of this continued flowing' (AOM 223). The traveller soon discovers that one cannot step into the river of one's most intimate being twice. Moreover, the one who becomes adept in the 'subtler art of travel' will rediscover the adventurous migrations of his ego, 'in the process of becoming and transformation', in many countries and ages, in Egypt and Greece, Byzantium and Rome, 'in the Renaissance and the Reformation, at home and abroad, indeed in the sea, the forests, in the plants and in the mountains' (AOM 223). One rediscovers the flows of the past in oneself with every fresh encounter, finding within *this world* hitherto unguessed-at depths:

> We need history, for the past continues to flow within us in a hundred waves; we ourselves are, indeed, nothing but that which at every moment we sense of this continued flowing. ... The last three centuries very probably still continue to live on, in all their cultural colours and cultural refractions, *close beside us* [*in unserer Nähe*]: they want only to be *discovered*. (AOM 223)

Directly after this passage in *Assorted Opinions and Maxims*, Nietzsche speaks of ages in which the senses are so blocked that they are incapable of hearing the voice of reason and philosophy or of seeing 'wisdom that wanders in bodily form [*die leibhaft wandelnde Weisheit*] whether it bears the name of Epictetus or of Epicurus' (AOM 224).[10] 'Wisdom walking in bodily form' implies a thinking relationship with the material environment, an alertness to the sensory richness of air, temperature, fragrance and light. Like Epicurus, who embodies this wisdom, Nietzsche traces thought-streams which meander through the countryside and byways, through buildings and gardens, translating themselves into stones and plants. Whatever is read or heard by Nietzsche is carried into the open where it quickly sloughs off its scholarly scent. His habit of thinking outdoors [*im Freien zu denken*] also manifests itself as 'walking, jumping, climbing, dancing, preferably on lonely mountains or close by the sea where even the paths become thoughtful' (GS 366).[11] This practice testifies to the power of 'walking as enabling sight and thought' and the power of paths as yielding 'not only means of traversing space, but also ways of feeling, being and knowing' (Macfarlane 2013: 24). Certain thoughts belong to a particular atmosphere, to a time and place of their genesis. In asking what one can know in a place that is unreachable elsewhere one is effectively asking, 'What does the place know?'[12]

Indeed, it is a rationalist prejudice to separate ideas from their conditions as if their blossoming were independent of all nutrients. When Nietzsche declares that paths become 'thoughtful', this is not a metaphor for an intellectual journey but a description of how thinking is part of a climate and a landscape. A provisional title for *The Wanderer and His Shadow* was 'Thought-paths of St Moritz' (KSA 8:610). Almost all of it was written in six pocket-sized notebooks that Nietzsche carried with him on hikes through the hills and around the lakes of St. Moritz, Silvaplana and Sils Maria (Krell and Bates 1997: 122–3). Among the few fragments gathered under this title in Nietzsche's private notes, Nietzsche describes a sublime experience of 'heroic-idyllic' power.

> The day before yesterday, towards evening, I was completely immersed in Claude Lorrainian raptures and finally burst into lengthy, intense crying. That I was still to experience this! I had not known that the earth could display this and had believed that good painters had invented it. The heroic-idyllic is now the discovery of my soul; and everything bucolic of the ancients has become all at once unveiled to me and made manifest – until now I did not understand anything of this. (KSA 8:43[3])

Nietzsche's discovery of the 'heroic-idyllic' in St. Moritz is an encounter with ancient forces 'living on' *close beside him*. According to Robert Macfarlane, certain paths have the capacity to conduct the walker back into deep time, 'as if time had somehow pleated back on itself, bringing discontinuous moments into contact' (Macfarlane 2013: 24). This profound experience in St. Moritz is the inspiration for a striking passage in *The Wanderer and His Shadow* entitled 'Et in Arcadia ego' (WS 295), in which Nietzsche describes stumbling upon an uncannily mythic landscape. Like the 'Epicurus' section of *The Gay Science* (45), this passage details a sun-lit scene of tremendous beauty. The ground is vivid with flowers and grasses, 'waves of hills' cascade to a 'milky green lake'. Overwhelmed by the loveliness of the place, he trembles in wordless adoration of 'the moment [*Augenblick*] of its revelation':

> Unconsciously, as if it were only natural, one transposed Hellenic heroes into this pure, clear world of light (which had nothing about it of yearning or expectancy, no looking forward or backward); one had to feel it as Poussin and his pupil would have done – at once heroic and idyllic. And so too have individual people *lived*, and have constantly *felt* themselves to be in the world and the world in them and among them one of the greatest men, the inventor of a heroic-idyllic form of philosophy: Epicurus. (WS 295)

Epicurus is 'experienced' on Nietzsche's thought path in the midst of the Swiss mountains. Charged with ancient sensibilities, the traveller conjures Hellenic spirits from a newly enchanted earth. Without forethought Greek heroes are summoned forth, with no trace of yearning or expectancy, no 'looking forward or backward'. To live without desire or expectation, without longing for the future or lingering in the past, is to live in the eternity of the moment. In St. Moritz, Nietzsche realizes that this is how individuals have actually lived; more, this is how 'they have enduringly *felt* they existed in the world and the world existed in them' (WS 295). When Epicurean affects are transmitted in this entrancing 'clear world of light', heroic-idyllic philosophy is lived and felt as a profound affirmation of the earth. The character of Epicurus, one 'of the greatest men', is experienced by Nietzsche as overwhelming love of fate: 'My formula for greatness in a human being is *amor fati* ... that one wants nothing to be other than it is, not forwards not backwards, not in all eternity' (EH 'Clever' 10).

Love of fate is only possible when one feels oneself to be part of the world. To live without *ressentiment*, to love the things of the earth, is to achieve a state of Epicurean tranquillity. On the untitled page that lies between the foreword and the first section of *Ecce Homo*, Nietzsche expresses a supreme gratitude to his 'whole life'.[13] The image is a rich and fertile one, a perfect moment of sun-lit brilliance:

> On this perfect day, when everything has become ripe and not only the grapes are growing brown, a ray of sunlight has fallen on to my life: I looked behind me, I looked before me, never have I seen so many and such good things together.

This 'goodwill to all nearest things' is an expression of gratitude for the bounty of the earth. To become 'so well disposed' to life that you would fervently desire its eternal return it is necessary to make an affirmative pact with fate. As Joseph P. Vincenzo writes, for both Nietzsche and Epicurus, 'the world can show itself as it is only when one steps out of the subjective, servile will and into the state of cessation of all need' (1994: 394). To feel oneself to be in the world and to embody its vital forces, is to '*realize in oneself* the eternal joy of becoming' (TI 'Ancients' 5).

> For Epicurus, *ataraxia* is an experience of the maximum pleasure of the aesthetic world and of oneself. It is a direct experience of the intrinsic pleasure of life itself,

of the active forces of a life freed from the reactive force of desire. (Vincenzo 1994: 392)

The announcement of eternal return in section 341 of *The Gay Science* is prefaced by 'The Dying Socrates' (GS 340), a section in which Nietzsche presents his ultimate indictment of Platonism. Facing death, Socrates asks to make an offering to the god of medicine. The words, 'O Crito, I owe Asclepius a rooster' betray his secret suffering of the 'disease' of life (GS 340), his craven desire to live 'beyond'. The judgement that Socrates passes on life reveals that this mortal earth is fundamentally deficient, so compensation for suffering must be sought beyond. The contrast with Zarathustra's 'sickness of bounty' (GS 342) revealed at the end of *The Gay Science* could not be stronger. Between the dying Socrates and the advent of Zarathustra, the possibility of life affirmation bears the 'greatest weight' (GS 341).

For Epicurus, the adage, 'Look to the end of a long life' betrays a lack of gratitude for past blessings.[14] Both Nietzsche and Epicurus affirm the joy of the present, irrespective of the ills that assail them. Indeed, there is an essential connection between the nearest things and the ability to profoundly affirm transience. In *The Gay Science*, Nietzsche offers a hymn of thanks to the bounty of 'brief habits' (GS 295). Having loved a certain thing with 'faith in its eternity', he declares that a time will come when it will depart, 'peacefully and sated with me as I am with it – as if we had reason to be grateful to each other' (GS 295). This happens with a host of things: 'Dishes, ideas, human beings, cities, poems, music, doctrines, ways of arranging the day, life styles' (GS 295). Life is deemed intrinsically pleasurable and not found lacking when things fail to endure. In fact, Nietzsche expresses profound gratitude for the illnesses which have compelled him to become so reconciled to transience.

> Yes, at the bottom of my soul I feel grateful to all my misery and bouts of sickness and everything about me that is imperfect, because this sort of thing leaves me with a hundred backdoors through which I can escape from enduring habits. (GS 295)

Taking 'a step further in convalescence', the 'free spirit' in Nietzsche's preface to *Human, All Too Human* (1886) professes gratitude for his expeditions: 'He looks thankfully back, grateful to his wandering, to his hardness and self-alienation' (HH P: 5). Slowly returning to health, he is full of wonder: 'Where *had* he been? These near and nearest things: how changed they seem! What bloom and magic they have acquired in the meantime!' Thankful for not having stayed muffled up at home, he concludes, 'he had been *beside* himself [*ausser sich*] no doubt of that'. In spite of his old sickness and relapses of health he feels immense happiness as he lies in the sun: 'They are the most grateful animals in the world, also the most modest, these convalescents and lizards again half turned towards life.'

Perhaps as Nietzsche lies in the sun, embarking on 'adventures of the spirit', he journeys with Epicurus through archaic-idyllic regions where landscape merges with timescape.

It is reputed that on the last day of his life Epicurus wrote to Hermarchus of his suffering and imminent death:

> I am suffering from diseases of the intestines and bladder which could not be more severe. ... However, all these sufferings are compensated by the joy of remembering our principles and our discoveries. ... My joy compensates the totality of pain. (Gaskin 1995: 66)

Whatever torments they may each have known, there is no hint in the writings of Epicurus or of Nietzsche of ill will towards fate. Nietzsche to Peter Gast, 22 January 1879:

> My health is abominable – rich in pain, like before; my life much more severe and lonely; I myself live on the whole almost like a complete saint, but almost with the disposition [*Gesinnung*] of the complete, genuine [*ächt*] Epicurus – very calm in soul and patient and yet watching life with joy. (KSB 5:799)

When Nietzsche claims to experience the character of Epicurus differently than perhaps anyone else he feels a resurgence of the extraordinary effects of Epicurus, a stirring of the 'past within'. It seems likely that when he extolls the pleasures of the afternoon of antiquity he is recounting his rapturous experiences in the thought paths of St Moritz. This delight resurfaces on many an afternoon when on the rocky Genovese coast he lies like a lizard in the sun, watching life with joy.

To 'want' something, to 'strive' after something, to have a 'goal', a 'wish' in view – I do not know this from experience. Even at this moment I look out upon my future – a *vast* future! – as upon a smooth sea: it is ruffled by no desire. I do not want in the slightest that anything should become other than it is; I do not want myself to become other than I am. But that is how I have always lived (EH 'Clever' 9).

Notes

1. Translations are my own.
2. See Paolo D'Iorio's discussion of this connection (D'Iorio 2016: 75).
3. See letter to Franz Overbeck, 10 February 1883 (KSB 6:373).
4. See Book II of Lucretius's *De Rerum Natura* (Gaskin 1995: 120).
5. See 'Letter to Menoeceus' (Gaskin 1995: 45).
6. According to Keith Ansell-Pearson, it is 'from Epicurus that Nietzsche gets the inspiration to give up on what he calls the first and last things, the questions of a theologically inspired metaphysics, and devote attention to the closest things' (2013: 104).
7. The thoughts that correspond to these three great things are by turns, 'soothing', 'elevating' and 'illuminating'. Thoughts that share all three qualities are those in which 'all things earthly are transfigured' and which partake of the kingdom of the great '*trinity of joy*' (WS 332).

8 Gary Shapiro makes a similar point when he argues that the garden is 'a deliberate shaping and arranging of earthly elements. It is a form of thinking with the earth, a realization of its possibilities, and a mode of giving the earth a direction (Sinn)' (2013: 74).
9 See Gaasterland (2016: 74). Gaasterland argues that *amor fati* is not a Stoic directive.
10 As Pierre Hadot explains, for both Epicurus and Epictetus, philosophy was primarily about the 'art of living' (1995a: 267).
11 He gives the example of the mountains at Portofino 'knowing how to end', sloping into the sea with proud and calm harmony 'where the bay of Genoa ends its melody' (GS 281).
12 A related question would be 'How does this thought move?' In GS 282 Nietzsche suggests that crude thoughts are betrayed by their 'gait and stride': 'They cannot *walk*.'
13 Richard Bett notes that Pierre Hadot includes Nietzsche in his discussion of the value of the present instant in ancient philosophy, citing a passage on saying 'yes' to eternity by saying 'yes' to a single moment. However, he does not see any relevant link to Epicurus: 'The thought is clearly connected with the attitude expressed in Nietzsche's contemplation of the eternal recurrence; but this is not especially relevant to Nietzsche's view of Epicurus' (Bett 2005: 70).
14 'Ungrateful towards the blessings of the past is the saying, "Wait till the end of a long life"' (Gaskin 1995: 53).

4

Epicurean gardens and Nietzsche's white seas

Babette Babich

Over tranquil seas: Hermeneutics and palimpsests

For more than a century, the Kroner edition of 1913 served as the source for scholars interested in Nietzsche and classical philology, despite the mainstream judgement of the classical tradition, which had by then for more than thirty years deemed him unworthy of engagement (Nietzsche 1913).[1] I am not going to retell the disastrous history of the famously non-collegial reception of Nietzsche's first book among his peers (and still). But the advantage of a book, containing scholarly work one is not meant to read, and certainly not to cite, just as analytic philosophers read past colleagues deemed insignificant, is that one can borrow with abandon and a certain lack of rigour. Thus, Nietzsche shows up here and there in classical scholarship throughout the past century, unflagged, or, even casually, adduced. Finding such references would require inventing yet another subdiscipline of classics. Scholarly 'ghosting' is a thing, of course, and Nietzsche is its poster child.

In that 1913 edition, one can find Nietzsche's lectures on the pre-Platonic/pre-Socratic philosophers, and a version of *Philosophie im tragischen Zeitalter der Griechen* had already appeared in 1896 (Nietzsche 1896: 1–132). Nietzsche offered his own lecture course, featured in the Kroner edition as well, on Ritschl's favourite disciplinary study of bio-bibliography, that is, pinakography (after Callimachus' listing of titles in the Library of Alexandria), (Pfeiffer 1949),[2] with a course on philosophical succession (διαδοχή) in 1873–74 (Nietzsche 1913: 305).[3]

Epicurus appears in Nietzsche as part of a listed array connected to Nietzsche's earlier lectures on Plato's dialogues concluding with a discussion of Plato's physics, in which Nietzsche argues that the association of Epicurus with the atomists follows Diogenes Laertius who appends Epicurus after Nausiphanes and Nausikudes (Nietzsche 1913: 310). Earlier, Nietzsche was able to begin his *Democritea* reflecting that for a Christian (and 'anti-cosmic') age, the writings of both Democritus and Epicurus could be regarded as the incarnation of 'heathendom' (Nietzsche 1913: 327).[4]

Pinakographic of names and lists, authors and books and, especially, of citations is key to any reading of Epicurus, as he is counted among the leading 'polygraphs', that is, more than ordinarily prolific. For the Greeks, Nietzsche explains, this kind of claim is so routine that Socrates's ascribed ascesis, whereby he writes nothing, stands out by contrast (and has thus to mean something). Thus, there was a competition on bookish productivity, whereby Chrysippus's high achievement ('705 books') would spark Epicurus' jealousy, outclassing him as Chrysippus did by '100 books' (Nietzsche 1913: 338).[5] Nevertheless, and for Nietzsche, this is part of the same culture of contest: Epicurus' followers insisted that written out in Epicurus' books are the equivalent of the writings of 'many Greek philosophers, including Chrysippus', as Epicurus

> in all his writerly undertakings remained original and independent, disdaining in aristocratic self-regard, the cheap fashion others had of filling books with citations. (Nietzsche 1913)

Some scholars today seem to channel this Epicurean–Chrysippean sniping, as Stanley Cavell once divided philosophy not into analytic and continental kinds but instead into those who sought to give the appearance of having read everything as opposed to those who wished to appear as if they had read nothing.

Nietzsche lists the ranking, starting with Zeno (after pointing out that from Zeno we have 'one book and a couple of inauthentic ones') (Nietzsche 1913: 342),[6]

Zeno = 100
Xenocrates = 200
Democritus = 300
Aristotle = 400
Epicurus = 600
Chrissippus 700. (Nietzsche 1913: 343)

After this listing, Nietzsche traces Democritus as palimpsest for Epicurus – so much for originality (Nietzsche 1913: 375) – while still insisting on the same originality, this Nietzsche tells us repeatedly, that led Epicurus to deny the existence of Leucippus altogether. The 'autodidactic-affectation' (Nietzsche 1913: 380), as Nietzsche names it, remains significant for the science of classical philology as such. Later Nietzsche invokes the image of heedlessly brushing the dust from the butterfly of history to express a similar rage not of authorly ego, or claims of non-influence for one's hero, but politically and on the historical stage: in this case Rome against its predecessors, all of them, Etruscans, Greeks, etc.

There are hints here of how one might (quite without offending the classic powers that be), in philology or in philosophy, use Nietzsche for research profit. Thus the classicist, Diskin Clay is able to cite, in a footnote no less, Nietzsche's reference to the sea when speaking of Epicurus, usefully reminding us of the important connection in Greek between ἀταραξία (tranquillity, unperturbedness) and the (untroubled) sea.[7] In another essay, Clay foregrounds the question Nietzsche highlights concerning attribution with respect to a discovery Nietzsche could only have, with minimal likelihood, known (he could have, the dates work for that, but we lack positive certainty), to wit: Diogenes of Oinoanda, a name unknown to/unmentioned by Nietzsche's Diogenes Laertius, man of names as he was, man of lists.[8] The reference is to an archaeological discovery, coincidentally mirroring Nietzsche's own emphasis on the influence of Epicureans and not less the issue of the relation between, or succession of, teachers and followers – the world's 'most massive inscription'[9] (more than 2.37 metres high and 80 metres wide), the legacy of the second-century CE Epicurean, Diogenes of Oinoanda, discovered in Turkey in 1884.[10]

As for Nietzsche, he will ask us to pay attention to the great difference between ourselves and antiquity. Thus Nietzsche, expert on Pindar, highlights the 'significance of water and the sea for the Greeks' (KSA 8: 118). At the conclusion, I will return to Nietzsche's striking description of the sea in such ecstatic moments – these are vistas from a distance, sometimes literally from the perspective of flight – in addition to underscoring its unruffled character: he several times repeats the same descriptive reference to a vista of rocks and sea, a landscape of olive or fig trees, along with 'purple melancholy' and the whiteness of the sea.

Reading ambiguity: Between Nietzsche and Epicurus

Epicurus was well known in antiquity as an important interlocutor for Cicero and Seneca and notably foregrounded in Lucretius' *De Rerum Natura*.[11] To this same extent, Epicurus had Alexandrian affinities, magnified, as Nietzsche emphasizes, by 'Roman philhellenism', that is, a 'Hellenization in fourfold coarsening and oversimplification'.[12]

Today, Epicurus appeals to us for his apparently 'modern' focus on sense observation, his avoidance of myth, matched with a tendency to mock 'other people's myths', and his proclivity for *simple* reasoning. To this, as mentioned earlier, one may add his contribution to/dependence on Democritean atomism (Nietzsche 1913: 202),[13] with his παρέγκλισις, the declination or swerve, better known as the *clinamen* in Lucretius' *De Rerum Natura*.[14]

Epicurus' cosmology is influential in Anglophone circles, letters and philosophy. Tennyson epitomizes the Epicurean gods in his poem *Lucretius* and the humanely naturalistic schematism 'of settled sweet Epicurean life'. In addition to Reid and Hume, Epicurus inspired Locke and Mill and Bentham,[15] among those interested in what analytic philosophy dubs 'naturalism'. On the continent, Epicurus' influence is manifest in thinkers from Montaigne to Gassendi, Molière, La Fontaine, Casanova (of course, of course, if we are thinking of a life of pleasure) as well as Queneau,[16] continuing in Henri Bergson, Gilles Deleuze, Michel Serres, Pierre Hadot, Michel Foucault (who alludes to Epicurus and repeats Epicurus, while conspicuously failing to reference Epicurus, ergo, so Hadot, a proof of influence).[17] And after more than a century of monumental discovery, additional scholarly discoveries continue to surround Epicurus.[18]

In the tradition of German philosophical reception of Epicurus, Fritz Bornmann notes that prior to Marx, Epicurean studies from a German language perspective were fairly spare and it is useful to read Volker Ebersbach's more recent discussion.[19] Hermann Usener's *Epicurea*, (1887),[20] would itself profit from, as Usener also praises, Nietzsche's *Laertiana*.[21] What is here essential is that, Usener originally planned to work together with Nietzsche on a joint project on Early Greek philosophy , so Nietzsche writes to Rohde (16 June 1869), subsequently becoming, as Hermann Diels tells us, a joint project between Nietzsche and Diels. As it transpired, given Nietzsche's call to

Basel, the project would be completed by Diels alone, who published his *Fragmente der Vorsokratiker* in 1903.[22]

To be sure, Diels drew upon[23] – just as Usener's *Epicurea* drew upon while going beyond – Nietzsche's source work on Diogenes Laertius, in studies he published in the foremost journal of the day, *Das Rheinische Museum für Philologie* (1868–1869: 632–53 and 181–228).[24] Thomas Brobjer famously speaks of 'Nietzsche's Forgotten Book'[25] or better said: forgotten *books*. For not only did Nietzsche establish source scholarship as such, as it were, for Diogenes Laertius, the source of sources, but and especially relevant in the case of Epicurus, given the lengthy concluding chapter Diogenes Laertius dedicates to him, Nietzsche also did not stop at that but went on to write on history including reflections on historical persons (Jesus) in the *Untimely Meditations*.

Nietzsche's 1869 inaugural lecture at Basel already laid out the foundational question of classics in terms of the historical 'person', that is, the 'Homer question', quite as if Nietzsche meant to match Diels' doxographic focus thereby.[26] Nietzsche continued to foreground the same notion of 'personality', highlighting the 'personal' by contrast with the doctrines (*doxa*) of the 'pre-Platonic philosophers' (including Socrates) as biographical texts (Diogenes Laertius) can very often be the only material available to scholars: the raw stuff of ancient philology. Underscoring the force of the scattered, 'concentrated' fragments we do have, Nietzsche emphasizes that 'the greatest part of philosophical prose is lost to us' (KGW II/4, 214). But in spite of this absence, that is, on the basis of no evidence whatsoever, deriving as we scholars, 'we philologists' are wont to do, the 'unknown on the basis of the known', we also proceed to 'discount these [same missing or lost works] in our valuation of them' (KGW II/4, 214). Nietzsche, specialist in source scholarship, expert on matters of missing work, noted thereby that in consequence we must count the greater part of Heraclitus, Empedocles and, not less, Democritus 'whose writings the ancients paralleled with Plato', as lost quite by comparison with the 'voluminous' (KGW II/4, 214) legacy of Plato and Aristotle – we may go back to Nietzsche's list of prolific writers – abandoning us to take what 'comfort' we can in, note both Nietzsche's irony and his listing of, the 'Stoics, Epicureans, and Cicero' (KSA 8: 107–8).[27]

Nietzsche's reflections on Epicurus run throughout *The Wanderer and His Shadow* after the first volume of *Human, All Too Human*, as well as *Thus Spoke Zarathustra*. And if we are thinking about Epicurus, we are following the doxographic or doctrinal succession typical of scholarly classifications as we still speak of these: that is, as we speak of Epicureans and of Platonists and of neo-Platonists, which is to say that we think in terms of schools, sometimes in sheer metonymic contiguity, invoking Aristotle's Stoa, Plato's academy, Epicurus' *kepos*, 'the garden'.

Prescribing happiness: The list

Epicurus' teaching has been epitomized in brief summaries, including the concise *Tetrapharmakos* summarized in Philodemus, *To the Friends of the School*:

1. Don't fear the gods.
2. Don't worry about death.

3. What is good is easy to get.
4. What is terrible is easy to endure.

Brevity enhances the appeal of these counsels and brevity is the test of the aphoristic as a focus for Nietzsche.

In 1879, writing *The Wanderer and His Shadow*, eventually to appear as a capstone to the second volume of *Human, All Too Human*, Nietzsche employs Epicurus' teachings to criticize Wagner as an exemplary artist of the very small in his ambition to be an artist of the very large. But at this juncture, circa 1886, and here we might recall the above-mentioned discovery of Diogenes of Oionanda (1884), Nietzsche begs the reader's indulgence: 'I have dared to paint my happiness on the wall' (GS 56). Earlier, in The *Wanderer and His Shadow*, written just as he would conclude his ten years in Basel, a striking apothegm for Epicurean happiness: '*The philosopher of opulence [Ueppigkeit]* – A tiny garden [*Gärtchen*], figs, little cheeses, and to that three or four good friends – that was the opulence [*Ueppigkeit*] of Epicurus' (WS 193).

Nietzsche draws this listing from Diogenes Laertius, but here we may note less an attestation to diet (we return to this later) than a meditation on luxury *qua* luxury, whereby the reader is to conclude, and this is the Protestant ethic of capitalism for those who do not have as for those who do: *less is more*. Indeed, in an era of late capitalism, our oceans full of floating garbage, and a world replete with environmental pollution of every elemental kind, fires raging, air and aether, water and earth, we might do well to think abstemiousness as opulence. Surely so, yet it is also key to reflect this as a challenge: What are the resources needed simply to attain the luxury of such modesty?

Similarly, we may pose a question to the famous *Tetrapharmakos*: Why only four rules? Why not three? And why merely a small garden, could it not be a little bigger, why figs, why little cheeses, is that not a matter of taste and dietary sensibility? And if the former is nugatory, why so *few* friends? Three or four?[28] Is *four* too many? Would *three* be too spare?

Nietzsche, who emphasizes the negative above all,[29] also tells us that Epicurean 'happiness is negative' (KSA 9: 151). Thus privative, sufficiency *is* opulence. The argument from Epicurus has yielded a tradition of those who argue for the luxury of simplicity and who thereby also maintain, in principle, that that same luxury is universally available. Other reflections include economics, minor and major,[30] as well as a certain democratic tone. And in this spirit, along with slaves, Epicurus' school counted women.

Living on the edge of Athens, not unlike the outskirts of any major town, we can ask again about what it would take such that one would have access to a garden? Presumably, on the model of the friends and the figs and the cheeses, this is to be a garden of one's own. Clearly, this personal reference mattered for Nietzsche, as he was fond of the reference, invoking it in letters to Paul Rée and also to Heinrich Köselitz.[31] It could not quite be a communal garden (if only because another group of friends might commandeer it first). A 'little thing' of this kind thus turns out to be a fairly substantive achievement. In this fashion, Hölderlin's *An die Nacht* (*To the Night*), the first verse of *Bread and Wine*, refers to the gardens attached to the privileged houses along the Neckar and little alleys around the market (these are largely the same) and when it comes to cities and their gardens in Berlin or in London or in New York, not much has changed.

We are also to think beyond little cheeses (beyond the time and knowledge conditional for the same) to the figs. Some readers have claimed these as Nietzsche's favoured fruit (apart from grapes). Further, we know that figs put Nietzsche in mind of the seasons, as Nietzsche foregrounded ripened figs, metaphors for the passage of time. Foresight is involved, required for the garden and the cultivation of happiness, a matter of circumspection: figs can be fresh or dried, relative to the *little cheeses*, maybe a Marcellin, an *époisse* or a little *crottin* wrapped in a certain leaf (perhaps of asphodel – the same powdered root of which was mentioned by Professor Severus Snape with its allusion to Homer and his Elysian fields) in J. K. Rowling's *Harry Potter and the Philosopher's Stone*.[32] The leaf-wrapped cheese announces its own time, drying out to underscore the brevity of life, as Seneca, himself influenced by Epicurus, will write. Much of this comes under meteorology, as Caygill beautifully reminds us, garden moments have good weather as a prerequisite.[33]

Again: minimalism is key to luxury: the right thing, the right measure, no superfluity – all George Gordon precision, *one shade the more, one ray the less*. A corollary would be Nietzsche's *everything is needful* – it's the constellation, everything together, that is opulence.

Thus, the Nietzsche of *The Gay Science* reflects on what he calls 'the happiness of the afternoon of antiquity' and gives us the vista of the sea to do it, telling us the sea, as Epicurus' eyes might have seen it:

> A wide white sea, across rocks at the shore that are bathed in sunlight, while large and small animals are playing in this light, as secure and calm as the light and his eyes. Such happiness could be invented only by a man who was suffering continually. It is the happiness of eyes that have seen the sea of existence become calm, and now they can never weary of the surface and of the many hues of this tender, shuddering skin of the sea. Never before has voluptuousness been so modest. (GS 45)

Later, Nietzsche's reflections on 'his happiness', *Mein Glück*, will come back again, after the interval that sees the publication of *Thus Spoke Zarathustra* in the poems appended to the second edition of *The Gay Science*, the poems of Prince Vogelfrei, but the above word painting also recurs in several loci, outlined in a poem dedicated to becalmed being in the south: *Im Süden*.

In *The Wanderer and His Shadow*, Nietzsche's reflections are not of happiness gleaned after suffering, abstracted from the 'sea of existence' (contrasting with the beginning of *The Gay Science* with its Aeschylean 'waves of laughter'), nor, indeed, a reflection on the rare 'modesty' of voluptuousness, but, and just, '*the simple life*',

> Nowadays a simple mode of life is hard: it requires much more reflection and inventive talent than is possessed by very clever people. (WS 196)

Nietzsche's aphorism to follow, '*The Epochs of Life*', highlights the relevance of Epicurus' cosmological theory for his life principles. The cyclical, seemingly eternal return or exchange between delight *and* desire, highlights the volatility of perfection as consummation – Nietzsche tells us that only one's twenties, thirties and forties are the decades to be counted in life, the years before being preludes, the years after discounted for reflection: 'Here one has attained a state of satisfaction. All else is hunger and thirst – or satiety' (WS 193).

Garden gods and Epicurean skies

Epicurus' divinities are often discussed: Perhaps one criticizes the gods by simultaneously proposing that gods, if they are divine, and note the Platonic lineage of the argument, will not/cannot concern themselves with humanity (Nietzsche traces the connection with some care), such that ataraxia, the smoothness of an untroubled soul, might be a godlike condition worthy of emulation. But what about the garden?

Epicurus is associated with horticulture in antiquity,[34] and (in England) with John Evelyn, along with Sir Thomas Browne and Sir William Temple.[35] In Nietzsche, this is exemplified by the Arcadian ideal with reference to Poussin and Claude Lorraine.[36] Invoking Lessing and Biedermeier culture, Nietzsche thematizes the garden in his first *Untimely Meditation*. David Allison, echoing Freud and Alice Miller, turns to a reflection on Daniel Paul Schreber and the little gardens that Schreber's father, Moritz Schreber, had prescribed as therapeutic loci for citizens: *Schrebergarten*.[37] In the present, think of the work of Gary Shapiro,[38] but also Paolo D'Iorio,[39] as well as of Stefan Günzel;[40] there are additional references we can make with respect to Nietzsche and his 'garden god', including complex sexual allusions as I have sought to trace these[41] – and, more esoterically, Dionysian/Zarathustran/Lucianic associations.[42]

In the first of Nietzsche's *Untimely Meditations*, 'David Strauss, the Confessor and Author' (which remains little discussed in comparison with his other meditations),[43] Nietzsche highlights the aversion to the mention of war (key at the time) as matched by an enthusiasm for 'German' culture. In the process he offers a relatively exhaustive indictment of philistine, that is, burgher culture. Reading 'David Strauss, the Confessor and Author', we follow Nietzsche on a tour through the '*House and Garden*' mentality of the bourgeoisie, focusing rather more on the house, including proper libraries and music rooms fitted out for the briefest of the owner's sojourns, including, for the seeming edification of visitors, 'the most famous piece of music arranged on the music stand', ready to be played (DS 9), no matter the injury wreaked on the composer, and a garden, complete with – this is a reference to a herm[44] – what Nietzsche calls an 'Epicurean Garden-God'.

Ancient architectural motifs, herms, are crucial for Nietzsche, who closes the later-written second volume of *Human, All Too Human* by reminding his reader of his own blood sacrifice: the blood he writes in, the blood given to the ghosts, echoing an allusion to Homer's *Odyssey* from the second of his *Untimely Meditations*.[45]

In addition, herms exemplify Nietzsche's reference to a dual nature in the third *Untimely Meditation*. For his part, Hermes, the deity who moves between life and death, communicating between mortals and divinities via Hades, complete with a hat to shade the traveller, sandals for the journey and wings to effect the translation between realms that is also sexuality: nature. The very fact that we have fragments of the hundreds of writings ascribed to Epicurus enhances the sardonic context of Nietzsche's reflection in *Beyond Good and Evil* on the nastiness [*boshaft*] philosophers indulge in one to another. Little 'could be more poisonous' than the jest Epicurus 'permitted himself contra Plato and his followers', naming them, as Nietzsche goes on to explain: *Dionysokolakes*, lickspittles or flatterers of Dionysus (BGE 7). Reference to tyrants and flattery was freighted in antiquity but, as Cornel West has learnt with respect to Obama, might hold even more for today's attempts to mix philosophy and politics.[46]

In addition to its then political significance, to be a 'flatterer of Dionysus' [*Dionysokolakes*] leads to its philosophical association with Plato as author of dialogues, including, hence the joke, a reference to the stage: 'The term *Dionysokolax* was a popular description for actors' (BGE 7). Theatre is *the* Dionysian art, even as and even if matched to Apollo in all his savagery, as Nietzsche dedicated his first book to this conjoint expression and as he would continue to argue throughout his life, and in order to read this aphorism one cannot dispense with the aphorism to follow, alluding to Apuleius and his mystery tradition, an ass, '*pulcher et fortissimus*', beautiful and strong, on stage, just where for Nietzsche (and hence Epicurus' joke at Plato's expense) the *conviction* of the philosopher routinely appears (BGE 8). In this esoteric context, Nietzsche also reflects on the status of the Greek woman, particularly the mother who was, he writes, 'condemned to live in darkness', precisely for the sake of fertility, to vegetate, like a plant, in a limited sphere, 'as a symbol of Epicurean World wisdom: λάθε βιώσας' (KSA 7: 172).

The Epicurean maxim, 'live in obscurity', is precise when it comes to the life, status, *fate*, as Nietzsche says, of woman in ancient Greece. To be urged to live masked – concealed, without drawing attention to yourself – is as much a reference to woman's modesty as to any other kind of unobtrusiveness. The later Nietzsche's reflection on the Chinese motto, supposedly inculcated by a mother in her children, *Keep your heart small* (BGE 267), may show the ongoing significance of this reflection. In this sense, the cult of Epicurus, the garden cult out of which Epicurus grows, the cult of the mother (there is a reference here to Bachofen) is pendant to the cult of Dionysus.

As Epicurus was a contemporary of Plato, we may understand his teasing of Plato as the fruit of his jealousy, as Nietzsche suggests – Epicurus would also be liable to a certain tradition of misunderstanding, as Nietzsche himself always worried about the *rareness of being understood*. If Nietzsche also argued that the Stoics levelled (and thus misrepresented) their Heraclitus (KSA 7: 456),[47] he would argue that Epicurus diminished the rigour of Democritus. Thus, for Nietzsche, Epicurus represents a mature conception of the ancient sciences as what 'point for point' Christianity will go on to reject (HH 68). At the same time and in the realm of religiosity contra science, 'fulfilled Christianity' likewise features Epicureanism, by way of a natural law in accord with which God may not demand more of his creature 'than what is possible for him' (AOM 96; cf. *Balm and Poison*, AOM 224). Neatly, Christianity and Epicureanism go together – in spite of Christian anxieties – and Nietzsche matches Epicurus with Epictetus, both as exemplars of the same worldly wisdom that our increasingly Christian and Roman era – Nietzsche's reference here is to Juvenal – tends to co-opt.

There is some justification for reading Nietzsche's aphorism on 'Epicurus: Cynic and Epicurean' (HH 275) as one palimpsest for Hadot's *Philosophy as a Way of Life*, namely *qua* tactic for reading between seemingly opposed schools. In abandoning himself to the world, the Cynic, for Nietzsche, becomes hardened against it, whereas the Epicurean transcends it and sees it, not via the perturbation in his own soul – here the soul is also often compared to the sea – but the figure recurs through ruffling movements obliquely, like the 'violent movements of the treetops' outside in the storm (HH 275). Thus the Epicurean had a decided advantage: 'Reinstitution of peace and stillness [*Ruhe und Stille*] in the realm of the intellect, displacement of modern noise' (KSA 8: 304), echoing his *Sanctus Januarius* resolve in the first edition of *The Gay Science*: to look away (KSA 8: 405).[48]

It is in this sense that we might approach Nietzsche's reflections on Epicurean consolation concerning the so-called hinterworlds, that is, metaphysical realms, and the anxiety our concern with the same elicits when it comes to what are typically called 'last things' (title of the first section of *Human, All too Human*) and the fate of the soul.[49] Thus it is argued that Nietzsche admired Epicurus' technique for appeasing worry about the existence/non-existence of the gods and thereby also concerning the fortunes of the soul in the afterworld. Thus, as Epicurus discovers this, 'to those tormented by "fear of the gods" it sufficed to him to say "if the gods exist they do not concern themselves with us"' (WS 7). The tactic was complemented by yet another, adverting to theoretical indeterminacy.

Today's philosophers of mind read Epicurus on metaphysics in this fashion (often without the liability of invoking Nietzsche,[50] certainly without Nietzsche's 'philosophy of science').[51] For Nietzsche, it would be Epicurus' epistemological solace that constituted the ultimate benefit of *ataraxia*, sea calm, as *perspectivalism*: 'Firstly, if that is how things are, they do not concern us; secondly, things may be thus but they may also be otherwise' (WS 7).

Caygill observes that Nietzsche anticipates a certain approbative trend in Francophone scholarship on Epicurus.[52] What is at stake for Caygill is not a matter of a disinclination to attend to the cosmological – almost as if echoing the debates between the 'Acusmatici and Mathematici', among the Pythagoreans, to cite a section title from the English translation of Burkert's *Weisheit und Wissenschaft*[53] – but an atmospheric parsing of the heavens of

> divinity, blessedness, friendship and philosophical regimen around the focus of the ancient science of this world or 'meteorology'. His reading of Epicurus thus takes place under the sign of the weather, identifying its significance in Epicurus's texts and assigning it a key role in Epicurus's conception of blessedness.[54]

Burkert's Epicurean science includes terms typically associated with the religious, as Nietzsche amalgamates both sensibilities in his *On the Genealogy of Morals*. For Caygill, Nietzsche's reference to the weather in this Greek context is another word for *divination*.[55]

'How little is needed for happiness'

The happiness of the Epicurean is 'negative'. Similarly, Nietzsche highlights what we can and cannot do, dependent upon the vitality of any specific moment in our lives.[56] This is different from Foucault who teaches the *Use of Pleasure*, *qua* guidelines for managing excess *and* indulgence, whereas Nietzsche emphasizes the subtle and often error-prone art of 'backwards inference'.

Nietzsche's reflections on music, no matter how minor (tone or key) – that is, the sound of a bagpipe – are matched by his reflections on midday slumber in the fourth parodic (and subsequently disowned) book of *Thus Spoke Zarathustra*, borrowing from Epicurus and Marcus Aurelius. '*How little already suffices for happiness?*' thus foregrounds what is very little: 'the softest, lightest, a lizard's rustling, a breath, an instant, the blink of an eye', as an imperative to be underlined, '*little* makes up the quality of the *best* happiness' (Z:IV '*Mittags*') (KSA 4: 344).[57] Thus Nietzsche's 'divine lizards', lightning flashes of insight, thoughts that appear from outside, seemingly of themselves, dart, like the tiny lizards that are also totems of Apollo.[58] And again we read: 'How little it takes to be happy', illuminated with a reflection on error: '*Without music, life would be a mistake*' (TI 'Maxims' 33).

This reflection on the small is nicely Epicurean. But Nietzsche also emphasizes the Greek prayer: *three times everything beautiful* together with a reflection on the abundance and wealth of the world, resplendent in a brocade of brilliance, of joy, of wonderful things, a world deficient only in the coordination of all the things necessary in order to *appreciate* the same abundant beauty. In this perfect precision, like the sharp light of an October afternoon, 'the happiness of the afternoon of antiquity' (GS 45), one must, for its sake, be rightly disposed *and* rightly placed *and* rightly minded to be able to grasp such multifarious abundance.

This is not unlike the concept of hope as such, as Kafka once reflected (as Max Brod recollects this), by comparison with the darker gnostic or shadow image of the world. Thus illuminated, the world might be seen as 'a bad mood of deity, a bad day' [*eine schlechte Laune Gottes, ein schlechter Tag*], to which the optimistic Brod queried, wondering whether, apart from the world in its apparent form, there might still be hope? To which question came Kafka's smiling reply: 'Oh, hope enough, infinite amounts of hope – only not for us'.[59]

For the Christian, again as Nietzsche notes, is 'actually only a kind of Epicurean'. Thus the counsel offered in *What is Romanticism?* where one is urged to learn the art of 'backward inference from the work to maker, the deed to the doer, from the ideal to those who need it' (GS 370). The passage appears, nearly word for word, in *Nietzsche contra Wagner*, in the section entitled *Wir Antipoden*. Nietzsche prefaces the comparison he still names 'Romantic', to link the Epicurean and the Christian, by noting the tendency to narrower and ever more limited horizons, never forget the little garden, as the prime condition for '*making stupid*' [*Verdummung*] (KSA 6: 426). Nietzsche cautions against the danger wreaked 'by forcing his own image, the image of his torture, on them', the alternative he celebrates could be named 'Dionysian pessimism', not as a past form or classical achievement but as 'the pessimism of the future' (GS 370).[60]

Here we read Nietzsche's reflection added to the second edition of *The Gay Science*, explicating *Why We Look Like Epicureans* as surfactant iridescence, in a book dedicated to the praise of surfaces, highlighting the 'slight tightening of the reins as our urge for certainty races ahead, this self-control of the rider during his wildest rides' (GS 375). This quasi-Epicureanism recurs in the inclination to knowledge, and yet there is a difference. Now, 'the wanderer speaks', as health is regained again and again – because relinquished again and again – and rather than a garden, rather than a new Epicureanism, Nietzsche forges a new set of laws, an 'as yet undiscovered country whose boundaries nobody has yet surveyed … a world so overrich in what is beautiful, strange, questionable, terrible, and divine that our curiosity as well as our craving to possess it has got beside itself' (GS 382).

The new ideal Nietzsche sees here is not a 'free spirit' of the kind described with a certain mocking in *Human, All Too Human*, *qua* free spirit flouting conventions thereby confirmed, like the fashionista who can only dress in such and such a way, but

> a spirit that played naively – that is not deliberately but from overflowing power and abundance – with all that was hitherto called good, untouchable, divine … the ideal of a human, superhuman, well-being and benevolence that will often seem *inhuman* – for example, when it confronts all earthly seriousness so far, all solemnity in gesture, word, tone, eye, morality, and task so far, as if it were their most incarnate and involuntary parody – and in spite of all this, it is perhaps only with him that *great seriousness* really begins, that the real question mark is posed for the first time, that the destiny of the soul changes, the hand moves forward, the tragedy *begins*. (GS 382)

Nietzsche's white seas

I suggested earlier that it matters that in the interim between finishing the first edition of *The Gay Science* in 1882 and writing the fifth book to be appended to the second edition in 1887, Nietzsche, a former student of Otto Jahn, the leading historical philologist of physical inscriptions, artefacts and monuments, might have been more than keen to know of the 1884 French discovery of Diogenes of Oinoanda's Epicurean inscription. Certainly, Usener himself would write on just this in 1892, yet we've no way of knowing whether Nietzsche did (or did not) have news of this discovery: there are, so far as I know, no indications of this. Yet, it is always crucial for philological hermeneutics, as Nietzsche explains to his students, when it comes to ancient history, that a lack of information does not permit us to conclude anything with positive certainty save and only that we lack positive certainty one way (or the other). What we can be sure of, perhaps, is that this would have interested Nietzsche and we know for a certainty that he was still thinking about his discoveries of ancient Greek metre in his later correspondence, quoting these same metric discoveries *verbatim*.[61] And if only to underscore this (dates are dates of publication not rumor) I paralleled Nietzsche's Epicurus with his references to his own painting on his wall.[62]

The figure 'painted', and this too is quasi-Epicurean (the true Epicurean has vastly more certainty), is a 'question mark'. But as Nietzsche reminds us in dark tones, admonishing his readers, reminding them of forgotten virtues, noting that even the spirits of his book admonish him, pulling his ears: '"We can no longer stand it" they shout at me, "away, away with this raven-black music!"' (GS 383) and now the note of the bagpipe returns, [*einfältigen bäurischen Dudelsack*], the note of which also appears in *Twilight of the Idols* as part of the little that is needed for happiness (TI 'Maxims' 33).

Are we right? Are we wrong? Nietzsche's worries about the reader return. If one 'misunderstands the *singer*, what does it matter? That happens to be the "singer's curse"' (GS 383). Such misunderstanding only helps one 'better' to hear the music – all the better to dance.

The cheap, ontic challenge, 'knowing how to end', Nietzsche had already given himself, alluding to a specific harbour, a melody of trees, rocks and sea, invoking the achievement that is beyond 'the mark of the second-rate' that is restlessness, 'to slope into the sea in such proud and calm harmony, as for example, the mountains of Portofino' (GS 281). Whereupon, to close the supplemental fifth book of *The Gay Science*, the reader is supplied with a musical garden, *Songs of Prince Vogelfrei*, and in that musical garden, almost as if made to order, with a white sea, becalmed, with a vista of rocks and fig trees, tower and harbour, an idyllic surround.

> Das weisse Meer liegt eingeschlafen,
> Und purpurn steht ein Segel drauf,
> Fels, Feigenbäume, Thurm und Hafen,
> Idylle rings, Geblök von Schafen, —
> Unschuld des Südens, nimm mich auf!
> [The white sea lies fallen asleep,
> And purple stands a sail upon it,
> Rocks, figtrees, tower and harbor,
> Idyll around, bleating sheep, –
> Innocence of the south, take me!]
> —*Im Süden* (Nietzsche 1887: *Lieder des Prinzen Vogelfrei* (my translation))

Notes

1 Nietzsche (1913), and see Nietzsche (1921).
2 This is derived from the title: Πίνακες τῶν ἐν πάσῃ παιδείᾳ διαλαμψάντων. See Pfeiffer (1949) and Pfeiffer (1968).
3 See also KGW II/4, 613–32.
4 Nietzsche also uses the characteristic 'Venusberg' from the perspective of the Middle Ages. See Nietzsche (1913: 376).
5 Nietzsche (1913: 338).
6 Nietzsche (1913: 342).
7 Clay (1972: 59–66).

8   'At the end of his biography of Diogenes of Sinope, Diogenes Laertius (VI.81) lists five notable men by the name of Diogenes; our Diogenes is not one of them. But then we know of no one who had heard of Diogenes of Oenoanda until a century ago when his name was discovered on an inscribed block in the mountain city of Oenoanda in Lycia: … And then it became apparent that Diogenes of Oenoanda was well known to a large group of fellow Epicureans or "friends" (φίλοι) who were equally unknown to Diogenes Laertius and to posterity' Clay (1989: 313–35, here 314–15).
9   Powell (2015). See too Zick (2008).
10 For an overview, see Hammerstaedt, Morel and Güremen, eds (2017). Of especial interest, although not referring to Nietzsche, is Roskam (2017: 241–70). See too, Powell, Undershell and Barber (1921), and Smith (1996). See Hicks (1910: 104). In its time, Oinoanda was a site of competition and thus of social and political significance, like Olympia and Pythia.
11 Thus, Lucretius names Epicurus as a paragon: 'A shining light, illuminating the blessings of life, O glory of the Grecian race, it is you I follow', Lucretius (1992: III.1-8). See, for example, Sedley (1999) and Clay (1983), as well as Nuovo (2017).
12 See Erler (2009) and Schofield (2007). Despite general scholastic condemnations, this can be extended to the church. See Jungkuntz (1962). See too, the significance of the coordinate use of Greek in Latin, including the oft-times 'lampooning' as Gordon (2012) says of Epicurus.
13 Nietzsche highlights this denial, naming Epicurus and Epicharmus in his Basel lectures on Leucippus/Democritus in *Nietzsche's Werke* (1913: 202), as well as in the material dating from his commentaries on Diogenes Laertius, 1866–8, entitled 'Democritea' in the Crusius/Nestle edition, emphasizing that Leucippus is considered to have been Democritus' 'teacher solely for the sake of the διαδοχαί' (1913: 381). Here Nietzsche highlights the attestation through Aristotle ('apparently one had concluded the unknown from what was known') (KGW II/4, 329), a resolution Nietzsche tracks throughout his Basel lectures on the pre-Platonic Philosophers.
14 The term is Lucretian. But see Asmis (1970), as well as her chapter on 'Motion' in: Asmis (1984: 277–81), and see, Wasserstein (1978) and, overall, Bloch (2009), in addition to another account, in this case via Deleuze, Bennett (2013). And see, albeit innocent of a good deal, Greenblatt (2011).
15 See, for discussion, Annas (1987) and Scarre (1994).
16 See the contributions to the huge collection edited by Delattre and Pigeaud (2010). In addition, see Gigandet and Morel, eds (2007), in addition to Brun (1993). Older accounts looked to Epicurus on love as this was often associated with his name (he corresponded famously, infamously, with courtesans), Flacelière (1954).
17 See Hadot (1995a). That Hadot means to uncover the Epicurean Foucault in connection with Nietzsche is clear, as Hadot cites Nietzsche's *amor fati* as a specifically universal, non-excluding yes-saying: 'not only to ourselves but to all existence' (1995a: 212).
18 See Németh (2017).
19 See Bornnmann (1984: 177–88) and Ebersbach (2014).
20 See Usener (1977).
21 Ebersbach (2014: 44). Reading Epicurus directly as he also could and did do, as Ebersbach also reminds us that Nietzsche himself would be spared certain misrenderings of Epicurus (Usener 1887: 219, 169). See for discussion, the first chapter of Mansfeld and David (1997).

22 Diels (1903). That there are elements of a certain *Wirkungsgeschichte* to be reflected (more is needed than can be offered here) may be evidenced by the publication of Diels (1879). See Heidegger ([1950] 1975) on this constellation – it is not the subject of his discussion but a prelude to his reading of 'The Anaximander Fragment'.
23 See, again, Mansfeld and Runia, *Aetiana*, (1997).
24 Nietzsche (1868–1869), 'De Laertii Diogenis fontibus', Rheinisches Museum für Philologie. Neue Folge, 23 & 24 Jahrgang, Frankfurt am Main: Verlag von Johann David Sauerländer: 632–53, 181–228 [in Latin]; Nietzsche, Friedrich (1870), 'Analecta Laertiana', Rheinisches Museum für Philologie. Neue Folge, 25, Frankfurt am Main: Sauerländer: 217–31 [in Latin]. Cf. Nietzsche, Friedrich (1868), 'Beiträge zur Kritik der griechischen Lyriker', Rheinisches Museum für Philologie. Neue Folge, 23, Frankfurt am Main: Sauerländer: 480–9 as well as Nietzsche, Friedrich (1870–1873), 'Der Florentinische Tractat über Homer und Hesiod, ihr Geschlecht und ihren Wettkampf', Rhenisches Museum für Philologie. Neue Folge, 25. & 28, Frankfurt am Main: Verlag von Johann David Sauerländer, 528–40, 211–49.
25 See Brobjer (2000: 157–61). And see further, Benne (2012).
26 See Babich (2007). For a more comprehensive discussion, see Zanker (2016), especially 'The Metaphor of Text = Person', 123ff.
27 Here 'Sie verlieren durch Socrates die Unbefangenheit. Ihre Mythen und Tragödien sind viel weiser als die Ethiken Plato's und Aristoteles'; und ihre ‚stoischen und epikurischen' Menschen sind arm, gegen ihre älteren Dichter und Staatsmänner' (KSA 8: 107–8).
28 Dinner parties can borrow from the same restraint: three friends plus oneself and perhaps one's companion, would be five, which can be ideal, with four friends that is a garden repast for six. But even so many friends is a rare thing, as Nietzsche reflected constantly, borrowing from Montaigne's reflections on the nature of the friend. See Nehamas (2016) on Montaigne, and Babich (2003).
29 See for a discussion, Babich (2020).
30 See most notably, Derrida (1974), as well as Helmer (2011). See too Asmis (2003), and Bartlett (2002), as well as Groff (2014), and cf., more broadly, Porter (forthcoming).
31 See again Ebersbach, Volker (2014) and Treiber (1992).
32 See for references, Babich (2018: 8, 18).
33 Caygill (2006: 107–15).
34 Cilliers and Retief (2009: 1–10), as well as Giesecke (2001).
35 See Small and Small (1997). And see Temple (1908), which also includes 'The Garden of Cyrus; Miscellanies' by Sir Thomas Browne, as well as Miller (2006). One can only await an as yet unarticulated connection with plant philosophy and, if this is only limitedly begun, a reflection on trees. See, for example, Young (2012) and Marder and del Caro (2004). In German, among other studies, see Borchardt, Rudolf ([1937–1938] 2016).
36 See especially Gary Shapiro (2013), in addition to Babich (2015).
37 See here the contributions to Allison, Oliveira, Roberts and Weiss eds (1988), as well as Santner (1997) and Freud ([1911] 2003). And on the elliptical edge, in the German tradition see Pelz (1996) as well as Kudrass (2017).
38 See perhaps in the first line, again, Shapiro, especially his discussion of Nietzsche and Epicurus' 'garden philosophy' in Shapiro (2016). To be sure, a recent collection reflecting on architectural theory is not above blaming Nietzsche (or his French epigones, that is, Derrida, Foucault, Deleuze) for a certain becalmed aura in the field, which the current author would ascribe to the sheerly homeopathic presence of

Nietzsche (with the exception of Wohlfarth's discussion of Max Weber) in Kostka and Wohlfarth eds. (1999). See Lahiji ed. (2014). Lahiji is correct that the left has trouble with Nietzsche in general but it is not clear that the trouble is Nietzsche. Indeed, apart from the editors' introductory complaints, Nietzsche makes no further appearance in the collection.
39 D'Iorio (2012).
40 Günzel (2003: 78–91).
41 I discuss this in Babich (2009b: 7–43).
42 In particular, see again, Shapiro (2013), in addition to Ebersbach (2014), and, overall, Vercelloni and Vercelloni (2010). To this, but esoteric (failing connection with literature and rife with unintentional replication and not specifically devoted to Epicurus), see Riedel (1998). More scholarly, more broadly focused on Nietzsche and antique literature in general, specifically Theocritus, and noteworthy as it raises the question of genre, see Forrer (2017).
43 Perhaps because most scholars assume reading a matter of redundancy, Strauss being, for the most part, at least in Anglophone Nietzsche scholarship more than a little obscure, many scholars assume the theme to be obvious.
44 See for a discussion of herms the essays on both sculpture and Greek Bronze above, as well as Babich (2009a).
45 See for an overview, Burkert ([1962] 1972), see especially for a discussion of shamanism and metempsychosis, in connection with Plato and Empedocles, 124ff. as well as Burkert ([1972] 1983).
46 Cornel West offers the best account of this himself. See West (2017). See West's earlier interview in medias res with Frank (2014). On Plato and the political, there is an immense literature.
47 'Die Stoiker haben Heraklit in's Flache umgedeutet und mißverstanden. Auch die Epikureer haben in die strengen Principiendes Democrit Weichliches eingeschwärzt (Möglichkeiten). Die höchste Gesetzmäßigkeit der Welt, aber doch kein Optimismus bei Heraclit' (KSA 7: 456).
48 The vulgar understanding of Epicureanism is thus not without an element of truth. As Nietzsche writes in an apothegm denouncing a common tendency to mythologize the idea/ideal of Nature (he includes Rousseau to be sure, along with Wagner, while he is at it, so to say, although as he is speaking of the art of song and rigour as such, it is not clear that this is solely meant as an afterthought). See KSA (8: 405).
49 See in addition to Amicus (2010), the Lucian expert, Branham (1984) and Graham (2016). Most helpful in connection with Nietzsche might be Nuffelen (2011).
50 Annas (1994: 203).
51 Babich (1994). If this is also a Peircean point, regrettably enough in the long tradition of Nietzsche scholars in the Anglophone tradition who have thought about Nietzsche and Epicurus, few engage Nietzsche on science. But see, however, Knight (1993).
52 Caygill refers to Festugière (1946) in English as André-Jean ([1946] 1956), and Hadot (1995a).
53 Burkert ([1962] 1972: 192–207).
54 Caygill (2006: 107).
55 Thus, Caygill can go on to note the 'broad and systematic mobilisation of meteorology throughout the writings of Nietzsche, one so ubiquitous as to become nigh invisible, part of the climate of his thought' (2006: 108). Caygill also underscores the therapeutic value of Epicurean optimism in terms of Nietzsche's variously ambivalent

account, within which Epicurus would exceed both 'Dionysus and the Crucified' (2006: 109).
56 This can be related to the special alchemy of which David Allison writes in his discussion of Nietzsche (2001: 115).
57 KSA (4: 344).
58 See Babich (2004: 264–83, esp. 280).
59 Cited from: Brod (1922: 55–62): 'So gäbe es außerhalb dieser Erscheinungsform Welt, die wir kennen, Hoffnung?' – Er lächelte: 'Hoffnung genug, unendlich viel Hoffnung, – nur nicht für uns.' I am grateful to Tracy Strong for the variant: *Nicht für uns, Max: nicht für uns.*
60 Note to be sure that Nietzsche uses almost the same metaphor of coast and sea and pine and olive trees to describe the tactics for reading a book; discovery but also distance and calm are essential.
61 An initial published report would not appear until 1992 and a comprehensive account not until 1897: Heberdey and Kalinka (1897). And see for a discussion, as well as a reconstruction, Clay (1989).
62 For a discussion, see Usener's (1892). See too, again, Hammerstaedt, Morel and Güremen, eds (2017).

5

What reason is there in the body?
Bodily suffering and happiness

Céline Leboeuf

To the 'despisers of the body', Nietzsche declares in *Thus Spoke Zarathustra*, 'there is more reason [*Vernunft*] in your body than in your finest wisdom' (Z I 'Despisers').[1] This statement coheres, I argue, with the connections Nietzsche draws between health, illness and the activity of philosophizing. He views the striving for health in the wake of suffering as essential to philosophy.[2] Contrary to a modern conception of illness as a lapse of health lacking any inherent personal significance, Nietzsche develops a conception of illness according to which it not only has vital meaning but also one that is relevant to philosophy itself.[3] While I am not the first to discuss his reflections on the relationship between suffering and philosophy, I seek to enhance our understanding of these reflections by integrating them with Nietzsche's interest in Epicurus.[4] Nietzsche sees a direct connection between suffering and Epicurean philosophy when he avers in *The Gay Science* that Epicurus was 'continually suffering' (GS 45). Accordingly, the questions I explore in this chapter deal with Nietzsche's view that Epicurean philosophy can be born from suffering. Specifically, I address three questions: first, broadly speaking, why are both suffering and health integral to the activity of philosophizing? Second, why, in general, does Nietzsche take an interest in Epicureanism? And third, why does Epicureanism, in particular, speak to the connection he draws between suffering, health and philosophy?

What reason is there in the body?

Let me begin with the question concerning the connection between suffering and philosophizing. This is not simply a speculative methodological question raised by Nietzsche but one deeply rooted in the philosopher's own intimacy with bodily suffering. Nietzsche experienced intense migraines and eye problems throughout his life,[5] and at the age of forty-four, suffered a breakdown that left him largely physically incapacitated for the last eleven years. According to our contemporary, commonplace conception of physical sickness, all there is to say about Nietzsche's repeated illnesses is that these episodes were unfortunate events that befell him. Full stop. But not for Nietzsche's philosophy or his life. For him, physical suffering played a crucial role in the elaboration of his philosophy. He explicitly probes the significance of bodily illness to philosophizing at several points in his oeuvre.

To grasp this, I work backwards from *Ecce Homo*, Nietzsche's summation of his writings and life, which is, unsurprisingly, rich in reflections on the connection between his physical illnesses and philosophizing. There Nietzsche expresses this connection succinctly: 'I created my philosophy from out of my will to health, to *life*' (EH 'Wise' 2). But this declaration does not offer much help! An earlier passage elaborates the relations between philosophy, suffering and health in exceptional detail:

> A long, all-too-long succession of years meant recuperation for me – it also unfortunately meant relapse, decay, the period of a type of decadence. After all this do I need to add that I am *experienced* in questions of decadence? I know it inside and out. Even that filigree art of grasping and comprehending in general, that finger for nuances, that psychology of 'looking around the corner', and the other specialties of mine, I only learned then, they were genuine gifts of that time when I refined everything, observation itself as well as all the organs of observation. To be able to look out from the optic of sickness towards *healthier* concepts and values, and again the other way around, to look down from the fullness and self-assurance of the rich life into the secret work of the instinct of decadence – that was my longest training, my genuine experience, if I became the maker of anything, it was this. I have a hand for switching *perspectives*: the first reason why a 'revaluation of values' is even possible, perhaps for me alone. (EH 'Wise' 1)

We learn here that convalescence makes Nietzsche's form of philosophizing possible. This is because recovery affords two perspectives: the perspective of the suffering individual who 'look[s] around the corner for', and yearns for, health, and that of the individual who possesses 'self-assurance' and who can 'look the other way around' at his sickness. Nietzsche directly links the ability to switch between the perspectives of illness and health to his project of a revaluation of values: such a project requires looking from the vantage of our present values, our sick contemporary value system, bred from Christianity, towards new, healthy anti-Christian values. Moreover, for healing to lead to philosophy, such healing must unfold over time. Put bluntly, recovering overnight from a cold after a good sleep does not offer material for philosophizing. Healing that brings forth philosophy must enhance the thinker's capacity for *observation*, which is not something that a transient harmless illness can do. What is the object of such observation? While Nietzsche's critiques of religion and morality depend on observing life, this passage leads us to believe that observing oneself, detecting the nuances in one's body in sickness and in health, lays the ground for observing the world around oneself. But I shall return to this point.

Ecce Homo not only synthesizes Nietzsche's reflections on the philosophical value of healing from physical suffering but also analyses the physical conditions conducive to health and thus philosophy. Nietzsche describes how location, climate and diet, among other factors, provide life energy and are thus crucial to the activity of philosophizing.

In the section titled 'Why I am so clever', Nietzsche asserts, 'dry air and clear skies are *conditions* for genius, which is to say its conditions include a rapid metabolism and the possibility of a constant supply of large, even enormous, amounts of energy' (EH 'Clever' 2). This assertion is clearly based on his peregrinations in search of a climate favourable to his health after the end of his teaching career.[6]

Yet, *Ecce Homo* is not our only source concerning the connection between physical suffering and philosophizing. If we look now to the period that will be of greatest interest to us, to what is referred to as Nietzsche's 'middle period', we learn that the connection between illness and healing described in *Ecce Homo* is already in the works. There Nietzsche judges that 1879 marked the 'low point' of his health. This is the year when he composes *The Wanderer and His Shadow*, the third part of *Human, All Too Human*.[7] *The Wanderer and His Shadow* (1880) is shortly followed by *Daybreak* (1881), described in *Ecce Homo* as a work that reflects 'perfect lightness and cheerfulness, even exuberance of spirit' (EH 'Wise' 1), and then by *The Gay Science* (1882), which Nietzsche also judges to be 'an affirmative book, deep but bright and good natured' (EH 'The Gay Science' 1). For our purposes, note that all three works mention Epicurus. This naturally raises the question of Nietzsche's interest in Epicurus during this period. Before broaching this question, let us explore how Nietzsche articulates the connection between philosophy and suffering in his middle period.

In the preface to Volume I of *Human, All Too Human*, Nietzsche explains that the free spirits to whom his book is dedicated 'do not exist, did not exist' as he suffered from such 'ills' as 'sickness, solitude, unfamiliar places, *acedia*, inactivity', but that he 'had need of them at that time' (HH P: 2). This desire for the companionship of free spirits during sickness first adumbrates the place of illness in the formulation of his philosophy and serves to outline the scope of the book's project. Nietzsche aims 'to speed the coming of [free spirits]' by describing the 'paths' upon which he sees them coming (HH P: 2). In simpler terms, the advent of free spirits would have aided Nietzsche's recovery, but a philosophy that invited them was first needed. A few lines later, taking aim at 'old idealists' and 'inveterate liars', he expands upon the role of illness and health for philosophy, adding that convalescence is a cure for pessimism: 'To become sick in the manner of these free spirits, to remain sick for a long time and then, slowly, slowly, to become healthy, by which I mean "healthier", is a fundamental cure for all pessimism' (HH P: 5). This statement is worth dwelling on for two reasons. First, Nietzsche emphasizes that the length of illness and the slowness of recovery matter to the philosophy of free spirits and that becoming healthy signifies becoming *healthier*. These reflections put forward the idea that sickness and health are not merely polar opposites, but that there is a continuum between these experiences. This continuum contrasts with our contemporary conceptions of illness and health. Consequently, familiarity with this continuum may itself be a piece of wisdom that the body offers and that a long suffering and gradual recovery allow us to discover. Second, Nietzsche's idea that a slow convalescence is essential to curing *pessimism* encapsulates the cheerful science in the works in his middle period.

Turning now to Volume II of *Human, All Too Human*, I highlight two decisive expressions of the connection between sickness, health and philosophy. First, in 'Assorted Opinions and Maxims', Nietzsche speaks to the role of *repeated* illnesses in philosophizing, thus anticipating his point in *The Gay Science* that Epicurus must have 'continually' suffered: 'He who is often sick does not only have a much greater enjoyment of health on account of the frequency with which he gets well: he also has a greatly enhanced sense of what is healthy and what sick in works and actions, his own and those of others' (AOM 356). This formulation indicates that the power for observation Nietzsche lauds in *Ecce Homo* concerns not only oneself but also what lies outside of oneself, and it suggests that this power, while it might develop from an attention to the body, extends beyond physical well-being to the healthiness of *works* and *actions*. This insight speaks to Nietzsche's preoccupation with the sick manner in which his contemporaries live. Second, he makes the relationship between our sickly value system and the striving for health explicit in *The Wanderer and His Shadow*, where he judges the chains that have made us sick to be 'those heavy and pregnant errors contained in the conceptions of morality, religion and metaphysics' (WS 350) and affirms that we 'stand now in the midst of our work of removing these chains' (WS 350). What is needed to remove these chains – namely, to 'salve' our 'wounds – is that the "ennobled man ... may be given freedom of spirit"' (WS 350); this would be a man who 'lives for the sake of *joy* and for the sake of no other goal' (WS 350). Again, we see that Nietzsche lauds gaiety of spirit and links this gaiety with the overcoming of illness.

Daybreak prolongs Nietzsche's reflections on convalescence and draws our attention to the task of taking one's recovery upon oneself. In the section, 'If possible live without a physician' (D 322), Nietzsche distinguishes between the 'frivolity' of those who adhere to the prescriptions of physicians and the 'conscientious view' of those who live without a physician. According to him, the latter must 'notice much more, order and forbid [themselves] much more, than would happen at the instigation of the physician' (D 322). Nietzsche's point is that having to care for oneself requires both attention to oneself and the self-command necessary to comply with a cure. The necessity to attend to oneself further clarifies Nietzsche's stress on the importance of observation in *Ecce Homo*: the capacity to observe *oneself* is paramount to convalescence and, by extension, to philosophy. The injunction to live without a physician encourages us to take on the rigours of self-observation, rather than to be frivolous. Nietzsche seems optimistic that we can achieve this since he adds at the end of the section that 'men' have never completely 'left everything in the hands of the divinity as their physicians' (D 322). This statement demonstrates that latent in us lies the possibility of developing our capacities for observation. These capacities, however, will lie dormant if we let ourselves be shepherded by physicians and by that supreme physician, whom Nietzsche identifies as God (D 322).

The task of self-consciously managing one's health is developed in *The Gay Science*, which strongly expresses the cheerfulness wrought from suffering. First, though, a few words about the very concept of a 'gay science'. This concept is opposed to traditional science, which conceives itself as the pursuit of knowledge in abstraction from personal qualities, including bodily characteristics. By contrast, Nietzsche considered his science to be rooted in the body – in *his* body and its convalescence. As Monika Langer explains, Nietzsche's project in *The Gay Science* rejects a traditional, rationalistic conception of the pursuit of knowledge: 'Plato, Descartes, Kant, Hegel, and Husserl claimed to put philosophy on a secure, scientific path to indubitable knowledge. By contrast, Nietzsche declares "gay science" signifies a convalescing spirit's revelry and his book is merely a little merriment. ... It means radically revaluating truth, knowledge, and philosophy – not foregoing them' (Langer 2010: 3). Quite simply, *The Gay Science* conceives of philosophizing in terms of the ways in which we navigate *illness* and *health*. Thus, in the preface, Nietzsche asserts that there are as many philosophies as there are passages through illness and health: 'A philosopher who has passed many kinds of health, and keeps passing through them again and again, has passed through an equal number of philosophies; he simply *cannot* but translate his state every time into the most spiritual form and distance: this art of transfiguration just *is* philosophy' (GS P:3).[8] This reveals the bodily dimension of philosophizing and the role narrating the body plays in the emergence of our philosophies. The 'distance' involved in 'translating' various states of health makes possible an 'art of transfiguration'. Put differently, states of illness and health are not merely successive conditions of the body, but *can* constitute stages in an education of the self. I say 'can', because such an education only happens when we self-consciously learn to observe life from the perspectives of illness and health. Most of us, Nietzsche might say, unthinkingly undergo illnesses without taking the step back that is necessary to learn from them. The sense of self gained from self-consciously navigating sickness and health demands the skill to transfigure these states, and this, in true Nietzschean fashion, requires a good dose of forgetfulness. For example, in Poem 4 of the 'Prelude in German Rhymes' of *The Gay Science*, Nietzsche maintains that loss of memory is the sign of someone who has recovered from illness. Referring to this passage, Langer explains that for Nietzsche, 'becom[ing] artists of our lives' involves a dance between forgetting one's past illnesses, unearthing their significance, but also letting go of their weight (Langer 2010: 16–17).

The Gay Science teaches that philosophy rests on actively constructing a narrative in light of one's suffering. To better appreciate the originality of Nietzsche's ideas concerning illness, let us compare them with our contemporary understanding of illness. Today we understand treating illness as the task of restituting well-being. Peter Sedgwick underscores this point in 'Nietzsche, Illness, and the Body's Quest for Narrative', when he explains that our 'restitutive model' of health and illness conceives of suffering as 'an inconvenience to be diagnosed, controlled and ultimately forgotten, rather than a painful encounter deserving of acknowledgement because it exposes us to the most human aspect of embodied experience' (Sedgwick 2013: 310). Modern medicine co-opts one's suffering, turning it into a symptom of bodily dysfunction, rather than an aspect of oneself, or as Sedgwick puts it, we treat illness in such a manner as to 'alienate the sufferer from their illness and hence, ultimately, from themselves' (Sedgwick 2013: 319). In contrast, Nietzsche resists the idea that it would be desirable to be alienated from one's suffering, instead, seeing suffering as important to the constitution of the self, for it allows us to develop multiple vantage points on our lives and, with that, multiple philosophies.

In sum, these middle-period writings depict a form of philosophizing that emerges from the 'the will to health'. Further, the idea of a will to health likely anticipates his later notion of a 'will to power', which describes our drive to affirm ourselves and to overcome resistance, a drive which is directly connected to happiness. Thus, in *The Anti-Christ,* Nietzsche equates the development of the will to power and happiness in a manner that echoes the connection between the will to health and the gaiety of his middle period. There, against the ideals of happiness of 'contentedness', 'peace', or 'virtue', Nietzsche defines happiness as 'the feeling that power is *growing*, that some resistance has been overcome' (A 2).

What reason is there in Epicurus?

Thus far, I have sketched in general terms the relationship between suffering and Nietzsche's conception of philosophy. I now tie this relationship to Nietzsche's interest in Epicurus during his middle period. Why does Nietzsche take an interest in Epicurus during his recovery from his lowest of lows?

Following Julian Young, I think that Nietzsche took an interest in Epicurus 'as a representative of ancient philosophy in general' (2010: 278). What is distinctive of ancient philosophy, especially of the Hellenistic schools, is that philosophy represents a *way of life* or an *art of living*. Thus, the appeal of ancient philosophy to Nietzsche, at his height of bodily suffering, lies in its capacity to give succour. Ancient philosophy aims at *happiness* – especially, happiness 'in the face of adversity' (Young 2010: 280). Consider one element of the *tetrapharmakos*, or four-part cure, in Epicurus: 'The limit of bad things either has a short duration or causes little trouble' is meant to deliver us from distress (LM 133).[9] In *The Wanderer and His Shadow*, Nietzsche relates the possibility that philosophy offers 'means of consolation' to Epicurus, where he mentions another part of the *tetrapharmakos*: do not fear gods. There, Nietzsche asserts that 'he who wishes to offer consolation – to the unfortunate, ill-doers, the hypochondriacs, the dying – should call to mind the two pacifying formulae of Epicurus' (WS 7).

Still, we need to consider which alternatives were available to Nietzsche to achieve serenity. As Young notes, by 1879, Nietzsche had abandoned the idea that either religion or the 'quasi-religious art' that he found in Wagner's music could provide solace (Young 2010: 280). It is evident from Nietzsche's repeated illnesses that the medical treatments administered to him were insufficient to relieve his suffering. Enter ancient philosophy as a cure.

Why Epicurus, though? His recommendation of a life of modest pleasures – the conjunction of his hedonism and a certain asceticism – offers a clue. For Epicurus, pleasure is 'the lack of pain in the body and disturbance in the soul' (LM 131). In the midst of illness, Nietzsche needed this: the absence of pain. Nevertheless, simply remedying pain is insufficient to understand the relation between philosophy and suffering. Thus, I claim that *the striving for health through the cultivation of modest pleasures* offers a better answer. Epicurus's injunction to develop only natural and necessary desires constitutes a *way of life* that not only relieves us from a form of mental anguish – produced by desiring luxury – but also leads to health: 'The unwavering contemplation of [necessary desires] enables one to refer every choice and avoidance to the health of the body and the freedom of the soul from disturbance' (LM 129).

What reason is there in Epicurus's body?

Although Epicurus makes a distinction between bodily health and the freedom from mental disturbance gained from contemplating only those desires that are natural and necessary, this distinction does not imply that he endorses an ontological dualism whereby the mind would be a non-physical substance. For Epicurus, the mind is physical, too. This rejection of mind–body dualism is a commitment that Nietzsche also holds. As Kristen Brown explains, Nietzsche 'heightens the stature of the body in the formation of the concept of the self' (Brown 2006: 7). To substantiate this, Brown highlights his early and forceful rejection of the distinction between subject and object in 'On Truth and Lying in a Non-Moral Sense', which puts pressure on the traditional conception of the mind as subject and the body as object (Brown 2006: 98–106). She draws attention to Nietzsche's inversions or subversions, in his later writings, of the attributes we typically give to body and mind. Appealing to material from *Beyond Good and Evil*, she writes that for him, 'The body interprets, evaluates, and thinks. The intellect tastes, digests, and eliminates' (Brown 2006: 108). Although Brown establishes this interpretation through an extensive reading of Nietzsche's corpus, her appeal to several concise and compelling passages from *The Will to Power* is especially suggestive. In these notes, Nietzsche states, it is essential 'to start from the *body* and employ it as a guide', and further that 'belief in the body is more fundamental than belief in the soul'.[10] It is crucial to note that Nietzsche's conception of the primacy of the body does not amount to a reductionist materialism according to which the mind is identical to the body and the body is an object governed purely by mechanical laws. Instead, Nietzsche's ontology of the body consists in a rejection of mind–body dualism, together with a 'devaluation of the intellect' (Brown 2006: 108). As the attribution of sensory and digestive qualities to the intellect and of intellectual qualities to the body indicates, Nietzsche conceptualizes the intellect through bodily metaphors. The intellect does not consist of a separate entity divorced from the body but is interpretable through bodily metaphors. Furthermore, he conceives of the body as living, spontaneous and intelligent: '[The body] is the much richer phenomenon.'[11]

Because of his rejection of mind–body dualism, pursuing an Epicurean way of life constitutes, first and foremost, a disciplining of the body. Characteristically for Nietzsche, the need for disciplining the body as a path to happiness is traced to the Greeks, and its corruption to Christianity. In the section of *Twilight of the Idols* titled 'Skirmishes of an Untimely Man', Nietzsche contrasts the Greek disciplining of the body to the German illusion that feelings and thoughts must be disciplined:

> Make no mistake about the method at work here: a simple discipline of feeling and thought amounts to practically nothing (this is the great misunderstanding of German education, which is totally illusory): you first need to persuade the *body*. Strict adherence to significant and refined gestures and an obligation to live only with people who do not 'let themselves go' is more than enough to become significant and refined: two or three generations later and everything is already *internalized*. It is crucial for the fate of individuals as well as peoples that culture

begin in the *right* place – *not* in the 'soul' (which was the disastrous superstition of priests and half-priests): the right places is the body, gestures, diet, physiology, *everything else* follows from this. ... This is why the Greeks are the *first cultural event* in history – they knew, they *did*, what needed to be done; Christianity, which despised the body, has been the greatest disaster for humanity so far. (TI 'Skirmishes' 47, original emphases)

This passage not only locates the need for disciplining oneself in the body but also highlights the prominent Nietzschean themes of diet and physiology. Furthermore, it echoes his response to 'the despisers of the body' in *Thus Spoke Zarathustra*. Nietzsche clearly rejects the idea that the body is irrelevant to living a good life, as Christianity (and the Germans) would have it. Let me add that Epicureanism might have been particularly attractive to Nietzsche, as opposed to the philosophies of other ancient schools, because of its attention to the health of the body. He did take an interest in other ancient schools, such as Stoicism. For example, in *Daybreak*, he expresses his sympathy for the Stoic conception of philosophy as therapy.[12] Yet, the Stoic way of life does not focus on the body in the way in which Epicureanism does. This is not to say that the Stoics never mention the body, but rather, that the vicissitudes of the body are to be tolerated and classed among the things to which one ought to be indifferent. By contrast, Epicurus describes health of the body as integral to a good life. This would explain why Epicureanism captivated Nietzsche as he developed a philosophy that put primacy on the body.

Although Epicurus offered a way of life focused on the health of the embodied self, Nietzsche's attitude towards him is not without ambivalence. There is evidence in later writings that Nietzsche appears so sceptical of Epicurean eudaimonia that he compares it with Christian happiness. For example, in *Beyond Good and Evil*, Nietzsche speaks of a man of 'late cultures and refracted lights' as embracing a 'notion of happiness' that 'corresponds to that of a medicine and mentality of pacification (for instance the Epicurean or Christian)' (BGE 200). There are clearly tensions between Nietzsche's statements about Epicurus. As Richard Bett (2005) notes, it does not come as a surprise that we cannot completely pin down Nietzsche's view of Epicurus! Nonetheless, Bett argues that we can explain Nietzsche's occasional sympathy for Epicurus if we notice that Nietzsche does praise him for *overcoming* suffering in order to achieve happiness (Bett 2005: 62–4). In other words, Nietzsche sometimes reads Epicurean happiness not as a pacifying philosophy, but as a triumph over suffering. To support his interpretation, Bett pays close attention to *The Gay Science* (45), where, as I indicated earlier, Epicurus is portrayed as 'continually suffering'. Nietzsche expresses his image of Epicurus's suffering in these terms:

Yes, I am proud to experience Epicurus' character in a way unlike anyone perhaps, and to enjoy in everything I hear and read of him, the happiness of the afternoon of antiquity: I see his eyes gaze at the wide whitish sea, across shoreline rocks bathed in the sun, as large and small creatures play in its light, secure and calm like the light and his eye itself. Only someone who is continually suffering could invent such happiness – the happiness of an eye before which the sea of existence has grown still and which now cannot get enough of seeing the surface and this colorful, tender, quivering skin of the sea: never before has voluptuousness been so modest. (GS 45)

In this light, Epicurean happiness appears more Nietzschean: this happiness is not a simple, placid satisfaction, but a hard-won experience of joy. Epicurus's happiness is that of someone who gazes at a sea that 'has grown still' – not a still sea! Simply speaking, the image of a sea that has become still stands as a metaphor for recovery. Thus, this passage crystalizes Nietzsche's conception of happiness during his middle period: happiness grows from overcoming suffering.

Still, there is a missing piece to the puzzle. Why must we imagine Epicurus to have suffered *continually*? To clarify, I appeal to Aristotle's ideas concerning the development of moral virtues, to argue that duration matters to the forging of a philosophy from suffering. *The Nicomachean Ethics* emphasizes the importance of cultivating habits over time in order to embody moral virtues and, thanks to this, become happy. Aristotle says: 'For one swallow does not make a summer, nor does one day; and so too one day, or a short time, does not make a man blessed and happy' (1098a).[13] Put differently, forming the traits of character upon which a good life rests requires repeated actions. Temperance requires repeatedly restraining one's desires for sensual pleasures. Courage demands of us that we stand our ground despite fear on multiple occasions, that we put ourselves in situations where we will feel fear.[14] Aristotle's description of the development of moral virtues concerns the health *of the soul*. However, for both Nietzsche and Epicurus refusing a soul–body dichotomy, and with that between virtues of the soul and bodily health, Aristotle's idea of the development of virtue over time speaks to the idea that repeated episodes of illness and transitions to health lead to an education of the concrete, embodied individual.[15] If this is true, then we should agree with Nietzsche that Epicurus must have suffered on many occasions. Epicurus's wisdom sprang from repeated lessons in suffering. Thus, Epicurus, like Nietzsche, must have suffered continually.

To summarize, when Nietzsche reads Epicurean happiness as predicated on suffering and not as tranquillizing, then the prescription of a life of simple pleasures provides not only a *way of life* but also a ground for *philosophizing* itself. It is only in this regard that we can make sense of Nietzsche's occasional praise of Epicurus and understand how it coheres with his perspectivism. If philosophy requires the capacity to switch between the perspectives of suffering and of health, and if Nietzsche – in some moods – reads an Epicurean way of life as a foundation for such changes, then we philosophers should join Nietzsche in admiring Epicurus.

Coda: What reason is there in my body?

While Nietzsche's conception of the importance of illness and health to philosophy might appear to romanticize bodily suffering, such appearances are deceiving. Tempting as it is to draw on another author's narrative of illness in order to defend my position, I instead, conclude in a Nietzschean fashion with a few personal reflections on illness. Unlike Nietzsche, I have suffered from few significant physical illnesses in my life. As a result, while writing this chapter, I have worried that I was not in a position to personally reflect on the power of suffering for philosophy. However, I, like some generally healthy people, have had brushes with health *scares*, moments when a physical complaint forebodes a serious or even terminal illness. I have had two such scares, both involving the possibility of breast cancer. The first occasion began when I found a lump in one of my breasts, which led to a series of ultrasounds and finally a biopsy that revealed that the lump was benign. The second occurred a year later when I experienced pain near the lump, and after another ultrasound and, this time, a mammogram, I learnt that the lump had not changed and was unlikely to have become cancerous. These two health scares, the first of which was drawn out over several months, and the second of which (mercifully) lasted only one month, did bring about a shift in my perspective on life. Before these health scares, I typically lived in denial of death that is common to many healthy persons, especially the young. I was immersed in daily activities with little awareness that death could affect me. The thought that 'I will die' really meant 'I will die *someday*'; it was not one worth considering at any length. During my brushes with breast cancer, I awoke to dying, to my mortality. There was a shift in my perspective on myself: the life that I took for granted revealed itself starkly in its *finitude*. Because of these health scares, I can now 'look around the corner', to echo *Ecce Homo*, to my naïve denial of death. I can switch to a different perspective, not necessarily that of *healing physical illness*, but that of reconciling myself with idea that *within my body* lie the seeds of its own ending. *Nascentes morimur.* I have learnt not only to observe my own *body* more closely, monitoring it to ensure that the tumour has not changed, but also to examine my existence as a whole. Potentially terminal illnesses carry with them the possibility of closing the 'point of view on the world' that I am, to borrow from Maurice Merleau-Ponty, another philosopher of the body (Merleau-Ponty 2002: 298). The possibility of terminal illnesses, of this closure, can lead to a more intentional mode of living, one where we become conscious of the weight of our actions and of our path through life. Instead of coasting on cruise control, we heed the call to exist authentically, a call that is usually drowned out by the daily hubbub of life. Out of my experience, I have taken a more deliberate stance towards life: I spend more time assessing my actions and deciding on how to live more fully. My health scares have proven to me that there is reason in the body, the reason born from encountering the body's fragility. Specifically, this reason consists in the lesson that I must use my time judiciously. I say 'lesson' deliberately, for prior to my breast cancer scares I could have assented to the truth that I should not squander my time as though my lifespan were infinite. Nevertheless, I could not yet feel this truth *in my bones*.

Epicurus tells us not to fear death because it is 'nothing to us'. While I am not sure that I have yet reached the acceptance of death he prized, it is now clear to me that awareness of one's finitude is a requisite step towards coming to terms with death, that is, towards embodying the Epicurean ideal. Philosophy does not spring from cleaving oneself *from* one's body, as Plato would have it, but from a deep immersion *into* the body. My body made possible an awakening to death and the birth of a philosophy of life.

Notes

1. I have used Graham Parkes's translation for the Oxford edition. All other references to Nietzsche's works are to the Cambridge editions.
2. Langer (2010) stresses the importance of healing from physical illness to philosophy: Nietzsche's rejection of science's 'relentless pursuit of truth' (61) in *The Gay Science* involves 'the relinquishing of absolutes' (such as truth and morality), and instead, 'offers a healing reintegration of mind and body' (62).
3. For example, Sedgwick argues that for Nietzsche, physical suffering should have a personal significance: 'Nietzsche's own response to suffering is not to flee from it, but to embrace it in its centrality to human experience' (2013: 317).
4. As is evident from the above endnotes, Langer and Sedgwick have attended to the relationship between bodily health, bodily illness and philosophy in Nietzsche's *oeuvre*. This is a relationship also discussed by Young (2010).
5. For details of Nietzsche's ailments, one might consult Kaufman (1974).
6. Wicks (2018) summarizes Nietzsche's many travels:
   His travels took him through the Mediterranean seaside city of Nice (during the winters), the Swiss Alpine village of Sils Maria located near the present-day ski resort of St. Moritz (during the summers), Leipzig (where he had attended university, and had been hoping to resume his teaching career in 1883), Turin, Genoa, Recoaro, Messina, Rapallo, Florence, Venice and Rome, never residing in any place longer than several months at a time.
7. The full quote from *Ecce Homo* reads: 'At that time – it was 1879 – I resigned from my post as professor in Basle, survived the summer in St. Moritz *like* a shadow, and then survived the following winter in Naumburg, the least sunny of my life, *as* a shadow. This was my low point: *The Wanderer and his Shadow* came out of this' (EH 'Wise' 1).
8. This passage is also cited by Sedgwick (2013).
9. I have used Inwood and Gerson's translation for Hackett.
10. Brown (2006: 108) provides these quotations from WP 532 (original emphases) and 491, respectively.
11. These are Nietzsche's words in WP 532, cited by Brown (2006: 108).
12. For a discussion of Nietzsche's interest in Stoicism as a philosophical therapy, see Ure (2009).
13. I have used the Oxford edition of *The Nicomachean Ethics* (Aristotle 2009).
14. Aristotle defends the idea that temperance, courage and other moral virtues require habituation at several points in Book II of *The Nicomachean Ethics*.
15. I owe this point to Langer (2010: 128–30).

Part Two

Comparative studies

6

Eternal recurrence

Epicurean oblivion, Stoic consolation, Nietzschean cultivation

Michael Ure and Thomas Ryan[1]

This chapter examines Epicurean, Stoic and Nietzschean accounts of the eternal recurrence and their ethical significance. Epicurean and Stoic physics commit both philosophies to a cosmology of recurrence. Lucretius and Seneca embed cosmological theories of recurrence in a philosophical tradition of consolation. Since both also conceive philosophy as a way of life, to borrow Pierre Hadot's terminology, they necessarily link their own formulations of this cosmological doctrine to their ethical theories. In other words, since they endorse the principle of living according to nature, and nature eternally returns to the same state, they must consider what it means to live according to recurrence. Nietzsche's commitment to the doctrine of the eternal recurrence is contested. Commentators dispute whether he holds it to be literally true, or he conceives of it in some non-literal sense, as an ethical thought experiment or spiritual exercise, for instance. Like the Stoics and Epicureans, however, Nietzsche aims to naturalize (or *re*naturalize) humanity. As an integral part of his naturalistic ethics he suggests that the best life is one that affirms recurrence.

We demonstrate that all three philosophies consider the eternal recurrence from a therapeutic and ethical perspective. That is to say, we show how they frame, interpret and mobilize the idea of recurrence in ways that suit their particular therapeutic or transformative ends. Yet we argue that each formulates a very different conception of its transformative effects. Though they share a conception of recurrence as a 'spiritual exercise', they attribute to it very different outcomes. We show that Lucretius uses it to derive pleasure from the prospect of eternal oblivion, Seneca to achieve tranquil contemplation of our fate and Nietzsche to incite an unquenchable craving for ourselves as works of art worthy of eternity.

Section 1 surveys Lucretius' use of the Epicurean doctrine of recurrence and the danger it poses to the Epicurean *pharmakos*. Lucretius examines recurrence in the context of an Epicurean consolation that aims to eliminate the fear of death. Drawing on standard Epicurean arguments Lucretius argues that a correct knowledge of nature ('physics') will enable us to achieve tranquillity in the face of death. Epicurean consolation depends on the mortality of the soul. Because death disperses our constituent atoms, it destroys the subject of any putative post-mortem harms. There is as much to fear in the post-mortem future as there is in the ante-natal past: nothing at all. In this context, Lucretius identifies not just the superstitious beliefs in eternal damnation, but also the idea of cosmological recurrence as a threat to tranquillity (3.1937).[2]

For Lucretius, the idea of recurrence threatens to jeopardize the tranquillity that he believes we must derive from the proper knowledge of death. For the Epicurean, eternal recurrence is an alarming prospect because it entails the repetition of pain. Lucretius faces the task of reconciling his therapeutic account of death as eternal non-existence with his cosmological commitment to belief in eternal recurrence. As we will see, to solve this problem he argues that the discontinuity of memory between our present and future selves insulates us from the eternal recurrence of suffering. Lucretius maintains that the truth of eternal recurrence does not undermine the consoling force of the mortality of the soul.

Section 2 shows how Seneca makes use of recurrence for a different ethical purpose. Drawing on Stoicism's providential cosmology Seneca challenges the Lucretian position that 'forgetfulness of the past' is necessary to confront recurrence with tranquillity (36). Seneca conceives recurrence not as a threat to tranquillity, but as a consolation that can spur us to remain true to the public virtues of courage and fidelity. Following the Stoic doctrine of *oikeiōsis*, Seneca claims that we have a natural drive to self-preservation.[3] We naturally love our own existence and therefore wish to preserve it for eternity. Unlike Lucretius, Seneca conceives recurrence as a consoling thought: we are not destined to die, but to return. On this view, the cosmology of recurrence satisfies our natural desire to preserve our own existence. Thanks to this solacing thought, he claims, we are able to heroically risk our lives or battle our grief for the sake of honouring our familial or patriotic duties.

Section 3 demonstrates that Nietzsche shares the Hellenistic idea that the thought of recurrence is a therapeutic and self-transformative practice. Unlike Epicureans and Stoics, however, he does not tie its transformative effect to belief in the literal truth of recurrence. Nietzsche maintains that the mere probability or even just the logical possibility of recurrence is sufficient for it to have a transformative effect.[4] In *The Gay Science* he implies that the thought of eternal recurrence has both a diagnostic function and a transformative effect. Diagnostically, he suggests, we can distinguish between the healthy and weak, those who are well disposed towards themselves and life from those who are ill-disposed, in terms of the desire for eternal recurrence (GS 341). Nietzsche suggests that the therapeutic and transformative effects of the thought of recurrence are very different from those sought after by Epicureans and Stoics. Above all else, Nietzsche's ethics values the creation of the self as a unique, immortal artwork. Nietzsche claims that the *wish* for eternal repetition is symptomatic of artistically fashioning a unique, unrepeatable life. However, he argues that the thought of eternal recurrence not only is a symptom of successful self-fashioning but also *cultivates* the self as an artwork. Let us consider these three cases in turn.

1 Epicurean oblivion

Lucretius countenances a cosmological notion of eternal recurrence in book three of *De Rerum Natura*. Lucretius' broader project in that book is to argue for the Epicurean doctrine that death is nothing to us. His aim is therapeutic: if death is nothing to us, then fearing it is irrational. Lucretius thinks that by exposing the irrationality of the fear of death he will free his readers from its otherwise debilitating clutches. He achieves this by demonstrating how the fear of death rests upon false, superstitious beliefs in an afterlife. More specifically, the fear of death depends on belief in the existence of a post-mortem self who might suffer the harms of death. The Epicurean's physicalist understanding of the soul precludes such a continuation of the self and thus rules out the harm of death. In the words of Epicurus, 'when we are, death is not come, and, when death is come, we are not' (LM). This demonstration is essential to attaining the freedom from disturbance that characterizes the Epicurean good life.

At 3.843 Lucretius breaks off this argument to discuss another possible fear, the fear of recurrence. Lucretius' discussion of recurrence is aimed at evaluating whether we ought to suffer distress at the idea of recurrence (Ansell-Pearson 2015a: 98). He argues that just as we should not fear death, we should also not fear recurrence. Nevertheless, he does conceive recurrence as a possible source of fear: one that we can eliminate through the exercise of reason. Lucretius holds that recurrence is a possible source of distress for us and he seeks to give reasons to allay our fear that we will return and suffer again. He identifies a recurrence phobia that Epicurean philosophy is able to treat.

Epicurean cosmology necessarily entails recurrence of the same. 'By the principles of Epicurean cosmology,' as Warren explains, 'this sort of palingenesis is not only possible, it is inevitable. Given the infinity of time, the atoms which now constitute me will arrange and rearrange themselves into an unlimited number of forms, and will go on to repeat these forms over and over again' (Warren 2001: 501). Lucretius considers such a case, in which 'time should gather together our matter after death and bring it back again as it is now placed' (3.849). Such a case seems to count against Lucretius' claim elsewhere that before birth and after death there is only eternal non-existence (3.972–5). The prospect that my atoms may recombine in the self-same configuration means that Lucretius must confront the possibility of post-mortem experience: Epicurean physics entails the eternal return of the same, or the possibility that 'the light of life will be given to us again' (3.849).

Should the prospect of post-mortem experience via recurrence trouble the Epicurean? At first glance the answer seems to be 'no'. Although the recombination of my atoms opens the door to post-mortem existence, this does not threaten the main thrust of the Epicurean argument against the fear of death. The post-mortem experience that recurrence makes possible is not the experience of a painful afterlife or a state of non-existence, since no experience of non-existence is possible. Instead, recurrence raises the prospect that we might experience the self-same life once again.

For Epicureans, the eternal recurrence of the same represents a danger because it seems to entail the repetition of life's suffering. When Lucretius compares everlasting non-existence after death to a peaceful sleep, he suggests that death heralds the permanent cessation of life's pains. Death takes away the possibility of 'misery and pain in the future' (Lucretius 3.862). The contrast between eternal oblivion and transient life is comforting because it shows that in the future there is nothing to fear. There is no possibility of pain in the future to eternity (as in the ante-natal past). The truth of recurrence causes problems for this comforting doctrine because it raises the prospect that the future does hold the possibility of fresh pains, namely the return of all those that one has already suffered and will suffer in this life.

Lucretius quickly discounts the threat that recurrence poses to our tranquillity. We should not fear recurrence, he argues, because between our present life and any other possible recurrences, past or future, exists 'a stoppage of life' (3.360). There are two ways of thinking about Lucretius' argument (Gill 2006: 69–70). The first is to take Lucretius as arguing that past and future recurrences are not 'us' (Alberti 1990: 151–206). This would be to read Lucretius as offering a criterion of personal identity in terms of memory and denying that the identity relation holds across recurrences. On this reading, being a self for Lucretius requires continuity of memory. The second is to read Lucretius' appeal to memory as part of an account of what concerns us as rational agents (Warren 2001: 499–508). We will not attempt to resolve this debate here. For our purposes, it is sufficient to show that on either interpretation, Lucretius' therapeutic argument fails.

On the first 'identity' reading, we have nothing to fear from the eventual return of our and the world's atoms back to their present state because the qualitatively identical individuals thereby produced would be numerically distinct from our present selves. That is, they are not us. Since they are not us, Lucretius implies, they are not the object of our self-directed concern. We have no grounds to fear the pain and suffering that inevitably afflicts their lives. Bernard Reginster explains this reading in his discussion of Nietzsche's doctrine of eternal recurrence: 'I have absolutely no reason to be concerned about the experiences of my self in recurring cycles of my life, since the self in those cycles is *not my self* in the relevant sense' (Reginster 2006: 211).

We might challenge the claim that Epicurean metaphysics is sufficient to demonstrate that we have no legitimate fears about future recurrences. Patricia Slatin (2014a), for example, explains why we might doubt whether Epicurean metaphysics really does demonstrate that recurrent selves are numerically distinct:

> Lucretius puts much emphasis on the idea that our consciousness comes to an end at death – there occurs 'a break in life' – as if that sufficed to guarantee that our life could not return. But what is consciousness, and what is our identity, according to Epicureans? Recall their metaphysical premise: nothing is real but atoms and void. I can be nothing over and above these particular atoms in this particular arrangement having these particular motions; my consciousness is nothing over and above the atoms of my soul moving thus and so. If my same atoms assume again the same arrangement and move again with the same motions, how can Lucretius deny that this is myself and my own consciousness returned to the 'light of life?' He will insist that the temporal separation makes all the difference: 'between then and now is interposed a break in life', but here's the catch – the Epicureans have to deny the reality of time, as time is neither the same as void

nor is it made out of atoms. Only a thing that does not really exist separates my present from my recurrent self. So is Epicurean metaphysics robust enough to give Lucretius the conclusion he wants?

If Lucretius is relying on the interruption of memory to numerically differentiate between qualitatively identical selves across recurrences, then his therapeutic conclusion is undermined by Epicurean metaphysics. The interruption of memory does successfully rule out the prospect of the infinite continuation of life. Lucretius also wants to rule out the prospect of the discontinuous immortality provided by eternal recurrence. It is this second prospect that Epicurean metaphysics fails to rule out.

On the second 'concern' reading, we have nothing to fear from recurrence, even though we do actually recur. To see why this is so, we can examine Lucretius' argument in more detail. Lucretius notes that if recurrence is true, then we would have already lived. This possibility, he claims, does not cause us distress, because we have no memory of previous recurrences. Any pains from a previous recurrence fall outside the scope of our concern. Since in the present we have no memory of experiencing the sufferings of past recurrences, we are not distressed by them anew. However, the fact that we have no memory of our past iterations does not prove that we have not had them, just as a failure to recall past experiences in our current life does not necessarily prove their non-existence. If we were to recall past iterations of our life that we had earlier forgotten, then this presumably would add to our present woes. Furthermore, recalling past experiences would not necessarily differentiate between the self in two recurrences (the subject and object of remembrance): under the recurrence hypothesis all experiences would be repeated, including acts of remembrance. Nevertheless, for Lucretius we have no reason to worry about our past selves because death permanently severs our chain of memory.

Lucretius argues that we should adopt the same attitude towards the prospect of future recurrences. In effect, he claims that memory acts to restrict the scope of our self-directed concern. What I cannot remember cannot distress me, and so what I cannot anticipate should not cause me fear. 'Even if, therefore,' as Warren summarizes, 'I am assured that one of these future selves will suffer terribly, each instantiation is psychologically insulated from all the others and therefore no concern could rationally be felt for the well-being of any instantiation besides the present one' (Warren 2001: 505).

Again, we can question whether Epicurean physics supports Lucretius' therapeutic conclusion. Lucretius accepts that one 'may easily come to believe' in the truth of recurrence after meditating on the 'motions of matter' or physics (3.854–5). While we lack direct access to the experience of previous recurrences in the form of a memory, Epicurean theory provides another non-mnemonic route to the knowledge that we have lived previously, and that we will live again. If we accept Epicurean physics then it appears we do have rational grounds to anticipate future recurrences.[5]

Let us sum up the Epicurean treatment of the doctrine of eternal recurrence. Lucretius claims that a proper grasp of recurrence demonstrates the irrationality of our anxiety about future recurrences. We believe that we have grounds for anxiety about our future selves because we assume that this recurrence of the same configuration of atoms means we will once again experience the same sufferings we presently endure. Yet, Lucretius argues, we ought to have no fear for the future because we are psychologically insulated from our future selves. Just as we will not be there when we die, so too Lucretius claims we will not be there when we recur. As we have seen, Lucretius' argument is flawed on two separate fronts: on an 'identity' reading, Epicurean metaphysics does not warrant the non-identity of recurrent individuals, and on a 'concern' reading, it provides non-mnemonic grounds for anticipating or fearing future recurrences

Indeed, against Lucretius, it seems that the Epicurean notion of recurrence must compound my present suffering. Epicurean physics requires that I must admit that I will suffer again, rather than sink into eternal oblivion at the moment of death. The knowledge of my return must intensify and compound my present suffering because I know that I will experience it again and again. I cannot live tranquilly in the knowledge of eternal oblivion, but I must suffer in anticipation of the repetition of my past, present and unknowable future sufferings.

Lucretius' Epicurean therapy aims to show that death is redemption from the recurrence of life. Epicureans do not want recurrence (the return to life) or, indeed, immortality (the extension of life). To Lucretius the prospect of definitive death is preferable to immortality or recurrence because it eliminates all possibility of pain and sorrow. Since the only pleasure Epicureans value is the absence of all pain, death delivers this end definitively. Lucretius suggests that death is not terrifying since it is like a restful sleep, except it is an eternal, unbroken sleep in which 'no longing for ourselves [will] trouble us' (3.920).

2 Stoic consolation

The Epicureans' main philosophical competitors, the Stoics, also took up the thought of eternal recurrence as an aspect of their philosophical therapy. Both schools share the commitment that philosophy ought to transform our way of life. In this context, we study nature in order to learn how to lead flourishing lives. 'The physics of antiquity' as Hadot explains '… is intended to bring about in its readers or listeners greatness of soul and inner peace' (Hadot 1995a: 245). We can compare the Epicurean and Stoic responses to the prospect of eternal recurrence.

In his *Letters*, Seneca addresses precisely Lucretius' therapeutic argument that the mortality of the soul ought not to be a source of fear or anxiety.[6] He furthermore considers Lucretius' corresponding claim that since death puts a limit on the scope of memory, the fact of recurrence also ought not to cause anxiety.

Following the standard Epicurean convention, Seneca suggests in *Letter* 36 that we ought to learn 'contempt of death' as a means of maintaining our equanimity in the face of fortune. Yet, he concedes that death has something in it that 'inspires terror, so that it *shocks even our souls*, which nature has so molded that they love their own existence' (36). Seneca stresses that even the Stoics are shocked by the thought of death because like all humans they naturally love their *own* existence. Seneca implies that this love is unqualified or unconditional: we love our own existence regardless of the quality of our lives – we love our own existence simpliciter. Our love of our own existence, he suggests, is evident in the fact that we must have courage to confront death and to perform our duties even at the risk of death. We would not need the virtue of courage unless we conceived death as an object of terror. Since our own existence naturally inspires love in us, and this love engenders a universal and unconditional desire to preserve it, its cessation must inspire terror.

Now it is precisely at this point in *Letter* 36 that Seneca assays the Epicurean cure for the fear of death, but he does so to show how it falls short of treating those who crave a longer life or immortality. If, as Seneca maintains on the basis of the Stoic concept of *oikeiōsis*, we have a natural and universal love of our own existence how can we learn to maintain equanimity in the face of our own death? Stoics' philosophical training, he suggests, requires meditating on death, or, as he notes in *Letter* 26.8, we must follow Epicurus' command: *meditare mortem*. It is the discipline that teaches one to despise death. Yet, Seneca's meditation on death leads us to a perspective very different from Lucretius' Epicurean perspective: we learn how to despise death not because it is eternal sleep, and therefore free of all painful sensations, but because we learn that it is only an interruption to our existence, not its end. We have nothing to fear from death, on this Stoic view, because it is merely a pause before we are restored to the light of day. Seneca argues that the Stoic philosopher correctly conceives recurrence as a consolation, not a threat. Seneca confronts the truth that Lucretius evades.

Addressing the philosophical discipline required to despise death, Seneca first recalls Lucretius' Epicurean argument that our own death should not be an object of terror because after death we will not exist to experience any harm. In *Letter* 36 Seneca glosses Lucretius' Epicurean argument that we ought not to fear death: 'In death there is nothing harmful; for there must exist something to which it is harmful.' In his *Consolation to Marcia* Seneca repeats the standard Epicurean therapy of the fear of death that the afterlife is a myth and death is equivalent to the state of never having been born, eternal non-existence, which can be neither good nor evil:

> Consider that the dead are affected by no evils, and that those things that instil in us fear of the underworld are fictitious. (19.4)

> Death is neither good nor evil. That can only be good or evil which is something. What is itself nothing and reduces all things to nothingness does not lead us into one condition or the other. (19–5)

However, in *Letter* 36 Seneca implies that Lucretius' consolation is effective only insofar as it liberates one from the natural desire for one's own existence. To put his point another way, Lucretius' consolation can have no traction for those who love their existence even if continuing to live entails suffering or longing. Seneca recognizes that death is harmful in the *present* for those who, motivated by their natural desire for self-preservation, wish for the *continuation* of their life. For those who love life their own death is terrifying precisely because it is the loss of themselves as a subject of experience. They fear it not because they irrationally believe they will continue to experience sensations after they are dead, but precisely because they will *not* experience sensations. To those who love their own life it is not consoling to learn that they will no longer experience it.

Seneca aims to show that we do not have to forgo the love of our own existence and with it the desire for more life in order to combat our terror of death. As we shall see, he argues that the natural desire for self-preservation is satisfied not by a longer life, but by a repeated life. Like the Epicureans, Seneca believes that one can achieve a form of self-completion or self-perfection that does not require added time: 'What a noble thing it is to round out your life before death comes and then await in peace the remaining portion of time, claiming nothing for yourself, since you are in possession of the happy life; for such a life is not made happier by being longer' (32.4). Unlike the Epicureans, however, Seneca implies, in a Letter, that both the ordinary person who fears death and is 'greedy for the future' and the sage who has achieved self-completion and does not crave more time can affirm the idea of recurrence (32.4–5).

For this reason, after glossing the Epicurean consolation Seneca sees the need for a new and *anti-Epicurean* consolation for death that answers to those who love their own existence and are therefore terrified rather than consoled by the thought of eternal non-existence, or definitive death. For Seneca, the thought of eternal recurrence is a part of the consolation tradition. In his *Consolation to Marcia*, for example, Seneca consoles Marcia for the loss of her son Metilius by imagining that in the interim before the world repeats itself he is happy. Here Seneca endeavours to console Marcia's grief not only by picturing her son's post-mortem happiness but also by claiming that he is happy specifically because he knows that he will return to repeat the same life. On this cosmological view, which Metilius knows is true, mother and son will be eternally reunited. In consoling Marcia for the loss of her son Seneca draws on the cosmology of recurrence. Here Seneca consoles Marcia with the suggestion that her son is happy in the knowledge that all shall return to the same life (26.7). Seneca shows that viewing the cycles of nature can help one view death with equanimity.

Seneca makes a similar case in his evocation of eternal recurrence in *Letter* 36. Here he suggests that we may not be able to have more life, especially if fate calls upon us to maintain our fidelity or virtue in the face of the enemy, but we can have life once more. Whereas for Lucretius eternal recurrence is an idea that has the potential to threaten, for Seneca it consoles. Even though the cyclical re-use of matter is both a Stoic and an Epicurean doctrine, each conceives its significance in a diametrically opposed way. In *Letter* 36 Seneca identifies the cosmological doctrine of recurrence as one of philosophy's universal weapon against the terror of death. For the Stoic our natural love of our existence, and desire for self-preservation, is satisfied by the fact of our recurrence. Seneca therefore proposes the eternal recurrence of the same as a consolation:

> And yet, if you are possessed by so great a craving for a longer life, reflect that none of the objects which vanish from our gaze and are re-absorbed into the world of things, from which they come forth and are soon to come forth again, is annihilated; they merely end their course and do not perish. And death, which we fear and shrink from, merely interrupts life, but does not steal it away; the time will return when we shall be restored to the light of day; and many men would object to

this, were they not brought back in forgetfulness of the past ... everything which seems to perish merely changes. Since you are destined to return, you ought to depart with a tranquil mind. (36)

For Seneca then we have no reason to fear death because the eternal recurrence of the same ensures that our own existence, which we naturally love and therefore wish to preserve forever, will return. Seneca reasons that even those who are possessed of a passion or craving for a longer life need not fear death if they possess the knowledge that they are bound to return. Seneca assumes that for those filled with this passion for more life, the return of their own life may be sufficient to moderate or still their craving for a *longer* life. They will learn how to despise death by following the Stoic imperative to reflect or meditate on the cosmic cycle of recurrence. In this respect Seneca uses the doctrine of recurrence as a 'spiritual exercise': it converts or transforms the self from a state of bondage to one of liberty. Seneca implies that by meditating on recurrence one can maintain constancy in the face of death. We should not fear death because it does not steal away our most loved possession, our own existence; death merely interrupts it.

In revisiting the idea of cosmological return later in the *Letters* Seneca stresses that it is the practice of reflecting on nature that enables one to remain constant in the face of death:

Whatever is will cease to be, and yet it will not perish, but will be resolved into its elements. To our minds, this process means perishing, for we behold only what is nearest; our sluggish mind, under allegiance to the body, does not penetrate to bournes beyond. Were it not so, the mind would endure with greater courage its own ending and that of its possessions, if only it could hope that life and death, like the whole universe about us, go by turns, that whatever has been put together is broken up again, and that eternal craftsmanship of God, who controls all things, is working at this task. (71. 13–14)

Contra Lucretius, Seneca judges the fact of eternal recurrence as a consolation rather than a source of distress. He observes that 'many men' would object to their own return to the self-same life if prior to their return they were offered a choice. 'Death', he explains, 'merely interrupts life ... the time will return when we shall be restored to the light of day; and many men would object to this, were they not brought back in forgetfulness of the past' (Cf. Augustine *De Civ.* 10.30). If they had the option to choose to return and repeat the same life and they were also to remember their past (identical) lives, he claims, these men would object to their own return. Seneca's argument implies that Epicureans belong to the many who cannot consent to the return of the same since they find consolation in the prospect of definitive death and the forgetting of past lives and with it the end of suffering.[7] Seneca maintains that even if Stoics were offered the choice of returning to the light of the same life in the full recollection of its travails they would consent to relive their lives again and again.[8] Epicureans consent to death, but not to recurrence; Stoics consent to death partly *because* of recurrence.

3 Nietzschean cultivation

Both Epicureans and Stoics share the view of the eternal recurrence of life, though on different metaphysical grounds. Famously, Nietzsche revisits the ancient doctrine and links it to his ethical perspective in ways that remain subject to ongoing, unresolved debate. As we have seen, the Epicureans and Stoics diverge in their response to the thought of eternal recurrence. Both endorse the truth of recurrence as a cosmological doctrine, yet Epicureans maintain that, properly conceived, we should be indifferent to this prospect since we are not connected with our future selves in any way that warrants concern, whereas Stoics claim that we should be consoled by the return of the same since it ensures we regain the object of our love, our own existence.

Nietzsche, like Lucretius and Seneca, puts the doctrine of the eternal recurrence to ethical use. In section 341 of *The Gay Science*, Nietzsche asks, 'How well disposed would you have to become to yourself and to life *to crave nothing more fervently* than this ultimate eternal confirmation and seal?' Rather than evasion or consolation, at stake in Nietzsche's approach to recurrence is fervent desire. Nietzsche's question in this section is how we can shape a life such that we want to return to it again and again. Nietzsche asks his reader to confront and evaluate the prospect of the eternal recurrence of the same. In doing so, he seeks to heighten and intensify his readers' concern over their own lives, in contradistinction to Hellenistic therapeutic goals. We argue that this concern is addressed by shaping a profoundly personal and distinctive life. The eternal recurrence motivates us to shape such a life.

Nietzsche, as we noted above, thought that the probability or mere possibility of recurrence was sufficient to engender concern about how one lives. Nietzsche assumes that as a thought experiment, the idea of recurrence can have a profound psychological significance. Putting aside debates over the correctness of Nietzsche's assumption, we want to address the question of the kind of transformative and therapeutic effect he attributed to this experiment.[9] We argue that Nietzsche believes that imagining and evaluating the prospect of our eternal repetition motivates us to cultivate ourselves as singular, immortal artworks. We can see why this is so by examining how Nietzsche personifies the thought of recurrence as the demonic voice of what he calls our 'ownmost conscience'.

Nietzsche links together the thought of eternity and self-transformation in the famous penultimate section of *The Gay Science*:

> *The heaviest weight.* – What if some day or night a demon [*Dämon*] were to steal into your loneliest loneliness and say to you: 'This life as you now live it and have lived it you will have to live once again and innumerable times again; and there will be nothing new in it, but every pain and every joy and every thought and sigh and everything unspeakably small or great in your life must return to you, all in the same succession and sequence – even this spider and this moonlight between the trees, and even this moment and I myself. The eternal hourglass of existence is turned over again and again, and you with it, speck of dust!' Would you not throw yourself down and gnash your teeth and curse the demon who spoke thus? Or have you once experienced a tremendous moment when you would have answered him:

'You are a god, and never have I heard anything more divine.' If this thought gained power over you, as you are it would transform and possibly crush you; the question in each and every thing, 'Do you want this again and innumerable times again?' would lie on your actions as the heaviest weight! Or how well disposed would you have to become to yourself and to life to long for nothing more fervently than for this ultimate eternal confirmation and seal? (GS 341)

We can understand the specific force or gravity Nietzsche gave this thought experiment by examining how he conceives the demon as the incarnation of personal conscience. Nietzsche frames the thought of recurrence not only such that you must suppose that your present self will re-experience the same life again and again but also that you must assess this prospect in light of what he calls just three sections prior your 'ownmost conscience' (GS 338). Nietzsche's demon challenges you to assess your present life and actions in light of your 'ownmost' or what in *Schopenhauer as Educator* (1874) he identified as your 'secret bad conscience'. In this earlier figuration Nietzsche suggested that we all have a 'secret bad conscience': 'the law that every man is a unique miracle', that implores us to fashion ourselves into a distinctive, personal unity (SE 1).

That Nietzsche wants us to assess the thought of our recurrence in light of our ownmost conscience follows from the mise en scène of GS 341: the demon confronts you in a moment of the profoundest loneliness when all that matters to you is your own singular fate independent of or standing apart from all others. Nietzsche suggests that our evaluation of our own recurrence, the weight it has for us, must ultimately derive from our 'ownmost conscience' (GS 338). He identifies the law or principle of this conscience in the imperative: 'You should become who you are' (GS 270). Our 'ownmost conscience', as he explains it, impels us to follow our own '*path*', a trajectory we follow independently of, and oblivious to, anything other than the realization and perfection of our own distinctive set of possibilities (GS 338).

We can illuminate Nietzsche's ideal of our 'ownmost conscience' by seeing how he defends it against the force of moral conscience. One of his key objections to Kantian and Schopenhauerian morality is that they both entail 'losing myself *from my path*' by compelling us to follow generalizable rules or to live for others (GS 338). Nietzsche's ownmost conscience censures us for betraying our own unique individuality. Nietzsche observes that this morality says, 'Live in seclusion so that you *are able* to live for yourself!' (GS 338) Nietzsche's *Dämon* creates this moment of seclusion and separation by stealing into your loneliest loneliness to announce the doctrine of recurrence. He stages the demon's challenge in such a way that we cannot take 'refuge in the conscience of the others' and we must therefore consider the prospect of recurrence strictly in terms of whether our present lives realize our 'personal infinity', an immeasurable gulf between our own individuality and others (GS 291).

The thought of eternal repetition is crucial to Nietzsche's ethics of self-cultivation because answering the question 'Do you want it again and again?' is the means by which we can disclose our ownmost conscience. We disclose our ownmost conscience by testing whether or not each and every action can bear the weight of eternity. By compelling us to imagine we have one and only one identical life and that we will repeat it to all eternity, Nietzsche's *Dämon* compels us to determine how we must live to abide by the imperative: become who you are. Eternity compels us to consider what we believe makes our transient lives worthy of this repetition.

Nietzsche supposes that when we examine our lives through the lens of eternity (or eternal repetition) we will judge that only a life that is singular or particular to ourselves is worthy of repetition. For each of us, he claims, what makes our lives worthy of eternity is living 'according to our own laws and standards' and in doing so shaping our nature so that it bears the 'monogram of our most essential individual essence, a work, a deed, an uncommon inspiration, a creation' (*HL* 3). If we take the view from recurrence, he implies, we must despair if we discover that our lives are merely replications or minor variations on a common theme. For Nietzsche, what evokes a despairing response to the thought of our own recurrence is not the return of our *suffering*, but the return of a life that is not our *own* (Cf. Reginster (2006: 217)). The thought of recurrence evokes the dread of not living a life according to our own laws and standards and in doing so failing to become the distinctive individuals we are. It arouses the dread, ultimately, of failing to become who one is. In this way, he implies, the thought of recurrence makes us hone in on our singularity and motivates us to pursue the ideal of creating our lives as immortal artworks.

Nietzsche also stresses that for the thought of recurrence to function as an instrument of self-cultivation we must employ it as an experiment or exercise. As Magnus rightly claims, mere belief in eternal recurrence 'does not cause or induce genuine affirmation … once the doctrine is "understood" no automatic liberation seems to follow' (Magnus 1978: 156). Yet, Nietzsche does not conceive eternal recurrence as a theoretical doctrine we simply need to understand, but as a 'spiritual exercise'. Nietzsche conceives the thought of recurrence as a particular spiritual exercise or practice: namely, a repeated meditation on the significance of the idea of recurrence. It is an exercise through which we transform our present life in such a way that it becomes such that we would desire its eternal repetition.

Following a classical analogy, we can conceive eternal recurrence as a spiritual gymnastics that makes us more adept at imposing the image of eternity on our lives. In this sense, as Hadot recognized, Nietzsche's philosophy follows in the footsteps of the ancient schools. Following the ancient model, Nietzsche rejects the idea of philosophy as the teaching of abstract theory – much less an exegesis of texts – and embrace it as an art of living (Hadot 1995a: 83, 108). We therefore miss something essential about his doctrine if we conceive it as imagining or believing in recurrence as a logical or theoretical possibility shorn of practical implications. Nietzsche does not ask us to contemplate recurrence as a theoretical doctrine, but to incorporate the thought of recurrence into our lives as a practice of self-cultivation. Rather than only contemplating or imagining recurrence, he asks how you might be transformed if 'this thought gained power over you' (GS 341).

In other words, the cultivating effect of the thought of recurrence hinges on its overpowering us, which is an entirely distinct proposition to idly contemplating it as a theoretical doctrine. Nietzsche stresses that the thought of recurrence must exercise the force of conscience: that is, it must exercise mastery over our lives. As Nietzsche conceives it, the thought of recurrence transforms or crushes us only if it exercises this mastery over our judgement and does so in the sense that 'the question in each and every thing: "Do you want this again and again and innumerable times again?" would lie on [our] actions as the heaviest weight!' (GS 341). Nietzsche implies that the thought of repetition is only cultivating insofar as it is overpowering, applies to all of our actions and becomes incorporated into our lives as a repeated practice. Nietzsche's thought of recurrence demonstrates how he adopted the ancient model of philosophy as a way of life. As he conceives it, the ethics of self-cultivation entails trying to see whether we can live in accordance with the thought of recurrence.

Yet, even as Nietzsche models eternal recurrence on the ancient conception of philosophy as a technique of self-cultivation, he believes it achieves the opposite of the ancient exercises. According to Hadot, the goal of the ancient exercises is to enable individuals to transcend their individual, passionate subjectivity and ascend to an impersonal, universal perspective (Hadot 1995: 97). 'Seneca', as he explains, 'finds joy not in Seneca, but in the Seneca identified with universal Reason. One rises from one level of the self to another, transcendent level' (Hadot 2011: 136).[10] The goal of Nietzsche's exercise, on the other hand, is to rise from the level of a common, collective self to a higher, singular level. If Stoics are necessarily uniform and unvaried, one who follows Nietzsche's teaching must be irregular and idiosyncratic. The Hellenistic schools more generally maintained that the ideal life is the realization of a universal human nature. In order to realize this ideal, they argued that philosophy must liberate us from false conventional values that encourage us to neglect a life in agreement with our universal nature. The Hellenistic idea, as Long puts it, 'is that an understanding of this nature can and should serve as the technologist of the self, shaping our innate potentialities in more life-enhancing ways than cultural norms themselves offer to us. This is not a project of making one's life into an artwork' (Long 2006: 27–8).

By contrast, Nietzsche maintains that the ideal life requires constructing ourselves as distinctive and personal artworks, not in agreement with any universal conception of human nature. In order to realize this ideal, he argues, philosophy must liberate us from the structures of consciousness that compel us to neglect the cultivation of our singularity. Nietzsche's thought of recurrence is a technique of self-cultivation that aims to counteract the limits of consciousness. Nietzsche explains the origins and evolution of consciousness as an instrument of social integration that belongs to our existence not as individuals but, rather, as what he disparagingly calls herd animals. What we 'know' of ourselves through consciousness, he argues, is only that aspect of ourselves that is dependent upon the community. The limits on self-knowledge are built into the evolutionary history of consciousness: it has been shaped by evolutionary pressure to allow us to know and communicate only 'that in ourselves which is "non-individual" or "average"', that is, those frailties and vulnerabilities that we share with all the members of our community (GS 354). Nietzsche explains this limitation through a political analogue: consciousness is the tyranny of the majority extended into our 'depths'. When we 'translate' our unconscious thoughts into consciousness, all that becomes visible is the general or herd-like. Our personal infinity is lost in translation. And yet, Nietzsche claims, 'at bottom all our actions are incomparably and utterly personal, unique and boundlessly individual, there is no doubt; but as soon as we translate them into consciousness, *they no longer seem to be*' (GS 354).

According to Nietzsche, the thought of recurrence is a technique or exercise that can help us to identify and cultivate this otherwise unrealizable singularity. The view from recurrence compels us to identify, value and cultivate our singularity or personal infinity, he suggests, because we suffer despair at the thought of the eternal repetition of commonality and take joy in the thought of our eternal singularity. Nietzsche's exercise motivates the desire to create an uncommon life because it implicitly draws on one of the most powerful modern ethical ideals. 'Artistic creation', as Charles Taylor observes, has become 'the paradigm mode in which people can come to self-definition. The artist becomes in some way the paradigm case of the human being, as agent of original self-definition' (Taylor 1992: 62). Nietzsche's belief that this exercise will cultivate our singularity is contingent on its mobilizing background values, specifically the romantic value of the self as artwork.

Conclusion

This chapter has charted the different ethical uses to which Lucretius, Seneca and Nietzsche put the thought of eternal recurrence. Lucretius seeks to allay the fear of recurrence by drawing attention to the discontinuity of memory between successive recombinations of one's body. Seneca embraces recurrence as a consoling thought: recurrence satisfies our natural desire to preserve our own existence. For him, the thought of recurrence overcomes the fear of death. Nietzsche connects his doctrine of the eternal recurrence to the fashioning of the self as artwork worthy of eternity or eternal repetition. In each of the three cases, eternal recurrence is deployed as a 'spiritual exercise' to suit its distinct therapeutic or transformative ends.

Notes

1. We would like to thank Keith Ansell-Pearson, David Konstan and John Sellars for their very helpful comments, criticisms and suggestions.
2. References to *De Rerum Natura* will be listed by book first and line second, which can refer to the Latin text or the numbers in the Loeb edition (Lucretius 1992).
3. See Cicero's account of the Stoic theory of *oikeiôsis* (appropriation): 'Every animal, as soon as it is born …, is concerned with itself, and takes care to preserve itself. It favours its constitution and whatever preserves its constitution, whereas it recoils from its destruction and whatever appears to promote its destruction' (Fin. 3.16); and Seneca (121.20–1).
4. In an unpublished note, he suggests that 'even if the circle-repetition is only probable or possible, the thought of such a possibility can disturb or transform us. … What an effect the possibility of eternal damnation has had!' (KSA 9:11 [203]).
5. Paul Loeb claims that Nietzsche develops a stronger objection to the Lucretian position. Nietzsche, according to Loeb, allows for the direct experience of recurrence. It is, in fact, an effect of our instincts for self-preservation that this experience is falsified into the non-eternal transient moment (Loeb 2017: 26). Our argument does not depend on this metaphysics.

6 Letters are referenced by number as found in the three volumes of the Loeb edition of Seneca's *Epistles*.
7 See Slatin: 'We may note that Seneca, like Nietzsche, believes the idea of eternal recurrence would be unwelcome to most people, and he seems also to agree with Nietzsche as to the reason for this when he says that many would object to reliving their lives, "were they not brought back in forgetfulness of the past" – that is, people shrink from suffering and have no creative means of transforming it into something affirmable; their only way of dealing with it is by forgetting. Seneca, however, is not addressing himself in his letter to the common run of people, but to a friend who is a reasonable man, who he is confident will see how the thought of eternal recurrence can just as well be a source of *comfort* as of fear, for if we have to get back all our sorrows, by the same token we will get back all our joys' (Slatin 2014b).
8 'If we were to come to life again and remember the sufferings of past lives, that would no doubt increase our suffering, but the fear of an afterlife is the fear that we will exist to suffer *again*, whether or not we remember having suffered before' (Slatin 2014b).
9 See, for example, Soll (1973); Clark 1990; Reginster (2006); Loeb (2010). For a defence of the psychological efficacy of recurrence as a thought experiment, see Ure (2018).
10 John Sellars (2019) rightly qualifies Hadot's claim by suggesting that the Stoics conceived their cosmic perspective as a means of cultivating the individual self and its virtues. Nietzsche, however, does not conceive the thought of recurrence as a means through which individuals cultivate their ability to exercise collective virtues or social responsibilities, but as an exercise in cultivating what he calls their 'personal infinity'.

7

Nietzsche and Guyau on the temporality of Epicurean pleasure*

Federico Testa

Following the path opened by Alfred Fouillée (1902b: 13–27),[1] I compare the works of Jean-Marie Guyau and Friedrich Nietzsche by situating the place of Epicurus and Epicureanism in their philosophies. Although both authors, in later writings, depart from the teachings of the philosopher of the garden, both the young Guyau and Nietzsche, in his middle-period writings, feel related to Epicurus.

Guyau, in *La morale d'Épicure*, explains the Greek philosopher's thought and its unfolding in modern ethics, from the perspective of a partisan intellectual engagement. Understanding Epicureanism as an important force in the development of the history of thought, which remerges every time that religious enthusiasm and intellectual servitude dwindle, Guyau emphasizes the figure of the Epicurean 'sage' as 'presenting an artist of happiness', fully embodying the idea of philosophy as a way of life. Although his study on Epicureanism is not systematic, middle-period Nietzsche finds in Epicurus a fellow traveller in the sea of suffering, who finds tranquil pleasure in the present. Nietzsche's Epicurus is the creator of a 'heroic-idyllic' model of philosophizing, a master of antiquity who found in a cultivated and modest voluptuousness a therapy for our passions and desires.

I present both Guyau's and Nietzsche's readings of the Epicurean notions of pleasure and happiness. I articulate the notions of time underlying Nietzsche's and Guyau's interpretations, relating these notions to their thoughts on temporality more generally. What are the divergences and convergences in their reading of the temporality of pleasure in Epicurus? Is it possible to see, in their readings of Epicurean happiness, the principles of their own notions of time and temporality?

Guyau and Nietzsche

After an earthquake in Southern France in 1888, 33-year-old philosopher Jean-Marie Guyau dies of an aggravation of his illness. That same year, Nietzsche leaves the French Riviera. This marks the end of a series of synchronicities regarding the trajectory of

---

* I am grateful to Keith Ansell-Pearson for his supportive and generous reading of this text. I would also like to thank my colleagues Andre Okawara and Thom Ryan for their helpful comments. Special thanks go to Ryan Johnson for his attentive and careful editing work.

these two philosophers. If Nietzsche's name would become widely known, Guyau remains an unknown figure in the history of philosophy.

For Ilse Walther-Dulk, the trajectories of their respective works remain connected even to today. She proposes that the erasure of Guyau's work is significantly linked to the history of the French reception of Nietzsche, since the former played a key role in setting the grounds for this reception (Walther-Duke 2008). In this process, she explains, 'philosophical trends close … [to] Nietzsche were thereupon attributed to [him], even when they took inspiration from other models … . This is how Guyau's philosophy was overshadowed by Nietzsche's' (Walther-Dulk 2008: 9). If such assimilation was possible, this was due to the striking similarities and the 'real intellectual proximity' between the two philosophers (L'Yvonnet 2008: 8).

Guyau never encountered Nietzsche,[2] but we do find material evidence of Nietzsche's reading of two of Guyau's books: the *Esquisse d'une morale sans obligation ni sanction* and *L'irréligion de l'avenir*. Nietzsche covered his copies of these books with marginal notes and exclamation marks (Fouillée 1902a: 11).[3] Following these traces, Alfred Fouillée was the first to propose a systematic comparative study of Guyau and Nietzsche (Fouillée 1902b: 13–27). While exploring the proximity of their projects, Fouillée's aim, however, is to show their divergences.

Fouillée is particularly critical of Nietzsche, whom he sees as an 'ancient reactionary' and a 'singer of praises of force and war' (Fouillée 1902b: 14). His elitist individualism made him 'the enemy of every democracy' and 'of socialism, which [for him] is a coalition of the weak and the miserable against this law of the strongest' (16). For Fouillée, Nietzsche's idea of *will to power* ultimately expresses a will to dominate others, who are seen from a perspective of opposition. In this sense, Fouillée argues, like the young Hegelian Max Stirner,[4] Nietzsche based his philosophy on the individual's egoistic will. Guyau, by contrast, believed that 'true individualism and true socialism were perfectly compatible because of the expansion of all sorts of free association' (16). For Guyau, the expansion of life implies what he calls *fecundity*, that is, the expansion towards others, which does 'not, as Stirner contended, [go] against the nature of life', but is, rather, 'the very condition of the truly intense life' (14).

Fouillée notes that, in his copy of the *Esquisse*, Nietzsche underlined a passage in which Guyau claims that 'from the physiological point of view, existence and life imply *nutrition*, consequently appropriation, transformation for itself of the forces of nature. Life is a kind of *gravitation upon itself*' (Fouillée 1902a: 81). This is precisely the point on which Nietzsche and Guyau converge. Following this principle of nutrition, Guyau explains, beings 'accumulate a surplus of force to ensure the amount necessary to maintain life. Thrift is a law of nature' (82). He asks, then, 'What will become of this surplus of force which is accumulated by every healthy being, of this superabundance which nature succeeds in producing?' (82) It is precisely in the answer to this question that the fundamental divergence between the two philosophers emerges. Fouillée reads this notion of accumulation, generated by the 'gravitation upon itself', in terms of power:

[Nietzsche] imagines that being accumulates power for the sake of power itself – as if power had a value independently of its usage and the final joy which is attached to it. He thinks that being accumulates life [*fait provision de vie*] in excess

> so as to deploy its power upon *others* ... . Guyau, on the contrary, sees in the superabundance [of power, of life] not the means to deprive others of what they need, but to join them. (1902a: 153)

According to Fouillée, for Nietzsche, 'the strong naturally love solitude and isolation; it is the weak who seek to associate themselves to others' (1902a: 88). If, for Guyau, the excess of power leads us to sociable expenditure, the expansion towards and *with* others, for Nietzsche, this excess manifests itself as a sort of sovereign solitude, a deployment of power *against* others. Fouillée sees no possible compromise: 'Placed as Hercules between these two paths, that of the natural expansion towards others, and that of the naturally aggressive expansion against others, each one of us must choose: one must necessarily follow either Nietzsche or Guyau' (1902a: 153).

While Guyau grounds 'altruism on the law of life itself', Nietzsche 'wants to remain in the state of primitive egoism and, therefore, preaches the deployment of power [*puissance*] upon and against others' (1902a: 153). One of Nietzsche's notes on Guyau's text shows that the highest intensity of life is equivalent to its largest expansion, but this expansion is 'inimical to every altruistic fact' (1902a: 153). Walther-Dulk (2014: 8) also stresses this tension in Nietzsche's readings of Guyau, by pointing to his copy of *L'irréligion de l'avenir*, where he writes '*Esel!*' ('ass'; 'donkey') every time Guyau mentions this essentially altruistic and social aspect of life.

Following the path opened by Fouillée, this chapter compares Guyau and Nietzsche. Fouillée, however, emphasized the differences between them by privileging their later works. This is clear if one looks at the concepts privileged in his analysis: *fecundity* in Guyau and *will to power* in Nietzsche, concepts that appear in the authors' later writings. I would like to propose a thematic and chronological shift in the way we consider this relation.

My proposition is to explore in parallel how Nietzsche reads Epicurus in his middle-period writings, and how the young Guyau reads the Hellenistic philosopher in his book *La morale d'Épicure*. In their later writings both authors depart from Epicurus' teaching: Nietzsche by opposing Dionysian joy to Epicurean delight (WP 19) and Guyau by showing the moral insufficiency of pleasure and self-interest. However, both the young Guyau and the middle-period Nietzsche feel strongly connected to Epicurus. This shared reference reveals that the two philosophers shared much more than Fouillée suggests, and that their divergences presuppose a shared background.

'The Afternoon of Antiquity': Nietzsche on Epicurus

Let us now look at a different reading of Nietzsche, which clearly departs from the kind of criticism articulated by Fouillée. In 1933, A. H. J. Knight revealed what Ansell-Pearson (2014b) called 'Nietzsche's commitment to a philosophy of peace, goodwill and serenity' (4) by highlighting the relations between Nietzsche and Epicurus. For Knight (1933: 436–7):

> Nietzsche, above all in his middle period, harboured a warm interest in Epicureanism, which he never completely lost. In both thinkers there is the

interest in an ideal of peaceful, scholarly, enjoyable rest in a beautiful environment, in friendship, in the society of the Few, who are able to give the philosopher all he ever requires. Still more certain, more lasting and more important, is Nietzsche's interest in Epicureanism as a system which sought to save the human spirit from the dread of a future existence, of a Divine justice or injustice, of the existence of a relevant God.

Knight's description shows us a figure completely different from Fouillée's 'singer of praises of force and war' (Fouillée 1902b: 14). Indeed, Knight emphasizes that which in Nietzsche's philosophy concerns peace, rest, lucid and simple pleasure. Referring to Epicurus, Hadot stresses Nietzsche's belonging to this tradition which conceived and practised philosophy as a 'way of life'; that is to say, as a constant occupation and work on oneself and one's passions in order to achieve happiness, wisdom and emancipation (Hadot [1987] 1995a: 59).

While Knight's reading inaugurates a different interpretation of Nietzsche linking him to Epicurus, we must not overlook the fact that the relation of the German thinker to the philosopher of the garden is ambiguous and complex. Nietzsche's reader, especially of his later writings, could easily link Epicurus to the decadence of ancient Greek culture and of its tragic and affirmative impetus.[5] Indeed, in *The Anti-Christ* (30), Nietzsche characterizes Epicurus as a 'typical decadent', who expressed an 'instinctive hatred toward reality', characterized by 'the fear of pain, even of the infinitesimal in pain'. Approximating Epicurus and Christianity, Nietzsche sees then in Epicurus the opposite of the tragic Greek – who was capable of a radical openness to the world and its risks.[6] Similarly, in the fragments grouped in *The Will to Power*, Nietzsche reaffirms the primacy of the tragic and of the Dionysian, and privileges the pre-Socratics as the 'true philosophers' (437).

Nevertheless, one could also speak, with Walter Kaufmann, of Nietzsche's 'sense of kinship with Epicurus'. In a note to *The Gay Science*, he writes:

> There are also many interesting references to Epicurus in Nietzsche's letters to Peter Gast, who was very much interested in Epicurus. All of these references express admiration and a sense of affinity, although it has often been suggested, falsely, that Nietzsche admired only the pre-Socratic philosophers. (110)

As Knight pointed out, Nietzsche's sympathy for Epicurus is clear in his so-called middle period. In *Human, All Too Human* (68, 275, 591), *Dawn* (71, 72, 150, 174, 433), *Beyond Good and Evil* (7, 20, 61, 62, 270)[7] and, especially, *The Gay Science*, Epicurus is a key avatar of a model of philosophizing that emphasizes the cultivation of modest pleasures. One finds here what Ansell-Pearson defines as an 'ethos of Epicurean enlightenment', a practical wisdom of moderate or 'small doses' (Ansell-Pearson 2018: 54).[8] Epicurus embodies rational temperance, in contrast with the absolute expenditure of Dionysian tragedy.

As an illustration of Nietzsche's engagement with the Hellenistic master, I propose to analyse that which different scholars[9] have identified as one of the most meaningful and enigmatic references to Epicurus, the GS 45. I propose we read this passage specifically stressing the notion of temporality it presupposes.

Nietzsche tells us that he is 'proud of the fact' that he 'experiences Epicurus quite differently from perhaps everybody else', and that he 'enjoys the happiness of the afternoon of antiquity' every time he reads or hears anything about him:

> I see his eyes gaze upon a wide, white sea, across rocks at the shore that are bathed in sunlight, while large and small animals are playing in this light, as secure and calm as the light and his eyes. Such a happiness could be invented only by a man who was suffering continually. It is the happiness of eyes that have seen the sea of existence become calm, and now they can never weary of the surface and of the many hues of this tender, shuddering skin of the sea. Never before has voluptuousness been so modest. (GS 45, 110)

I would like to stress two elements in this complex extract. First, the definitions of voluptuousness (or pleasure) and happiness that are based on an image of pacification and appeasement: the passage from trouble and pain to pleasure (which defines Epicurean *ataraxia*). Second, the temporal dimension that defines this passage, and which is opened to us in this process of pacification and appeasement. In this sense, with Robin Small, I consider Nietzsche as 'a philosopher of *time* in that much of his thinking on human life centres on this theme' (Small 2010: 2), although temporality is often expressed in his thought through metaphors and images.[10]

The first aspect appears in the characterization of Epicurus as someone who 'suffered continually'. This description reflects Nietzsche's sense of proximity to Epicurus, as expressed in a letter from 1879:

> My health is disgustingly rich in pain, as formerly; my lire much more severe and lonesome, I myself live on the whole almost like a complete saint, but almost with the outlook of the complete, genuine Epicurus ... – with my soul very calm and patient and yet contemplating life with joy. (GS 110)

Similarly, in GS 45 it is from within the experience of suffering that Epicurus discovers happiness. It is the departure from this condition, even if temporary and precarious, that immediately opens or unfolds the perspective of a modest but accomplished happiness. Following Nietzsche's image, the philosopher has seen the violent and tempestuous sea of existence becoming calm before his eyes. But if one considers the dynamism and instability of the sea, one realizes that this calm and this voluptuousness that the philosopher finds in the momentary disappearance of pain can only be transient and ephemeral.[11] And this aspect leads us to the second point I wish to stress: the temporal dimension of the passage – that is, the temporality which the 'appeasement of the sea' symbolizes – which is that of the present and a peculiar way to experience it. As soon as we liberate ourselves from pain, as soon as suffering dissolves into the past, the present opens itself to us as the sole possibility of happiness. The future may reserve new storms and tides, the past is always already lost, but real happiness can only be found in the present.

According to Hadot, several spiritual exercises were mobilized by the ancient schools to produce an awareness of time, an attention to the present and its uniqueness.

Especially in Epicureanism, the present is considered a joyful and gratuitous gift (Hadot 1995a: 209). The experience of the present moment (in which, in Nietzsche's image, one contemplates 'the surface of the sea') reveals a pure sentiment of existence that is already pleasure in the full sense of the term. Before a sea that has become peaceful, no struggle or toil is imposed upon us, and we can accede to this modest voluptuousness of dwelling or being present in the heart of the instant. The present appears then as a sort of suspension, as a different mode of experiencing time which is neither marked by the suffering of the past nor by the hopes and fears of the future, including the fear of death. When the moment of accomplished pleasure interrupts pain, we overcome, to use Howard Caygill's words, that 'resentment against time which infallibly accompanies the fear of death' (1994: 140). This experience acquires almost mystical undertones in Krzysztof Michalski's description of this dwelling in the present in Nietzsche as a way to experience eternity (2011: vii).

It is also curious to note that the figure of the sea reappears in a fragment from 1885 (WP 1067), but this time deprived of its moments of precarious contemplative tranquillity and happiness. The sea of the will to power is a violent 'sea of forces flowing and rushing together, eternally changing, eternally floating back' (WP 1067). In the same way that the figure of Epicurus acquires, in the later works and fragments, the ideal/typical traces of decadence and gives place to Dionysus, the peaceful sea of modest and contemplative pleasure gives place to the sublime and tempestuous ocean of the will to power.

Guyau on Epicurus: The time of a *lifetime*

For Guyau, rational emancipation and resistance to fear and superstition constitute the core of Epicureanism. Differently from Nietzsche's fragmentary and non-systematic approach to Epicurus, Guyau's 1878 work is situated in the field of a history of philosophical systems. Guyau's project, however, goes beyond the history of ideas. In his exploration of the history of Epicureanism, Guyau reactivates an image of philosophy as an art of living and an art of happiness, in which pleasure plays a fundamental role.

What I now propose is to analyse the way in which Guyau characterizes the Epicurean notion of pleasure. My analysis will present the notion of temporality underlying this interpretation, highlighting the singularity of Guyau's reading in relation to that of Nietzsche. Finally, I analyse the importance of the figure of the Epicurean *sage*.

For Guyau, pleasure is the 'key idea' of the Epicurean system: it constitutes the 'sole end of desire' (1878: 35). Following Guyau's explanation, 'any pleasure ... is in itself a good', and so are the means mobilized to obtain it. Given the priority that Epicurus attributes to sensation and sensibility, it is enough to attest the presence of enjoyment [*jouissance*] to understand it as *good*.[12] From this perspective, Epicurus' doctrine is similar to the hedonism of Aristippus and the Cyrenaic school.

Guyau characterizes Aristippus' position as a radical form of hedonism, roughly consisting in promoting an absolute fidelity to the present moment and, consequently, to the fleeting pleasure one can obtain in each ephemeral fragment of the present. After all, says Guyau's Aristippus, 'who knows if the future will be for us? Only the present is ours' (1878: 36). Aristippus strives to efface all thought that presupposes duration and succession, making ourselves fully present in the actuality of enjoyment.

Perhaps the Cyrenaic master thought that, by living with plenitude and full intensity each of the fleeting moments that the present offers us, it would be possible to liberate ourselves from the suffering caused by time and temporality – suffering that Nietzsche captured so well in the untimely meditation *On the Uses and Disadvantages of History for Life*, when he affirmed that our existence 'fundamentally is – an imperfect tense that can never become a perfect one' (UM 61). For Aristippus, when one realizes that the past lacks positive existence, one is delivered of the weight of one's errors and regrets. In the same way, he wanted to liberate us from the anxiety and fear (or hope) presupposed by the idea of the future. He shows that reflection on the consequences of pleasure removes us from the plenitude of present enjoyment. The present, however, is movement and flow, and enjoyment – depending on this movement – is as ephemeral as the fleeting instants that exist between the abstractions of past and future. If, consequently, everything we have is a myriad of pleasures enjoyed in a multiplicity of fleeting and discrete instants, we cannot establish any end beyond the moment, nor any principle that would be exterior to this ephemeral variety of instantaneous pleasures. This is how, in trying to free himself from time and the suffering it involves, especially in the figure of an uncertain future, Aristippus becomes a slave of time, of a time that is always fugacious, in which nothing solid can be constituted. According to Guyau, he 'does not realise that, by wishing to liberate us from the future, he becomes a slave of the present' (1878: 37).

If all pleasure is good, can the same be said about its consequences? Guyau explains that the divergence between Epicurus and Aristippus emerges precisely by considering the *consequences* of pleasure and *pain*, as well as the *temporality* in the ethical experience of pleasure in Epicurus. In other words, Epicurus proposes that we consider the possibility of a future pain when we consider whether to accept a certain present pleasure. He also invites us to reflect on the possibility of a future pleasure that could emerge from the choice of enduring a certain present pain. And this is precisely the singular role played by reason and 'intelligence' in the Epicurean system: it links present sensation – which is all that the *flesh* [*la chair*] knows – to its possible consequences.[13] In this sense, guided by intelligence, we can choose pain over pleasure under certain circumstances, sacrificing the instant in the name of a future pleasure.

For Guyau's Epicurus, one must thus consider pleasures and pains from the standpoint of temporality and, particularly, from the perspective of the totality of one's life or of *a whole life* (*hó hólos bíos*) (ibid.). Passions and desires can be experienced as absolute if considered in the present of sensation. However, Guyau argues, if we consider them in time, from the perspective of a whole life, we can assess their ethical significance and, finally, master them. The concept of the *whole life* expresses what Small characterized as a 'perspectival' interpretation of temporality, which depicts time through an analogy with space (Small 2010: 126). This analogy is clear in Guyau's explanation, according to which the duration of a whole lifetime is to our passions the same as infinite space or void is to the Epicurean atoms:

> Each of those tendencies and passions which, when restricted to the present instant, was absolutely a master [*maîtresse*] within us, we can master it, once we place it

in the whole of our lives [*le tout de la vie*] … . The passions no longer collide in indescribable tumult. Just like Epicurus' atoms have the space before them in which to operate their spontaneous movements …, so too the instincts and passions of the soul have *duration* [*durée*] before them: if restrained, imprisoned, they would erupt in revolt. But when they are spread over time, they subside. When they are not repressed by obstacles, they cease to obstruct one another. (1878: 41)

In Guyau's reconstruction, the introduction of the notion of temporality is linked to the discussion on the figure of the Epicurean *sage*. If pleasures and pains are viewed from the perspective of the duration of this *hólos bíos*, they are also referred to a same *telos* – happiness. The requirement for happiness is the constancy, coherence and consistency in the pursuit of this end throughout time. This is the existential choice of the Epicurean sage.

For the sage, each moment is filtered and purified by the contact with this unique end, which unifies his will, thereby making it capable of projecting itself beyond the present moment, beyond what Hadot has called 'the voice of the flesh' (1995: 180): 'Epicurus' ethics places before our eyes something which is superior to the present, a good that surpasses and encompasses all particular goods, in a word, a *whole* or a *totality* [*un tout*]' (Guyau 1878: 41).

This continuity in time and this coherence of the will of the sage is also an ethical continuity in terms of the *style* that one gives to one's existence, to use Nietzsche's phrase (GS 290). Indeed, crafting one's existence like one creates a work of art is an important aspect in Guyau's view of the sage, and we can thus grasp the aesthetic dimension of his reading of Epicurus. The Epicurean sage is, for Guyau, 'an artist of happiness' who rationally organizes the emotions and pleasures he experiences in a beautiful and harmonious unity:

Life then becomes this *cadre* of undetermined contours, in which the sage, this 'artist of happiness' groups his emotions to come, placing some of them in the second plane, some others in the first, bringing these to light, and casting the shadows of oblivion over the others. (1927: 42)

Modes of temporality: Guyau and Nietzsche on eternity and the instant

I have briefly analysed the way Guyau and Nietzsche read the Epicurean notion of pleasure, exploring how they articulate different notions or experiences of temporality. In my reading of Nietzsche's GS 45, I argued that the notion of time underlying the 'modest voluptuousness' discovered by Epicurus is that of the present, as is clear in Nietzsche's image of the 'appeasement of the sea' and the serenity of Epicurus' gaze. In fact, the experience of the present is a constant in Nietzsche's work. To illustrate this, one could consider the opposition between historical time – past and memory – and the present in the second *Untimely Meditation*.[14] Or, with Michalski, one could look at the image of a child at play in the *Zarathustra*, which, also marked by forgetfulness, is 'complete and perfect in every moment of its duration' (2011: 18).

Guyau's reading mobilizes another notion of time. Differently from Cyrenaic Aristippus, Guyau's Epicurus situates pleasure not in the fleeting and dying instant but, rather, in a different temporal axis which emerges from the consideration of the future (and the pain or joy it reserves to us according to our present choices). It is the time of our whole lives, in which we must situate our passions in order to master them. The Epicurean sage is, for Guyau, he who organizes his 'emotions' consistently in 'style' and throughout the succession of time.

Now, it is important to note that these readings of the temporality of pleasure entail what we could call, with Hadot, 'spiritual exercises' (1995a: 81–125) – in this case, exercises regarding the experience of temporality or two forms of 'exercises of time'.[15] The first, which appears in Nietzsche, consists in the full openness to the present – which is seen, in the Epicurean perspective, as a *gift* of chance, which we should welcome as such. The second, which is found in Guyau's reading, is the projection and anticipation of the future, which is somehow brought to the present by the effort of intelligence: the future filters each singular moment. It is the ideal of a coherent totality in which the instant is not thought of as a self-contained event, but as tied to the whole of one's lifetime. This whole, Guyau suggests, should be actualized at each moment through an active disposition and exercise, and it should also be the criterion for accepting pleasures and pains. Here, the present paradoxically passes through a deviation *via* the future. As I have shown, through the concept of *hó hólos bíos*, Guyau's Epicurus teaches us to master our present and actualize our future, which is wrested from uncertainty and blind chance and brought to our sphere of action. One must actively make the future present at each instant, in the same way the 'artist of happiness' groups 'his emotions to come', as if one were capable of exercising one's freedom to 'abolish, in the present, all distance between the pursuit and the end pursued' (Goldschmidt 2006: 207).

Nevertheless, and to conclude, I would like to suggest that, despite my emphasis on the present for Nietzsche and on the 'whole lifetime' for Guyau in their readings of Epicurus, our authors do not reduce the experience of time to these two figures. Both think of different temporal axes in their works, and both discuss the notion of *eternity*.

When reading GS 45, we saw that the openness to the present – the awareness of existing in the present – could lead us to a superior form of intensity: a form of presence and co-presence with and in the world, which Michalski characterized as 'eternity'. For Michalski, the notion of eternity is the 'the core of time, its essence, its engine', being present in 'everything Nietzsche wrote' (2011: 6). As he argues: 'Time, Nietzsche believes, cannot be understood without eternity; without reference to eternity one cannot understand how it flows, what we mean when we say it destroys and creates' (vi).

Indeed, if the notion of eternity is important throughout Nietzsche's work,[16] I should stress here that this notion takes the form of an *immanent* eternity, which can only be experienced in *this* very life. This is clear in one of Nietzsche's notes: 'Eternal life is no other life; it is the very life you are living' (KGA 411). This eternal life is discovered in the 'affirmation of the moment that life is' (Michalski 2011: 58). In this sense, eternity in this life could be understood as a moment of intensity that somehow escapes mere succession, a sort of break or interruption. As Michalski claims, 'each moment [...] conceals within itself the possibility of breaking free from the continuity of yesterday and tomorrow' (ix). One could describe this experience as a fulfilment of life in the present, when time is short-circuited by a desire of the *eternal return* of what one lives. In GS 341 this striking insight is announced by a demon:

> What if some day or night a demon were to steal after you into your loneliest loneliness and say to you: 'This life as you now live and have lived it, you will have to live it once more and innumerable times more; and there will be nothing new in it, but every pain and every joy and every thought and sigh and every unutterably small or great in your life will have to return to you, all in the same succession and sequence – even this spider and this moonlight between the trees, and even this moment and I myself.'

In this sort of thought experiment, when listening to the terrible words of the demon, one is faced with two possible reactions: an attitude of anger and resentment against this heavy thought and its messenger, or the affirmative and joyful celebration of the message as divine. As Nietzsche claims: 'The question in each and every thing, "Do you desire this once more and innumerable times more?" would lie upon your actions as the greatest weight.'

This weight could be understood as the importance and value of every action, every choice, every thought, against the nihilistic indifference of the 'All is empty, all is the same, all has been!' (Z 'The Soothsayer'). In the image of the eternal recurrence, eternity could be understood as the criterion for living in the present: loving what and how one lives in the present to the point of wishing to live it eternally (KSA 9, 11 [159], 503). In this sense, in what we live and do *now* 'eternity is at stake'. As Nietzsche explains:

> My doctrine declares: the task is to live in such a way that you must wish to live again – you will anyway! He to whom striving gives the highest feeling, let him strive; he to whom rest gives the highest feeling, let him rest; he to whom organisation, allegiance, obedience gives the highest feeling, let him obey. Only *let* him become aware of *what* gives the highest feeling and avoid no means! Eternity is at stake! (KSA 9, 11 [163], 505)[17]

Following this line of thought, Michael Ure characterized the eternal return as a form of spiritual exercise (2018). In this reading, not only is the eternal return 'a test of affirmation' (Clark 1990: 270) but it is also a spiritual practice mobilized in the constitution of eternity in one's life.[18] As Nietzsche wrote: 'Let us impress the image of eternity on our life! This thought contains more than all religions that despise this life as something fleeting and teach us to look to an indefinite *other* life' (KSA 9, 11 [159], 503).

On this reading, one relates to eternity in the constitution of the self as an 'immortal artwork', which entails the 'creation of a self worthy of eternity' (Ure 2018: 89). This reading situates Nietzsche's concern in the context of a sort of Homeric – or, as Ure claims, pre-Socratic – idea of glory according to which immortality and eternity are the marks one leaves in the world through *action* (Arendt 1958: 19). Ure, however, situates this theme within Nietzsche's concern with the constitution of oneself, which I think we could characterize as *epic*. In this *epic of the self*, 'we can immortalise ourselves through the creation of lives that we shape into singular, unrepeatable artworks' (Ure 2018: 88).[19]

In Guyau, one also finds complex reflections on temporality and eternity.[20] If, on the one hand, I emphasized a temporality of the 'whole of a lifetime' (in which the future plays an important role), on the other hand, we can also note that Guyau's reading of Epicurus does not neglect the present.

When discussing the Epicurean tranquillity in the face of death,[21] Guyau stresses Epicurus' rejection of immortality understood as an indefinite continuation or temporal extension of life, underlining its impossibility (given the Epicurean physical presuppositions) and its non-desirability. According to Guyau, we must turn away from this idea of a 'limitless duration' when thinking about our finite lives. He then shows how Epicurus dissociates time (as duration and extension) from *intensity*, claiming that, in Epicurean philosophy, 'happiness is a complete whole', self-sufficient and self-contained (113). Consequently, what is important in 'enjoyment is not its duration, but its intensity' (112). Guyau writes: 'There is therefore in enjoyment a sort of plenitude and inner superabundance, which make it *independent of time* as of all the rest: pleasure brings its infinity within itself' (113–14).

After having proposed a reflection on pleasure dependent on a certain conception of temporality that surpasses the fleeting instant (as was the case in the notion of *ho holos bios*), and after having dissociated the notion of pleasure from a sort of instant gratification, Guyau now re-situates enjoyment in the present, which is to say within a delimited and circumscribed temporal framework. What is more, dissociating intensity and the 'quality' of pleasure from its duration and extension in time ('quantity'), he finds in Epicurus a form of pleasure to which nothing can be added – the presence and accomplishment of pleasure cannot be enhanced (not even by its prolongation). Guyau quotes Cicero explaining that 'Epicurus denies that duration could add anything to the happiness of a life' (1878: 113).[22] The same is valid for pleasure: the latter is not less or more intense in a short time span than if it were to last eternally.

It is in this pleasure, experienced in the present, but somehow going beyond time itself, that Guyau finds the elements for proposing an analogy between Epicurus and Ludwig Feuerbach:

> This Epicurean doctrine which elevates happiness beyond time, and which somehow condenses it in a limited duration without taking away any of its inestimable value, has recently been taken up by a German philosopher that denied personal immortality: and we are here referring to Feuerbach. (114)

In Feuerbach, Guyau finds the modern analogy of Epicurus in the affirmation of a finite, yet intense and joyful existence – against the fears of eternal punishments and the promises of eternal life. Within this finite and limited life, Epicurus and Feuerbach find space for *eternity* – not as continuation in time, but as accomplishment and fulfilment in intensity – possible at every instant. As Feuerbach argues: 'Each instant is a full and complete existence, each instant is of an infinite importance, [an existence] satisfied and accomplished in itself, a limitless affirmation of its own reality' (114). For Guyau, 'Feuerbach's doctrine rests upon a particular conception of time and eternity; eternity which consists not of an infinite extension in duration, but of an infinite intensity of life; it would be thus found condensed in each instant of existence' (114).

Feuerbach's view seems to revive the Stoic notion of time, according to which, as Victor Goldschmidt explains: 'As soon as momentary happiness is achieved, the very question of its prolongation, the question of that which comes "after" it, loses all meaning' (2006: 208). Similarly, Feuerbach shows 'the rigorous equivalence, in happiness, between the instant and eternity' (208). This notion seems to echo an ancient conception of time, which is *qualitative* rather than mathematical (211). Through this analogy with Feuerbach's philosophy, Guyau reveals how Epicurus conquers our desire for eternity and immortal life with the perfection of pleasure, which opens the moment to eternity.

Conclusion

In both Guyau and Nietzsche, 'philosophers of time', we find a reflection on the temporal experience of one's existence and on the different modes of temporality it can entail. In their readings of Epicurus, the existential experience in question is that of pleasure. Different forms of relating to pleasure presuppose different forms of experiencing temporality and, conversely, different experiences of time could change our relationship to our pleasures. As we have seen, Guyau's perspective presupposes a singular view regarding the *future* and the Epicurean notion of *hólos bíos*, whereas Nietzsche emphasizes a perception of the present and an openness to the present moment, which somehow interrupts mere temporal sequence and the forms of suffering it causes.

Both authors emphasize, however, two important categories or forms of experience and practices to enact these experiences through spiritual exercises, namely, the *present moment* and *eternity*. In Nietzsche's reading of Epicurus in GS 45, the present appeared as the key dimension. Nevertheless, in the same book, Nietzsche proposes a singular relation between the present and the notion of eternity in the figure of the 'eternal recurrence' (GS 341). For Guyau, the present as a fragment of succession is the trap of Cyrenaic hedonism. However, through his reading of Feuerbach, Guyau reconsiders the present in Epicureanism from a different perspective, reconducting it from a predominantly utilitarian interpretation to its hedonist matrix: we touch eternity in the accomplishment of the instant, to which, given its perfection, nothing can be added. And here we can recall Victor Goldschmidt's text on the Stoics, in which he claims that 'it seems that the Stoics have insisted in the apparently paradoxical character of happiness in which momentary enjoyment [*jouissance momentanée*] is the same as [*vaudrait*] an eternal happiness', as if 'the perfection of a happy life' were subtracted from time itself (2006: 2015).

As a song that always passes away, unable to play on for eternity, so does life and every happy moment. To conclude, we could ask, with Feuerbach:

> What would you call someone who, while the sonata was being performed, did not listen, but only counted, who separated the length of the tone from its content, who, in this separation, took the temporality to be his object, and, when the sonata was over, made the fifteen minutes that it took to be played into the predicate of his judgement concerning the sonata, and, who, while other people, overcome with admiration at its content, sought to catch its significance in exact words, characterised the sonata as a quarter-hour sonata? Wouldn't you assuredly find the predicate *fool* too affirmative to define such a person? Then how should one call those who take transitoriness to be a predicate of this life, who believe that they say something, that they pass a judgment on this life, when they say that it is temporal, it is transitory? (1992: 172)

Notes

1 See Fouillée (1902b).
2 As Fouillée writes: 'Without knowing it, Nietzsche, Guyau and myself lived in Nice and Menton during the same period. Guyau did not have any knowledge of Nietzsche's name and work' (Fouillée 1902a: 11).
3 See Walther-Dulk (2014).
4 Cf. Stirner (1995).
5 See Vincenzo (1994). Vincenzo shows that this interpretation was promoted, above all, by Martin Heidegger. See Dennis and Testa (2017).
6 For a more nuanced reading of the place that Epicurus occupies in Nietzsche's late writings, see Conway (2016). Conway shows how Nietzsche's esteem for Epicurus goes beyond the middle writings. He argues that Nietzsche's positive assessment of Epicureanism against Christianity also presupposes the recognition of the impossibility of being an Epicurean after the hegemony of Saint Paul's doctrine in the West.
7 In effect, BGE shows the complexity and ambiguity of Nietzsche's relation to Epicurus. In BGE 20, for example, Nietzsche compares Epicureanism to a 'tranquilising medicine'. BGE 270, by contrast, depicts Epicureanism as a sort of heroic attitude of those who have 'suffered profoundly': 'An ostentatious courage of taste which takes suffering casually and resists everything sad and profound.'
8 The reference is to D 534.
9 See Ansell-Pearson (2013: 100) or Langer (2010: 67).
10 Small calls the constellation of these metaphors 'sign language' or 'semiotic' (5).
11 Langer reads this transient experience from a different perspective, namely of the uncertainty and precariousness of our beliefs. In Langer's reading, Epicurus symbolizes the joy of the possibility of abandoning reassuring certainties and, like the seafarer, leaving secure land for the adventures of the sea: 'Standing securely on firm ground, Epicurus gazes at the sea and enjoys the possibility of uncertainty it offers. Literally and figuratively he can float on the sea. He can chart his course or simply set sail and let the wind determine his way. In taking to the sea he might lose his bearings and even

his mind. He might suffer shipwreck and drown or survive. As Nietzsche portrays him, Epicurus is indeed the antithesis of modernity's shipwrecked man. The latter is overjoyed at leaving the insecurity of the sea for the solidity of dry land. Epicurus delights in the ever-present possibility of leaving that secure land for the perils of the sea' (Loeb 2017: 67). Ansell-Pearson challenges this interpretation claiming that it 'misses the essential insight that Nietzsche is developing into Epicurus in the aphorism. Rather than suggesting that the sea calls for further and continued exploration, hiding seductive dangers that Epicurus would not be afraid of, Nietzsche seems to hold to the view that Epicurus is the seasoned traveller of the soul who has no desire to travel anymore and for whom the meaning of the sea has changed' (Ansell-Pearson 2018: 136).

12 See Diogenes Laertius (1925: 651).
13 Guyau explains: 'Here, the role of intelligence is that of a means; however, without this means one cannot achieve the end. Not only have human thought [*dianoia*] and practical wisdom [*phrōnesis*] as their work to direct all actions of man towards pleasure, but they should also organize the pleasures themselves, and also the pains, aiming at a superior pleasure.'
14 'Then the man says "I remember" and envies the animal, who at once forgets and for whom every moment really dies, sinks back into night and fog and is extinguished for ever. Thus the animal lives *unhistorically*: for it is contained in the present, like a number without any awkward fraction left over; it does not know how to dissimulate, it conceals nothing and at every instant appears wholly as what it is; it can therefore never be anything but honest. Man, on the other hand, braces himself against the great and ever greater pressure of what is past: it pushes him down or bends him sideways, it encumbers his steps as a dark, invisible burden which he can sometimes appear to disown and which in traffic with his fellow men he is only too glad to disown, so as to excite their envy' (UM 61).
15 I owe this phrase to Luca Lupo, who employed this expression to characterize Foucault's reading of the Stoic meditation on death in his presentation 'A Matter of Time: The Stance of the Ancients Towards the Future in Foucault's Lectures at the *Collège de Framce*' at the conference *Government of Self, Government of Others* in Lisbon, 2017.
16 See, for instance, Nietzsche's discussion of Anaximander in *Philosophy in the Tragic Age of the Greeks*. An interesting discussion of this notion from the perspective of Nietzsche's cosmological sources is found in Paolo D'Iorio (2000: 361–89).
17 KSA 9, 11 [163], 505, quoted and translated by Small (2010: 143).
18 See Testa and Ure (2018).
19 Conway also highlights the notions of eternity and immortality in Nietzsche. Differently from Ure's epic notion of immortality, he sees in Nietzsche's idea a Dionysian form of immortality: 'Like Epicurus, Nietzsche promotes a way of life that delivers its adherents to a blessed state of tranquil self-enjoyment, free from the mental and spiritual perturbations incident to the fear of death. Unlike Epicurus, however, Nietzsche links the achievement of this blessed state to the affirmation of one's immortal existence – not as an indestructible soul …, but as an eternally recurring participation in the Dionysian flux of life itself' (Conway 2016: 5–6).
20 Guyau's reflections on time will constitute an important chapter of his work, and a central concern throughout his lifetime. The publication, by Fouillée and Bergson, of *The Genesis of the Idea of Time*, which would be an important and inspirational text to the latter, can be seen as a document of this concern.
21 See Guyau ([1878] 1927: Book 2).
22 De finibus, II.xxvii, 87, 88 apud Guyau ([1878] 1927: 113).

8

Nietzsche, Hobbes and the tradition of political Epicureanism

Morality, religion and the social contract

Paul Bishop

Introduction

As Michel Onfray has pointed out in *Décadence*, the second volume of his *Brève encyclopédie du monde*, the teachings in Epicurus' letter to Herodotus contain a number of theses that would have delighted Nietzsche because of their incompatibility with – or outright antinomial opposition to – some key doctrines in Christianity.[1] Likewise in his letter to Pythocles, Epicurus offers a rational and material account of natural phenomena, thereby rendering obsolete the supernatural, superstitious fables of organized religion. And in his letter to Menoeceus, Epicurus argued that impiety lay in believing that the gods were interested in or cared about human beings, whereas in fact the gods are not interested at all in human affairs, and thereby opposed the image of God as a judge and punisher. Epicurus argued that death was nothing to fear, because if it is there, I no longer exist, and if I exist, then death is still absent, thereby contrasting the way that religious belief plays on the fear of death and on the anxiety felt at the thought of death. Finally, Epicurus' core argument that pleasure is the sovereign good, that it resides in the satisfaction of natural, necessary desires, constitutes the complete antithesis to the asceticism, the self-abgenation and the self-mortification represented by such doctrines as original sin and the inheritance of guilt across the generations.

In this respect, Onfray argues, Epicureanism offered a startling contrast to other philosophical systems in the Greco–Roman world, which were more amenable to being recycled in order to support the core doctrines of Christianity.[2] There is much in Onfray's argumentation that would have been highly congenial to Nietzsche; indeed, Onfray describes himself as a follower of Nietzsche.[3] Yet, it is impossible to ignore Nietzsche's highly ambiguous attitude towards Epicurus. Seeking to address this and other ambiguities, this chapter triangulates Epicurus, Hobbes and Nietzsche in relation to their understanding of morality and politics in general and of the (social) contract in particular.

Nietzsche on Epicurus

In *Beyond Good and Evil*, Nietzsche refers to Epicurus dismissively as 'that old schoolmaster from Samos, who sat, hidden away, in his little garden at Athens and wrote three hundred books – who knows? perhaps from rage and ambition against Plato?' (7).[4] In *On the Genealogy of Morals*, Nietzsche aligns Epicureanism with Hindu and Buddhist conceptions of asceticism, describing it as a 'Hellenically cool' form of responding to suffering: 'The hypnotic sense of nothingness, the repose of deepest sleep, in short *absence of suffering* – sufferers and those profoundly depressed will count this as the supreme good, as the value of values' (18). And in *The Anti-Christ*, he describes Epicurus as 'a *typical decadent*' and as a 'pagan' anticipation of the (Christian) 'redemption doctrine' (30).

On other occasions, Nietzsche extensively praises Epicurus. In *Human, All Too Human*, Epicurus features (coupled with Montaigne, and Goethe and Spinoza, Plato and Rousseau, and Pascal and Schopenhauer) among the four pairs he encounters, like Odysseus, in the underworld: 'Upon these eight I fix my eyes and see theirs fixed on me'; in *The Wanderer and His Shadow*, Nietzsche calls him 'eternal Epicurus'; in a beautiful aphorism entitled '*Et in Arcadia ego*', he deems Epicurus 'one of the greatest of men, the inventor of an heroic-idyllic mode of philosophizing' (WS). In *The Gay Science*, Nietzsche reports experiencing the character of Epicurus 'quite differently from perhaps everybody else' and that, whenever he hears or reads of Epicurus, he enjoys 'the happiness of the afternoon of antiquity': 'Never has voluptuousness been so modest.' And here lies the rub: in WS 192, Nietzsche had described Epicurus as 'the philosopher of sensual pleasure', noting: 'A little garden, figs, little cheeses and in addition three or four good friends – these were the sensual pleasures of Epicurus.' As Heidegger recognized, 'The world is no garden, and for Zarathustra it dare not be one, especially if by "garden" we mean an enchanting haven for the flight from being', since 'Nietzsche's conception of the world does not provide the thinker with a sedate residence in which he can putter about unperturbed, like the philosopher of old, Epicurus, in his "garden"' (1991: v.2, 52). Or as Nietzsche himself put it in that part of his *Nachlass*, published as *The Will to Power*, 'I have presented such terrible images to knowledge that any "Epicurean delight" is out of the question. Only Dionysian joy is sufficient: *I have been the first to discover the tragic*' (KSA 11:25[95]).

The ambiguity in Nietzsche's response and this contrast between 'Epicurean delight' and 'Dionysian joy' perhaps reflects a core ambiguity in Epicurus himself, who argued for the existence of a supreme, blessed and imperishable form of divinity, and yet was widely regarded, both by his contemporaries and by later Christian writers, as an atheist.[5] This reflects a further core ambiguity in Nietzsche himself, who is widely regarded as being a key figure in the history of atheism, and yet who makes constant reference to pagan gods, notably Apollo and Dionysos. After all, another of the central contrasts in Nietzsche's thought is the one between Epicurean optimism and that pessimism placed by Nietzsche under the sign of a god – Dionysos. The reception of Epicurus by thinkers other than Nietzsche, notably Thomas Hobbes, enables us to discern more clearly the essential features of the affinities between Nietzsche and

Hobbes, particularly in their respective views of the relations among politics, morality and religion.

Epicurus on politics

Onfray's *contre-histoire* of philosophy seeks to reverse and overturn the centuries of Christian rejection of Epicurus' materialist, hedonist, sensualist and utilitarian principles. Among the 300 plus books reportedly written by Epicurus, he wrote political works, which included such titles as *On Just Dealing*, *On Justice and the Other Virtues* and *On Kingship*.[6] Though these works were lost or destroyed, we can regard Epicurus as a key figure in the history of Western political theory, and we can discern a distinct political stance from what remains in his *Vatican Sayings*: 'We must get out of the prison house of routine duties and politics' (206). This chapter thus responds to Onfray's question: What would an Epicurean political theory look like? (2017: 355–6). At its core, Epicurean politics is based on a theory of natural law that is utilitarian and contractualist, and has as its aim a communal way of life in which each person has nothing to fear from anyone else.[7]

Epicurus on the contract

At the centre of Epicurus' philosophy lies the study of nature as a reaction and a response to existential anxiety – that is, to being worried 'by apprehensiveness regarding the heavenly bodies, by anxiety about the meaning of death, and also by our failure to understand the limitations of pain and desire' (1963: 198). His political doctrine reflects this existential anxiety and his insight that 'it is possible to get protection against other beings, but when it comes to death, all of us human beings live in a city without walls' (1963: 205). In *Principal Doctrines*, Epicurus observes that 'any means by which it is possible to procure freedom from fearing other men is a natural good' (196). It is true that pursuit of a politics of *ataraxia* leads, paradoxically, to a stance that seems apolitical. In line with the principle that 'withdrawal into obscurity is the best form of security' (1963: 198), Epicurus proposes that 'the simplest means of procuring protection from other men ... is the security of quiet solitude and withdrawal from the mass of people' (1963: 198). Concomitantly, the economic principle that wealth can be both 'natural and unnatural' leads Epicurus to conclude that 'nature's wealth is restricted and easily won, while that of empty convention runs on to infinity' (1963: 198).

Epicurus' political theory is underpinned by his conception of the contract. The contract is an expression of 'the justice that seeks nature's goal', that is, natural justice, in the form of 'a utilitarian pledge of men to harm each other or be harmed' (1963: 201). For Epicurus, reciprocity in agreements is the foundation of justice (1963: 201). Epicurus' conception of justice thus is anti-Platonic, inasmuch as 'justice was never an entity in itself' but 'a kind of agreement not to harm or be harmed, made when men associate with each other at any time and in communities of any size whatsoever' (1963: 201–2). George K. Strodach notes that whereas, for Plato, justice is 'an eternal archetype', for Epicurus it is 'a social contract empirically arrived at in various times and places in human history' (1963: 250). As Epicurus himself puts it: 'In its general meaning, justice is the same for all because of its utility in the relations of men to each other, but in its specific application to countries and various other circumstances it does not follow that the same thing is just for all' (1963: 202). Equally, injustice is regarded by Epicurus as 'not an evil in itself', for 'its evil lies in the anxious fear that you will not elude those who have authority to punish such misdeeds' (1963: 202). This fear is, in Epicurus' eyes, entirely justified in the case of those who break the social contract.

Epicurus' conception of justice is also avowedly utilitarian: 'In the case of actions that are legally regarded as just, those that are of tested utility in meeting the needs of human society have the hallmark of justice, whether they turn out to be equally just in all cases or not', Epicurus writes, and he draws out the implication of this position: 'If someone lays down a law and it does not prove to be of advantage in human relations, then such a law no longer has the true character of justice.'[8] Consequently, 'where laws regarded as just have been shown to be inconsistent with the conception of justice in their actual workings, such laws are unjust' – because 'when they were no longer useful they became unjust' (Epicurus 1963: 202–3). In practical terms, Epicurean politics and ethics aim, so far as possible, at making friends, avoiding making enemies and staying as far away from one's enemies as possible. While embracing individualism, Epicurus' views on society are underpinned by a strong sense of community: 'All who have the capacity to gain security, especially from those who live around them, live a most agreeable life together, since they have the firm assurance of friendship' – a value which, it seems, can outweigh even the fear of death, for 'after enjoying their comradeship to the full they do not bewail the early demise of a departed friend as if it were a pitiable thing' (1963: 203). The notion of friendship, conceived on the model of a mutually agreed contract, grounds Epicurean politics.[9]

Social contract theory

While the notion of the social contract goes back at least to Epicurus, subsequent thinkers revived and refined the idea, most notably Thomas Hobbes.[10] Hobbes is a controversial figure in European political thought, even, or especially, to other thinkers interested in the notion of the contract.[11] Many of these critiques stem from the view that Hobbes's theory of the contract implies a godless world, of just the sort that we later see in Nietzsche. Yet the question remains: How much did Hobbes know about Epicurus' political theory?

Bernd Ludwig has proposed two major theses concerning Hobbes's intellectual development from *De Cive* to *Leviathan* and during his exile in Paris.[12] First, Ludwig argues that Hobbes's political theory was not significantly influenced by the 'resolutive-compositive' method of early modern natural science,[13] but that the intellectual roots of Hobbesian thought, reflected in *De Corpore* and *Leviathan*, are found in Aristotle and in philosophers with whom Hobbes associated in Paris, such as Pierre Gassendi (Paganini

2001: 9).[14] Gassendi is a remarkable figure: a priest, scientist and mathematician, who sought to reconcile the doctrines of Epicurean atomism with those of Christianity, and the author of a two-volume study of Epicurus.[15] Second, Ludwig proposes that, although Hobbes's theory of the state in *De Cive* and in *Leviathan* differs only in points of minor detail, *Leviathan* stands out because of its decisive break with accounts based on a theistic conception of natural law. While *De Cive* was, despite its secular rhetoric, implicitly based on theological elements borrowed from the natural law tradition of Stoicism and Christianity, *Leviathan* is a treatise proposing a secular conception of natural law based on Epicurean principles.[16]

On Ludwig's account, traces of Epicureanism are found in Hobbes's work before 1645. Even if Hobbes later distanced himself from Epicurus, as Arrigo Pacchi suggests,[17] and developed his own position more distinctly, as Charles T. Harrison argues,[18] Hobbes nevertheless drew throughout his career on the general pool of cultural knowledge shared by his contemporaries, which included Epicurean material. For instance, Hobbes's much-discussed distinction between 'faith' and 'confession' is thoroughly Epicurean in its conception, as F. A. Lange realized when discussing Gassendi's biography of Epicurus: 'Inwardly Epicurus could think whatever he wanted; in his outward behavior, however, he was subject to the laws of the state' ([1866] 2018: 237).[19] Hobbes developed this principle even more clearly, arguing that 'the state has unconditional power over matters of ritual; the individual must surrender his judgment; but *not inwardly*, for our thoughts are not subject to our whims, and for this reason no one can compel someone else to believe' ([1866] 2018: 237).[20] There are significant points of overlap between Epicurus' political philosophy and Hobbes's. Key tenets of Epicurus' political theory are echoed in Hobbes's account in *Leviathan* of some of his own political theoretical principles, especially his conception of the war of all against all (90).

On Ludwig's account, there are three main affinities between Epicurus and Hobbes in respect of their political views.[21] First, the state of nature is not so much a state of injustice as a state where there is an absence of obligations, commitments or other kinds of reciprocal agreements. Second, the capacity for justice or law is something that one does not find in humans as individual natural beings. Rather, it is something acquired through the process of civilization. And third, legal obligation is conceived as applying to relations between human beings, that is, exclusively as something that involves reciprocal obligation arising from mutual consent expressed through *contracts*. In other words, all forms of obligation arise from the ability of human beings to make agreements about their future behaviour, that is, that they will not harm each other in the future, and to stick to those agreements. (As Nietzsche later puts it, the 'paradoxical task' that nature had set itself in the case of humankind had been 'to breed an animal *with the right to make promises*' (GM II: 1).)

As Ludwig observes, a few years after *Leviathan*'s publication it was no secret that Hobbes's central ideas were Epicurean in nature, or even in origin. Harrison has noted that, in the second half of the twentieth century, Hobbes and Epicurus were 'almost universally treated together, whether to oppose them with' – in the words of Bishop John Wilkins – 'the reasonableness and the credibility of the principles of natural religion', that is, Christianity, or with some metaphysical system like that of Descartes', while at the same time adding that 'it is not uncommon for a teaching of Hobbes, to be ascribed to Epicurus, and vice versa, however it may clash with the actual doctrines of the other' (1934: 24). For instance, when the English political philosopher James Tyrrell sent a copy to John Locke of his newly published book on natural law, his accompanying letter remarked that he hoped his treatise would 'give the world a better account of the Law of Nature and its obligation, than what hath already been performed, as also to confute with better reasons the Epicurean principles of Mr Hobbes' (Locke 1988: 79). Nearly a century later, Kant recognized the Epicurean roots of Hobbesian thought: 'Hobbes followed the blueprint of Lucretius and of Epicurus, who had principles that were by far not so noble as those of the Stoics' (1974: 3). It is thus surprising in his view that few modern critics recognize this fact.[22]

While exiled in Paris, Hobbes became familiar with the thought of Gassendi, Galileo and Descartes.[23] He encountered their ideas in the 'Cavendish circle', an important intellectual circle centred on the mathematician Charles Cavendish, his brother William Cavendish and his sister-in-law, Margaret Cavendish.[24] On their return from exile in France, the members of the 'Cavendish circle' and their associates brought Gassendi's rediscovery of Epicurus back to England. In Ludwig's words, Epicureanism became 'not only an important trend in natural science' but also 'a significant influence in intellectual life as a whole', including Hobbes's own conception of the social contract (1998: 404).

Hobbes on the social contract

On Hobbes's account, prior to the social contract humankind lived in its 'natural condition', where there is 'no power able to overawe them all' or to 'keep them quiet', that is, 'men live without a common Power to keep them all in awe' (1996: 88).[25] While the natural condition is solitary, poor, nasty, brutish for some, for those Hobbes described as 'taking pleasure in contemplating their own power in the acts of conquest, which they pursue farther than their security requires', the state of nature might have been a golden age of *Übermensch*-like possibilities (88). Hobbes anticipates the dialectic of strength and weakness explored in Nietzsche's *Genealogy*, writing that 'even the weakest has strength enough to kill the strongest, either by secret machination, or by confederacy with others, that are in the same danger with himself' ([1866] 2018: 87). At the same time, Hobbes points to some of the dangers of the state of nature: it is characterized by a 'known disposition to fight' or, to put it another way, it is a state of war – the opposite of 'peace' ([1866] 2018: 89). One of the problems with Hobbes's account of the state of nature is to explain the transition from this state to the commonwealth; later, Nietzsche sought to explain the mechanism by which the binary of 'good'/'bad' became converted into the binary 'good'/'evil'. While Hobbes considers the link between morality and religion, it is unclear why Hobbes is interested in religion at all.[26]

The answer lies, in part, in the fact that the covenant, a central concept in Hobbes's political philosophy, is the basis for his philosophy of history, which is grounded in his reading of Scripture.[27] The Old Testament, which interests Hobbes far more than the

New Testament, is the story of one covenant (or contract) after another. In *De Cive*, Hobbes maintains that 'God reigned indeed, not only naturally, but also by way of covenant, over Adam and Eve', although he added that 'this Covenant was presently made void, nor ever after renewed' (201). In Genesis, Jehovah made a covenant between God and Abraham (or Abram as he was then known) that turned Him into the sovereign over Abraham. For the covenant, that involves Jesus Christ, Hobbes strips this precondition for salvation back to the barest of essentials, reducing the statement of faith required for salvation to the '*Unum Necessarium*', that is, the 'Onely Article of Faith, which the Scripture maketh simply Necessary to Salvation', to the proposition 'Jesus is the Christ' (1996: 407).[28] This reduction, rather than the attack on theology in *De motu*, was the chief cause of scandal to Hobbes's critics.[29]

In other respects, Hobbes's approach to biblical criticism anticipates Nietzsche's philological objections to conventional interpretations of the Bible. Hobbes was, for instance, one of the first major scholars to argue that the author of the Pentateuch is not Moses but Ezra.[30] Hobbes's technique of 'internal criticism', a sort of 'textual criticism', studies the language used in biblical accounts or points of inconsistency in detail to uncover pointers to their date of composition.[31] In explaining the source of authority of the Bible, Hobbes makes the key proto-Nietzschean move of using the immanent to explain the transcendent. People believe the Bible, he claims, for a variety of pragmatic reasons, including the integrity of those who teach it, its aesthetic beauty and its moral insights.[32] People do not actually know that the Bible is true, for knowledge has to do with science; rather, the answer to this question is tied up with another question, namely, '*From whence the Scriptures derive their Authority*' (Hobbes 1996: 267) – the answer to which lies in the decision of Christian sovereigns to use their given authority to make the Bible the basis for how subjects governed.[33] In other words, it is about *power*.[34]

For Hobbes, the social contract is a construction of public reason.[35] Justice derives from contracts, hence his suggestion that while ethics are a consequence of the passions, justice is a consequence of speech, specifically in the act of contracting.[36] This is so, because contracts concern language, and hence involve a performative element. Not only must the contract have to be spoken or written but the acts must also be consistent with what one has promised or be otherwise aligned with this expression of one's will.[37] Hence Hobbes describes it as one of the *laws of nature* that '*men perform their Covenants made*' (1996: 100). Thus, law is, Gerald F. Gaus explains, 'the lynchpin of justice and, indeed, the entire social contract, for in Hobbes's view justice is conceptually tied to covenants' (2013: 277).

Hobbes and religion

Gianni Paganini describes Hobbes's *De motu* as occupying 'a very special position in Hobbes's philosophy' and as representing 'a decisive *turning point* in his intellectual history' (2013: 286–303, 299).[38] This is because of its position on theological problems and because it argues against any 'possibility of rationally proving the existence of God' (2013: 299). In his critique of the work *De mundo dialogi tres* by Thomas

White, an English Roman Catholic priest and scholar in the fields of theology and philosophy, Hobbes reached conclusions that were probably too stark to publish.[39] Those conclusions grounded a materialist, mechanistic psychology,[40] cast in the form of a critique of White for having distinguished the spirit from the body only 'in word', while failing to say how the spirit can be separated from 'the mind'.[41] Since, for White, substance is 'identical to being a body and having magnitude', and since, for Hobbes, the only substance that can be 'conceived' is one that is extended in three dimensions, the question arises as to how the spirit, if it can be conceived as a substance, is not body.[42]

Hobbes explains the belief in 'the existence of innumerable daemons, both good and bad ones, and of other incorporeal substances' in psychological terms: 'Noticing that, not only when they slept but also when they were awake, certain images appeared before their eyes', people 'did not know that these were apparitions aroused by some violent mental passion' and 'were able to consider them as external things, possessing dimensions' (1976: 54). 'Wishing to give them a name for insubstantial bodies, they have called them spirits, for, being ignorant of nature, they recognise bodies not by their dimensions but by their opacity' (1976: 54). Since 'it is impossible to conceive of matter other than by the criterion of its magnitude', then belief in incorporeal substances is based on 'the authority of Holy Scripture', but not on 'the reasonings of philosophers' (1976: 54).[43]

De motu emphasizes the undemonstrability of God, coupled with an acquiescence in a belief in his existence *as a belief* – as a matter of faith, not reason; as an object of honorific language or the language of reverence, not as an object of declarative language or philosophical discourse.[44] In *Leviathan*, Hobbes distinguishes between 'pious' and 'dogmatic' language, equivalent to the distinction between honorific and philosophical discourse (77–8). Whether theological propositions are true or false is not something that the philosopher can judge, Hobbes writes, 'for how can anyone know whether a proposition is true or false that he does not understand?' (1976: 54).[45]

In *De motu*, Hobbes notes that Holy Scripture attributes motion and rest to God, but 'not in the same sense in which they are attributed to bodies, but in a manner that we cannot understand' (321). Apart from saying 'He *is*', or designating Him negatively as 'infinite' or 'incomprehensible', or speaking of Him metaphorically as 'good', 'just', 'wise', or 'blessed', we can say nothing about Him (1976: 54). Indeed, 'not even the pagans [*ethnici*] termed their gods, to honour them, "calm" or "placid" ("at rest"); they called them "indefatigable" ("tireless")' – that is, 'the Epicureans apart' (1976: 54).

Hobbes and the will

The will is also a central category for Hobbes.[46] As Jürgen Overhoff explains, Hobbes's will is one of the most controversial aspects of his thought both to his contemporaries and to later thinkers (2000). Descartes and Gassendi vehemently opposed the ontological premises of Hobbes's determinism. While agreeing with his mechanist physics and the physiological functioning of the human body, they demurred when it came to his psychological materialism. Descartes thought it necessary to introduce a metaphysical explanation in defence of the freedom of the will, arguing that each of us contains the image of God, while Gassendi thought that free will could only be understood as a gift from God.[47]

Hobbes's account of the will is dependent on his theory of the emotions or passions: 'In deliberation the last appetite, as also the last fear, is called WILL', that is, 'the last appetite will to do; the last fear will not to do, or will to omit' and 'it is all one therefore to say will, and last will' ((1969: 61–2). In other words, appetite, fear and the other passions are involuntary because they do not proceed from, but *are* the will, and the will itself is beyond volition – 'the will is not voluntary'. An individual 'can no more say, he will will, than he will will will, and so make an infinite repetition of the word will; which is absurd, and insignificant' ((1969: 62–3). If the will plays a crucial role in Hobbes's social contract, it becomes a central category in Nietzsche's politics and metaphysics.

Hobbes and Nietzsche

Nietzsche's explicit remarks about Hobbes in his writings are, while rare, telling. In *Untimely Meditations*, he praises Hobbes (in contrast to Strauss) for his 'intrepid mind' and 'grand love of truth', and he frequently cites the phrase *bellum omnium contra omnes* (30). In *Beyond Good and Evil* he dismisses Hobbes (along with Bacon, Hume, Locke and other 'unphilosophical' Englishmen) as having contributed to 'a debasement and lowering of the value of the concept of "philosophy" for more than a century' and he critiques Hobbes's allegedly dismissive attitude towards laughter (379, 421–3). Though Nietzsche says little about Hobbes, a point of contact lies in their shared interest in Thucydides, and their common adoption of a 'tragic realism' that is nurtured by the Epicurean tradition.[48]

In 1629, Hobbes published his translation of the entirety of the *History of the Peloponnesian War*, the earliest translation of Thucydides from the original Greek into English.[49] Hobbes retained his classical interests, publishing translations of Homer's *Odyssey* and *Iliad*, well into his eighties. His introductory essay to the translation of the *Peloponnesian War* argues that Thucydides was an authority on how to write history because his writings are characterized by 'two things', '*truth* and *elocution*', for 'in *truth* consisteth the *soul*, and in *elocution* the *body* of history'.[50] Combining these two qualities turned Thucydides into a master of his art, with the result that 'he affected least of any man the acclamations of popular auditories, and wrote not his history to win present applause, as was the use of that age: but for a monument to instruct the ages to come; which he professeth himself, and entitleth his book ΚΤΗΜΑ ΕΣ ΑΕΙ, *a possession for everlasting*' (Hobbes 1839–1845: xxi).

In *Twilight of the Idols* Nietzsche presented the historian Thucydides as a counterfoil to Plato: '*Courage* in face of reality ultimately distinguishes such natures as Thucydides and Plato: Plato is a coward in face of reality – consequently he flees into the ideal [*folglich flüchtet er in's Ideal*]; Thucydides has *himself* under control – consequently he retains control over things' (107).[51] This (political) realism is shared by Nietzsche and

Hobbes, as is their ontological outlook. For Hobbes, body represents 'a fundamental, if not *the* fundamental, metaphysical category' of his thought.[52] In *De Corpore*, Hobbes defines body as 'that which having no dependence upon our Thought is coincident or coextended with some part of Space',[53] and in *Leviathan* he extends this definition to cover everything that exists: 'The World (I mean not the Earth onely, that denominates the Lovers of it *Worldly men*, but the *Universe*, that is, the whole masse of all things that are) is Corporeall, that is to say, Body' (463). No less apodictic is Nietzsche's own *Zarathustra*, when he categorically declares in 'Of the Despisers of the Body': 'But the awakened, the enlightened man says: I am body entirely, and nothing beside; and soul is only a word for something in the body' (61). Consequently, Hobbes is clearly a materialist when he argues, in the Third Set of Objections to Descartes's *Meditations*, that 'the mind will be nothing more than motion occurring in various parts of an organic body' (126).[54]

Like Nietzsche, however, one could also describe Hobbes as a *vitalist materialist*, because he places great emphasis on the importance of the emotions or, as he calls them, the *passions*.[55] Passions are governed by the principles of appetite and aversion, and are thus 'beyond' good and evil: as Hobbes puts it in *Leviathan*, '*Pleasure* ..., (or *Delight*,) is the appearance, or sense of Good; and *Molestation* or *Displeasure*, the appearance, or sense of Evill' (40). In other words, Hobbes's view of morality reflects his nominalism, thus regarding good and evil as aspects of discourse: 'For these words of Good, Evill, and Contemptible, are ever used with relation to the person that useth them: There being nothing simply and absolutely so; nor any common Rule of Good and Evil, to be taken from the nature of the objects themselves' (1996: 39).

In *Leviathan*, Hobbes introduces the figure of the Fool, someone who tries to refute Hobbes's third law of nature by arguing that sometimes it might be reasonable to go against the social contract, that 'injustice ... may not sometimes stand with that Reason, which dictateth to every man his own good', and that if practical reason truly grounds self-interest, then it is perfectly rational to act in one's own interests by breaking the social contract and the covenant agreed with the all-powerful sovereign (101).[56] Hobbes's Fool might then be a forerunner to the Madman of *The Gay Science*: alluding to Psalm 14, 'The fool hath said in his heart, There is no God', the Hobbesian Fool 'hath sayd in his heart, there is no such thing as Justice' (Hobbes 1996: 101). While Nietzsche's Madman cries out, 'I seek God! I seek God!' then asks, 'Where is God?' and declares, 'God is dead. God remains dead. And we have killed him' (GS 181).

More generally, Hobbes's 'central idea' is, according to R. E. Ewin, '*disagreement*': 'People have different ideas of what is valuable or reasonable, and therefore different ideas about what natural law requires or allows' (1991: 27). Nietzsche's central idea is even more radical: it is not simply disagreement, but *Eris* or strife.[57] In *Philosophy in the Tragic Age of the Greeks* Nietzsche praises Heraclitus for elevating the contest or competition to the position of a fundamental principle of cosmic justice: 'Everything that happens, happens in accordance with this strife, and it is just in the strife that eternal justice is revealed. ... Only a Greek was capable of finding such an idea to be the fundament of a cosmology; it is Hesiod's good *Eris* transformed into the cosmic principle' (55). In *Human, All Too Human*, Nietzsche claims that 'the Greek artists, the tragedians for example, poetized in order to conquer', adding that 'their whole art cannot be thought of apart from contest: Hesiod's good Eris, ambition, gave their genius its wing' (90).

In *The Wanderer and His Shadow*, Nietzsche continued his meditation on the distinction in Hesiod between Eris, a goddess of peaceful competition and striving for excellence, and 'terrible' Eris, the bringer of war and strife (HH 314). In a discussion in *Daybreak* about how drives are transformed by moral judgements, Nietzsche observed that 'the older Greeks felt differently about *envy* from the way we do; Hesiod counted it among the effects of the *good*, beneficent Eros, and there was nothing offensive in attributing to the gods something of envy: which is comprehensible under a condition of things the soul of which was contest; contest, however, was evaluated and determined as good' (26). As Laurence Lampert points out, Alisdair MacIntyre misses the point when, in *After Virtue*, he accuses Nietzsche of misunderstanding heroic virtue by reading it in anachronistic terms as a kind of modern individualism or self-assertion (MacIntyre 2007: 121–30).[58] What Nietzsche admires in the heroic tradition exemplified by, say, Achilles is not so much their heroic virtues as the culture of admiration surrounding Achilles right up to Alexander. Thus Nietzsche aims 'not to duplicate ancient heroes, but to duplicate ancient admiration', and his admiration is not directed towards Achilles himself but, rather, involves 'that way of stationing oneself toward the admired which intends to surpass it' (Lampert 1986: 320). This positive aim forms the counterpart to the nihilist moment of the 'death of God' – an essentially atheist position.[59] Most significantly for our argument here, however, is Nietzsche's engagement, over and above his reception of Hobbes, with the notion of the contract in the *Genealogy*.

Nietzsche on contracts

In the second essay of the *Genealogy* Nietzsche claims that 'the major moral concept' *Schuld*, that is, guilt, has 'its origin in the very material concept' *Schulden*, that is, debts (498–99). We earlier saw this typically Nietzschean move that Hobbes also makes: to explain the ideal and the transcendent in terms of the material and the immanent. For Nietzsche, the desire for punishment (to give and receive) is rooted 'in the contractual relationship between *creditor* and *debtor*, which is as old as the idea of "legal subjects" and so points back to the fundamental forms of buying, selling, barter, trade, and traffic' (Lampert 1986: 499). In this way, Nietzsche tries to explain the relation between, on the one hand, 'contractual relationships', 'promises', 'guarantees' and 'obligations' and, on the other, 'severity', 'cruelty' and 'pain' (Lampert 1986: 500). What the debtor promises the creditor is not just something he possesses – such as his body, his wife, his freedom, his life or even (in the case of the ancient Egyptians) his bliss after death – but ultimately a kind of pleasure, 'the pleasure of being allowed to vent [one's] power freely upon [someone] who is powerless, the voluptuous pleasure "*de faire le mal pour le plaisir de le faire*", the enjoyment of violation' (Lampert 1986: 501).[60] Thus 'the moral conceptual world of "guilt", "conscience", "duty", "sacredness of duty"' originates in 'the sphere of legal obligations', and so 'its beginnings were, like the beginnings of everything great on earth, soaked in blood thoroughly and for a long time' (Lampert 1986).

In the *Genealogy* Nietzsche reaffirms his central argument that 'the feeling of guilt, of personal obligation, had its origin ... in the oldest and most primitive personal relationship, that between buyer and seller, creditor and debtor' (Lampert 1986: 506). This relationship is the oldest and the most primitive Nietzsche argues, because 'it was here that one person first encountered another person, that one person *measured himself* against another' (Lampert 1986). On Nietzsche's account (echoing Protagoras), Man is the measure of all other men, as the etymological root of the German 'Mensch', that is, *manas*, suggests: 'No grade of civilization, however low, has yet been discovered in which something of this relationship has not been noticeable. Settling prices, determining values, contriving equivalences – these preoccupied the earliest thinking of man to so great an extent that in a certain sense they constitute thinking *as such*' (Lampert 1986).[61]

Nietzsche argues that we must learn to see the world through the prism of the will-to-power; that it is, in terms of his core insight that

> whatever exists, having somehow come into being, is again and again reinterpreted to new ends, taken over, transformed, and redirected by some power superior to it; all events in the organic world are a subduing, a *becoming master*, and all subduing and becoming master involves a fresh interpretation, an adaptation through which any previous 'meaning' [*Sinn*] and 'purpose' [*Zweck*] are necessarily obscured or even obliterated. (Lampert 1986: 513)[62]

In short, punishment, Nietzsche contends, was not devised for punishing. Rather, the entire concept of punishment must be seen in terms of the logic of the will to power, since

> purposes and utilities are only *signs* that a will to power has become master of something less powerful and imposed upon it the character of a function; and the entire history of a 'thing' [*eines 'Dings'*], an organ, a custom can in this way be a continuous sign-chain [*Zeichen-Kette*] of ever new interpretations and adaptations whose causes do not even have to be related to one another but, on the contrary, in some cases succeed and alternate with one another in a purely chance fashion. (Lampert 1986)

The 'essence of life', he says later, is 'its *will to power*' and 'the essential priority of the spontaneous, aggressive, expansive, life-giving forces that give new interpretations and directions, although "adaptation" follows only after this' (Lampert 1986: 515).

Elsewhere in the *Genealogy*, Nietzsche explores the interface between these kinds of contractual thinking and the *ressentiment*-laden ethics of Judeo-Christianity. There is a direct link between the project of breeding 'an animal *with the right to make promises*' (Lampert 1986: 493), which is essential to the establishment of any kind of social contract, and what Nietzsche describes elsewhere as the process of 'the *internalization of man*', that is, how 'all instincts that do not discharge themselves outwardly *turn inward*' with astonishing results (Lampert 1986). The 'existence on earth of an animal turned against itself, taking sides against itself, was something so new, profound, unheard of, enigmatic, contradictory, *and pregnant with a future* that the aspect of the earth was essentially altered' (Lampert 1986: 520). For Nietzsche, the Greeks represented the antithesis of Christianity. With their gods, the Greeks 'warded off the "bad conscience"', 'rejoiced in their freedom of soul' and thus were 'the very opposite of the use to which Christianity put its God' (Lampert 1986: 529–30). These gods sound very much like Epicurean gods.

Here Nietzsche quotes a passage from the beginning of the *Odyssey* where Zeus addresses the immortals. Recalling several deaths and revengeful rulers, Zeus declares:

> Ha! how dare mortals tax the gods, and say,
> Their harms do all proceed from our decree,
> And by our setting; when by their crimes they
> Against our wills make their own destiny? (quoted in Hobbes 1844: 305–6)

This passage interests Nietzsche as much for what it does *not* say as for what it *does*. It does *not* talk about sin but about 'foolishness', 'folly' and 'a disturbance in the head'. This leads Nietzsche to conclude, albeit ironically, that 'the gods served in those days to justify man to a certain extent even in his wickedness, they served as the originators of evil – in those days they took upon themselves, not the punishment but, what is *nobler*, the guilt' (GM 530). These gods could be seen to stand as an emblem for what, in *Esquisse d'une morale sans obligation ni sanction*, Jean-Marie Guyau proposed as a new theory of ethics – a morality without obligations or sanctions. There is a link here back to Epicurus, for Guyau was also the author of *La morale d'Épicure*, a work arguing for the originality of Epicurus' utilitarian moral account of pleasure and tracing the history of Epicurean and utilitarian thought down to modernity.[63]

Although Nietzsche is not an Epicurean inasmuch as he rejects the conception of the contract as something beneficent, he nevertheless embraces the ethics of the Epicureans' conception of the gods. He shares with Hobbes a behavioural account of human beings that understands them in terms of their desire for – no, their *will to* – power, although he rejects the collectivist ethics behind Hobbes's conception of the state, preferring, instead, the 'radical individualism' of the *Übermensch*. Triangulating Epicurus, Hobbes and Nietzsche as political thinkers enables us to appreciate better the specificities of each man's thought, as well as to discern the continuities (and discontinuities) in the tradition of European political thought to which each has made a distinctive contribution.[64] As Paul Nizan – the French philosopher and writer who so presciently opposed Epicurus and his Garden to the figure of *l'Homo Economicus* or the bureaucratic, administrative, bean-counting and profit-obsessed individual typified by the banker, the salesman, the industrialist, the stock trader, the manager, etc. – put it,[65] Epicurus 'has not stopped being regarded as a liberator'.[66] It is this liberating aspect of his thought that makes him, over and above areas of specific agreement and disagreement, such a significant thinker for Hobbes and Nietzsche over and above *their* areas of specific agreement and disagreement, then as now.

Notes

1. Onfray (2017: 323).
2. Onfray (2017).
3. For Onfray, to be Nietzschean means 'to take Nietzsche as a starting point for thinking – not to think as he does' (*être nietzschéen, c'est penser à partir de Nietzsche – pas comme lui*) Onfray (2001: 281).
4. I have used the Kauffman translations for BT, BGE, GM, CW and EH for Random House.
5. See Festugière (1956), Festugière (1946), Obbink (1989: 187–223); cf. Winiarczyk (1984) and David Konstan (2011: 53–71).
6. See Klosko (2012: 178–82).
7. Klosko (2012: 356).
8. See Rosen (2003: 15–28).
9. See Thrasher (2013: 423–36).
10. See D'Agostino, Gaus, and Thrasher (2017).
11. See Ryan (1996: 208–45).
12. Ludwig (1998).
13. See Jesseph (1996: 86–107).
14. See Paganini (2001: 3–24).
15. Gassendi (2006).
16. Ludwig (1998: 9–10). See Goldsmith (1996: 274–304).
17. Pacchi (1978: 54–71). See also Paganini (2010: 1–5), introducing a special volume of *Hobbes Studies* on this theme.
18. Harrison (1933: 191–218).
19. See Gassendi (2006: 18–25).
20. Cf. Hobbes (1996: 15–20).
21. Ludwig (1998: 402–3).
22. Haas (1896).
23. See Rogers (2007: 413–40).
24. See Clucas (1994: 247–73), and Hutton (1997: 421–32).
25. See Hoekstra (2007: 109–27) and Sreedhar (2013: 219–22).
26. See Tuck (1996: 175–207), Sorell (2007: 128–53) and Lloyd (2013: 117–43 and 233–62).
27. Martinich (2013: 255–60, 257). See Springborg (1996: 356–80) and Lessay (2007: 243–70).
28. See Farneti (2007: 291–308).
29. Martinich (2013: 257). See Martinich (2007: 375–91).
30. See Hobbes (1996: 260–9). See Malcolm (2004: 241–64).
31. Martinich (2013: 258–9).
32. 'The causes why men believe any Christian Doctrine, are various' (Hobbes 1996: 405).
33. Martinich (2013: 259).
34. See Patton (1993: 144–61).
35. Hobbes (1996: 121). See Sreedhar (2013: 214–18) and Gaus (2013: 215, 263–78).
36. Hobbes (1996: 61); cf. Gaus (2013: 320n.40).
37. Gaus (2013: 272).
38. See Paganini (2015: 99–28).
39. Paganini (2013: 289).

40 See Paganini (2013: 294), and the note on mechanistic psychology on 322n.91.
41 Hobbes (1976: 53).
42 Paganini (2013: 299).
43 See Martinich (2013: 255–60). It is true that, in the appendix to *Leviathan* and in his debate with Bishop Bramhall, Hobbes affirms the doctrine of a corporeal God and that of the corporeality of spirits; and in the English edition of *Leviathan* Hobbes uses Scripture to support his own non-biblical, metaphysical notion of the incorporeal (Paganini 2013: 299).
44 Paganini (2013: 300).
45 See Tuck (1993: 120–38).
46 See Overhoff (2013). For the texts of the debate itself, see Chappell (1999). For discussion of the impact of this and other debates on *Leviathan*, see Sommerville (2007).
47 See Overhoff (2013: 122).
48 See Patton (2001: 99–116) and Kirkland (2010: 55–78).
49 Sommerville (2013: 24–8).
50 See Lemetti (2013: 88–91).
51 See Polansky (2015: 425–48), as well as Mann and Lustila (2011: 51–72).
52 Frost (2013: 29–31).
53 Cited in Frost (2013: 29).
54 Cf. Duncan (2013: 55). See Duncan (2005: 437–48) and Frost (2008).
55 See Krom (2013), Miller (2013) and Frost (2013).
56 For discussion of Hobbes's Fool, see the debate about the significance of this figure in Hoekstra (1997: 620–54), Hayes (1999: 225–9) and Hoekstra (1999: 230–5). See Rhodes (1992: 93–102), LeBuffe (2007: 31–45) and Springborg (2010: 29–53).
57 For an overview of the concept of strife in Nietzsche, see Lampert (1986: 319–320n.76).
58 See also Casey (1990).
59 For further discussion of nihilism and the 'death of God' in Nietzsche's thought, see E. Osborn (2017) and van Tongeren (2018).
60 Cf. Mérimée (1874: 8).
61 Compare Zarathustra, who tells us in 'Of the Sublime Men': 'But all life is dispute over taste and tasting!' (Z 140).
62 See Schrift (1990: 181–94).
63 See Guyau (2008) and Guyau (2002).
64 For a discussion of Nietzsche in relation to the tradition of German political thought, see Bishop (2019).
65 Nizan (1960: 150). See Onfray (2013: 120–1, 136–8 and 436–7).
66 Nizan (1982: 44).

9

Passionate individuation

Epicurean self-cultivation in Mill and Nietzsche

Matthew James Dennis

I Introduction

> The same strong susceptibilities which make the personal impulses vivid and powerful, are also the source from whence are generated the most passionate love of virtue, and the sternest self-control. It is through the cultivation of these, that society both does its duty and protects its interests: not by rejecting the stuff of which heroes are made, because it knows not how to make them. (Mill 2003: 125)

Contemporary virtue ethicists have not deeply scrutinized the topic of the individuation of character. Nevertheless, the question of which character traits distinguish us from others is a great source of everyday intrigue and speculation, one which motivates a whole spectrum of evaluative emotions from love to pride, from shame to disgust. When the character traits constituting individualized differences between persons have been discussed, commentators have tended to focus on traits connected to self-expression and creativity, traits that distinguish persons in a secondary sense insofar as they give rise to cultural artefacts or ways of living that are individually distinctive. While this kind of individual distinctiveness might furnish the content of a person's creative oeuvre or the events constituting their life story, it does not pertain to the character traits that constitute character itself, and so could only be thought of as the individuation of character indirectly. Most significantly, however, virtue ethicists tend not to discuss the individuation of character in the context of human flourishing, which again is odd given that the free expression of individual character is often thought to be inextricably connected to living a choiceworthy life. Perhaps this is because philosophical accounts invariably seek to offer a model of the good life that applies to us all, one which is necessarily immune to what is taken to be irrelevant idiosyncratic quirks, but nonetheless such an oversight is striking. Furthermore, most contemporary accounts of human flourishing have been guided – or misguided – by a historical tradition from Socrates onwards that primarily understands flourishing in terms of exercising one's moral virtues. Undoubtedly there are many reasons for this, but one might be tempted to ascribe it to the long-standing reliance of modern virtue ethicists on Aristotle, along with the moral and intellectual virtues he picks out as important. This is still so prevalent that most virtue ethicists who identify as neo-Aristotelians have not thought more deeply about individuation in other senses. While recent literature still grapples with questions of how individuals must use their practical wisdom (*phronesis*) imaginatively in the exercise of these virtues, according to changes in circumstances, there is widespread agreement that the virtues themselves must remain the same, and that there is little room for individual distinctiveness in the profile of character traits that lead to the flourishing life.

Of course, there are many ways to think about what distinguishes us from others, so to get this discussion into sharper focus I will specify in advance the kind of individuality in which I'm primarily interested: first, rather than moral obligations, I am going to focus on the kind of individuality that applies at the level of those things we care about or *love* – which I will refer to as our passionate attachments; second, I am concerned with the question of how these passionate attachments impact upon our flourishing, especially on the claim – which I believe we can locate in Mill and Nietzsche – that having a unique constellation of passionate attachments is essential. To do this I will depart from the texts that the virtue ethical tradition typically draws on, and will seek the philosophical resources for an account of how the individually distinctive nature of our passionate characters is necessary for flourishing elsewhere. Fortunately, I shall argue, both these nineteenth-century philosophers provide the resources to do this, especially if we consider the parts of their work that were most influenced by the Hellenistic philosopher, Epicurus.

In contrast to the paucity of interest in these questions in the Aristotelian tradition, both Mill and Nietzsche make powerful and explicit claims regarding the fundamentally important nature of individuality for the flourishing life, both for the well-being of individual persons and for the prospering of those societies to which these individuals belong. Contrary to Aristotle's disinterest, both nineteenth-century philosophers insist that the specific nature of our passionate character decisively distinguishes us from others, as well as providing the conditions for a far greater degree of flourishing than we would otherwise enjoy. Moreover, both offer hypothetical sketches of the historical processes that have traditionally quashed individuality, reasons relating to the survival of primitive societies, and both philosophers suggest that it is now of vital importance to provide institutions and contemporary ways of living that foster and encourage individuality in human beings. Most significantly, however, both philosophers locate the domain for this kind of individual expression as belonging to our love relationships, as they think that individuality is most meaningfully expressed in the context of our passionate characters. We do not become most distinctively ourselves in the context of how we meet our moral obligations or exercise our ethical virtues, these philosophers think, but, rather, in how we refine and cultivate our passionate attachments in ways that makes us the persons that we are.

Before delving into the texts of these thinkers, however, we will do well to think of how this might work in everyday life, by thinking about folk approaches to how we best come to know ourselves and others. Using broad brushstrokes, we might identify two schools of thought here, which are not unconnected, but are nonetheless distinctive.

The claim of the first school is that we best know what makes a person the person they are when we know their moral character, as mentioned earlier. This is a school of thought that has been deeply influential in the philosophical tradition. Socrates advocates the view that true knowledge of a person concerns their moral character, and Aristotle's views about the highest form of friendship as being virtue friendship – knowing another person on the basis of their virtuous character – can be thought of as part of the same tradition. There is another school of thought, however, one which has perhaps been more influential in depth psychology, as well as in the philosophical influences of this tradition. Freud, for example, advocates a route to knowledge of his patients, and self-knowledge on the part of the patients themselves that is resolutely non-moral, as the moral virtues or the seeming-credence one gives one's moral obligations are regarded as mere symptoms covering a more pertinent and telling set of investments. Indeed, while these investments may well be constituted by many kinds of desires, at least some of them could be described as passionate attachments, an idiosyncratic set of love investments that make up a patient's passionate character. As we will see, both Nietzsche and Mill are closer to Freud than Plato on this question, although they add a normative dimension to the problem insofar as they also claim that pursuing the distinctive nature of our passionate attachments will draw us ever closer to the flourishing life.

In what follows I compare Nietzsche's account of how one 'becomes what one is', a major theme in his middle-period writings, alongside Mill's account of the importance of fostering what he calls 'originality' and 'individuality', extensively explored in *On Liberty* published twenty years earlier (1859).[1] I then move to examine the influence of Epicurus on both thinkers, especially how he offers an account of how we can cultivate our passionate attachments, one which provides the practical guidance to support the claim that both philosophers make that our passionate attachments can be most closely aligned with flourishing when they are actively cultivated.

II.1. Mill on 'originality' in human flourishing

Whereas there has been little engagement with Mill's emphasis on 'originality' within the utilitarian literature, it plays a vital role in his moral philosophy, especially in the comprehensive account of the good life that we find in *On Liberty*. In the third chapter of this work – 'Of Individuality, as One of the Elements of Well-Being' – Mill discusses what he considers to be the 'chief ingredient of individual and social progress', which he designates with the synonyms 'originality' or 'individuality', sometimes glossing this with the phrase that which makes a human being 'the best thing it can be' (2003: 128). Although Mill stresses that the expression of individuality has social, legal and political limits – 'free scope should be given to varieties of character, short of injury to others' (2003: 122) – he also thinks that our social lives and collective institutions are obliged to organize themselves in a way that safeguards this dimension of human flourishing. Moreover, as we will see below, he incorporates this understudied aspect of his ethics into his celebrated utilitarianism, proposing that we all enjoy a net gain in collective utility if we provide the social and political conditions for individuality to thrive. So what does Mill understand individuality to be? And is his claim that it is an invaluable dimension of the good life one that can be supported by plausible arguments?

Perhaps the best way to understand what Mill means by individuality is to set it against those social, legal and political constraints that are necessary to ensure that the expression of individuality is benign. For Mill, we must add to this the constraining force of one's moral obligations, which must constantly be borne in mind, in order not to trespass on the 'limits imposed by the rights and interests of others' (2003: 127–8). All these kinds of obligations apply to all members of the community; no exceptions for the individuality of any one member can be made. In sharp contrast to this, individuality pertains to those aspects of our lives that distinguish us from others but have no negative moral consequences, such as our passionate attachments. Mill calls such attachments those things for which we have 'desires and impulses' (2003: 125). Indeed, he gives some rather wholesome examples of these – 'rowing', 'smoking', 'music', 'athletic exercises' and 'chess' (2003: 132) – but his claims about individuality gain greater traction if we think of our love relationships with specific persons, our commitment to a long-cherished project, or our assiduous commitment to a non-moral passion. Each of these things makes us distinctive in a way that our moral, social or political obligations do not – they are unique to us alone, non-fungible, and we would lose a vital part of our identity if out passionate attachments were exchanged for those of another. Of course, at the most basic level we can readily understand that having a choice in these things is necessary for flourishing – or at least the counterclaim that not having this kind of choice would seriously impoverish our lives – but why is it necessary that our passionate attachments are individualized, that is, unique to ourselves in a way that distinguishes us from other individuals? Surely, one might think, the important thing is that we have freedom to pursue what we are passionate about, and even the most rudimentary anthropological survey would show that there is a good deal of similarity in the passionate attachments human beings choose to take up and pursue.

To banish such worries, Mill offers three reasons why individuality is important in the flourishing life, each of which responds to the everyday observation that – although there is some diversity at the extremes – for the most part human beings typically love a relatively narrow range of things. In the first instance, Mill acknowledges that our choices about which passionate attachments to pursue are clearly informed by the 'traditions and customs of other people', and that such 'presumptive evidence' should have a 'claim to [one's] deference' (2003: 123). In fact, he adds, it would be 'absurd to pretend that people ought to live as if nothing whatever had been known in the world before they came into it' or that no 'one mode of existence, or of conduct, is preferable to another' (2003: 123). Second, he notes that, due to the diversity of human physiology, what may be a suitable passionate attachment for one person may not be suitable for another. As Mill puts it – in a decidedly Nietzschean register – just as 'all the variety of plants [cannot 'exist healthily'] in the same physical environment, atmosphere and climate', 'different persons also require different conditions for their spiritual development' (2003: 132). Lastly – offering a reason that would perhaps resonate most strongly with Nietzsche – Mill tells us that there is something unhealthy about acting in correspondence with customs that have not been thoroughly sifted and incorporated into one's own practical identity, something that negatively impacts upon human flourishing itself. He writes:

> Though the customs be both good as customs, and suitable to him, yet to conform to custom, merely as custom, does not educate or develop in him any of the qualities which are the distinctive endowment of a human being. (2003: 124)

This is an astonishing claim, which Mill supports by suggesting that individuality concerting our passionate attachments is important because it provides the necessary conditions for human autonomy, which he regards as a vital part of the flourishing life. He writes:

> The human faculties of perception, judgment, discriminative feeling, mental activity, and even moral preference, are exercised only in making a choice. He who does anything because it is the custom, makes no choice. He gains no practice either in discerning or in desiring what is best. The mental and moral, like the muscular powers, are improved only by being used. The faculties are called into no exercise by doing a thing merely because others do it, no more than by believing a thing only because others believe it. If the grounds of an opinion are not conclusive to the person's own reason, his reason cannot be strengthened, but is likely to be weakened by his adopting it: and if the inducements to an act are not such as are consentaneous to his own feelings and character (where affection, or the rights of others, are not concerned) it is so much done towards rendering his feelings and character inert and torpid, instead of active and energetic. (2003: 123–4)

So now that I have shown what Mill thinks individualization is, and why he thinks of it as important, I am ready to ask how he thinks we can go about achieving it. I discuss this practical question more fully when we examine below the Epicurean influence on Mill and Nietzsche, but for now we should note how Mill also thinks individuality is deeply connected to self-cultivation.

Mill's view on the necessary role of autonomy in human flourishing is at the heart of his account of how we can practically become distinctive individuals in the sense that we have outlined earlier. He sees it as a consequence of an active cultivation of one's passionate attachments. In contradistinction to how the cultivation of character is thought of in the Aristotelian tradition, Mill thinks that the qualities required to manifest individuality must be gained in a strictly *self*-directed process. As I show in the next section, Nietzsche also stresses the self-directed nature of self-cultivation, and it is interesting to compare his reasons with those that Mill adduces for this. First, Mill emphasizes that individuality is not just the absence of conformity to customary practices, emphasizing that we should understand it positively. Our characters do not become distinctive by 'wearing down uniformity' but by 'cultivating [individuality] and calling it forth', he writes, and it is only by the active participation in self-directed practices of cultivation that 'human beings [can] become a noble and beautiful object of contemplation' (2003: 127). Just as artworks 'partake in the character of those who [create] them', so too

> human life also becomes rich, diversified, and animating, furnishing more abundant aliment to high thoughts and elevating feelings, and strengthening the tie which binds every individual to the race, by making the race infinitely better and worth belonging to. In proportion to the development of his individuality, each person becomes more valuable to himself, and is therefore capable of being more valuable to others. There is a greater fullness of life about his own existence, and when there is more life in the units there is more in the mass which is composed of them. As much compression as is necessary to prevent the stronger specimens of human nature from encroaching on the rights of others, cannot be dispensed with; but for this there is ample compensation even in the point of view of human development. The means of development which the individual loses by being prevented from gratifying his inclinations to the injury of others, are chiefly obtained at the expense of the development of other people. (2003: 127–8)

On this view it is the active role of the individual in their own cultivation that is vitally important. We cannot flourish by allowing other processes to discover the nature of our individuality for us; we must find it for ourselves, in a way that requires a painstaking process of self-cultivation. After examining Nietzsche's account of individuality, I speculate *how* Mill thinks we can do this, a practical topic that Mill himself does not touch on, but one that I suggest we can find the resources to answer in one of his acknowledged philosophical influences: the work of Epicurus.

II.2. Nietzsche's individualized ideal of 'becoming what one is'

Compared to Mill's notion of 'originality', Nietzsche gives a rather more dazzling title to his injunction to flourish through individuality, which he terms with typical panache 'becoming what one is'.[2] As commentators note,[3] this phrase first appears in the middle period, derives from Pindar's enigmatic phrase, γένοι' οιος εσσί μαθων (become the one you have learnt to be) (Snell and Maehler 1978: 72),[4] and is first used by Nietzsche, albeit in truncated form, in his letter to Erwin Rohde of 3 November 1867.[5] Here, Nietzsche recounts some of his recent exploits in the artillery division, reminisces at length about their last meeting and concludes by telling Rohde how delighted he is to have found a friend, οιος εσσί (such as you are). While this is a reference that Rohde, also an aspiring philologist, would have immediately grasped, Nietzsche reminds him that these 'joyous [*festlichen*] words' are especially apt as they have already 'proved propitious' in an equestrian context. The context and thus the precise meaning of these lines is still contested by contemporary philologists, but they are believed to have been directly addressed to Pindar's patron, Hieron of Syracuse, both to celebrate his recent chariot victory at the Pythian Games of 470 BCE and to urge him to ignore the flattery of other court poets.⁶ It is interesting to note that Pindar's English-speaking commentators have typically translated γένοι' οιος εσσί μαθων μαθων (become the one you have learnt to be) into English in much the same way as Nietzsche translated it into German, although they have often included the idea that 'becoming what you are' is related to pedagogy,⁷ another significant connotation given Nietzsche's keen interest in the question of education in nineteenth-century Germany.

Versions of 'become what you are' also feature prominently in the third and fourth *Untimely Meditations*. *Schopenhauer as Educator* begins with the contention that we are fundamentally estranged from ourselves, urges us to 'live according to our own laws and standards' (1) and offers 'Be yourself!' as an essential existential imperative. In *Richard Wagner at Bayreuth*, Nietzsche uses the formulation again in his description of Wagner's artistic development. Wagner is implored to 'become what he is' by unifying his markedly disparate drives, and as long as this process continues, he will become 'what he will be' (1).

The next significant version of the formulation appears two years after the publication of the Wagner essay, in the fifth book of *Human, All too Human*. In §225, Nietzsche relates the independence of free spirits to the fact that they 'come to be what they are', in defiance of the dominant views of the age and attendant social, economic and political factors. In §263, when discussing the nature of talent or ability (*Begabung*), Nietzsche suggests that although 'everyone *possesses inborn talent*', such a capacity is not sufficient in order to be talented. Instead, to 'become a talent' (*ein Talent wird*) one must first 'become what one is' (*wird, was er ist*) as this is vital for any latent talent to be realized.

Partial or fragmented versions of the imperative are scattered throughout the rest of the Free-Spirit Trilogy: Goethe must 'become Goethe' in §227 of *Assorted Opinions and Maxims*; and in §366 of the same work Nietzsche connects 'becoming what you are' with an act of the will, proposing that one must '*will* a self [to] *become* a self' (wolle *ein Selbst, so* wirst *du ein Selbst*), and remarks that – in contrast to the Delphic imperative to 'know thyself' (*kenne dich selbst*) – his is the guiding imperative (*dem Spruche*) for 'active, successful natures'. The formulation prominently appears next in *The Gay Science*. Here, in §270, Nietzsche pairs it with the conscience, asking 'What does your conscience say?' ('*Was sagt dein Gewissen*?'), and answering immediately with the rejoinder 'You must become what you are' ('*Du sollst der werden der du bist*'). The connection with the conscience is re-emphasized in §335 where Nietzsche suggests that although many different forces can elicit the conscience, we should prioritize our 'intellectual conscience' (*intellectuale Gewissen*) as it is this which urges us to 'become what we are'. Finally, GS §335 connects 'becoming what you are' with creating one's own values; the imperative is for those 'who give themselves laws, who create themselves!'

Moving on from the Free-Spirit Trilogy, 'become what you are' appears conspicuously in Nietzsche's later work: in *Thus Spoke Zarathustra* it is explicitly linked to the thought of eternal return when the eponymous hero is addressed using a version of the formulation, 'Zarathustra, who you are and must become' ('*Zarathustra, wer du bist und werden musst*') and, in the fourth and final part of the same work, Zarathustra explicitly adopts the formulation as his own motto, declaiming 'Become what you are!' ('*Werde, der du bist!*').⁸ In addition to these direct references, there are several allegorical versions of the formulation in Nietzsche's oeuvre – several of which are contained within *Zarathustra* – which do not explicitly invoke the words of the formulation itself. The first significant appearance of these allegorical versions in the 'On Beholding Virtue' (*'schenkenden Tugend'*)⁹ section at the end of Book I. The passage was published in the original 1883 imprint of *Zarathustra*, but readers are quite familiar with it since Nietzsche reused the final lines as the epigraph for the second book, published the following year, and as a foreword to *Ecce Homo*.

The section begins with a short discussion of allegory in which Nietzsche remarks on the allegorical nature of the terms 'good' and 'evil'. For Nietzsche, these terms do not refer to robust qualities of acts or individuals; rather, they are allegories or parables (*Gleichnisse*) that only indicate an analogous relation between what naturally attracts or repels us and that to which we would give a more weighty normative term. Nietzsche suggests that such allegories should be treated in the same way as the ancients treated the pronouncements of their oracles insofar as they can only *indicate* (*winken*), and thus must be carefully interpreted. Indeed, we could say that the delicate hermeneutic work of deciphering the allegorical nature of the terms 'good' and 'evil' shares much in common with Heraclitus' well-known characterization of the Delphic oracle, which Nietzsche himself discusses at the end of the second *Untimely Mediation*. In this passage, Nietzsche *follows* Heraclitus by suggesting that the imperative to 'know thyself' is empty until furnished with a specific context. Similarly, we fail to understand the terms 'good' and 'evil' if we elide their indicative nature; as Zarathustra rails: 'A fool [*Ein Thor*] is he who wants knowledge of them [directly].' We could add that what is foolish is seeking knowledge of 'good' and 'evil' *in themselves*, abstracting them from, and failing to analogize them to, our own individual concerns. By abstracting and analogizing these terms, however, we are able to understand them in the only sense we truly can; that is, we understand them by grasping their essentially figurative nature.

From this we can see that Nietzsche prioritizes the idea of 'becoming what one is' throughout his middle-period oeuvre, but if we want to understand how he views the practical process taking place we need to look for clues for this in his middle and earlier period works. Two aphorisms stand out in this regard, both from *Assorted Opinions and Maxims*, which discuss the importance of fostering individuality in the pedagogical process. Nietzsche hints at the idea that it is vitally important to respect the autonomy and the particularities of pupils' psycho-physical make up in AOM 268, where he notes – perhaps to the consternation of the less maverick pedagogues among us – that

> a good educator knows cases in which he is proud of the fact that his pupil remains true to himself *in opposition to him*: in those cases, that is to say, in which the youth ought not to understand the man or would be harmed if he did understand him. (AOM 268)

This builds on the core idea of self-development in WS 267, where Nietzsche discusses 'self-education', proposing that as a 'thinker one should speak only of self-education' because of the inherent psycho-physical differences that make us distinctive as individuals. Developing and accentuating our individual differences, Nietzsche argues, is the point and purpose of an enlightened model of education (WS 267). For Nietzsche education is all too often either an 'experiment carried out on an as yet unknown and unknowable subject' or – *à la* Mill – a 'levelling on principle with the object of *making* the new being ... conform to the customs and habits then prevailing', but this will not facilitate an individual's passage to the highest state of flourishing that Nietzsche associates with 'becoming what one is' (WS 267). Rather, the vital thing is to encourage the accentuation of the idiosyncratic differences which enables one to '*discover oneself*' (WS 267; emphasis in original), which, as we will see in the next section, Nietzsche explains in an Epicurean-inspired way in *Schopenhauer as Educator*.

III Two views on contemporary human flourishing

To understand why both Nietzsche and Mill think we are in the midst of a crisis of individuality, we should situate their respective analyses on the importance of human distinctiveness – either in terms of 'originality' or in terms of 'becoming what one is' – within a broader set of critical complaints that each thinker directs towards the ways that flourishing is typically prescribed in his respective society. Although scholars typically focus on Nietzsche's later genealogical studies with regard to this question, his interest in this matter began far earlier in his middle-period works. Although preceded by the sketches found in the 'On the History of Moral Sensations' section of *Human, All Too Human*, Nietzsche's first sustained engagement with the genealogical method appears in *Dawn* in an aphorism entitled 'Concept of Morality of Custom'. In this potted history of morality, Nietzsche identifies a deep similarity between prehistoric systems of morality, and what he regards as the constitutive moral systems of the Western world: the Roman Empire, Christianity and – from the eighteen century onwards – Kantianism. Conducting oneself strictly according to the established dictates of custom is the hallmark of prehistoric systems of morality, Nietzsche argues, an attitude he views as permeating more recent moral systems. As he puts it, customs are just a 'traditional way of behaving and evaluating', and 'morality is nothing other ... than obedience to customs, of whatever kind they may be' (D 9). But whereas today we tend to think of moral obligation as generating one kind of – more or less overriding – consideration among others, Nietzsche proposes that everything about collective life was once viewed as under the auspices of morality. 'Originally ... everything was custom', he writes, and even practices as diverse as 'education', 'care of health', 'marriage', 'cure of sickness', 'agriculture', 'war', 'speech', silence', 'traffic with one another and with the gods' were squarely regarded as 'within the domain of morality' (D 9). The flipside of this is that actions that depart from the customs of these grim times were regarded with suspicion and hostility. Those who managed to 'depend upon [themselves] and not upon a tradition', Nietzsche writes, were considered to be immoral, and the adjectives applied to those who had achieved this kind of independence – 'individual', 'free', 'capricious', 'unusual', 'unforeseen', 'incalculable' – were regarded as synonymous with 'evil' (D 9).

For Nietzsche, the reason for such a resistance for any conspicuous display of individuality was that it was viewed as threatening the very foundations of those early social communities. In an earlier remark in HH – one which has a decidedly Millian ring to it – Nietzsche tells us that, like custom, the impersonal has traditionally been viewed as the 'distinguishing mark of the moral action', and, indeed, we should view Nietzsche's account of the role of 'custom' and 'impersonalness' in morality as actively complementing one another. 'It was on account of their *general utility* that impersonal actions', along with related selfless character traits, were 'universally commended and accorded distinction', and eventually prized as moral phenomena (emphasis added; HH 95).[10]

Before turning to Nietzsche's account of how the advent of individuality allowed human beings to become more interesting animals, I will compare it with Mill's similar account of the suppression of individuality which we find in *On Liberty*, which he wrote with Harriet Taylor Mill (his then wife) who although officially uncredited in the original 1859 text, he elsewhere warmly acknowledges as a vitally important contributor. In the relevant section, 'On the Role of Individuality in Well-Being', Mill offers a similar speculative sketch of the likely historical precedents that led to a suppression of individuality in prehistorical societies. Mill writes:

> In some early states of society, these forces might be, and were, too much ahead of the power which society then possessed of disciplining and controlling them. There has been a time when the element of spontaneity and individuality was in excess, and the social principle had a hard struggle with it. The difficulty then was, to induce men of strong bodies or minds to pay obedience to any rules which required them to control their impulses. To overcome this difficulty, law and discipline, like the Popes struggling against the Emperors, asserted a power over the whole man, claiming to control all his life in order to control his character – which society had not found any other sufficient means of binding. (2003: 125–6)

From this we can see that Mill's account deals with the struggle that early primitive societies had in taming the wild drives towards self-satisfaction that he regards as typifying the conduct of human beings before they organized themselves within communities which depended on the rule of law ('the difficulty ... to induce men ... to pay obedience to any rules which required them to control their impulses'). In the same manner as Nietzsche's account of the de-individualizing role of the 'morality of custom', therefore, the account of the development of morality that Mill presents also proposes that early societies were necessarily fixated with minimizing individuality to ensure the rule of law, which was also a condition of their own survival. Although Nietzsche emphasizes the later stages of this process (when customs had been established), Mill's account deals with an earlier stage of this process – the stage when customs still needed to be enforced.

But in addition to sharing a similar historical world view about how the role of shared custom-making is deeply connected to present-day morality, Nietzsche and Mill also share a view about the state of development of this historical process, a view which is connected with their account of the role of individuality in flourishing. To understand this view we must follow what they both regard as trends and currents that have guided the historical development of collective moral behaviours up until the nineteenth century. While the process of destroying the individuation of character, life styles, conduct, ways of behaviour, was a necessary consequence of the formation of collective societies where custom provided the conditions for social life, when this process runs too far – for both Nietzsche and Mill – it is seriously detrimental to the capacity of a given society to function. Perhaps because he is so vociferous, Nietzsche's views on this are fairly well known, but Mill's have undergone rather less scrutiny. Once human communities have been successful in the 'hard struggle', that is, as Mill himself puts it, once 'society has … got the better of individuality', then the 'danger which threatens human nature is not the excess, but the deficiency, of personal impulses and preferences' (2003: 126).[11] Collective human endeavours are not existentially threatened by too little conformity, in the way Mill and Nietzsche describe above, but, rather, by too much social cohesion. Today, Mill writes, when the 'opinions of masses of merely average men have everywhere become, or are becoming, the dominant power, the counterpoise and corrective to that tendency would be, the more and more pronounced individuality of those who stand on the higher eminences of thought' (2003: 131). The problem is that those cultural outlets, which had to be narrowed as a condition of society's existence in the first place, are now so narrowed that individuals are becoming too rare.[12] To counter this, a remedial process needs to take place. Exceptional individuals, 'instead of being deterred, should be encouraged in acting differently from the mass' because 'in this age the mere example of nonconformity, the mere refusal to bend the knee to custom, is itself a service' (2003: 131).

IV Epicurean self-cultivation in Mill and Nietzsche

While Epicurus is an influence that Mill routinely cites as important to him – albeit in the context of differentiating the former's conception of 'pleasure' from his own conception of 'utility' – we would be hard-pressed to find an explicitly Epicurean account of cultivating our originality in Mill. Some scholars such as Wendy Donner (2010) have paid attention to Mill's account of self-cultivation in *The Art of Life*, but the focus has been on Mill's prominent comments on self-directed aesthetic cultivation, rather than the cultivation of those passionate attachments that we have seen he views as integral to his account of originality. By contrast, Epicurus' influence on Nietzsche has become an increasingly important topic of scholarly interest. Recent scholarship has offered both convincing and powerful accounts of Nietzsche's middle-period engagements with the Hellenistics, and readers who are familiar with Nietzsche often cannot escape the impression that many implicit references to Hellenism appear throughout his texts. These references occur in his later works, but – as commentators from Heidegger onwards have pointed out – these references are predominantly negative. But despite Heidegger's influential reading that claims that Nietzsche is adamantly opposed to Epicurus (1991: v.2, 52),[13] recently a new wave of Nietzsche scholars have shown that a close reading of his middle-period works reveals a deep Hellenistic influence. Within this debate, scholars typically favour one or other of the Hellenistic schools as being most influential; Michael Ure directs attention to the Stoics, Jessica Berry to Pyrrhonian Skeptics, whereas Keith Ansell-Pearson argues that the subtexts of Nietzsche's middle-period works typically prioritize Epicurean themes.

Whether it was Epicurus, Epictetus, Seneca, Cicero or Sextus Empiricus who most influenced Nietzsche, however, this literature has shown beyond doubt that both his extensive reading and note-taking covered many figures in the Hellenistic schools, much of which eventually permeated his own practical philosophy. Furthermore, thinking back to Mill, although we saw him offering a comprehensive account of the value of 'originality' for flourishing, when we turn to a practical conception of how this could be done, we are given few clues, and understanding how such an ideal might be achieved involves seeking the resources within the work of his influences. Can the figure of Epicurus offer us the resources to furnish a practical account of how we attain 'originality' or engage in the process of 'becoming what one is', then? And if so, how could such an account function?

Against the mainstream Anglophone reading that Hellenistic philosophers such as Epicurus were opposed to all passionate attachments, Pierre Hadot has argued that while a historical engagement with the Hellenistic philosophers reveals that although they certainly viewed our passionate attachments as potentially dangerous, there was some significant leeway in this attitude. This aimed to bring the philosophical and practical resources of the Hellenistic schools to those who were interested in their ideas but chose to remain 'lay-philosophers'. These persons did not want to relocate to Epicurus' famed Garden or to the various establishments of the Stoic or Skeptic schools. Furthermore, Hadot proposes, by focusing on the Hellenistic account of the 'spiritual exercises', we can find evidence for them in thinkers in the Modern European Tradition, as well as showing how these exercises hold the resources to offer us new ways to think about self-cultivation in the contemporary world. Hadot only provides a sketch of both these projects, however, since he does not give concrete examples of how they appear in the work of Modern European thinkers such as Mill and Nietzsche, nor does he develop a comprehensive account of how Hellenistic self-cultivation could play a substantive role in the philosophical studies of our own era. Nevertheless, Hadot's account of the exercises that were most prevalent in the Hellenistic world does offer us a way to think about how to cultivate our individuality in terms of our passionate attachments, in a way that may satisfy the demands that we do so, which we have seen both Mill and Nietzsche advocate. The exercise I will focus on in this section is one Hadot terms the 'view from above', partly because he argues that this exercise was especially important for Epicureanism, and partly because we can find traces of this in the writings of both Mill and Nietzsche.

Hadot's most detailed account of the 'view from above' occurs in *Philosophy as a Way of Life*, in which he tells us that this exercise featured in the practical philosophy of all the Hellenistic schools. This exercise was an imaginative one in which the 'imagination speeds through the infinite vastness of the universe', one which required the practitioners to contemplate themselves among ever larger circles of time and space, and so to better contextualize themselves, and to rightly regard their existence as just one part of an otherwise magnificent and glorious natural world (1995a: 242). In the Epicurean school, Hadot continues, the 'lives and activities of sages' were openly discussed with much interest as the sages – especially Epicurus himself – was considered as a source of valuable information concerning how to live. Perhaps imitating the notoriously aloof Epicurean gods, the Epicurean sage was generally unconcerned with 'mundane affairs' and the bulk of their existence was spent 'contemplating the infinity of space, time, and the multiple worlds' (1995a: 243). Imaginatively taking up the 'view from above' within the context of a Hellenistic exercise, therefore, was a way to temporarily participate in how the sage viewed the world.

Taking the image further, Hadot speculates that the Epicureans may have regarded his exercise as permitting access to the view of the Epicurean gods, those lofty celestial beings that Epicurus claims view the activities of humans with unconcern. Hadot writes:

> The view from above thus leads us to consider the whole of human reality, in all its social, geographical, and emotional aspects, as an anonymous, swarming mass, and it teaches us to relocate human existence within the immeasurable dimensions of the cosmos. (1995a: 245)

But in addition to being a striking imaginative image, the view from above is intended to focus the mind by engendering a reappraisal of how one is living one's life. Viewing ourselves from this point of view encourages us to re-evaluate how we are living, especially our commitment to whatever considerations our life is guided by. The partial and fragmentary nature of the desires of 'society and the individuals who comprise it' is revealed when viewing them from above, because we are able to see these desires from 'the point of view of universality' (1995a: 242). At times Hadot calls this the 'philosophical way par excellence of looking at things' (1995a: 242), at times the ability to see things 'as they really are' (1995a: 247).

Interestingly, among the Epicureans, the exercise took remarkably different forms, sometimes being thought of in terms of duration instead of space. To 'observe human affairs from above means', Hadot tells us, 'to see them from the point of view of death', because like the observation of oneself from the perspective of the heavens 'this perspective [also] brings about the necessary elevation and loosening of the spirit' because it provides another kind of 'distance ... in order to see things as they really are' (1995a: 247). This line of thought is taken up in the work of Michel Foucault's exploration of the Epicurean exercises of 'meditation on future ills [*praemeditatio malorum*]' and the 'meditation on death [*meletê thanatou*]', both of which aim to precipitate the practitioners' realization of what is fundamentally important to them, and to ensure that they are actively leading their life accordingly (1997: 103). So how can we think of this exercise as offering a practical answer to the question of achieving the kinds of individual ideals that both Mill and Nietzsche advocate? How might a 'spiritual exercise', as Hadot puts it, one that isolates and contextualizes our existence in terms of the extremities of either time or space precipitate in us a sense of individuality, one which encourages us to pursue the idiosyncratic nature of our passionate attachments?

While Mill only indicates that originality is a fundamentally important part of the good life, and does not provide a detailed account of how we can cultivate such originality in ourselves, Nietzsche offers an account that contains some similar elements to Hadot's description of the 'view from above'. Furthermore, if we take into account Hadot's claim that this exercise took radically different forms in the Epicurean school, defining it in wide enough terms to include Foucault's account of the *meletê thanatou* or the *praemeditatio malorum*, then we can identify a version of the thought in Nietzsche's early *Untimely Mediation*, 'Schopenhauer as Educator'. In this essay, Nietzsche begins with a rapt account of the importance of individuality, which in II.2 I showed contains an early version of the imperative to 'become what one is'. Here Nietzsche addresses his reader by surmising that 'all you are now doing, thinking, desiring, is not you yourself', and – as we saw – admonishes him or her to 'be yourself' (1). The reason for such a plea, he tells us, stems from the 'law that every man is a unique miracle', that he is 'uniquely himself to every last movement of his muscles' and that when he is 'strictly consistent in uniqueness', he reaches his highest possibilities.

What is most useful for the aim of this article, however, is the sketch Nietzsche gives of how this kind of individuality is cultivated. Just like his remarks on education in AOM, this is necessarily a self-directed process in which the individual must identify and then accentuate their radically unique psycho-physical heritage. He writes:

> Your true educators and formative teachers reveal to you that the true, original meaning and basic stuff of your nature is something completely incapable of being educated or formed and is in any case something difficult of access, bound and paralyzed; your educators can be only your liberators. (1)

Education is not a formative process of one world view upon another, therefore, but, rather the teacher acts more in the manner of a facilitator who points one towards the conditions for the expression of one's individual nature. Indeed, we could think of one of the conditions for such a process as the teaching of spiritual exercises, in which the pupil learns to engage in practical processes aimed at revealing the nature of their passionate attachments, both past and future.

This is why it is appropriate that in his answer to the questions 'How can we find ourselves again?' and 'How can man know himself?', Nietzsche suggests that we can do this by engaging in a spiritual exercise in which one 'looks back on [one's earlier] life' to discover what one has 'truly loved up to now, what has drawn your soul aloft, what has mastered it and at the same time blessed it' (1). Taking a global and retrospective view of the historical trajectory of one's passionate attachments has the effect of allowing one to plot a line towards those future attachments at which one should aim. By instigating a self-directed practice of recalling and evaluating the passionate attachments to which we have been previously truly committed, we are able to see more clearly which passionate attachments stand out for us as truly important. Furthermore, in contrast to much recent literature on discovering one's passions within the self-help community,[14] Nietzsche's promotion of an Epicurean-inspired spiritual exercise does not offer a 'one-size-fits-all' approach, but one which is explicitly tailored to unmasking what is unique and singular in the passionate attachments of whoever engages in this exercise. Engaging in an evaluation of one's life in which one scrutinizes one's historical trajectory for patterns of attachment through which the uniqueness of one's character is revealed allows one to come to a fixed understanding of who one is on the basis of those passionate attachments that one routinely prizes. In response to the two schools of thought regarding how one comes to 'know oneself' better, mentioned in 1.0, this way of discovering and knowing one's individuality firmly sides with the idea that we come to know ourselves better (and therefore others) by knowing what we love, rather than through 'practical knowledge' of our moral character.

V Conclusion

From what we have seen above, there is much merit in turning to Epicurus' spiritual exercises to understand how we can practically achieve the individualized conception of flourishing that both Mill and Nietzsche strongly advocate. We have seen that both Mill and Nietzsche were deeply influenced by Epicurus, and I noted in Section 1.0 that Nietzsche's middle-period writings may well have been influenced by Mill's *On Liberty*, in a way that has not enjoyed the scholarly acknowledgement that it deserves, even among leading Nietzsche historians such as Brobjer. Despite this, if we follow Hadot's analysis of Epicurus' exercises of self-cultivation, we can see that the exercise of the 'view from above' offers at least one account of how we could be said to cultivate our passionate attachments, one which Hadot suggests can be reactivated, as well as claiming that it has been influential to thinkers in the modern philosophical tradition. Furthermore, thinking imaginatively about this exercise, especially how it was relatively protean in the Epicurean world, capable of taking different shapes or forms, allows us to understand Nietzsche's proposal that we should recall which passionate attachments we have been previously drawn to in the project of attaining our individuality. While Mill does not address this question directly, insofar as his account of human flourishing includes a strong commitment to individuality, we can furnish him with a practical account of how to achieve this aim by recalling Hadot's claim that the Epicurean exercises can be re-actualized. This allows us to employ their resources to philosophical questions, which gives contemporary philosophy a practical use, and concreteness was a hallmark of philosophical enquiry in the Hellenistic period.

Notes

1 The question of Mill's influence on Nietzsche is difficult to answer conclusively. Even a scholar as assiduous as Thomas Brobjer concedes defeat in trying to 'determine [the precise date] when Nietzsche acquired the Mill volumes', although he notes that by the 'summer of 1880 [Nietzsche] had read at least three of the five volumes he possessed' (1995: 160). Furthermore, elsewhere Brobjer notes that 'Nietzsche carefully read and studied [and] annotat[ed] almost every page of the five volumes in Mill's collected works that Nietzsche possessed' (2008: 184). As Brobjer diplomatically notes, 'Nietzsche as a reader was much more tolerant and better informed than one would perhaps have guessed from knowing only his published statements. This can be seen, for example, in his reading of J. S. Mill, Lecky, and the brothers Goncourt, all of whom Nietzsche curtly dismissed in his published writings and letters. Nietzsche's heavily annotated copies of books written by Mill, Lecky, and Goncourt, respectively, are heavily annotated and full of positive exclamations but contain relatively few negative words and comments' (2008: 16).

2 A note on translations of Nietzsche's works: I have used R. J. Hollingdale's translations for Cambridge in citing from D, HH and UM. For EH, GS and Z, I have used Walter Kaufmann's translations for Random House and Viking, and for GM and WP, Kaufmann and Hollingdale translations for Random House.
3 See John Hamilton (2004: 54–69) and Babette Babich (2003: 29–58).
4 B. Snell and H. Maehler (1978: 72).
5 E. Förster-Nietzsche and F. Schöll (1923: 52).
6 As R. W. Burton notes, 'The poet holds up to Hieron a mirror in which he may look and know himself, urging him to be what he is' (1962: 121).
7 For example, W. H. Race translates it as: 'Become such as you are, having learned what that is' (1997: 239). Whereas Glen Most favours: 'Show yourself in your action as the sort of man you have learned that you are' (1985: 102). Interestingly, Most refers to Nietzsche's translation, specifically to the absence of a reference to $\mu\alpha\theta\omega\nu$ (learning), and notes that, 'those who have most celebrated this sentence have on occasion simultaneously most abused it' (1985: 102).
8 See 'The Honey Sacrifice'.
9 Kaufmann translates *schenkenden Tugend* as 'gift-giving'.
10 Nietzsche's full remark reads, 'Ought a significant alteration in this point of view not to lie just ahead, now when it is realized more and more that it is in precisely the most personal possible considerations that the degree of utility is at its greatest also for the generality: so that it is the strictly personal action that corresponds to the current conception of morality (as general utility)? To make of oneself a complete person, and in all that one does to have in view the *highest good* of this person – that gets us further than those pity-filled agitations and actions for the sake of others' (HH 95).
11 He continues, 'Things are vastly changed, since the passions of those who were strong by station or by personal endowment were in a state of habitual rebellion against laws and ordinances, and required to be rigorously chained up to enable the persons within their reach to enjoy any particle of security. In our times, from the highest class of society down to the lowest, every one lives as under the eye of a hostile and dreaded censorship' (2003: 126).
12 See later in the text, 'Already energetic characters on any large scale are becoming merely traditional. There is now scarcely any outlet for energy in this country except business. The energy expended in that may still be regarded as considerable. What little is left from that employment, is expended on some hobby; which may be a useful, even a philanthropic hobby, but is always some one thing, and generally a thing of small dimensions. The greatness of England is now all collective: individually small, we only appear capable of any thing great by our habit of combining; and with this our moral and religious philanthropists are perfectly contented. But it was men of another stamp than this that made England what it has been; and men of another stamp will be needed to prevent its decline' (2003: 134).
13 See Dennis and Testa (2017: 95) for a summary of the scholarly literature relating to Heidegger's reading of Epicurus.
14 Recent bestsellers relating to this theme include Attwood (2006), Robinson (2009), Juntilla (2013) and – the *New York Times* award-winning bestseller – Duckworth (2016).

Part Three

Appropriations and ambivalences

10

'And Epicurus triumphs anew'

On Nietzsche's *Daybreak*

Vinod Acharya

I Introduction

Epicurus is explicitly mentioned in only two[1] of *Daybreak*'s 575 sections.[2] Yet, this work is arguably the most Epicurean[3] of Nietzsche's middle-period writings.[4] Throughout it, Nietzsche employs Epicurean concepts and metaphors – 'fear', 'security', 'chance', 'knowledge', 'anonymity', 'living modestly', 'garden', 'even pleasure' or 'happiness', among others – often exhibiting Epicurean attitudes towards them. *Daybreak* analyses the historical development and decline of morality, which underlies Nietzsche's critique of the present. Positively, Nietzsche seeks to safeguard the contemporary subject against moral decay, as he attempts to redirect it towards a new future.[5] Epicurus, who fought against embryonic forms of Christianity, is one of the few figures who is reviewed favourably in Nietzsche's history. But what, besides a pro-science, anti-Christian philosophy, does Nietzsche see in Epicurus? *Why* Epicurus, given Nietzsche's radical critique of history and the present?

I argue that Nietzsche views Epicurus' late antiquity as a morally deteriorating age similar to his own. Correspondingly, he appropriates Epicurus' critique of false security, fear and politics for his own critical diagnosis of late modernity. Further, Nietzsche finds in Epicurean thought a different path to individuation, involving nature, knowledge and pleasure, than in the history of morality, where cultural mores, superstition and suffering produced moral subjects. Nietzsche's revival of contemporary subjectivity, therefore, involves creatively transforming and cultivating in the modern context key Epicurean virtues such as *phronēsis* (practical wisdom), self-sufficiency, magnanimity, honesty, courage and gratitude.

II Situating Epicurus; confronting modernity

In section 72,[6] Nietzsche applauds Epicurus for attacking the idea of punishment in hell, which came into prominence later in Christianity, but which was already circulating among numerous religious cults during Epicurus' time.[7] Since Christianity emerged victorious, the Epicurean triumph 'came too early'; but Nietzsche concludes that Epicurus has the final word – 'and Epicurus triumphs anew' – in the present age insofar as with the decline in Christianity, scientific thought comes to reject the idea of life after death (72).[8]

Nietzsche here is hinting at a likeness between late antiquity and the contemporary era. Keeping in view the larger historical narrative of *Daybreak*, section 72 may be interpreted as commenting on a transitional, declining culture to which Epicurus belonged,[9] sandwiched between the classical Greek age (still largely defined by an older form of morality) and the advent of Christianity. According to this narrative, Socratic thought signifies history's turning point by offering 'the *individual* a morality of self-control and temperance as a means to his own *advantage*, as his personal key to happiness' (9). In all previous eras of 'morality of custom' (*Sittlichkeit der Sitte*), in contrast, morality centred on community and tradition. The individual was expected to sacrifice herself, tame her intellect, regulate her bodily and sexual impulses, submit herself to various rituals of discipline, cruelty and voluntary suffering such that her way of life conformed to the customs of her community. Morality was originally nothing but 'obedience to customs', and customs were '*traditional* ways of behaving and evaluating' (9). Tradition represented a 'higher authority', which inspired 'fear' (*Furcht*) 'of an incomprehensible, indefinite power' (9), and which 'one obeys, not because it commands what is *useful* to us, but because it *commands*' (9). Nietzsche thus places fear – the target of Epicurean therapy – at the basis of morality.

The attempt to configure morality around the individual – which Christianity also represents, arguably more blatantly, in encouraging its followers to primarily seek their own salvation (9) – is symptomatic of and presupposes the historical enfeeblement of the power of customs and the general decline of the moral sense in the post-Socratic era. This latter historical development is also the presupposition of the Epicurean intervention,[10] although, I argue, it charts a different path to individuation than both customary morality and post-Socratic moralities such as Christianity. The Epicurean path is based on the practice of self-cultivation and relies on pleasure and knowledge, in contrast to the moral tradition, which stipulated the contours of one's individuality through mechanisms of fear, paralysis of the intellect and the imposition of suffering and punishment. Christianity borrows and enforces these latter moral techniques, albeit with key transformations – it invents novel fears (of punishment in hell (72) or for one's eternal salvation (57)), and more extreme modes of tormenting the body and the soul (76–8, 86); it subscribes to metaphysical intoxications that comprehensively condemn the experiential self (50, 52, 87), and correspondingly promotes a crude intellect, which ignores or opposes honesty, doubt and intellectual rigour (70, 84, 89). However, simultaneously, in encouraging its follower to 'abandon all customary modes of behavior' (87), promising, instead, a '*shorter way to perfection*' (59), involving faith in miracles, 'a sudden change in all value-judgments', conceived as the work of God (87), Christianity also signifies an era of the great weakening of morality.

This contradiction reveals the absurdity of individual-centric morality, especially considering that in prehistoric ages, a community defined itself as 'moral', only by opposing and excluding the 'individual', who would take exception to the prevailing customs, and was thus perceived as 'evil', 'capricious', 'free', 'unusual', etc. (9). Fear of the individual is one form in which the fear of tradition manifested itself in the daily workings of the moral community. When periodically the exceptional individual did emerge – perhaps as a symptom of waning customs (9) – she had to embody 'madness' in order to overcome great self-doubt, despite the threat of punishment or death, to earn the right to personify new ideas and evaluations that could eventually transform the moral community (14). The Christian attempt, therefore, to normalize madness, the exceptional, not only betrays the general depletion of the moral sense, but also actively contributes to its further rarefaction in modernity. This prompts Nietzsche's comment that present-day humans live in an 'immoral' and 'evil' age (9, 14).

Moreover, renouncing the obligation to follow worldly customs, or to fulfil the moral 'law' (68), Christian metaphysics enacts a wholesale condemnation of earthly reality (39). In contrast, under morality of custom, the cultural process of subjugation to traditional practices effected a sublimation of the feeling of fear to that of power, ultimately justifying moral and communal existence. Morality helped 'secure' oneself against nature, tools, animals and other humans 'by force, constraint, flattering, treaties and sacrifices' (23); it provided a framework to make sense of the world, nurtured a sense of belonging in it, thereby increasing one's feeling of confidence and power (26). Rewards and punishments were devised to promote adherence to prevailing customs, not to renounce them. For similar reasons, were cruelty and voluntary suffering counted as virtues (18), and innovative, but perverse, usages of the intellect invented (for instance, fabrication of imaginary (divine or otherworldly) causalities (10, 33), misinterpretation of cause and effect as cause and punishment (11, 13), leaps in inferences and blindness to experiential refutation (21, 24, 27), conclusions based on moods and feelings (28), and projection of teleological principles onto nature based on human utility (37)). The gratification of power does not happen without humans weaving all their 'higher feelings (of reverence, of sublimity, of pride, of gratitude, of love) *into an imaginary world*: the so-called higher world' (33). Although a metaphysical flight is inevitable – that ultimately values this-worldly reality only as a 'symbol' (33) – for a system of values founded on fear, nevertheless, there was no sweeping renunciation of reality.

These considerations, especially about the novel Christian innovations, inform Nietzsche's depiction of late modernity, which he views as also a transitional, morally decadent age. In a section entitled 'Moral Interregnum', Nietzsche writes that today the 'foundations of [moral feelings and judgments] are all defective and their superstructure is beyond repair' (453). Nevertheless, morality still wields a certain normative power. The only way we can do away with it is if the forces of reason and science continue to grow; and if they do, Nietzsche argues, they might even lead to new future ideals (453). Contemporary humans live '*prelude* or [ ] *postlude*' lives (453), contributing to a cultural struggle with uncertain outcome. However, the detour through Christianity has accentuated the terms of this struggle. On the one hand, the further erosion of the power of customs makes us more susceptible to a mishmash of historically transmitted values. Nietzsche describes the contemporary human as tasteless, able to 'digest ... almost everything', stuck between a past that had a more stubborn taste and a future that could perhaps be more discriminating (171).[11] On the other hand, the passage through

Christianity has further resolved the scientific spirit, making our age greatly receptive to the Epicurean affirmation of nature and knowledge than Epicurus' own (another reason why the Epicurean triumph 'came too early' (72)). Nietzsche, therefore, hails the 'passion for knowledge' as the distinguishing mark of contemporary humankind, which holds the key to future happiness and exaltation (429).

These historical connections and deliberations provide the necessary framework to explore, as we shall do below, Nietzsche's appropriation of certain key elements of Epicurean thought. For example, Epicurean writings recommend distance from, if not rejection of, the mores of the existing political sphere. But in stark contrast to Christianity, Epicurus undertakes a this-worldly justification of existence. Individuation is an achievement, not a given; and one must earn it through pursuing pleasure as our natural good, which entails living a simple, contemplative life with its unique virtues. Nietzsche finds such teaching instructive for resisting the ongoing moral decay, and for redirecting humanity onto an affirmative path.

III Moral decay and modernity

Contemporary degeneration lies not only in the defectiveness of moral foundations but also in our tendency to conceal this from ourselves while desperately (if unconsciously) clinging to past evaluations. Nietzsche's critique attacks this hypocrisy while exposing the cracked foundations.

He derides today's common mantra that the goal of morality is the 'preservation and advancement' of humankind. But it is seldom specified what exactly must be preserved and to what end we are advancing (106). The host of cliché responses (longest possible existence; de-animalization of humankind; highest degree of rationality; or highest happiness (average-happiness of all?)) are either unclear or inconsistent with each other; and they do not teach us what our duty is that is not already 'tacitly and thoughtlessly, regarded in advance as fixed' (106). If the goal is average-happiness, why should morality be the means, since, as history reveals, morality 'opened up such an abundance of sources of displeasure [*Unlust-Quellen*]' (106)? If the goal is individual happiness (*Glück*), Nietzsche reminds us that moral prescriptions have always been 'directed against individuals' (108). Presupposing that evolution has the 'unconscious' goal of promoting 'highest happiness' is only an old moralizing mischief (108). Nietzsche argues that 'from fear' we adopt evaluations and pretend that it is our own and habituate ourselves to this pretence (104). But at a time when traditions and customs have long receded, what sort of fear is this?

We no longer live in continual fear of wild animals, barbarians and gods (5); the Christian fear for our eternal salvation is also lost on us (57); for the intellectual middle class today, what remain of Christianity are not 'God, freedom and immortality', but a lukewarm 'benevolence and decency of disposition' (92). Our 'pride' (arguably a Christian inheritance), 'which resists the theory of descent from the animals and establishes the great gulf between man and nature' is rooted in a 'prejudice', which is the opposite of the prejudice of prehistoric times which assumed that 'spirit' existed everywhere in nature and therefore was not exclusively human (31). Despite these transformations, contemporary humans are still vulnerable to past evaluations, which produce metaphysical exaltations. For instance, our pride also prefers to 'suffer for the sake of morality', and resists being 'told that this kind of suffering is founded on an *error*', thus obstructing a new understanding of morality (32). We surrender to the oldest mode of evaluation here: valuing the gratification of the feeling of power more than knowledge. It is preferable to subscribe to errors, voluntarily suffer, affirm a 'profounder world of truth' and thereby feel exalted above reality, than not suffer and affirm this-worldly truth (32; also see 18, 215, 425). Nietzsche observes that feelings are the conduits of past judgements and evaluations (35); and especially since the feeling of fear was constantly stimulated throughout history, the feeling of power has evolved to a great degree of subtlety, becoming our 'strongest propensity' (23). Habitually yielding to this feeling and the opportunities for its gratification, we unconsciously subscribe to the many perversities of the intellect, inherited from our Christian and pre-Christian past, which have the overall effect of condemning earthly reality, while endorsing otherworldly projections (33, 99).

However, intellectual errors and metaphysical exaltations do not contribute to a coherent ethos of meaning and practices today, which may justify individual existence, or promote individual happiness. Our *'drive to knowledge* has become too strong for us to be able to want … the happiness of a strong, firmly rooted delusion' (429). These exaltations only provide fleeting solaces, outside of which contemporary individuals take very little 'pleasure' (*Freude*) in themselves and their everyday lives (174), similar to the Christian who suffered restlessness and self-loathing when her intoxicating 'visions' subsided (50, 52). The sign of the defectiveness of moral foundations is that adhering to moral precepts generally leads to world-weariness, individual misery, discontent with one's neighbour, mutual persecution and suspicion without greater redemption (425). Hence Nietzsche, appealing to our distinguishing stronger knowledge drive, calls for suspicion regarding *'all higher feelings'* (33).

Failing to take this critical stance, the modern self seeks to unburden its self in 'sympathetic, disinterested, generally useful social actions' (132).[12] In this context, Nietzsche attacks the overestimation of pity (132–9), the current commercial society – in which one 'understands how to appraise everything without having made it, and to appraise it *according to the needs of the consumer*, not according to his own needs' (175) – and the work ethos of 'hard industriousness', which keeps everyone in bounds, expending a wealth of nervous energy, hindering 'the development of reason, covetousness and the desire for independence' (173).[13] What is attempted in these trends is the 'weakening and the abolition of the *individual*' (132). But also, what is sought is universal 'security' (*Sicherheit*), which apparently busy work (through easy, regular satisfactions), other-oriented culture of commerce and political revolutions are supposed to guarantee (173–5, 179). Nietzsche exposes the underlying phenomenon as the oldest fear: the 'fear of everything individual [*Furcht vor allem Individuellen*]' (173). It inspires a 'tyranny of timidity [*Furchtsamkeit*], [which] prescribes to [modern humans] their supreme moral law', as they 'allow themselves to be ordered to look away from themselves but to have lynx-eyes for all the distress and suffering that exists elsewhere!' (174). This fear ultimately drives the modern individual to thoughtlessly adopt past evaluations, which only contributes to a more desperate attempt to renounce the self, which then reinforces the dependence on the past, and so on.

But because the attempt to relinquish the self is never entirely successful, it does not unburden the self from anxieties. Instead, we achieve the neglect of the 'nearest things' – 'the everyday, hourly, pitiableness of our environment which we constantly overlook, the thousand tendrils of this or that little, fainthearted sensation which grows out of our neighborhood, out of our job, our social life, out of the way we divide up the day' – allowing things foreign to our nature and detrimental to our individual needs ('little plants', 'weeds', and 'grass') to creep upon us (435). This results in further self-discontentment, while simultaneously diminishing any possibility of true exceptionality or greatness (435).

One is, instead, better off critically confronting the impoverishment of morality rather than concealing it. Imposing moral demands upon humankind is 'irrational and trivial' since 'for the present there exists no [universally recognized] goal', which can propose the right course of action (108). Historical knowledge, therefore, is key to Nietzsche's attempt to arrest the ongoing trend of self-renunciation and to revive the self anew. The decline of morality in modernity implies the relative inner *freedom* of the self to shape itself, which must therefore be affirmed and cultivated. The individual is free to affirm her right to folly, and to pose '*individual* questions as to How? and To what end?', which morality hitherto has banished from thought (107). From the perspective of this freedom, the contemporary fear of the individual is irrational since, unlike in prehistoric times, it betrays an absence of morality rather than its genuine presence.

IV Epicurean triumph

Epicureanism represents, for Nietzsche, a different path to individuation. The individual is neither opposed nor regulated through communal mores. Individuation is also not assumed but is earned through a lifelong practice of virtues – especially, self-sufficiency, magnanimity, honesty, courage and gratitude and, above all, *phronēsis* (practical wisdom or prudence) – with 'nature' as guide. Nietzsche's text creatively transforms and develops these virtues in the modern context, as it undertakes the two intertwined projects of resisting the squandering of the self (overcoming fear and false securities) and cultivating it anew. Nietzsche, like Epicurus, views the pursuit of knowledge itself as ennobling, and therefore as key to both of these projects.

A. *Epicurean phronēsis; Nietzsche's experiment*

Epicurus taught that the world is a product of chance combinations of rapidly moving atoms, without an inherent or overarching purpose, especially in alignment with human utility (LH 40–5);[14] that the gods do not interfere with the terrestrial or the celestial world, during life or after death (LH 76–80); that the soul, composed of atoms like all corporeal bodies, is mortal (LH 63–8); and so we should not fear death since it means nothing to us (LM 124–5). Human existence is no exception to nature's laws. Nature does not reward or punish human efforts nor is it an intentional or 'spiritual' force, with 'evil' qualities, which disrupted communal life (an assumption which in prehistoric eras prompted metaphysical speculations and modifications to prevailing customs) (13, 17, 33). Nietzsche would find the Epicurean affirmation of chance a necessary corrective to the moral interpretation of nature, which 'robbed of its innocence the whole purely chance character of events' (13).

Equally, nature is not a realm of pure mechanical determinism in relation to which the human being is a passive 'disinterested' observer. No great chasm exists between humans and nature. For Epicurus, as we shall discuss below, nature not only sanctions the starting point and the goal of the good life but also facilitates the means to live it (natural goods are easy to obtain, bodily pain and natural desires have limits, etc.). Still, natural limits are not static or fixed, which ultimately leaves space for and necessitates the cultivation of an active subjectivity, a project of freedom and individuation, corresponding to the lifelong task of maintaining the Epicurean good life. *Phronēsis*, which Epicurus interprets as the 'source of all other virtues' (LM 132), is indispensable for this purpose, insofar as it is attuned to this nature–human nexus.

I argue that the equivalent of Epicurean *phronēsis* in *Daybreak* is Nietzsche's 'experimentalism'.[15] As beings living prelude or postlude lives, Nietzsche encourages us to found little *'experimental states [Versuchsstaaten]'*: 'We are experiments: let us also want to be them' (453). Being an experiment primarily means affirming and nurturing the freedom that one is, which is particularly critical in our transitional era. This entails *not* treating one's subjectivity as if it is a *'full-developed fact[ ]'* (560). Accordingly, Nietzsche advises against pious and blind identification with even the new virtues to avoid reverting to the myth of the immutability of character. He writes: 'What is a thinker worth if he does not know how to escape from his own virtues occasionally! For he ought not to be "only a moral being"' (510). Such an attitude is necessary for maintaining the self's freedom from morality, which grounds the pursuit of the virtues in the first place. In a passage that contrasts strikingly with the one on the creeping 'little plants' and 'weeds' (435), Nietzsche invokes the Epicurean metaphor of the 'gardener':

> One can dispose of one's drives like a gardener, and though few know it, cultivate the shoots of anger, pity, curiosity, vanity as productively and profitably as a beautiful fruit tree on a trellis ... one can also let nature rule and only attend to a little embellishment and tidying-up here and there ... one can ... let the plants grow up and fight their fight out among themselves – indeed, one can take delight [*Freude*] in such a wilderness. ... All this we are at liberty to do. (560)

Experimentalism, therefore, is a fundamental virtue that regulates the practice of the other virtues. It involves 'reasoning out' when to employ what virtues, to what extent and the possibility of integrating the virtues together in shaping one's self. Hence the significance of Nietzsche's declaration: 'We may experiment with ourselves' (501).

Since Epicurean *phronēsis*/Nietzschean experimentalism are manifest in the active exercise of the other virtues, we further comment upon their importance, along with the respective interpretations of nature, as we conduct a comparative study of these other virtues in the following. We begin with Epicurean self-sufficiency (*autarkeia*), a central value of the good life, particularly because of the decisive role *phronēsis* plays in its attainment.

B. *Epicurean self-sufficiency; Nietzschean solitude*

In both thinkers, these virtues represent a practice of inwardness, where the self gathers itself from its anxiety and dispersion, surveys and understands its essential needs, and lives a simple life in fulfilling those needs.

For Epicurus, knowledge primarily serves an ethical end. The scientific knowledge of nature entails self-knowledge, indispensable for resisting and dispelling irrational fears – pertaining to the significance of death, post-mortem punishment, divine agency and nature's capriciousness – that disturb the soul, preventing it from embarking on the pursuit of tranquillity (*ataraxia*) (LH 81–3, PD XI-XIII). Dispelling fear of death especially entails the experience of a unique pleasure inherent to being alive, which is not artificially generated by 'unnatural' desires (LM 124–5, 128–31). The removal of pain in itself results in pleasure (LM 132, PD III), which corresponds to the consciousness of being alive in the present moment.[16] Pleasure is 'our first innate good', and it has a 'nature congenial to [us]' (LM 129). It signifies freedom from fear and pain, and the affirmation of existence without the aid of otherworldly constructs.

An Epicurean dictum links the study of nature to self-sufficiency and pride: 'Natural philosophy does not create boastful men nor chatterboxes nor men who show off "culture" which the many quarrel over, but rather strong and self-sufficient men, who pride themselves on their own personal goods, not those of external circumstances' (VC 45). PD XI attests that the study of nature, in addition to physics and cosmology, includes knowing the limits of pain and desire, and this knowledge is essential to practise self-sufficiency. Maintaining the inherent pleasure of being alive by keeping the body and the soul free from pain and agitation is itself the goal (*telos*) of life (the life of tranquillity) (LM 128–9, 131–3). To do this, one must know the limits of pain and the division and limits of desire. And nature is a guide here.[17] Satisfying 'natural' and 'necessary' desires (for food, water, etc.) ensures freedom from bodily discomfort and the maintenance of life (LM 127), while one should only moderately indulge in 'natural' and 'unnecessary' desires (for sex, finer foods), and avoid the 'unnatural' and 'unnecessary' desires (for money, power, fame), which are generated due to society's 'groundless opinions' (PD XXIX, XXX).

Since simple and inexpensive foods are sufficient to satisfy the necessary desires, Epicurus rejoices that 'everything natural is easy to obtain' (LM 130).[18] The corresponding pain due to unquenched necessary desires is, therefore, limited and easily overcome (PD IV, LM 133). Since removal of this pain yields the quantitative limits of bodily pleasure (PD III, XVIII), there is no need for extravagant pleasures. Epicurus' crucial insight is that in the ethical sphere, everything natural has limits (PD XV).[19] The natural way of life is easily secured, while 'whatever is groundless is hard to obtain' (LM 130). Nature itself facilitates a self-sufficient life. Pursuing pleasures, particularly those corresponding to unnatural desires – since they lack limits – might lead to frustration and addiction, which beget more pain and discontent, making tranquillity impossible. One succumbs to the fear of death, as the belief in the possibility of an indefinite amount of pleasure legitimizes the idea that the soul has infinite time left, thereby endorsing the fear of interminable punishment after death.[20]

Self-sufficiency is secured through habituation: one gets used to simple, not extravagant ways of life, which are easily obtained, and finds enjoyment in it (LM 130–1). Epicurus observes that one must also develop 'prudence' (*phronēsis*) and 'sober calculation', to 'search[ ] out the reasons for every choice and avoidance and drive[ ] out the opinions which are the source of the greatest turmoil' (LM 132), keeping in view the 'goal of nature' (PD XXV). Hence, prudence is the source of all the other virtues, themselves 'natural adjuncts of the pleasant life' (LM 132). As Stephen Rosenbaum has written, 'As the faculty which uncovers the means to good living, [Epicurean] *phronēsis* distinguishes between the desires which are good for people to have and which conduce to living well and those desires which are not good for people to have and which detract from living well' (1996: 402). The specific criterion it relies on is: 'The desires which do not bring a feeling of pain when not fulfilled are unnecessary' (PD XVI). However, this leaves room for interpretation regarding the limit to which natural and unnecessary desires in particular could be satisfied without compromising tranquillity. Epicurus' qualifications only confirm this impression. PD XVI reads further: 'But the desire for them is easy to dispel when they seem to be hard to achieve or produce harm', which makes many merely natural desires, *if* they can be easily dispensed with, compatible with the tranquil life along with the necessary desires. And if it is true, as some scholars argue,[21] that variations in pleasure introduced by satisfying easily dispensable merely natural desires are ultimately essential components of the Epicurean good life – because they keep things like boredom at bay, which might otherwise compromise this life – one might conclude that the limits of those desires that could be considered 'necessary' for the good life are not objectively fixed. Further, PD XXX claims that when 'an intense effort' is required to satisfy natural and unnecessary desires and they fail to be dissolved, it is 'not because of their own nature but because of the groundless opinions of mankind'. Merely natural desires *can become* unnatural due to superimposed groundless opinions.[22] Thus, prudence has a crucial role to play in 'reasoning out' these various limits by keeping in view the 'goal of nature'.[23]

Finally, an essential aspect of practising this self-sufficient, contemplative life is withdrawal from the 'the prison of general education and politics' (VC 58).[24] For Epicurus, 'security' from fellow humans is not gained through fame or power (PD VII) or through the political process, but through a 'quiet life' (PD XIV) (or 'quiet solitude' in Strodach's translation (1963)), retreating from the multitude into the 'Garden', where one could live the philosophical life surrounded by a hospitable community of friends.

Nietzsche, too, endorses solitude (*Einsamkeit*) and modest living shielded from the public gaze, often using Epicurean metaphors and concepts, and associates this life with that of the thinker. Solitude is Nietzsche's existential cure to combat the contemporary culture of self-renunciation triggered by the fear of everything individual. Nietzsche ridicules the marketplace of opinions, which our political and economic spheres embody, that torments one's ambition, and makes solitude difficult through constant distraction (177, 179). He laments the squandering of 'gifted spirits' (179), and the loss of all genuine productivity (177), given the lack of sufficient time or energy for 'reflection, brooding, dreaming, worrying, loving, hating' (173). Like Epicurus, Nietzsche calls for distance from the politico-economic sphere in order to preserve the individual (179). Embracing solitude resists the self-alienating and normalizing mechanisms, which our work and commercial culture represent (491). Solitude also helps one to recuperate from public clamour and judgement, which might otherwise make one fear the other (see PD VI) and become embittered towards life (323, 491). The primary task, therefore, is not to ensure 'common security', but to turn inwards and feel secure within oneself. Nietzsche relates solitude to courage (249), which fearlessly affirms the freedom of the individual from the disciplinary mechanisms of social mores. But solitude can also be restorative, not only corrective:

> One should take care not to live in an environment in which one can neither preserve a dignified silence nor communicate what is of most moment to us. ... In this condition one grows dissatisfied with oneself and one's environment. ... One ought to live where one *is ashamed* to speak of oneself and does not need to. (364)

Solitude fulfils this requirement. In it, one attends to one's inner needs by choosing and managing those 'nearest things', 'what is around us and in us', which 'display[s] colors and beauties and enigmas and riches of significance of which earlier mankind had not an inkling' (44), and so which hold the key to self-flourishing.[25] For Nietzsche, solitude is necessary to the life of the thinker pursuing knowledge, as it allows the latter to leap into her element and gain 'cheerfulness' (*Heiterkeit*) (440). In clearly Epicurean terms, Nietzsche describes the thinker's life of simplicity and self-sufficiency:

> The cheapest and most inoffensive way of living is that of the thinker ... [who is] easily pleased and has no expensive pleasures; his days and nights are not spoiled by pangs of conscience; he moves about, eats, drinks and sleeps in proportion as his mind grows even calmer, stronger and brighter; he rejoices in his body and has no reason to be afraid of it; he has no need of company, except now and then so as afterwards to embrace his solitude the more tenderly. (566; also see 553, 482)

By dwelling in solitude the thinker's thoughts slowly mature and come to fruition (552), perhaps intimating a new evaluation of things (534).

C. *Magnanimity and anonymity*

In solitude the self is replenished, ready again for a more genuine encounter with the other. Nietzsche writes: 'To let some of one's property go, to relinquish one's right – gives pleasure when it indicates great wealth. Magnanimity [*Grossmuth*] belongs here' (315). It is important that one *is* ready to bestow, that one is secure with oneself and has gained self-mastery, that one is 'first benevolently and beneficently inclined *towards* [*oneself*]', not fearfully fleeing from oneself using the other as pretext (516). Only then one enjoys 'an even higher festival' of giving away 'one's spiritual house and possessions' to somebody in distress, and '*make light*' of their troubled soul (449; also see 471).

Generosity towards the other necessarily presupposes an 'egoistic' concern with one's own self. Nietzsche's argument is consonant with the Epicurean view expressed in VC 44: 'When a wise man is brought face to face with the necessities of life, he knows how to give rather than receive – such a treasure of self-sufficiency has he found.' Arguably, such magnanimity, compatible with self-interest and an outgrowth of self-sufficiency, informs the Epicurean attitude towards friends (VC 39) and neighbours (or society in general, see VC 67).[26]

Nietzsche certainly invokes magnanimity to show how 'helping others' and 'neighborly love' are still possible, despite his attack on the Christian approach to these concepts. Frequent pitying increases overall misery (134), as one ends up suffering from one's own 'ego' (137); moreover, being pitied 'divests one of all virtue' (138). Eager compassion for the neighbour's suffering also betrays a profound suspicion of their joy (80). Loving the neighbour when one suffers from oneself makes the neighbour suffer the ill effect of one's self-suffering (516). For Nietzsche, in co-suffering or Christian self-sacrifice one is still secretly enjoying one's own ego in multifarious ways (133). Instead of denying it, affirming its inevitability might lead to a healthier relation to the other. Nietzsche wonders by invoking Epicurean metaphors

> whether one is of *more use* to another by immediately leaping to his side and *helping* him … or [alternatively] by *creating* something out of oneself that the other can behold with pleasure: a beautiful, restful, self-enclosed garden perhaps, with high walls against storms and the dust of the roadway but also a hospitable gate. (174)

A 'garden' offers the other a recuperating, contemplative space, cordoned away from the marketplace of opinions, where one could heal from one's suffering and replenish. It represents a 'gentle, reflective, relaxed friendliness' (471). Such offering transcends pity and expects from the other what one expects from oneself: pride in sacrificing oneself for a greater purpose if needed, but also conscious regard for one's innermost needs (146, 133). Such an attitude, Nietzsche argues, is more suitable for the pursuer of knowledge, and it will raise 'the general feeling of human *power*', which would be 'a positive enhancement of *happiness*' (146).

Furthermore, Nietzsche stresses the importance of anonymity when the giver bestows upon the other. The giver is not looking for fame or gratitude: 'What he seeks is to live nameless and lightly mocked at, too humble to awaken envy or hostility … a poor doctor of the spirit aiding those whose head is *confused with opinions* without their being really aware who has aided them!' (449). Fame and gratitude lack 'respect for solitude and silence' – suggesting there is no question now of abandoning the 'selfishness and self-enjoyment', which solitude makes possible, in order to become one with the masses (449). Also, those who are 'serious in their passion for knowledge and for honesty' have no time or desire for fame (482), since the latter distracts from the former qualities. Simultaneously, to receive gifts from someone with 'no name, like nature', is also delightful for the receiver (464; also see 470). Anonymity honours the solitude of the receiver (464), without spoiling their virtues (466).

The experimental attitude is crucial for the thinker to gain the appropriate distance from solitude and magnanimity, and therefore to strike the right balance between these virtues and anonymity. Over-identification with one's solitariness might make one 'damp and gloomy' (382). And to find relief from it, one must give away one's 'spiritual possessions'. But the thinker has to 'reason it out', when she is 'rich' enough to do this so that giving is, indeed, pleasurable; hence, the thinker is also the 'gardener', not just the 'soil of the plants that grow' in her (382). However, through anonymity the thinker maintains the capacity for solitude, gaining the proper distance from her function as a giver, while upholding her passion for knowledge, honesty and inner freedom.

D. *Honesty*

The key to Nietzsche's goal of the 'purification of the higher feelings' of humankind (33) is to cultivate the passion for knowledge:

> Knowledge has in us been transformed into a passion which shrinks at no sacrifice and at bottom fears nothing but its own extinction; we believe in all honesty that all mankind must believe itself more exalted and comforted under the compulsion and suffering of *this* passion than it did formerly. ... Perhaps mankind will even perish of this passion for knowledge. (429)

History bequeaths to us this passion, given that the very fear that paralysed human intellect in history, also, over time, promotes knowledge and the development of the intellect (309, 142).[27] With the decline of Christianity and the birth of the modern sciences – 'physiology, medicine and sociology', but also 'solitude' (*Einsamkeitslehre*) (453), and especially, history – knowledge becomes critically important to scrutinize feelings, and help gather and secure the self from its otherwise fear-ridden, irrational scattering. So similar to Epicurus, Nietzsche interprets knowledge as having ethical, 'therapeutic' implications. The primary object of knowledge is the self itself, the effect of which is to affirm the self's freedom from morality.

Therefore, going beyond a mere conserving function, for Nietzsche, the passion for knowledge produces a new 'exaltation' (*Erhebung*) (45, 429) or enhancement in the 'feeling of power' of humankind (146). However, those operations of the intellect, which in earlier times individually produced 'exaltations' and 'happiness' in the thinker – for example, abstraction from experience, invention of a metaphysical world, impersonal style of thinking, dialectics, presentiment, etc. – no longer have the same effect (43). They are the means that the thinker employs today, as befitting her passion for knowledge, to the knowledge of truth, of this-world reality (see 45, 433), although such knowledge leads to no easy consolation (424). In this context, Nietzsche claims honesty (*Redlichkeit*) as the novel virtue of his age, neither Socratic nor Christian, still in the 'process of becoming', which resists easy gratifications of our desire for happiness (456).

Honesty implies that exaltation cannot be superimposed upon knowledge but is inherent to the pursuit of knowledge. In arguing for this, Nietzsche associates the Epicurean terms 'pleasure' and 'happiness' with exaltation (429). In section 433, Nietzsche wonders whether our 'happiness' does not lie in the '*knowledge of reality*' itself. Elsewhere, he suggests that the future seeker of truth has real 'pleasure' in scientific study (424). The passion for knowledge elevates and rejuvenates us, and the pleasure or happiness knowing engenders keeps us affirmatively oriented towards life: happiness 'enhances the beauty of the world and makes all that exists sunnier; knowledge casts its beauty not only over things but in the long run into things' (550). The knowledge–pleasure–elevation nexus may also be discerned in the Epicurean experience of tranquillity.[28] Scientific knowledge of the genesis and the disintegration of worlds, which brings pleasure by overcoming the fear of death, also compels us to recognize our relative insignificance in the cosmos. Although humbling, Pierre Hadot argues, such recognition elevates Epicureans above mundane anxieties to a 'cosmic consciousness', which serenely contemplates the infinity of space and time.[29]

Epicurean philosophy upholds honesty ('frankness' or *parresia*) in the study of nature, without trying to pacify anyone's feelings. VC 29 reads: 'Employing frankness in my study of natural philosophy, I would prefer to proclaim in oracular fashion what is beneficial to men, even if no one is going to understand, rather than assent to [common] opinions and so enjoy the constant praise that comes from the many.' One commentator views Epicurean honesty as 'enjoined by Nature', as anti-Platonic and apolitical in its opposition to rhetoric, dialectic and sycophancy in politics, but also to 'smugness and hypocrisy in private life', while promoting 'unreserved self-revelation' (DeWitt 1954: 303).

However, for Nietzsche, honesty must be tempered and creatively nurtured so that new modes of living and evaluating (new future ideals) may be sustained, although there is no guarantee of success. His experimentalism is particularly evident in his innovative attitude towards truth. He warns against the 'tyranny of the true', and recommends finding '*relief* from time to time in untruth', so that truth – especially this-worldly truth – does not become 'boring, powerless and tasteless to us' (507). Compare this attitude to the Epicurean one that recommends satisfying certain natural and unnecessary desires as integral to living well, as it helps avoid things like boredom. Paradoxically, for Nietzsche, periodic immersion in untruth is key to maintaining the passion for truth. Truth should be made congruent with power: 'In itself truth is no power at all – whatever its flatterers of the Enlightenment may be accustomed to say to the contrary! – It has, rather, to draw power over to its side, or go over to the side of power, or it will perish again and again!' (535). This approach is consistent with Nietzsche's recommendation to 'act humanely' with one's sense of honesty, and – consonant with one's solitude and inner freedom (and others', too) – not to impose one's belief onto the whole world (536).

E. *Courage*

A closely related and important virtue is courage (*Muth*), particularly given the Epicurean-inspired critique of fear throughout *Daybreak*. In a section called 'Mortal Souls', Nietzsche claims that the abandonment of the belief in immortality is greatly conducive to the promotion of knowledge (501). Formerly, since the salvation of the eternal soul depended on knowledge acquired in a finite life, knowledge possessed frightful importance. But now, 'we have re-conquered our courage for error, for experimentation, for accepting provisionally', and we need not timidly gulp down half-baked ideas (501; also see 551). Part of the experimental attitude is to realize that there are 'no scientific methods which alone lead to knowledge'; instead, we must 'tackle things experimentally, now angry with them and now kind, and be successfully just, passionate and cold with them' (432). Sympathy, force, reverence for secrets, indiscretion and roguishness are possible attitudes the experimenter adopts to attain knowledge of the world, self and morality (432). Courage, therefore, complements honesty.

In WS 7, Nietzsche celebrates Epicurus for realizing that 'it is absolutely not necessary to have solved the ultimate and outermost theoretical questions' in order to console the heart; he credits Epicurus for proposing a '*multiplicity* of hypotheses' to explain the same phenomenon (ethical or scientific), and thus to lift fear and gloom from the soul.[30] Assuming that entertaining multiple hypotheses involves accepting things provisionally and/or adopting several methodological strategies, we conclude that for Nietzsche, Epicurean thought also represented an experimental courage for knowledge.[31]

F. *Gratitude*

Since the world is a product of chance, death imminent and each instant of existence a unique pleasurable occasion, Epicureanism embodies a profound gratitude for the gift of life.[32] Because nature itself facilitates the self-sufficient, good life, we read Epicurus expressing gratitude, in a surviving fragment, to 'blessed nature'.[33]

Nietzsche writes in an aphorism, which celebrates many virtues together, that he seeks the company of those who 'expect little from life, and would rather take this as a gift than as something they have earned' (482). Nietzschean gratitude may also be traced back to his affirmation of chance (see 122–3, 130); it opposes and releases one from the embitterment and discontent towards life, which morality generally breeds. Gratitude to nature is discernible when Nietzsche claims that unlike in previous ages, today's knower finds the 'knowledge of even the ugliest reality [ ] itself beautiful', and therefore finds delight (*Entzücken*) in it (550; also see 427). The knower need not renounce reality or artificially embellish it with errors to be exalted by it (550). But simultaneously, Nietzsche emphasizes the inevitability of error, untruth, approximation and simplification for life (see 117 and 119), for the experience of beauty and pleasure: 'Every thinker paints his world in fewer colors than *are actually there*, and is blind to individual colors', and only then 'he introduces harmonies of colors *into the things themselves*, and these harmonies possess great charm and can constitute an enrichment of nature' (426). The only way to reconcile these two conflicting standpoints is to avoid clinging to a single method or perspective, but, instead, to experimentally multiply them (recruiting the resources of the various sciences), while maintaining gratitude towards life and a rigorous will to knowledge that may lead to genuine exaltation. Nietzsche, like Epicurus, is therefore compelled to reject the uncritical spiritualizing of nature (attributing to it will or purpose), but also a perspective-free objectivity.

Notes

1 Sections 72 and 150.
2 I use R. J. Hollingdale's translations for Cambridge University Press in citing from D and WS, and Walter Kaufmann's translation for Vintage in quoting from GS and EH.

3 See Ansell-Pearson (2010), who holds a similar view about *Daybreak*.
4 During the period 1878–1882, one generally finds in Nietzsche's works an attitude of admiration towards Epicurus and his philosophy. Beyond *Daybreak*, see HH 68; AOM 224, 408; WS 7, 192, 227 and GS 45 and 277. Nietzsche's letters during these years also testify to his appreciation for Epicurus and to his fondness for the Epicurean 'garden'. See KSB 5:799, 5:826 and 5:899. Some important scholarly works that discuss Nietzsche's references to Epicurus in his middle writings include Knight (1933), Bett (2005) and Ansell-Pearson (2013, 2018).
5 Reflecting back on *Daybreak*, Nietzsche writes: 'My task of preparing a moment of the highest self-examination for humanity, *a great noon* when it looks back and far forward, when it ... poses, *as a whole*, the question of Why? And For What?' Further: 'The question concerning the origin of moral values is for me a question of the very first rank because it is crucial for the future of humanity' (EH 'Dawn' 2).
6 Since *Daybreak* is the primary source for this essay, all references are to this text, unless indicated otherwise.
7 Morgan Rempel's (2012) discussion of section 72 is informative about the pre-Christian secret cults (Isis and Mithras), which gained popularity in the Greco-Roman world.
8 Also see HH 68. In his later writings, Nietzsche highlights the decadence of late antiquity, and tends to criticize *both* Epicurus and Christianity as partaking in its corruption – and therefore, ultimately decadent themselves – despite their effort to combat or gain victory over the mystery cults. See BGE 200, A 30 and GS 370. See Shearin (2014: 71–2) for a discussion of the similarities between Epicureanism and Christianity from Nietzsche's perspective. However, in *Daybreak* and the middle writings, Nietzsche emphasizes the positive aspects of the Epicurean intervention in late antiquity: he admires its anti-Christian spirit, and he finds the Epicurean effort to justify earthly existence in a declining epoch instructional for combating the maladies of his own age. For a discussion of Nietzsche's overall ambivalent attitude towards Epicurus, see Shearin (2014) and Knight (1933).
9 See GS 45 and WS 7, where Nietzsche describes Epicurus as the philosopher of the 'afternoon of antiquity', and as the 'soul-soother of later antiquity'.
10 See Howard Jones (1992: ch. 1) for a discussion of the factors accounting for the glory of the Athenian culture of the sixth and fifth centuries BCE, and also of the symptoms of its decline beginning in late-fifth century BCE.
11 On Christianity's conceptual tastelessness and 'heathen' character, see section 70.
12 Nietzsche argues that as one liberated oneself from the Christian belief in 'eternal *personal* salvation', one sought '*justification* for this liberation in a cult of philanthropy', which also has its origin in Christian teachings such as 'love of one's neighbor' (132).
13 Consult Ansell-Pearson (2014a) for more on this line of critique in *Daybreak*.
14 See Lucretius (2001: II.1050–1067, 1090–2); Hadot (1995a: 208–9); and Long (1977: 67).
15 See Bamford (2016) for a recent treatment of Nietzsche's experimentalism.
16 For more, see Hadot (1995a: 69, 87–8, 209, 222–6). Also see, DeWitt (1954: 223, 237–40) and Tsouna (2009: 260).
17 On this issue, see Deleuze (2017), DeWitt (1954) and O'Keefe (forthcoming).
18 Also see, LM 133 and PD XV, XXI.
19 Arguably, the theme of limits is the unifying thread of Epicurean thought, the determination of which is the task common to the different domains of ethics and

natural science. See Deleuze (2017) and De Lacy (1969). Also see, Lucretius (2001: I.75–7, 584–8; V.1430–33; VI.24).
20 See Lucretius (2001: III.47–73, 978–1024) and Deleuze (2017: 250).
21 See Cooper (1998) and Rider (2019).
22 On this point, I am persuaded by Benjamin Rider's interpretation. See section V in Rider (2019) for discussion of these two aphorisms of PD.
23 VC 63 reads: 'There is also a proper measure for parsimony, and he who does not reason it out is just as badly off as he who goes wrong by total neglect of limits.' In addition to highlighting the importance of *phronēsis*, this aphorism offers further support for the interpretations of Cooper and Rider. Also see Phillip De Lacy (1969) who argues for the radical conclusion that Epicurean thought presupposes that limits to desires or pleasures exist without being able to locate precisely where those limits are.
24 Epicurus believes, unlike Aristotle, that it is possible – and even necessary – to cultivate oneself and fulfil one's goal as an ethical subject without active contribution to the *polis*. See Nussbaum (1994). Also see Brown (2009), who qualifies this apolitical position.
25 On the 'nearest things', also see WS 5, 6, 16. Refer to Ansell-Pearson (2013) for a discussion of the attention to 'nearest things' in Nietzsche's middle-period works.
26 See Long (2006) and Rider (2019).
27 Nietzsche's argument is the following: owing to the aura of mystery surrounding the initial formulation of prescriptions in prehistoric communities, there results, over time, constant speculation upon their usages and limits – fear being the catalyst – precisely in order to ascertain their validity. Such speculation provided fertile ground for the growth of not only religions but also prehistoric science; and 'here is where the poet, the thinker, the physician, the lawgiver first grew' (40). The emergence of the exceptional, 'mad' individual – often in the guise of one or more of these figures – presupposes the above development.
28 It must be noted that the later Nietzsche is critical of Epicurean *ataraxia*, often depicting it as a nihilistic doctrine, similar to Christianity, signifying a fear of pain and strife, and hence, a longing for rest, inactivity and absence of suffering. See BGE 200, GM III: 17 and A 30. However, also see Joseph Vincenzo (1994), who argues for a similarity between the Epicurean experience of tranquillity and the joy of Dionysian world-affirmation implied by the Nietzschean conceptions of *amor fati* and eternal return.
29 See Hadot (1995a: 59, 243–4, 266).
30 Epicurus's Letter to Pythocles provides several examples of multiple explanations of cosmological phenomena.
31 Arguably, the Epicurean 'multiple hypothesis' approach is the inspiration for Nietzsche's later 'perspectivism'. See Shearin (2014: 73–6) for more on this connection.
32 See Hadot (1995a: 87–8, 224–6) on the importance of gratitude in Epicureanism. Also see, Rider (2019) for a detailed exposition of gratitude as a vital Epicurean virtue.
33 See Inwood and Gerson (trans.) (1997: 99). As Hadot puts it, the Epicureans are grateful towards the 'miraculous coincidence between the needs of living beings and the facilities provided for them by nature' (1995a: 225).

11

Enjoying riddles

Epicurus as a forerunner of the idea of gay science*?

Patrick Wotling

I How are we to gain an insight into what 'Epicurean' means in Nietzsche's writings?

Quite a few Epicuruses are to be found in the modern philosophical tradition. As a matter of fact, the Greek thinker seems to have been one of the favourite interlocutors of many different trends. These, in return, have shaped varied images of his thinking. Epicurus plays an important part in Hume's reflection, for instance.[1] But Hume's Epicurus is not exactly that of Marx.[2] As is well known, references to the Greek atomist also pervade Gassendi's thought, and Bayle focuses on him in his *Dictionnaire historique et critique*. La Mettrie's is, in turn, quite a different character.[3] Hegel provides another, renewed, interpretation. However, all of these thinkers are interested in the Greek philosopher primarily in that he stands as the advocate of pleasure, and therefore as a firm and reckless opponent of asceticism, first of all of Platonic thought, but as a consequence, he can also yield an efficient weapon to fight (or to cure) Christian beliefs and values. Secondly, although this is not systematically the case, he is interpreted as an advocate of atomism.

At first sight, to come across an interest for Epicurus in Nietzsche's writings may not seem to make him much different from his colleagues. Nietzsche might just be seen as bringing this already long tradition a few steps further. His Epicurus, however, might well provide a very original version of the philosopher – moreover, one of its most entangled and complicated iterations. After a long period during which Nietzsche's analysis of Epicurus was generally overlooked on the grounds that the only Greeks who captured Nietzsche's attention were those of the tragic age – in particular the pre-Platonic philosophers – a good deal of illuminating scholarship has been carried out for some decades now that investigates Nietzsche's strange, perhaps even groundbreaking version of the Greek philosopher.[4] In this respect, one of the most

---

* My warmest thanks to Martine Béland for rereading this chapter, with her usual kindness and competence.

persistent conclusions from this scholarship emphasizes that two different and even incompatible appreciations of Epicurus seem to live side by side within Nietzsche's corpus. On the one hand, there is a well-known critical attitude that severely discards his praise of pleasure, which is interpreted as amounting to nothing more than sheer fear (or hatred) of pain[5]: this is Epicurus as 'a typical decadent', 'first recognised as such by me', as Nietzsche has it in A 30. On the other hand, one finds in Nietzsche a most enthusiastic approach to Epicurus, more typical of the works from the turn of the 1870s (namely HH, D and GS), that celebrates the discoverer of a special way of practising philosophy, as both an 'idyllic' and a 'heroic' attitude, which Richard Roos's celebrated paper first analysed: it pertains to Epicurus as one of the very few thinkers 'I will let … judge when I am right and wrong', making him one of those rare and precious minds to whom the *Assorted Opinions and Maxims* pays homage in its closing aphorism (HH 408).

But when it comes to the Ancient Epicurean School, the original and important point to be noted is that we do not just encounter one, or perhaps even two Epicuruses in Nietzsche's writings: we also come across quite a few 'Epicureans'. These, in turn, are motives for perplexity. If the reliability of Nietzsche's image of Epicurus may well be discussed, there at least is no doubt as to whom this name is supposed to refer. But the situation is totally different as regards the second term: Who exactly are these 'Epicureans' whom Nietzsche mentions and – this has to be noticed – enthusiastically praises from time to time? More to the point, why does he call these people 'Epicurean' at all when it is perfectly obvious that they do not belong to the historical Epicurean circle? This happens to be a turning point where things really take on a strange appearance. Throughout the modern philosophical tradition, both in Britain and on the continent, to mention Epicurus or the Epicurean school was intended to bring into discussion some of the distinctive features of Epicurean doctrines. But contrastingly, the characters that Nietzsche describes as 'Epicurean' do not advocate a strictly hedonistic stance, nor do they hold pleasure to be a fundamental principle of all living creatures. They do not claim either that reality as a whole is to be understood in terms of combinations of atoms. As a matter of fact, they are not even interested in this type of issue pertaining to the principles of physical epistemology. Why then are they called Epicureans? An accurate rereading of the texts might suggest that Nietzsche makes a very specific use of this term, namely a displaced, consequently figurative, metaphorical use. This process is even known to be one of the basic traits of Nietzsche's philosophical writing technique or, as he sometimes calls it, of 'our new language'.[6]

If we are to understand who these mysterious characters really are, it is of the utmost importance to begin by asking what exactly the meaning of the *word* 'Epicurean' in Nietzsche's new language is. This is exactly the type of question that a careful reader is regularly compelled to raise when confronted with a collection of other, sometimes funny but always puzzling, Nietzschean designations. This is notably the case with the adjective 'English' (*englisch*), which certainly does not strictly refer, in Nietzsche's way of writing, to nationality – and not just because he often mistakes 'English' for 'British', as has long been stressed, but, more radically, because in the most determined way he classifies a German thinker like Paul Rée among the 'English psychologists'.[7] This intentional mistake suggests that when making such a claim, Nietzsche aims at conveying a specific meaning that he attaches to the word 'English'. In other words, it is his purpose to single out a feature or a group of features that he holds to be typically exemplified in the kind of philosophizing that he encounters in a collection of celebrated contemporary or almost contemporary thinkers: Bentham, Mill, Spencer or Darwin – a group to which his fellow countryman Rée also belongs, as far as philosophical methodology is concerned. What is characteristic of these philosophers is that they emphasize habit, instinct and non-rational processes in the genesis of the so-called moral phenomena.[8] The same goes for the meaning of 'Chinese', which, for similar reasons, cannot be taken to denote a particular nationality. It is well known that according to Nietzsche's texts, Kant ranks among Chinese people, whereby the author of *Beyond Good and Evil* mainly seems to be suggesting a hidden attraction to complication, and in this particular case, to useless unconvincing complication.[9]

Let us suppose, as must be the case, that Nietzsche makes exactly the same kind of unorthodox, offbeat and puzzling use of the adjective 'Epicurean'. What then is the meaning of this designation when he uses it in contexts where it is obviously not referring to historical Epicureanism? This is the mystery to be solved if we are to discover who on earth these 'Epicureans' may be, they who have nothing to do with void and atoms as epistemological principles, and who do not advocate pleasure as the sole rule of living beings. In other words, what does Nietzsche intend to refer to? What features does he have in mind when he calls someone an Epicurean? And more importantly, what does he thereby insist on making clear to his reader? To address these questions, in other words to decipher the meaning of this term, it may first be helpful to have a closer look at the contexts in which Nietzsche introduces the characterization of his Epicurus. We can then move on to an analysis of the passages that refer to 'Epicureans'.

As a matter of fact, it is always a relatively limited collection of characteristic features that is involved in the passages dealing with Epicurus. The first one concerns his hypersensibility, even his hyper-excitability, as opposed, in particular, to 'insensitivity' in accordance with the Stoics' basic search for *apatheia*. The Epicurean stance thus implies, in Nietzsche's view, a certain form of delicacy, which may give rise to both weakness and fragility, or to fineness of appraisal. A series of texts stress this general feature, in particular a few posthumous ones (for instance, KSA 8:38[1] and KSA 9:10[B22], as well as section GS 306).

Secondly, Epicurus' way of thinking is often paralleled with (genuine) science: 'The awakening sciences have allied themselves point by point with the philosophy of Epicurus but point by point rejected Christianity', as is observed in the first volume of *Human, All Too Human* (68).[10]

Independence is another distinctive trait of Epicurean reflection – and one must not overlook the fact that independence is considered by Nietzsche to be the main requirement (or virtue, to put it another way) of the genuine philosopher. This point is underlined again in *Human, All Too Human*[11]. Besides, detachment, which may be considered relatively close to independence, is seen as another feature typical of the Epicurean attitude – both as wise men and as gods themselves are concerned. The detachment praised in this way is, of course, strongly evocative of *ataraxia*, and it is in a way embodied in the habit of soberness, which is mentioned in particular by *The Wanderer and His Shadow*.[12]

Two further features are of great importance, as has been mentioned earlier: a cause for paeans of praise on the one hand, and one for continuous harsh criticism on the other hand. Distancing himself from the earlier, ascetical, Platonic practice, Epicurus is to be acknowledged as the inventor of a renewed understanding of philosophical reflection, of a way of thinking pervaded with courage and fighting spirit, and at the same time with refinement and sensitiveness to the fulfilment that human life can experience in this world. This is precisely the type of attitude – for which we have no proper name – that Nietzsche tries to portray in a famous aphorism of *The Wanderer and His Shadow*, where he suggests describing it as 'heroic-idyllic': 'Individual beings also *lived* in this way, persistently *felt* themselves to be in the world, and the world in them, and among them', he goes on, 'one of the greatest human beings, the inventor of a heroic-idyllic form of philosophizing: Epicurus' (295).[13]

It may seem puzzling, but it is an indisputable fact that, at the same time, this highly praised philosopher is constantly reproached with an untenable, utterly negative conception of pleasure and happiness – pleasure, Nietzsche means, as amounting to nothing more than the avoidance of pain, and therefore implying the condemnation of pain.[14]

What about Nietzsche's 'Epicureans'? Are they friends or disciples of the master of the Athens Garden? Nietzsche's writings doubtless indicate that he does not always use the name of Epicurus as strictly restricted to the Greek philosopher. An aphorism from *The Wanderer and His Shadow* makes this point perfectly clear. Beneath the real, historical Epicurus, there is, indeed, another reality, a general type of man, a type of thinker, a sort of 'eternal Epicurus': '*The eternal Epicurus*. – Epicurus has lived in all ages and still lives on, unknown to those who called and call themselves Epicurean, and without any reputation among the philosophers. He himself forgot his own name, too: it was the heaviest burden that he ever cast off' (227).

II Why are Nietzsche's 'Epicureans' called Epicurean?

When Nietzsche considers this eternal Epicurus, that is the basic type of man characterized by a certain structure of dominant drives, to whom he refers when he uses the adjective 'Epicurean', he does not retain all the traits that he identifies in the historical Epicurus. Some traits are, indeed, privileged, as becomes obvious if we collect the most important passages where this type of man is presented. For instance, who is described as an 'Epicurean' by Nietzsche? One of the most conspicuous cases is that of Stendhal, a character he admires most, as is well known: BGE 254 is a crucial text in that respect. Another example is the set of persons referred to as 'we', particularly in the writings of the late 1880s[15] – this important 'we' which is very present in the period when Nietzsche feels he now is in a condition to further his experimental works and formulate hypothetical conclusions from his former inquiries: that is, from 1885 or 1886 on, particularly in the fifth book of *The Gay Science* and, simultaneously, in *Beyond Good and Evil*.

Although Nietzsche much admires Stendhal, it is not easy to understand what he and the French writer may have in common in his own view. But it is extremely striking that when he praises Stendhal and calls him an 'Epicurean', the aphorisms at the same time stress the importance of enigmas and of a certain attitude towards them: concerning 'Henri Beyle, that remarkable anticipatory and precursory human being' who explored several centuries of the European soul, Nietzsche claims that 'it required two generations to *catch up* with him in any way, to figure out again a few of the riddles that tormented and enchanted him, this odd Epicurean and question mark of a man who was France's last great psychologist' (BGE 254). In other words, a riddle himself, attracted to the fight against riddles. On closer scrutiny, this particular feature happens to be frequently associated with Nietzsche's hints at Epicureanism. This is the case in another very important aphorism, GS 375, one of the texts that bring the puzzling 'we' to the foreground:

> *Why we look like Epicureans* – We are cautious, we modern men, about ultimate convictions. Our mistrust lies in wait for the enchantments and the deceptions of the conscience that are involved in every strong faith, every unconditional Yes and No. How is this to be explained? Perhaps what is to be found here is largely the care of the 'burned child', of the disappointed idealist; but there is also another, superior component: the jubilant curiosity of one who formerly stood in his corner and was driven to despair by his corner, and now delights and luxuriates in the opposite of a corner, in the boundless, in what is 'free as such'. Then an almost Epicurean bent for knowledge develops that will not easily let go of the questionable character of things; also an aversion to big moral words and gestures; a taste that rejects all crude, four-square opposites and is proudly conscious of its practice in having reservations. For this constitutes our pride, this slight tightening of the reins as our urge for certainty races ahead, this self-control of the rider during his wildest rides; for we still ride mad and fiery horses, and when we hesitate it is least of all danger that makes us hesitate.

Confronting these texts sheds light on Nietzsche's analysis. It appears to be his firm contention that there is a link between the love of knowledge, that is the desire to understand, and a mistrust of the absolute – and most particularly, a mistrust of the belief in absolute knowledge. Indeed, his reflection shows that the so-called absolute knowledge, for which philosophers have been craving so intensely, is always based on unnoticed, deeply rooted prejudices – on 'ultimate convictions'.

It should be stressed that Nietzsche concentrates on Epicurus precisely at the time when he embarks on redefining philosophy – freeing it from the prejudices that have always led philosophers so far to betray its radical ambition – and on specifying what a genuine philosopher is. It is interesting that Epicureanism should be promoted just when Nietzsche begins to elaborate the notion of free spirit and to portray this real philosopher as being one, that is a man endowed with the ability to be independent.[16] And it is revealing that, in *Human, All Too Human*, Epicurus should be described first and foremost as an independent spirit:

> The Epicurean likewise employs his higher culture to make himself independent of dominating opinions; only he lifts himself above them, while the Cynic remains

at the stage of negation. It is as though he wanders along still, sheltered, twilight pathways, while above him the tops of the trees whirl about in the wind and betray to him how violently buffeted the world outside is. (HH 275)

How 'knowledge' is to be understood, or rather how its understanding has to be reformed, proves to be one of the leading questions that Nietzsche is concerned with in the years when Epicurus surfaces and is praised in his writings. But another, and more basic, problem is whether philosophy can be defined as the quest for knowledge at all. And this may certainly be the main reason for Nietzsche's trip to Hades to visit the Greek philosopher. For, as we have just mentioned, the understanding of knowledge that has prevailed in philosophy, but that arouses Epicurus's suspicion, now has to be discarded.

As a matter of fact, it must be noticed that one of the features that Nietzsche mentions at the time when he grants renewed attention to Epicurus, and above all one of the very few (if not the only) basic constituents of Epicureanism that he comments upon at some length, is the doctrine of multiple explanations that is exposed in an important passage of the *Letter to Pythocles*. Nietzsche doubtless considers it a decisive landmark of the Epicurean turn of mind. However, the way he himself describes it might reveal something more, namely how he is prone to reinterpret and thus understand Epicurus. The important aphorism from *The Wanderer and His Shadow* referring to the multiple explanations theory should be reread carefully:

> Epicurus, the soother of souls in late antiquity, had the wonderful insight that is so rarely found nowadays, that solving the ultimate theoretical questions is not at all necessary for soothing the disposition. So it was sufficient for him to tell those who were tormented by 'fear of the gods': 'Even if gods do exist, they do not concern themselves with us' – instead of disputing fruitlessly and from afar about the ultimate question of whether the gods exist at all. That position is much more favourable and more powerful: one gives the other person a few steps' advantage and thus makes him more willing to listen and to take it to heart. But as soon as he sets about proving the opposite – that the gods do concern themselves with us – into what labyrinths and thorn bushes the poor fellow must fall, all on his own, without any cunning on the part of his interlocutor, who only has to have enough humanity and refinement to conceal his compassion at this spectacle. Eventually the other person reaches a point of disgust, the strongest argument against any proposition, disgust with his own assertion: he grows cold and goes away in the same frame of mind as the pure atheist; 'what do the gods really matter to me! To the devil with them!' – In other cases, especially if a half-physical, half-moral hypothesis had cast a pall over the person's mind, he did not contradict this hypothesis, but instead conceded that it could well be so: but that there is *still a second* hypothesis for explaining the same phenomenon: something different could perhaps still be the case. A *multiplicity* of hypotheses concerning the origin of pangs of conscience, for example, is still sufficient in our time for removing from the soul the shadow that so easily arises from brooding upon a single, solely visible and thereby hundred times overrated hypothesis. –

Hence anyone who wishes to dispense comfort to those who are unhappy, to wrongdoers, hypochondriacs, or dying, should recall the two calming formulations of Epicurus, which can be applied to a great many questions. In their simplest form, they would go something like this; first, even supposing that this is the case, it matters nothing to us; second, it may be so, but it may also be otherwise. (7)

If we turn to the recommendation Nietzsche seems to allude to, as written by Epicurus, we are, in fact, confronted with a text that sounds a bit different:

[Our aim is] neither to achieve the impossible, even by force, nor to maintain a theory which is in all respects similar either to our discussions on the ways of life or to our clarifications of other questions in physics, such as the thesis that the totality [of things] consists of bodies and intangible nature, and that the elements are atomic, and all such things as are consistent with the phenomena in only one way. This is not the case with meteorological phenomena, but rather these phenomena admit of several different explanations for their coming to be and several different accounts of their existence which are consistent with our sense-perceptions. (LP 86)

To stick to the main point, it is extremely important to see how Nietzsche here, in fact, extends the methodological doctrine to a much broader field. In Epicurus' letter, it was presented as a means to deal with a limited, very specific class of phenomena, namely those relating to meteorology and celestial processes, but ruled out as far as the principles of physics or the outlines of ethics were involved. Without giving any explicit justification, Nietzsche associates the Epicurean philosophical attitude, generally speaking, with the acceptance of multiple explanations. Whatever the possible textual support (or the absence of it all) for such a reading, it is obvious that Nietzsche first and foremost perceives in Epicurus both a cautious and a defiant mind, and therefore something of a genuine philosopher; that is, a thinker who has caught a glimpse of the prejudices that are ordinarily attached to the search for truth. The ineradicable belief in the absoluteness of truth might well have been the basic prejudice of philosophers so far;[17] for Nietzsche, this position is supported by the discovery of the overall interpretive character of reality (and not just of human thought), and the impossibility to walk any step past the '*erroneousness* of the world' (BGE 34). Epicurus is certainly no philosopher of interpretation as Nietzsche is. However, it is the latter's firm conviction that Epicurus is, indeed, defiant about the idea of an attainable absolute truth – and still more about the impact of such an idea, for both epistemological and ethical reasons. First, the belief in the pricelessness of truth means a subtle but unacceptable blindness, in particular concerning the hypothetical status of some of our 'explanations': in other words, it involves overlooking the interpretive status of our 'knowledge'. Secondly, it induces a certain form of fanaticism, and therefore can cause trouble of mind to emerge.

And precisely one of the recurring features that characterize the way that Nietzsche feels about Epicurus at the time he rediscovers him is the absence of any form of fanaticism – which turns out to be so frequent among the rest of philosophers – the taste for measure, and the virtue of moderation.[18] This is also the reason why the Epicurean gods, retaining the important traits of this philosophical position, are described as endowed with 'mocking and aloof eyes' (BGE 62).

What Nietzsche discovers, then, is the fact that it is necessary to radically reconsider the way in which we (including philosophers) ordinarily understand knowledge. Meeting this urgent requirement results in the notion of a 'passion for knowledge', which is the first stage bound to lead to the subsequent, original idea of 'gay science'. At the very core of this notion, which Nietzsche elaborates at the time of *Human, All Too Human* and *Daybreak*, is the regained awareness that the search for knowledge is above all an activity performed by living beings – not by pure spirits – and thus conditioned by the basic regulations of life. Therefore, it is to be reassessed in accordance with this status. And this is precisely the striking point of connection with Epicureanism, as Nietzsche claims several times: 'Philosophy, art of living, *not* art of discovering truth Epicurus' (KSA 13:12[1])[19] or: 'Philosophy as an art of discovering truth: as Aristotle has it. *Quite contrarily*, the Epicureans, who knew to take advantage of Aristotle's sensualist theory of knowledge: quite ironic towards the search for truth and opposing it; "philosophy as an art of *living*"' (KSA 12:9[57]).

Unlike Plato, Epicurus never lost sight of the sensible condition of the philosopher, nor of its consequences. So it may be no accident that Nietzsche's attention should be drawn to the Greek philosopher at the time when he works out his renewed version of knowledge: for Epicurus is seen above all as the only philosopher who succeeded in maintaining a vivid interest for this activity while refraining from the excesses that the quest of knowledge almost always entails. When Nietzsche departs from the dangerous idealistic view that has long prevailed, he commits in *Human, All Too Human* to re-examining the very nature of this activity, and elaborates the notion of 'passion for knowledge' to sum up his conclusions. He thereby tightly binds together the same couple of requirements: 'Our drive to knowledge has become too strong for us to be able to want happiness without knowledge' (D 429),[20] but at the same time, '"must take things more cheerfully than they deserve; especially since we have for a long time taken them more seriously than they deserve' (D 567).

Is Epicurus, then, to be considered as a forerunner of Nietzsche's philosophical revolution? Is he to be regarded as an ancestor of the 'gay science', since this is the final version of Nietzsche's reappraisal?[21] As we suggested, several features might support this view. There certainly is a certain degree of consonance between Epicurus' mistrust of abstract idealistic philosophizing and Nietzsche's claim to put knowledge at the service of the fulfilment of life; as well as between the pursuit of the peace of mind in Epicureanism and the acknowledgement of cheerfulness as the basic effect of life-enhancing philosophy – hence Nietzsche's constant criticism of heavy and clumsy thinking, mistaken for seriousness: '"Where laughter and gaiety are found, thinking does not amount to anything": that is the prejudice of that serious beast against all "gay science"' (GS 327). In this respect, introducing some subtlety and some lightness – which certainly does not mean superficiality – into the understanding of knowledge is one of the main benefits brought about by Epicureanism.

III 'Epicureanism' as an affirmative philosophical drive: The mask as a deity

The rejection of fanaticism results in the refusal to find and grant explanations at any cost, as is the consequence of blind belief in the unquestionable value of truth, and of the related conviction that any explanation is better than none at all. Excessive craving for knowledge exposes one to fall back into superstition under the pressure of the need to find a solution – any solution whatsoever – that would unravel the mysteries one is confronted with. This is why Epicurus' theory of multiple explanations, as mentioned in *The Wanderer and His Shadow*, is so important to Nietzsche: indeed, 'solving the ultimate theoretical questions is not at all necessary for soothing the disposition' (7). It takes more strength, and it is a symptom of greater health, to be able to admit the limitation of the present state of our knowledge rather than to despair. It is better to accept the presence of riddles – better, even, to learn to enjoy riddles – than to be the victim of the rancour instilled by the fanciful claim to absolute knowledge!

Hence this consequence, which is crucial for the understanding of the genuine philosopher, and the reason why 'Epicurean' becomes an image referring to it: the delight in the question mark. A delight intensely experienced by the new species of philosophers: for 'we are cautious, we modern men, about ultimate convictions' (GS 375). In other words, the commanding drive in us, which makes us philosophers, is not the desire for the absolute, but 'the Epicurean instinct of the friend of riddles' (KSA 12:2[162]), or as *The Gay Science* puts it: 'An almost Epicurean bent for knowledge develops that will not easily let go of the questionable character of things' (375).

Ultimately, such an attitude relies on a finer analysis of the status of reality that involves respect for the '*rerum concordia discors*' that is found to be dwelling at the core of everything that exists, as *The Gay Science* puts it, thus making meaningful use of another Epicurean-minded phrase:[22] 'But to stand in the midst of this *rerum concordia discors* and of this whole marvellous uncertainty and rich ambiguity of existence *without questioning*, without trembling with the craving and the rapture of such questioning, …, that is what I feel to be *contemptible*' (2). With such a description of what it takes to act as a real philosopher, it now becomes clear why Stendhal, the 'odd Epicurean', may rightly be referred to as a 'question mark of a man'.[23] To recognize our share of ignorance is not a defeat; it is, rather, the counterpart of honesty and of a subtler, unprejudiced approach to what reality is: there is a sort of 'deliberate Epicureanism of the heart', which 'worships the mask as its deity' (KSA 12:2[33]). In Epicurus, then, Nietzsche detects a nascent form of affirmative thinking that enjoys the complexity of reality, and above all feels this indomitable complexity as an attractive situation: according to Nietzsche, this is the direction that the Epicurean attitude points to, although less radically so than his own way of thinking.

However, 'friend of riddles' does not mean obscurantist. It is even quite the opposite. This type of thinker identifies and sets aside the so-called explanations that do not explain anything or, in philological terms, the untenable interpretations, particularly the predetermined ones, which distort the text to be deciphered by injecting a personal prejudice into it. This (metaphorical again) understanding of philology is first theorized in *Human, All Too Human*, by the time of the rediscovery of Epicureanism. Nietzsche defines it again in *The Anti-Christ*: 'What is here meant by philology is, in a very broad sense, the art of reading well – of reading facts without falsifying them by interpretation, without losing caution, patience, delicacy in the desire to understand. Philology as *ephexis* in interpretation – whether it is a matter of books, the news in a paper, destinies or weather conditions, not to speak of the "salvation of the soul"' (A 52).

The ability to reject certain types of (pseudo-)interpretations, or 'explanations', may sound more evocative of scepticism than Epicureanism. In fact, the notion of '*ephexis*', the suspension of judgement, is typical of the sceptic's vocabulary, as Nietzsche is perfectly aware. However, his investigations have a tendency to connect Epicurus and the sceptical attitude. When he brings the Greek philosopher to the foreground in *Human, All Too Human*, Nietzsche simultaneously puts a stress on the sceptical spirit that informs sound philosophy, and appeals for 'the spirit of science, which on the whole makes one somewhat colder *and more sceptical* and in especial cools down the fiery stream of belief in ultimate definitive truths' (HH 244, emphasis added).

As we have seen earlier, *The Gay Science* specifies what is eliminated by this *ephexis*: 'An aversion to big moral words and gestures; a taste that rejects all crude, four-square opposites and is proudly conscious of its practice in having reservations' (375). The characteristic feature of the real philosopher is both his rapture at enigmas and his ability to refrain from doing violence to them in his efforts to decipher – in other words, his ability to abide by the rules of honest and faithful reading.

In this respect, the Epicurean recommendation to remain open to multiple explanations under certain circumstances may be regarded as a form of *ephexis*, of scepticism in the sense accepted by Nietzsche.[24] If it is basically aiming at practical purposes, it is very likely that Nietzsche associates it with the philological viewpoint, too, so that it finally refers to intellectual probity. This means that by way of the philological perspective, the Epicurean idea of multiple explanations is considered as having an ethical meaning but in the deeper sense of the 'intellectual conscience'[25] the 'conscience behind your "conscience"' that Nietzsche frequently invokes (GS 335). This Epicurean theory is in accordance with Nietzsche's (more radical) rejection of the problematic of truth. It makes it possible to avoid the fanatical excesses and dishonesties that are typical of the 'lack of philology' which has spread over the practice of philosophers, and in a way is echoed in Nietzsche's constant effort to pluralize interpretative hypotheses, whereby he underlines that they are, and cannot be more than, hypotheses.[26]

In summary, an Epicurean riddle lover is thus someone who shows great restraint in interpreting. This is the key to identifying and neutralizing deep-rooted prejudices such as have tainted philosophical thinking so far. Therefore, he must be recognized as a firm defender of intellectual integrity – a virtue that Nietzsche always associates with the practice of the philological 'art of reading well'. The important point is that the Epicurean sceptical tendency that Nietzsche thinks he can identify is not at odds with the attraction towards knowledge, which is the first feature that characterizes the type of person that Nietzsche has in mind.

A last point must be made to complete the general outline of Nietzsche's 'Epicureans'. Although Nietzsche constantly rejects hedonism (as well as pessimism),[27] which is nevertheless crucial to the Epicurean understanding of philosophy, it is obvious that a certain form of joy is at the core of his interpretation of Epicureanism. That is also why he establishes a parallel between Stendhal and Epicurus in BGE 62: Stendhal is well known for his extreme insistence on cheerfulness, 'gaieté d'esprit', or 'caractère gai', although these are not to be equated with hedonism *stricto sensu*.[28] An important remark should be made here: for when it is time to suggest parallels between Nietzsche's positions and those of another philosopher, the one who is the most frequently brought up by scholars is Spinoza.[29] On close scrutiny, however, it is my opinion that Epicurus is a much more interesting candidate – due in particular to the presence of this affirmative drive to cheerfulness which Nietzsche believes is at the basis of his philosophizing,[30] whereas he is reluctant to grant Spinoza any really affirmative, let alone cheerful, way of thinking. In this respect, similarities with Spinoza appear to be mostly illusory, whatever Nietzsche's first enthusiastic comments upon (re)discovering him may have been.[31]

As we have seen, when Nietzsche uses the term 'Epicurean', he generally does not give it its usual meaning, namely 'hedonistic' as referring to someone stating that pleasure is the principle of all living beings, or defending a strictly naturalistic analysis of reality based on void and atoms as ultimate principles. An 'Epicurean', in Nietzsche's new language, is something quite different: a riddle lover. It refers to a person who takes delight in the process of thinking – that is of confronting and trying to solve the world's enigmas – but who in doing so never indulges in the fanaticism that the ordinary blind worship of truth always evokes. An Epicurean knows how to remain defiant towards the persistence of prejudices; and above all, an Epicurean enjoys the seducing inventiveness of life – life that always finds a way of escaping our attempts to capture and enclose it within a rational frame. He acknowledges the seduction operated by the 'the questionable character of things': the Epicurean, therefore, substitutes 'gay science' for the usual, naive yearning for absolute all-encompassing knowledge that is blind to the interpretive character of reality. And as such, an Epicurean is a genuine philosopher.

But exactly how *Epicurean* are these reinvented 'Epicureans'? From Epicurus to Nietzsche, enemies have changed – partly, at least. It is no longer the epistemologically unfounded fears projected on death and gods that must be relentlessly opposed, but, rather, and at a much deeper level, the devastating conclusions spreading from idealistic values, and in particular those involving an inadequate understanding of knowledge, namely the religious worship for truth – truth considered priceless, worthy of any sacrifice, in an all too pious way, venerated in complete unawareness of its interpretive character. Something remains common however: the passion for knowledge, the passion to dissipate dishonest interpretations, alongside the high esteem of cheerfulness. So there may be an emerging form of gay science in the way of thinking developed by Epicurus and his school, although there is no perfect fulfilment of what Nietzsche considers to be gay science, which involves understanding 'life as a means to knowledge' (GS 324) and justifying all the aspects of existence. In other words, it would be the subject of another inquiry to understand why, notwithstanding his probity and approval of joy, Epicurus was not, after all, 'Epicurean' enough, and remained in Nietzsche's view 'the opposite of a Dionysian pessimist', 'a typical decadent' (GS 370).

Notes

1 See, for instance, 'The Epicurean', in the second volume of the *Essays, Moral and Political*. But references to Epicurus are to be found in most of Hume's major works, in particular (2007, 1983), and, of course, in the important eighth part of (1998). I shall not address here the much-debated problem of how much Hume really draws on Epicurean philosophy.
2 His 1841 doctorate dealt with the *Difference Between the Democritean and the Epicurean Philosophy of Nature*.
3 Julien Offray de La Mettrie's *Système d'Epicure* was published in Berlin in 1750. Epicurus is frequently discussed throughout La Mettrie's works, in particular in *L'homme-machine*, in his *Traité de l'âme* and his *La volupté*. Concerning the uses of Epicurean thought in the eighteenth century, see Leddy and Lifschitz (2009).
4 Some recent studies have shed precious light on Nietzsche's special understanding of this character. The turning point in this respect certainly was Roos ([1980] 2000). Among recent scholarship, Ansell-Pearson (2018) is of particular import.
5 No matter, for the time being, if this is acceptable or not on strictly philosophical grounds.
6 On this crucial aspect of Nietzsche's philosophy, see in particular Blondel (1991), Denat and Wotling (2013: 7 ff.), and Schacht (1985). As Schacht rightly points out: 'The terms of which Nietzsche avails himself in this connection – such as "force", "system", "power", "master" and "slave", "herd", "spirituality", "affect" and "instinct" – are all borrowed from existing forms of discourse. They are transformed and refined in the course of his appropriation and employment of them, however, and are held to serve to bring out something important about the matters indicated. Unquestionably and indeed openly metaphorical at the outset, they are taken to be *illuminating* metaphors, admitting of development into concepts which are appropriate and revealing with respect to various features of the world, life and human existence' (113).
7 See in particular GM P4. It should be noted in addition that Rée was not a psychologist either! Another striking example of Nietzsche's particular use of language.
8 For a deeper insight into Nietzsche's analysis, see GM I: 1, and above all 2.
9 Regarding Kant's attraction to inefficient and useless complication, see, for instance, BGE 5: 'The equally stiff and decorous Tartuffery of the old Kant as he lures us on the dialectical bypaths that lead to his "categorical imperative" – really lead astray and seduce – this spectacle makes us smile.'
10 See also, for instance, KSA 8:33[9], or KSA 8:23[56], which acknowledges the same fact concerning wisdom.
11 See HH 275 in particular. We shall have to examine this point below.
12 See WS 192.
13 On Epicurus' 'refined heroism', see KSA 8:28[15]; on his delicacy and nobility, see also for instance, KSA 10:7[97].
14 See, for instance, the following judgement: 'The same appraisal as that of the clear, cool Hellenically cool, but suffering Epicurus: the hypnotic sense of nothingness, the repose of deepest sleep, in short *absence of suffering* – sufferers and those profoundly depressed will count this as the supreme good, as the value of values' (GM III: 17). The first instances of this assessment can be traced back at least as far as the late 1870s:

see, for example, posthumous note 4 [204] in KSA 9. Some of the clearest verdicts are to be found in KSA 11:25[17]) and A 30.
15 That is, a period when Nietzsche is particularly prone to use the adjective Epicurean.
16 Independence is always considered by Nietzsche the fundamental virtue of the genuine philosopher, alongside intellectual honesty. See, for instance, BGE 26, 29, 42–44, as well as the splendid discussion of Shakespeare in GS 98.
17 The reasons for this are discussed, in particular, in the first aphorism of BGE, to limit ourselves to a single synthetic text.
18 This topic has been precisely discussed by Ansell-Pearson (2015c).
19 Translations of KSA are mine, unless otherwise noted.
20 The notion of 'passion for knowledge' is introduced for the first time in this aphorism. For an analysis of this idea, see Brusotti (1997).
21 On the meaning of the notion of gay science, see in particular, Denat and Wotling (2013: 139 ff.)
22 'Rerum concordia discors', that is 'the discordant concord of things', is a phrase coined by Horace, and is to be found in the first book of his *Epistles* (I, xii). Nietzsche takes it over for his own purpose in the second aphorism of GS.
23 It should be kept in mind that Nietzsche borrows nothing less than the description of the 'good philosopher' from Stendhal (see BGE 39).
24 Nietzsche insists more explicitly on the parallel between scepticism and Epicureanism in his late posthumous notes, particularly in 1888, often bringing Pyrrho and Epicurus together (see KSA 13, 14[87], 14[99], 14[116], 14[129], 14[141], among others). However, in this context, he concentrates rather more on their ways of living and the signs of nihilism that they are supposed to reveal.
25 On the notion of intellectual conscience, see in particular, HH 109; AOM 26; GS 2 and 335; and BGE 45 and 205.
26 This feature of Nietzsche's philosophizing would, of course, require a longer discussion. Let us just mention that pointing out this peculiar status of his thinking is the function of the frequent 'vorausgesetzt, daß', 'assuming that' in his writings. BGE 1, 2 and 36 are good examples of this process.
27 See BGE 225, for instance.
28 Stendhal is at the same time a perfect example of the sceptical restraint Nietzsche praises as a crucial philosophical virtue.
29 See Schacht 1994.
30 Regardless of how excessively enthusiastic he may be in his interpretation of Epicurus' *ataraxia* and *galenismos*.
31 In particular in the postcard he sends to his friend Franz Overbeck on 30 July 1881, where he lists five theoretical points that he feels he shares with Spinoza. But the vast majority of the further developments about Spinoza in Nietzsche's later corpus are sharply critical and point to irreconcilable divergence. The claims of this celebrated postcard should therefore be considered with some critical reservation.

12

Great politics and the unnoticed life

Nietzsche and Epicurus on the boundaries of cultivation

Peter S. Groff

After more than a century of neglect, Epicurus has in recent years come to be recognized for the profound influence he had on Nietzsche and the central, if ambivalent, place he holds in his thought.[1] Their affinities are many, but two points of intersection in particular deserve mention: a staunch naturalistic opposition to metaphysico-moralistic interpretations of the world[2] and an understanding of philosophy as a 'way of life' or 'art of living'.[3] As is sometimes pointed out, Epicurus looms largest in Nietzsche's middle-period works, where select aspects of his thought and life are valorized and appropriated: his vitality, modesty, 'heroic-idyllic' mode of philosophizing, therapeutic technique of multiple explanations, embrace of a death-bound soul and rejection of an afterlife, preemptive critique of Christianity and anticipation of a modern scientific, de-deified world view.[4] Here, however, I will focus on one aspect of Epicurus' teachings that has received little attention: his controversial advice to 'live unnoticed' (*lathe biōsas*).[5] Nietzsche was familiar with this credo and took it to heart, but it ultimately stood at odds with, and lost out to, his irresistible temptation to engage in great politics.[6] The following discussion attempts to track and illuminate Nietzsche's conflicted appreciation for the virtues of the unnoticed life.

A buried Epicurean teaching

As traditionally interpreted, the *lathe biōsas* doctrine counsels us to avoid the political life and opt, instead, for a quiet, sequestered life of contemplation and ethical perfectionism. Most of what we know about it comes to us through doxographies and later critics of Epicurus, but one can, nevertheless, find comparable sentiments scattered throughout his corpus.[7] For instance, he repeatedly warns against the limits of attaining security through other people (*asphaleia ex anthrōpōn*) (PD VI, VII). He urges his adherents not to seek happiness in fame or honour and to shun the multitude (VC 64, 81; cf. PD VII). He contends that 'the purest security is that which comes from a quiet life and withdrawal from the many' (PD XIV).⁸ Elsewhere, he encourages his followers to 'free themselves from the prison of daily duties and politics' and avoid the political life (*mē politeuesthai*) (VC 58).⁹

Unsurprisingly, Epicurus' doctrine of the hidden life was wildly unpopular in its time and remains so even today. It ran against the grain of not only common opinion (which placed great emphasis on traditional civic values, as well as fame and honour) but also the views of most philosophers. Socrates himself eschewed political offices, but, nonetheless, provided an even greater public service though his zetetic activities in the marketplace – ultimately, at the cost of his life. Plato, envisioning the ideal coincidence of political power and wisdom in the wake of Socrates' death, placed philosophers at the very centre of the city as its rulers.¹⁰ For Aristotle, the human being is the *zōon politikon*: we require political association and genuine flourishing is impossible shorn of certain social advantages and perks.¹¹ The Stoics, despite their withdrawal into the 'inner citadel', acknowledged the duties we have to our communities as rational and virtuous beings, and so saw an ethical obligation to participate in politics. Even the outlandish Cynics, who despised conventional morality, remained dialectically bound up with the traditional values of the city they sought to overturn. In this respect, Epicurus' unapologetically apolitical stance is unique among the ancients. It represents such a striking divergence from the norm that it is sometimes explained away in historicist or psychologistic terms, for example, as a function of the political malaise following Alexander the Great (the retreat from the polis to the individual), or a shortcoming of his character (excessive gentleness, softness, etc.), or perhaps some pivotal traumatic episode that soured him on politics once and for all. But bearing in mind the comparably heretical status of Epicurus' other teachings within the tradition, there is no reason to assume his rejection of the political requires some ad hoc explanation. As Geert Roskam argues, it is a reasoned philosophical teaching proceeding from his fundamental commitment to pleasure as the highest good. Specifically, Roskam links it to three components of Epicurus' ethical thought: (1) his therapeutic attempt to cure the soul of painful irrational fears and vain desires, (2) his analysis of desire (and recognition that desires for fame, honour, power, influence, or even to contribute to the public good are neither natural nor necessary) and (3) his prudential calculus of pleasure (2007: 34–5).¹² Put simply, if one seeks tranquillity of the soul (*ataraxia*) and wishes to minimize mental anxiety, a private life off the radar is far preferable to a public, political one. But if the human being is for Epicurus not necessarily a political animal, we, nonetheless, require some degree of sociality to lead good lives. Hence Epicurus's garden: a small, relatively independent community of friends hidden away from the city and its empty distractions, engaged in revivifying philosophical therapy, cultivating themselves into godlike beings who pursue lives of quiet, simple, stable, tranquil pleasure in accordance with the 'deep-set boundary stone' of nature.¹³

Great politics and the Platonic philosopher-legislator

There is an obvious sense in which Nietzsche shares Epicurus' dismissive views on the political. He repeatedly distances himself from the interests of the state even in his early writings: 'He who has the *furor philosophicus* within him', he writes, 'will already no longer have time for the *furor politicus* and will wisely refrain from reading the newspapers every day, let alone working for a political party' (SE 7:181).[14] And he frequently reminds us of his disdain for the vulgar nationalism of Bismarck's *Reich*, pointing out that the growth of political and military power inevitably comes at the cost of cultural degeneration and 'spiritual flattening' (BGE 241; cf. TI, 'Germans' *passim*). In these respects, Nietzsche aptly describes himself as 'the last *antipolitical* German' (EH 'Wise' 3).[15] Still, being *antipolitisch* is not the same as being *unpolitisch* – apolitical, indifferent to politics – an attitude that arguably aligns more closely with Epicurus' maxim. Put differently, the relevant choice for Nietzsche is not between politics or no politics, but between petty politics (*kleine Politik*) and great politics (*grosse Politik*). Politics becomes great when an actual 'revaluation of all values' is at stake, when it involves a cultural 'war of spirits' (*Geisterkrieg*) rather than merely a crude power conflict over legal systems, economic policies, material resources or national boundaries (EH 'Destiny' 1).[16]

'It is only with me', Nietzsche contends, 'that the earth knows *great politics*'(EH 'Destiny' 1). An immodest, self-mythologizing claim perhaps, since elsewhere he recognizes that initiating such world-transforming revaluations is the true task of the *philosopher*:

> *Genuine philosophers, however, are commanders and legislators* [*Befehlende und Gesetzgeber*]: they say, '*thus* it *shall* be!' They first determine the Whither and For What of humankind. ... With a creative hand they reach for the future and all that is and has been becomes a means for them, an instrument, a hammer. Their 'knowing' is *creating*, their creating is a legislation, their will to truth is – *will to power*. (BGE 211)

In the *Nachlass* drafts for this passage from 1884–85, Nietzsche points to Plato and Muhammad as paradigmatic examples of commanders and legislators, despite the residual self-deception under which they were labouring (KSA 11:26[407], 38[137]). Nietzsche sees these predecessors as involved in the same sort of transformative world-historical task that he himself is *qua* philosopher; they are simply less self-aware of the radically creative nature of their legislations. And, indeed, it seems appropriate for Nietzsche to place himself in the lineage of Plato, since the conception of philosophers as 'commanders and legislators' – even *prophets* in the manner of Zarathustra – is a fundamentally Platonic idea. Nietzsche's nomothetic great politics can thus be understood as a late-modern radicalization of Platonic political philosophy, aiming at the ideal coincidence of wisdom and political power epitomized by the philosopher-king.[17] His new philosophical legislators, however, do not pretend to transmit some pre-existent, universal Good to us, nor are they trying simply to realign the human soul with the rational and moral order of things; rather, they are bringing into being a new table of goods according to which we might live, and in doing so are experimentally attempting to transform humanity. They must accordingly prepare 'great ventures and over-all attempts of discipline and cultivation' in order to determine the future of the human (BGE 203). This ambitious project of transfiguration is crystallized in the dramatic image of Zarathustra attempting to produce his *Übermensch* from the ugly, uncarved stone of humanity (Z II 'Blessed' cf. BGE 62 and 225).

Concealment and the discreet therapeutic philosopher

Yet Platonic as this sounds, one can, nevertheless, find deeper Epicurean reservations in Nietzsche's thought. For the Nietzschean philosopher-lawgiver is a shadowy, unobtrusive, hidden figure who dwells far from the centres of conventional political power, shunning fame and the recognition of the masses. As Zarathustra says in his initial condemnation of the city: 'Around inventors of new values the world revolves – invisibly [*unsichtbar*] it revolves. Yet around play-actors the people and fame revolve: that is "the way of the world"' (Z I 'Flies'). This same line is repeated after he and his students have abandoned the city, with a small alteration: 'Not around the inventors of new noise', he says, 'but around the inventors of new values does the world revolve, *inaudibly* [*unhörbar*] it revolves' (Z II 'Great Events', cf. II 'Stillest Hour'). A powerful but confusing image: What would it mean for the world to revolve 'invisibly' or 'inaudibly' around something or someone? The suggestion seems to be that it is the inventors of new values who themselves remain invisible or inaudible to the world, even as they shape it. Certainly Nietzsche saw himself that way as he wandered anonymously throughout southern Europe, and despite his occasional frustrated desire for recognition, believed – in a residually Epicurean spirit – that it was probably for the best.[18] Indeed, Nietzsche's early retirement from the academy in 1879 and the inconspicuous, nomadic regimen that shaped the next ten years of his life were prompted not only by chronic health issues but also by his growing Epicurean inclination to 'free [himself] from the prison of daily duties and politics' (*VC* 58) and become a genuine philosopher.[19] It is perhaps not entirely coincidental that his withdrawal from that world left him literally stateless.[20]

As mentioned earlier, it is in Nietzsche's middle-period works (1878–82) that one finds the richest trove of Epicurean insights, and the siren call of the sequestered life is no exception. In describing the 'prudence' of free spirits Nietzsche observes:

> [They] will easily be content with, for example, a minor office or an income that just enables them to live; for they will organize their life in such a way that a great transformation of external circumstances, even an overturning of the political order, does not overturn their life with it. Upon all these things they expend as little energy as possible .... There is in [the free spirit's] way of living and thinking a *refined heroism* which disdains to offer itself to the veneration of the great masses, as his coarser brother does, and tends to go silently [*still*] through the world and out of the world. Whatever labyrinths he may stray through, among whatever rocks his stream may make its torturous way – if he emerges into the open air he will travel his road bright, light and almost soundlessly [*geräuschlos*] and let sunshine play down into his very depths. (HH 291)[21]

The mood and language of this passage are deeply Epicurean: consider the emphasis on prudence or caution (*Vorsicht*, a common German rendering of *phronēsis*, which is for Epicurus the root of all other virtues), the desideratum of minimizing interaction with, and dependency upon, the city, the strategy of creating stabilizing bulwarks against social and political disruption, the evocation of refined heroism,[22] the avoidance of the masses, the ideal of going silently-soundlessly through and out of the world (*lathe biōsas, lathe apobiōsas*) and the themes of open air and sunlight.[23] But who is the 'coarser brother' of this Epicurean free spirit who seeks popular veneration – the meddling Socratic gadfly? The Platonic philosopher-ruler? The vain Peripatetic seeking recognition as a knower? More likely, it is either the theatrical Stoic- or Cynic-type, both of whom Nietzsche elsewhere compares unfavourably to the more discreet, nuanced, cultured and spiritualized Epicurean.[24]

One finds reminders of this Epicurean prudence even in the post-Zarathustran works. In *Beyond Good and Evil*, for example, he counsels his nascent free spirits in similar terms:

> Take care, philosophers and friends, of knowledge, and beware of martyrdom! Of suffering 'for the truth's sake' [that is, in the manner of Socrates, Spinoza, Giordano Bruno, etc]! ... Rather, go away. Flee into concealment [*Verborgene*]. And have your masks and your subtlety, that you may be mistaken for what you are not, or feared a little. And don't forget the garden, the garden with golden trelliswork. And have people around you who are as a garden ... choose the *good* solitude, the free, playful, light solitude that gives you too the right to remain good in some sense. (BGE 25)

Apart from the obvious Epicurean tropes of withdrawal and concealment – earlier in the same book, he describes Epicurus as 'hidden away [*versteckt sass*] in his little garden' (BGE 7) – it should be noted that Nietzsche sometimes associates Epicurus with having an unknown or obscured identity: being mistaken for what one is not.[25] Even the emphasis on solitude here – an ascetic practice that looms large throughout Nietzsche's corpus[26] – is construed in Epicurean terms: the 'good' and 'light' solitude is the garden, where one is not entirely alone and never lonely, because there are always healing friends and kindred spirits.[27]

Sometimes this Epicurean withdrawal-concealment strategy is cast as a necessary prologue to more ambitious cultural or even political projects: a desire to be useful on a grander scale. In an aphorism entitled '*The buried*' (*Die Vergrabenen*), he writes:

> We withdraw [*zurückziehen*] into concealment: but not out of any kind of personal ill-humor, as though the political and social situation of the present day were not good enough for us, but because through our withdrawal we want to economize and assemble forces of which culture will *later* have great need ... . We are accumulating capital and seeking to make it secure: but, as in times of great peril, to do that we have to *bury* it. (WS 229)

The predominant emphasis in the middle-period writings, however, is on a more modest task: cooperative therapy and pluralistic experiments in self-cultivation among a close circle of like-minded free spirits.[28] This is often juxtaposed with the imprudent desire (rooted in sympathy or pity) to eliminate danger and suffering from the lives of others. An aphorism in *Daybreak* concludes:

> The question itself remains unanswered whether one is of *more use* to another by immediately leaping to his side and *helping* him – which can in any case be only superficial where it does not become a tyrannical seizing and transforming – or by *creating* something out of oneself that the other can behold with pleasure: a beautiful, restful, self-enclosed garden perhaps, with high walls against storms and the dust of the roadway but also a hospitable gate. (D 174)[29]

Interestingly, the Platonic strategy of 'tyrannical seizing and transforming' is considered here, but quickly passed over in favour of a more voluntary, private Epicurean cultivation. A year later in *The Gay Science* Nietzsche returns to this idea and unpacks it more carefully. Observing the ways in which the causes and inner logic of a person's suffering are generally inaccessible or incomprehensible to others – and thus why pity is an ineffective and even counterproductive response to suffering – he encourages philosophical therapists to prioritize their own self-discovery and cultivation and then, by extension, focus only on kindred souls who they can genuinely understand and help. The primary concern is never to lose 'one's own way':

> How is it possible to keep to one's own way? Constantly, some clamor or other calls us aside; rarely does our eye behold anything that does not require us to drop our own preoccupation instantly to help. I know, there are a hundred decent and praiseworthy ways of losing *my own way*, and they are truly highly 'moral'! Indeed, those who now preach the morality of pity even take the view that precisely this and only this is moral – to lose one's *own* way in order to come to the assistance of a neighbor. I know just as certainly that I only need to expose myself to the sight of some genuine distress and I am lost. And if a suffering friend said to me, 'Look, I am about to die; please promise to die with me', I should promise it; and the sight of a small mountain tribe fighting for its liberty would persuade me to offer it my hand and my life. ... All such arousing of pity and calling for help is secretly seductive, for our 'own way' is too hard and demanding and too remote from the love and gratitude of others, and we do not really mind escaping from it ... while I shall keep silent [*verschweigen*, that is, hide, conceal, keep secret] about some points, I do not want to remain silent about my morality which says to me: Live in concealment [*Lebe im Verborgenen*, that is, live secretly, discreetly, in hiding or seclusion] so that you *can* live for yourself. Live in *ignorance* about what seems most important to your age. Between yourself and today lay the skin of at least three centuries. And the clamor of today, the noise of wars and revolutions should be a mere murmur for you. You will also wish to help – but only those whose distress you *understand* entirely because they share with you one suffering

and one hope – your friends – and only in the manner in which you help yourself. (GS 338; cf. SE 1)

The conclusion to this passage ('live in concealment so that you can live for yourself') is an elegant summation of the *lathe biōsas* maxim, and more generally, of the kind of refined egoism that drew Nietzsche to Epicurus.[30]

Even when the theme of philosophical *therapeia* is expressed in a more generous, expansive and inclusive mood, the Epicurean watchwords remain. In one such passage, Nietzsche speaks of the desire to 'give away one's spiritual house and possessions' in assisting those working on themselves. Such a therapist, he suggests,

> is not merely not looking for fame: he would even like to escape gratitude, for gratitude is too importunate and lacks respect for solitude and silence [*Stillschweigen*]. What he seeks is to live nameless [*namenlos*] and lightly mocked at, too humble to awaken envy or hostility. ... To be like a little inn which rejects no one who is in need but which is afterwards forgotten or ridiculed! ... Forever in a kind of love and self-enjoyment! To be in possession of a dominion and at the same time concealed and renouncing! To lie continually in the sunshine and gentleness of grace, and yet to know that the paths that rise up to the sublime are close by – That would be a life! That would be a reason for a long life! (D 449)

The emphasis on (relative) solitude, namelessness, silence and concealment is obviously Epicurean, as is the indirect utility of refined egoism, the sunshine motif, the reference to the sublime and even the evocation of a long life.[31] But in a *Nachlass* note from the same period (Autumn 1880), we find a link tethering this passage even more closely to Epicurus. There he offers a strikingly resonant portrait of the type sketched out above: those who are in possession of a dominion and at the same time concealed and renouncing. 'I found strength', he writes, 'in the very places one does not look for it, in simple, gentle and helpful human beings, without the slightest inclination to rule ... powerful natures *dominate*, that is a necessity, even if they do not move one finger. And when they bury themselves, in their lifetime, in a garden house [*Gartenhaus*]!' (KSA 9:6[206]).[32] Once again, one feels the magnetism of the hidden Epicurus, and with it, Nietzsche's desire to play a similar role.

Beyond the garden

It is hardly surprising, then, that Nietzsche dreamt of founding a kind of modern Epicurean Garden. One finds anticipations of the idea in his pivotal 1876–77 trip to Sorrento, where he lived together with Malwida von Meysenbug, Paul Rée and his pupil Albert Brenner in a small friendship community for almost a year.[33] There Nietzsche and his friends spoke fervently of creating a 'monastery of free spirits' that they called the School of the Educators (D'Iorio 2016: 24–43). This project, which excited

Nietzsche greatly, never came to fruition, but the possibility of establishing his own Garden school stuck with him, and he would revisit the prospect at various junctures in letters to his amanuensis Peter Gast (KSB 5:826, 6:457, 7:651).[34] As we have seen, the image of the Garden figures prominently in his middle-period writings. Curiously, it reaches its fullest and most sustained expression in *Zarathustra*, when the prophet-legislator and his select group of co-creator disciple-friends retreat from the city to the 'Blessed Isles' (*glückseligen Inseln*) in order to cultivate and perfect themselves.[35] The locale's namesake seems intended to evoke the ancient Greek dream of the 'Isles of the Blessed' (*makarōn nēsoi*): an eschatological paradise located in the far Western streams of Okeanos where the elite few – originally heroes, later the righteous, in Platonic dialogues, philosophers – live eternally and happily.[36] This is surely right, but while some commentators have taken this as evoking Hesiod, Pindar or Plato, it is more likely a homage to Epicurus. For Zarathustra's *glückseligen Inseln* are essentially the *makarōn nēsoi* made concrete in the here and now, which is precisely how the Garden was originally presented (Frischer 1982: 38).[37] Moreover, in a letter to Gast from this period, Nietzsche disclosed that he had Epicurus specifically in mind when he invented the Blessed Isles (KSB 6:446).[38]

Virtually all the speeches and actions of the Part Two of *Zarathustra* take place on the Garden-like Isles. However, by the time Nietzsche began work on Part Three of *Zarathustra*, he was already beginning to doubt the wisdom and efficacy of such tight-knit, sequestered friendship communities.[39] Despite its rich residual Epicurean imagery, *Zarathustra* signals a shift away from the modest privatized and pluralistic experiments in self-cultivation that characterized Nietzsche's middle-period writings, and a move towards the obsession with great politics that marked his later works.[40] The model of the philosopher-therapist is replaced by the philosopher-commander, now concerned with the legislation of new values and the consequent determination of the future of the human being. One might say that here Nietzsche grows weary of Epicurus and flees back into the arms of Plato.

While it is difficult to give a full account of the reasons for this change, one detail merits mention: Nietzsche's increasing impatience and inability to abide the unperfectible human types produced by the blind impress of nature and millennia of uninformed self-experimentation.[41] He can no longer passively observe the diminution of the human being with 'the mocking and aloof eyes of an Epicurean god' (BGE 62).[42] In Nietzsche's first post-Zarathustran work, he writes:

> Anyone ... who approached this almost deliberate degeneration and atrophy of the human being represented by the European Christian ... feeling the opposite kind of desire, not in an Epicurean spirit but rather with some divine hammer in his hand, would surely have to cry out in wrath, in pity, in horror: 'O you dolts, you presumptuous, pitying dolts, what have you done! Was that work for your hands? How you have bungled and botched my beautiful stone! What presumption!' (BGE 62; cf. Z II 'Blessed')

Here we see a surprising inversion. As mentioned earlier, Epicurus and Nietzsche are, each in his own way, philosophical naturalists. Epicurus' naturalism takes as its measure the deep-set boundary stone of nature, avoiding the political sphere in favour of the private project of therapeutic self-cultivation. Nietzsche's ostensibly more radical and ambitious naturalism demands the creation of new values, ultimately requiring a decisive intervention in the grand politics of shaping the human future. From an Epicurean perspective, however, the desire to transfigure humanity (or à la Zarathustra, to 'redeem' the earth) is no more natural or necessary than amassing wealth, or earning public honours, or gaining power over one's fellow citizens, and to exchange peace of mind or equanimity of the soul for such conceits is a bad trade, indeed. For better or worse then, Epicurus will not be vulnerable to the pain and anxiety that Nietzsche experiences when he witnesses 'that gruesome dominion of nonsense and accident that has so far been called "history"' (BGE 203). Both Epicurus and Nietzsche are, of course, deeply anti-teleological thinkers who recognize no overarching intelligence, purpose or meaning at work in the various productions of nature. There is no one at the wheel, so to speak. The crux of their difference lies in this: Epicurus is content to leave natural history without a driver; Nietzsche ultimately is not. And it is this that finally tempts him away from the intimate boundaries of the unnoticed life towards the imprudent task of grand politics.

The hidden, helpful Life

To engage with Nietzsche's writings as though he offers a series of claims that might be simply true or false is to lose the power of philosophy as a way of life and, indeed, to overlook the importance of philosophers as interlocutors, educators and examples (SE 1:129–30, 3:136–7). It is tempting when observing Nietzsche's post-Zarathustran descent into grand politics to conclude that he somehow lost his way – that he should have stuck with his Epicurean experiments in private self-cultivation and not worried about redeeming humanity.[43] Yet what is the point of such criticisms? Nietzsche made the moves he made and there's no sense in pronouncing upon what he should have said or done. But that does not mean we have to give up what Nietzsche himself abandoned. Nietzsche took what he wanted from the Greeks in the construction of his own art of living (KSA 9:15[59]), and we, in turn, can take what we want from him. Some of it will be useful to us, some of it not. I believe that his middle-period experiments, when he was closest in spirit to Epicurus, are the ones we can profit from the most. Nietzsche is most helpful when he wants least to be noticed, when he is discreet and modest like the powerful philosopher-therapist hidden in the garden: 'In possession of a dominion', as he says, 'and at the same time concealed and renouncing' (D 449). This is the Nietzsche who is the genuinely transformative educator, who liberates and invigorates and augments the lives of his readers. George Eliot, that other great modern Epicurean, perhaps put it best when she observed that 'the growing good of the world is partly dependent on unhistoric acts; and that things are not so ill with you and me as they might have been is half owing to the number who lived faithfully a hidden life, and rest in unvisited tombs' (Eliot 1972: 896).

Notes

1 While Nietzsche's relationship to Epicurus was sometimes acknowledged in passing, there were until recently few sustained discussions. Some noteworthy exceptions are Knight (1933) and Bornmann (1984).
2 On this affinity, see Caygill (2006), Groff (2014), and most notably, Ansell-Pearson's recent articles and chapters on Nietzsche and Epicurus.
3 Ansell-Pearson (2018: 1–46 and 135–50). On the recuperation of this ancient model of philosophy as way of life (*bios*) or art of living (*technē tou biou*), see, for example, Hadot (1995a).
4 On the centrality of Epicurus to Nietzsche's middle-period works, see Young (2010); Ansell-Pearson (2013); and Ansell-Pearson (2015d). On the continuing vitality of Epicurus' thought, see AOM 48 and WS 227; on his modest (quasi-ascetic) hedonism, see WS 192 and GS 45, as well as Roos (2000); on his greatness and heroic-idyllic mode of philosophizing, see WS 295 and WS 332, as well as Milkowski (1998) and Ansell-Pearson (2014b); on his higher cultural-spiritual status compared to other Hellenistic philosophers, see HH 275 and GS 306; on his multiple explanations (*pleonachos tropos*) technique, see WS 7 and GS 375, as well as Shearin, Wilson H. (2014); on his embrace of a death-bound soul and rejection of an afterlife, see D 72 and Z P: 6, as well as Rempel (2012); on his pre-emptive war on Christianity, see A 58 and KSA 13:16[15]; on his anticipation of a modern scientific, de-deified world view, see HH 68 and Groff 2014; for an Epicurean anticipation of the death of God, see WS 84. Nietzsche's later writings take an increasingly unsympathetic view of Epicurus, specifically his atomistic materialism (GS 109, 373, BGE 12, TI, 'Reason', 5), his hedonism (BGE 225), and his sickness and decadence (BT P4, GS P2 and 370, GM III.6 and 17, TI 'Morality', 3, A 30, KSA 11:25[95]).
5 Usener (2010), Fragment 551. For the most comprehensive discussion of the *lathe biōsas* teaching, see Roskam (2007). *Lathe* has been rendered variously as 'hidden', 'inconspicuously', 'in obscurity', 'unobtrusively', 'secretly', etc.
6 Nietzsche mentions the phrase *lathe biōsas* only twice explicitly in his writings. Both are *Nachlass* entries from the period of *The Birth of Tragedy* (late 1870) and have to do specifically with the political status of women in ancient Greece (KSA 7:7[31] and 7[221]). The passages liken this 'symbol of Epicurean world wisdom' to living in the dark or vegetating like a plant in close circles. However, one finds the idea scattered throughout Nietzsche's subsequent writings – especially in the middle-period works – where it is expressed indirectly via metaphors of silence, withdrawal, concealment, obscured identity and, of course, the Garden.
7 As Roskam points out, 'One of the sad consequences of the manuscript tradition of Epicurus' works is that the maxim *lathe biōsas* has in the end applied its own advice. For indeed, it nowhere appears in the extant writings of Epicurus, leading, as it were, to its own hidden life, far away from inquisitive or boring scholars' (33). Epicurus' lost *Peri Biōn* ostensibly provided a more detailed account of this doctrine; see Schofield (2000).
8 Note that all Epicurus translations are from *The Epicurus Reader* (2010) Fragment 187.
9 VS 58 and Diogenes Laertius X.119 (henceforth DL); see. DL X.10: 'So gentlemanly was [Epicurus] that he did not even participate in political life.'
10 *Republic* 473c-e and Bks VI-VII *passim*; see. *Laws* 712a, 713e. Plato also contrived to mould existing rulers into something resembling a philosopher-king, for example,

his ill-fated engagement with Dionysius II – which led Epicurus mockingly to describe his canonical antipode as 'golden' and his followers as 'flatterers of Dionysius' (*Dionysiokolakes*), that is, tyrants' sycophants. See Plato, Seventh Letter 326a-b, 328a and DL X.8; cf. BGE 7. For a more nuanced view, however, see Carter (1986), which envisions Plato's contemplative life as an outgrowth of a minority tradition of apolitical quietism (*apragmosynē*) in classical Greek life.

11 The *Nicomachean Ethics* X.6-8 famously sketches out an ideal of self-sufficient theoretical contemplation, but even this way of life arguably presupposes a degree of recognition and acknowledgement – an intellectual fame of sorts – from a community of expert knowers.

12 One might invert the primacy here, as for example, Arendt does, but the essential connection nonetheless remains: 'Hedonism … is but the most radical form of a non-political, totally private way of life, the true fulfillment of Epicurus's *lathe biōsas kai mē politeuesthai*' (Arendt 1958: 112–13).

13 Cf. DL 10.121b: '[The sage] will found a school, but not so as to draw a crowd.' On the 'deep-set boundary stone' (*alte terminus haerens*), which indicates the necessary limitations of nature according to which we should think and live (and thus rules out vain fears and desires), see Lucretius 1992, I.77, cf. I.596; II.1087; III.787, 794, 990 and 1014.

14 I use Walter Kaufmann's translations for Penguin/Vintage and R.J. Hollingdale's translations for Cambridge University Press (with occasional emendations in favour of greater literalness), the single exception being Graham Parkes' translation of *Thus Spoke Zarathustra* for Oxford. Translations of passages from the notebooks or letters are my own. Cf. SE 6, 165, where he defends a conception of education 'that makes one a solitary, that proposes goals that transcend money and money-making, that takes a long time', characterizing it (affirmatively, in spite of popular opinion) as '"refined egoism" and "immoral cultural Epicureanism"'.

15 On this, see Bergmann (1987). I set aside here the deeper and more difficult question whether Nietzsche does have a political philosophy in any traditional sense, and if so, how it ought to be understood.

16 Nietzsche's use of the expression *grosse Politik* is sparse and polysemic. Sometimes it's loosely associated with any agent – princes, rulers or masses – spurred by the need for the feeling of power (D 189); sometimes it's used ironically and in scare quotes to describe the shallow, petty, provincial power politics of the *Reich* (BGE 241, 254); sometimes it has to do with the 'the struggle for the dominion of the world', which at first may seem to indicate simply a more ambitious transnational European or world political power conflict (BGE 208). But it increasingly comes to signify an ambitious world-historical revaluation of values, that is, in the *Genealogy*, where he describes the Judeo-Christian inversion of Noble morality as 'the secret black art of a truly *grand* politics of revenge' (GM I: 8). His final usage of it in *Ecce Homo* cements this sense, inasmuch as it has to do with a spiritual–cultural struggle for the future of the human (EH 'Destiny' 1). Drochon (2016) offers the most extensive discussion of this aspect of Nietzsche's thought.

17 On Nietzsche as Platonic political philosopher, see Strauss (1983) and Strauss (2017); Rosen (1995); any of Laurence Lampert's excellent books on Nietzsche, but especially Lampert (2004) and Lampert (2017); Hutter (2005); and Groff (2006).

18 See letters to Heinrich Köselitz, 26 August 1883 (KSB 6:457) and 10 December 1885 (KSB 7:651).

19 On the turn in Nietzsche's life from disenchanted university professor to nomadic philosopher, see D'Iorio (2016). His middle-period works – especially *Human, All Too Human* – are strewn with warnings against the petty, obsessive *vita activa* of modern life; see, for example, HH 283.
20 As D'Iorio points out, due to an unusual combination of circumstances, Nietzsche was by this time no longer a citizen of any country – an appropriate status for a self-proclaimed 'good European' (2016: 9).
21 As Nietzsche makes clear in his 1886 preface to *Human, All Too Human*, 'such "free spirits" do not and did not exist'. Nietzsche invented them as a kind of life-preserving illusion at the time – a 'hermit's shadow play', he calls it – but even his late period works are predicated on the possibility that 'such free spirits could *someday* exist'.
22 Cf. SE 6, p. 165 and WS 295. On Nietzsche's appropriation of Epicurus' 'refined egoism' as a kind of naturalistic care of the self, see Ansell-Pearson (2013); on Epicurus's exemplification of the 'heroic-idyllic mode of philosophizing', see note 4.
23 Nietzsche often associates Epicurus with sunlight (specifically a clear, bright exterior light); see, for example, WS 295, 332 and GS 45. Cf. implicitly Epicurean passages where Nietzsche describes his own predilections, for example, D 553.
24 Cf. GS 306, which purports to compare the Stoic and the Epicurean as types. The passage has an inescapably autobiographical or even confessional tone: 'The Epicurean selects the situation, the persons, and even the events that suit his extremely irritable, intellectual constitution; he gives up all others, which means almost everything, because they would be too strong and heavy for him to digest … the Epicurean would rather dispense with [the Stoic's theatrical cultivation to insensitivity], having his "garden"! For those with whom fate attempts improvisations – those who live in violent ages and depend on sudden and mercurial people – Stoicism may, indeed, be advisable. But anyone who foresees more or less that fate permits him to spin a long thread does well to make Epicurean arrangements. That is what all those have always done whose work is of the spirit.' Cf. HH 275, where the Epicurean type is favoured over the crude and unreceptive Cynic. For a comparative discussion of Nietzsche's understanding of Epicureanism, Stoicism and Skepticism, see Bertino (2007).
25 On Epicurus' mistaken identity, see WS 227, GS 45 and BGE 7; cf. Letter to Heinrich Köselitz, 3 August 1883 (KSB 6:446).
26 Despite Nietzsche's well-known critique of ascetic ideals, he was attentive to the transformative value of ascetic practices, appropriated them himself and recognized them clearly in Epicurus' philosophy. See, for example, KSA 9:3[53]: 'One thinks of asceticism as something superhuman, forgetting that an asceticism belonged to every ancient morality, even to Epicureanism.' Cf. GM III.7-8, where Nietzsche's emphasis on the merely hygienic meaning of ascetic ideals for philosophers is cast in deeply Epicurean terms. On solitude as an ascetic strategy in Nietzsche, see Hutter (2005: 47–74).
27 As D'Iorio points out (2016: 16), the original projected title for *Human, All Too Human* was 'The Light Life' (*Das leichte Leben*). The initial sketches from 1876 are again strikingly Epicurean in spirit, describing an 'art of living' (*Lebenskunst*) that aims not at lightening life (i.e., making it easy for us), and certainly not at making it even harder (so as to offer afterwards some supreme soteriological solution), but, rather, helping us 'to take life lightly', like the gods, standing before the truth in vivid rapture. See KSA 8:16[7], 17[74] and 17[85].
28 On this theme, see Parkes (1994); Abbey (2000); Ure (2008); and again, Ansell-Pearson's extensive recent work on Nietzsche and Epicurus.

29 Cf. BGE 25, where one's friends are the garden in a '*good* solitude'; here one becomes the healing, inspiring garden for other like-minded spirits. See also D 194, which similarly contends that instead of offering moral prescriptions for everyone, one should focus on helping limited circles or even lone individuals cultivate themselves. This more modest, conservative, selective approach to transfiguration can be seen in other passages from *Daybreak*, for example, D 534, where he emphasizes 'small doses' rather than great revolutions, or D 462, where he advocates 'slow cures' of the soul, focusing again on the overlooked 'little' things (cf. WS 5–6, 16; D 435, 553). On this theme, see Ansell-Pearson (2015b) and D'Iorio (2016: 86–8).

30 A beautiful aphorism from *Daybreak* entitled '*Do not perish unnoticed*' (435) would at first seem to suggest an explicit repudiation of Epicurus' teaching, insofar as his counsel to live unnoticed was often understood as entailing that we should die unnoticed (*lathe apobiōsas*). However, D 435 has more to do with the ways in which we gradually get ground down to nothing by the seemingly small, everyday, repetitive details of our lives about which we are inadequately cognizant. In this sense it should be understood against the background of passages like WS 5–6 and 16 – Epicurean passages which emphasize the importance of attending to the 'nearest' (*nächsten*), 'smallest and most everyday things', for example, diet, housing, clothing, nutrition, place, climate, recreation, etc. (cf. D 553, and EH, 'Clever', 10). In the notebooks we find an outline for several potential chapters, scribbled down when Nietzsche was writing *The Wanderer and His Shadow* (June–July 1879), which suggest the Epicurean dimension of such concerns and link them with the *lathe biōsas* doctrine. The first outline, entitled 'Doctrine of the *Nearest Things*', reads as follows: '*Division* of the day, goal of the day (periods). Food. Company. Nature. Solitude. Sleep. Earning of Bread. Education (of one's own and others'). Utilization of mood and wealth. Health. Withdrawal from politics [*Zurückgezogenheit von der Politik*]' (KSA 8:40[16]).

31 On the Epicurean compatibility between self-realization and helping select others, see D 174 and GS 338, as well as Ansell-Pearson (2015a); on sunshine as an Epicurean symbol, see again WS 295, 332 and GS 45; on Epicurus and the sublime, see WS 295; on the association of Epicureanism and a long life, see GS 306.

32 On Epicurus' 'powerful nature', see Letter to Heinrich Köselitz, 1 July 1883 (KSB 6:428); cf. Letter to Heinrich Köselitz, 22 January 1879 (KSB 5:799). On the image of being 'buried' and 'concealed' in an Epicurean sense, see WS 229; cf. D 449 and BGE 25.

33 Not coincidentally, this is also when he began work on his first middle-period book (*Human, All Too Human*) and decided to free himself from academia (D'Iorio 2016: 1–5).

34 See, for example, Letters to Heinrich Köselitz, 26 March 1879, 26 August 1883 and 10 December 1885.

35 See Z II 'Child with the Mirror', 'Blessed', but also Z II *passim*, III 'Wanderer', 'Vision and the Riddle':1, 'Blissfulness Against One's Will' and IV 'Cry of Need', 'Welcome'. For a nuanced and illuminating reading of Z II 'Blessed', see Bishop (2017).

36 The Isles of the Blessed begin as a conception of the afterlife (in opposition to Hades; later merged with Elysium), but in some versions become merely a place where life is easiest and best for mortals on earth. See Olshausen (2006), as well as Inwood (2006).

37 For an interpretation of the Blessed Isles as a modern Epicurean garden, see Groff (2018).

38 Letter to Heinrich Köselitz, 2 August 1883. Strangely, Epicurus himself is cast here as a 'negative argument' due to the supposed indiscriminate permeability of his original

Garden. It should be noted as well that the Blessed Isles were modelled on Ischia, a volcanic island located in the Gulf of Naples, which had fascinated and inspired Nietzsche during his time in Sorrento (Letter to Heinrich Köselitz, 16 August 1883 [KSB 6:452]). Sadly, the island was partially destroyed by an earthquake in July 1883. This event dealt a symbolic but painful blow to Nietzsche's Epicurean hopes and is reflected in various drafts for Part Three and Part Four and of *Zarathustra*, which envision the death and sinking of the Blessed Isles (KSA 10:15[17], 17[54], 20[8], 2[4] and 11:29[23]; cf. *Z* IV 'Cry of Need'). See D'Iorio (2016: 79–88) for discussion.

39 Zarathustra leaves the Blessed Islands at the end of Part Two for a variety of reasons that might be categorized into two groups. On the one hand, his departure can be seen as an attempt to overcome his prophetic loneliness in the midst of community, weariness with gift-giving, and softening in the absence of struggle (*Z* II 'Night-Song', II 'Stillest Hour', III 'Return Home', KSA 10:16[89]); on the other, it can be understood as a sacrifice of personal happiness for his world-historical work, that is, his attempt to perfect himself, articulate and embrace the doctrine of the eternal recurrence, reshape the future of the human and redeem the earth (*Z* III 'Blissfulness Against One's Will', cf. the previous limitations of his teaching exposed in *Z* II 'Soothsayer', 'Redemption').

40 For a rich reading of the Epicurean elements of Nietzsche's thought in *Zarathustra*, see Vincenzo (1994).

41 See, for example, Zarathustra's notion of the 'last human' (*Z* P, 5) and his nausea at the prospect of the eternal recurrence of the 'small human being' (*Z* III 'Convalescent').

42 On the unconcern of the Epicurean gods, who serve as models for human life, see D 150 and GS 277; compare the famous shipwreck observer motif in Lucretius II.552–64. On Nietzsche's use of the distant, unconcerned Epicurean gods as a half-way house between Abrahamic monotheism and Nietzsche's new Dionysian religion of the earth, see Groff, (forthcoming).

43 In this respect, the sentiment contained in Nietzsche's final letter is doubly poignant: 'In the end, I would much rather have been a Basel professor than God; but I did not dare to push my private egoism so far as to avoid the creation of the world for its sake' (Letter to Jacob Burckhardt, 6 January 1889, KSB 8:1256).

Part Four

Critical assessments

13

Nietzsche con/tra Epicurus

The necessity of noble suffering for intoxication with life

Michael J. McNeal

Introduction[1]

The evolution of Nietzsche's thinking on and persistent affinity for Epicurus, from whom he 'took the willingness to enjoy [life] and the eye for where nature has set the table for us' (KGW 1881: 15[59]), raises questions pertaining to significant developments in his thought. Among Epicurus' philosophical positions that Nietzsche found compelling – particularly in his middle period, which he retrospectively dubbed a 'series whose common goal is to establish a new image and idea of Free Spirits'[2] – were his proto-positivist/empiricist epistemological stance, view of the gods, rejection of any final judgement after death and immortality and his ethical stance of cultivating tranquillity, solitude and friendships for happiness (HH-WS 7, 192).[3] This chapter considers how the resonance of Epicurus' way of life with Nietzsche and his acceptance of certain of the Hellenistic philosopher's principles in his middle works are prima facie at odds with key aspects of his mature thought. It then seeks to explain the abiding attraction Nietzsche felt for Epicurus in light of this dissonance.

Nietzsche's thinking about Epicurus evolved in ways that informed his conception of suffering and its role in his free spirits' self-overcoming. Noble suffering entails a discipline of dangerous experimentation, cunning, self-squandering, forgetting and laughter in the face of pain and the horror of existence to achieve pleasure in oneself and intoxication with the entirety of existence. This discipline, and the pleasure in the agon it enables, requires great health. Rather than eschewing the strife of contest, those with the strength for it welcome struggle, particularly that entailed in opposing the dissipative values of a decadent age (McNeal 2018: 163–4). The agonies free spirits undergo correspond with their potential for growth, which when fulfilled augments the pleasure they take in and from existence. Out of this development he emerges as philosophically opposed to Epicurus in important and interesting ways.

With these matters in mind I consider the function of anguish in the free spirits' radical affirmation of life and how it conditions their prospects for intoxication with it.

This subject comprises an important piece of Nietzsche's mature philosophy. I further consider the 'marvelous cunning' (GS 291) and 'experimental imagination' (GS 345) that inform the free spirit's 'discipline of suffering' (BGE 225). Can such a self-mastery through suffering be squared with Nietzsche's lasting affection for Epicurus and his thought? 'Why', Vincenzo queried, 'did Nietzsche admire and feel a sense of affinity with Epicurus', who denied the value of suffering? (Vincenzo: 383). While Nietzsche's late reassessment of Epicurus' quasi-hedonic, eudaemonic philosophy did not significantly diminish his affection for a certain *ethos* evident in Epicurus' thought, it did change his view of that philosophy's value for life. As Nietzsche stated, 'There are problems that are higher than any problems of pleasure, pain, or pity; and any philosophy that stops with these is a piece of naïveté' (BGE 225). However, although he called Epicurus 'the antithesis of a Dionysian Greek' (NCW 'Antipodes'), Nietzsche's fondness for him persisted through his late works. As Shearin observes, 'There exists a significant, if partial, identification between Nietzsche and Epicurus' (2014: 72).

Surveying the evolution of Nietzsche's interest in Epicurus, it becomes evident that his implicit and explicit engagement with it tracks the development of these interrelated ideas. The *euthumia* (ευθυμία) – good passion or spiritedness – promoted by Democritus corresponds with Nietzsche's understanding of Epicurus and is manifest in his gay science.[4] In holding that Nietzsche's thinking aligned with important aspects of Epicurus' thought despite his opposition to key features of it, I agree with Ansell-Pearson that a cheerful disposition extolling a qualified form of *ataraxia*, or unperturbed tranquillity, was one means by which he sought to regulate emotional and mental turbulence in his own life. Ansell-Pearson asserts that 'the aim of philosophy for Nietzsche is to temper emotional and mental excess, and [towards realizing this] Epicurean teaching has a key role to play' (2014b: 239). A jovial spiritedness (*euthumia*) in combination with corresponding practices of life affirmation – including, importantly, suffering – serve as Nietzsche's method for productively challenging anti-human values and the life-denying moral systems they promulgate. In so doing Nietzsche tacitly encourages free spirits to adopt that attitude and related habits, to engage in 'dangerous exercises in self-mastery' (NCW 'Epilogue 1)' and overcome 'the highest resistance' (TI 'Skirmishes', 38).

Nietzsche espoused a jocose temperament that he considered key to the realization of happiness, or intoxication with life, a conception with echoes of Epicurus' concern for attaining happiness – the necessity of friends, critical reflection upon one's existence, and a modicum of self-sufficiency and control over one's desires (living wisely). This disposition accords with the free spirits' 'enigmatic longing' (BGE 56), which impels them, through an agonic 'striving for distinction' (D 113), to affirm themselves and existence. This cheerfully undertaken struggle – an unqualified embrace of life – is ultimately at odds with Epicurus' vision of a good life, and explicit resonances between Nietzsche's thought and Epicurus' decrease significantly in the mature, post-Zarathustra works. By the end of his productive career Nietzsche rejects Epicurus' ethics of self-care via *ataraxia*, despite remaining affectionate towards the Hellenistic philosopher.

I

In what sense should we understand Nietzsche as having been both 'with' and 'against' (that is 'con/tra') Epicurus? Nietzsche explicitly identifies with Epicurus, particularly in his so-called 'middle' period, in which he mustered Epicurus' proto-positivist/ empiricist view in support of his own quite sanguine views of science. As with his rejection of Epicurus' ethics of self-care, Nietzsche's mature works dispense with the quasi-positivist/empiricist epistemological stance of his middle period in which he celebrated science, a stance informed by Epicurus (cf. D 72 and GS 123 with GS 344 and BGE 204).

There have been numerous attempts to explain Nietzsche's abiding interest in Epicurus, which like many other subjects Nietzsche engages, entails a broad range of interpretations. Milkowski sees the sociopolitical implications of his critique of decadence: the 'acceptance of the Epicurean lifestyle', he asserts, 'can preserve the masses from decay. ... Nietzsche thinks that Epicureanism as a worker's lifestyle is safer for the aristocrats of the spirit than any other way of life, especially the one that lets the proletariat retain some hope' (72). Caygill contends that 'Nietzsche "gradually learnt to understand Epicurus as a savior figure"' (109), citing GS-370, due to the Samian philosopher's optimism. Ansell-Pearson recently demonstrated 'that an ethos of Epicurean enlightenment pervades Nietzsche's middle period texts' (Ansell-Pearson 2014: 239). Suffering, which Nietzsche understood as 'an agitation of the will (towards action, defense, revenge, retribution)', was a persistent concern he shared with Epicurus (GS 127). As Acharya notes, Nietzsche 'considered suffering an inescapable condition [... and the] ambiguity associated with the problem [it] implies the "great question mark over the value of existence"' (Acharya 2014: 19–20, citing BT-Attempt-1). Irrespective of how Epicurus' extant fragments may have influenced Nietzsche's works, the latter delineate the problem of suffering far more deeply than the former.

Notwithstanding his late reassessment, Nietzsche remained fond of the ethos of Epicurus' philosophical outlook and sensibility, which Ansell-Pearson praises as useful for 'show[ing] us how to quieten our being and so help to temper a human mind that is prone to neurosis' (Ansell-Pearson 2014b: 239). Claiming to be 'proud to experience Epicurus' character in a way unlike perhaps anyone else and to enjoy, in everything I hear and read of him, the happiness of the afternoon of antiquity' (GS 45), Nietzsche concurs with Epicurus 'in believing that death is nothing to us' (LM), insofar as we can accept the thought experiment and practice of affirming the eternal return, and uphold the view that 'evils' – or woe – must, as an ineliminable feature of existence, be expected. The aforementioned evolution of his view of science (from sanguine to critical) runs parallel to the transformation of his views towards Epicurus' thought. Following *Thus Spoke Zarathustra* and the development of his critique of decadence, he identifies Epicurus' rejection of suffering, advocacy of withdrawal and the pursuit of tranquillity with a decadence that '*desires* nothing' (KSA 13:11[365]). While stating no position on Epicurus' view that 'physical pain does not last long' (PD-4), Nietzsche saw pain as a necessary spur to self-overcoming and perfection that strong individuals strove to increase. Living means desiring, which prompts striving, foments resistance and produces apprehensions and pains, which generate new desires, until death. He therefore objected to any contention that 'pain [in any of its forms] is the chief evil of life (PD-10)'. As Abraham observed, 'For Nietzsche ... pain is the major condition of all creation: "all becoming and growing", all that exceeds the present and "guarantees the future". Pain is no negative force but represents an affirmative power. Like suffering renders birth, pain is a force creating reality' (116, citing TI 'Ancients' 4). Furthermore, as denying the fecundity of pain and benefits of suffering falsifies reality, Epicurus' ethics were an expression of his sickness: 'Who are the only people motivated to lie their way out of reality? People who suffer from it. But to suffer from reality means that you are a piece of reality that has gone wrong' (A 15).

Despite Nietzsche's recognition that Epicurus was a decadent, remainders of his affection for the Epicurean sensibility in his middle period are evident in his mature works:

> Profound suffering makes you noble; it separates. One of the most refined forms of disguise is Epicureanism, and a certain showy courage of taste that accepts suffering without a second thought and resists everything sad and profound. (BGE 270)

The central tenet of Epicurus' philosophy that Nietzsche rejects is his emphasis on avoiding sources of suffering to minimize pain and cultivate maximal pleasure.[5] Instead, Nietzsche concludes – in keeping with a key feature of his therapeutic philosophy – that pleasure is a *product* of the chosen suffering entailed in attempts at self-creation and squandering, as exemplified in the wastefulness characteristic of the Renaissance, 'the last great age' (TI-'Skirmishes', 37). Nevertheless, Epicureanism may serve as a mask to conceal and/or deflect attention from the suffering one has undertaken (BGE 270).

Epicurus wrote, 'The magnitude of pleasure reaches its limit in the removal of all pain. When such pleasure is present, so long as it is uninterrupted, there is no pain either of body or of mind or of both together' (PD 3). He considered the elimination of discomfort and anxiety necessary for the achievement of imperturbability, which he considered proper to a happy, well-lived human life. Hence, he took the preservation of pleasure via the eradication of pain as universally desirable. Contra Epicurus, Nietzsche asserts that 'happiness is neither the purpose of existence, nor its natural end':

> Insofar as the individual is seeking happiness, one ought not to tender him any prescriptions as to the path to happiness: for individual happiness springs from one's own unknown laws, and prescriptions from without can only obstruct and hinder it. – The prescriptions called 'moral' are in truth directed against individuals and are in no way aimed at promoting their happiness. (D 108)

Nietzsche maintains that happiness – and pleasure – is a second-order motive of free spirits that results from invigorating agonic engagements, rather than a striving to avoid pain. Tranquillity is not sought as an unceasing state of being but enjoyed in times of peace as an opportunity to gather oneself in anticipation of future agonic struggles.

As Epicurus' tempered advocacy of pleasure relates to happiness, his 'prescriptions' are quite general: 'No pleasure is a bad thing in itself, but some pleasures are only obtainable at the cost of excessive troubles' (PD-8). This conditionality of pleasure – 'the cost of excessive troubles' – may provide Nietzsche some latitude in maintaining his partiality for Epicurus' related conceptions of pleasure and happiness. Being symptomatic of their involuntary drives and essential to their growth/becoming the free spirits, agonistic pursuits – the means by which they seek the good by opposing decadence values – do not impose an undue burden upon them, nor does the suffering they undergo in consequence cause them undesired distress. Reginster correctly explains that 'saying that suffering is valued for its own sake [is not to say that it] is not valued *by itself*, but only as an ingredient of the good. The good life involves not only resistance (and therefore suffering) but also its overcoming. Nietzsche considers that pain, as well as suffering, can be sources of affirmation' (Reginster 2006: 234).

Conversely, Nietzsche arguably affirms Epicurus' association of pleasure with happiness and virtue, albeit by reversing Epicurus' premises. Pleasure and the consequent happiness and virtue it affords, is indirectly attained – not deliberately striven for – in resistances and agonic striving generative of suffering and the growth it facilitates, rather than its avoidance or the pursuit of pleasure/happiness for its own sake. Nietzsche distinguishes between life-enhancing spiritualization and the 'wretched contentment' pursued by the all-too-many whose 'religion of snug coziness' typifies decadent ages (GS 338). He scorns the plebeian pursuit of happiness, quipping, 'people don't strive for happiness, only the English do' (TI 'Arrows' 12). While Nietzsche does not associate the latter with Epicurus, it corresponds with the avoidance of suffering for the sake of a narrow ideal of pleasure and the narcotizing desire for tranquillity born of a hatred of existence (GM III 17).

Nietzsche's critique of morality is predicated upon interconnected psychological motivations. Contending with the affliction of nihilism in post-Christian Europe, he denied that there are universal ethical principles and that the assertion of such old fictions indicates a decadence born of *ressentiment* for difference. He argued that in a decadent culture free spirits should not be constrained by the reigning, albeit abased, values of their society, particularly when those values assist the 'mediocritization and depreciation of humanity in value', but he does think it behooves them in a practical sense to *appear* to conform with decadence values as they 'struggle with constant unfavorable conditions' to overcome themselves and revalue those values in the process (BGE 203, 262). Epicurus acknowledges that his system of disciplined withdrawal for the cultivation of tranquillity and concurring pleasures that conduce a superior quality of happiness is undesired by – and unattainable – to most. While Nietzsche's view of how such a heretofore unknown happiness may be realized would strike most as undesirable, it contrasts with Epicurus' because it requires free spirits to 'bear and to be able to bear [the] monstrous sum of all kinds of grief' (GS 337). He further associates the highest joy conceivable with the '*tragic* feeling' attained by 'saying yes to life, even in its strangest and harshest problems' (TI Ancients 5).

While Epicurus considered the absence of bodily pain and emotional anxiety necessary for happiness and the *telos* of a well-ordered human existence, Nietzsche maintained that 'humankind as a whole has no goal' (HH I 33). He affirmed the necessity of pain as part of the work free spirits undertake to perfect themselves and to contribute to the flourishing of their culture. They strive to overcome the type 'man', which entails squandering themselves without concern for preservation. It is through productive strife that 'free spirits' achieve what for them constitutes happiness.

> There are people [for whom] pain itself gives them their greatest moments! They are the heroic human beings, the great pain-bringers of humanity, those few or rare ones who need the same apology as pain itself – and truly, they should not be denied this! They are eminently species-preserving and species-enhancing forces, if only because they resist comfort and do not hide their nausea at this type of happiness. (GS 318)

These passages illustrate a tension within Nietzsche's own thought and between his views and those of Epicurus, namely, their differing views on the utility of tranquillity and the avoidance of pain for happiness and the realization of the best life.[6]

Nietzsche does not deem Epicurean happiness – peacefulness and the evasion of pain it fosters – desirable. Instead, it disgusts him as symptomatic of weakness and nihilistic resignation. Yet, Nietzsche recognized a fellow decadent in Epicurus, hence his sustained affection for the philosopher of the garden. Against the imperative to discover the truth, which was then (as now, via faith in science) being encouraged by 'the prejudice of reason [and...] faith in grammar' (TI 'Reason' 5), he asserted: 'To acknowledge untruth as a condition of life ... means resisting the usual value feelings in a dangerous manner; and a philosophy that risks such a thing would by that gesture alone place itself beyond good and evil' (BGE 4). In an unpublished note from the next year he links this idea with the 'Epicureans [... asserting that they] rejected the search for truth with irony [in pursuing] "Philosophy as an art of *living*"' (KSA 12:9[57]). Given his identification with such an ironic stance towards truth claims and value judgements (BGE 191) and his view that Dionysian philosophy serves the flourishing of life (TI 'Ancients', 4; NCW 'Antipodes'), this indicates how appreciative of Epicureanism he remained. It also echoes Nietzsche's earlier contention that Epicurus was 'the inventor of an heroic-idyllic mode of philosophizing' (HH 295) that left his ethics open to misinterpretation, most famously in the form of its appeal to crass hedonists through the intervening centuries, which associated Epicureanism with drunkards, whore-mongers and gluttons, as well as today's mindless consumers, shallow bourgeois gourmands and self-styled 'creatives'. However decadent it was for denying the needfulness of suffering and creativity born of pain, as an art of living it was conceived to foster friendship, composure and contemplation (see: Verkerk 2017).

II

Both Epicurus and Nietzsche were concerned with the best life for individuals according to the social life – or future world – they, respectively, imagined. Nietzsche echoes Epicurus on the desirability of solitude and the necessity of spiritual friendships for the best life as well as avoiding complete ostracism as a pariah (GM III 14). Some dangers should be embraced tactically, such as challenging the reigning values of one's age, which is certain to jeopardize one's security. Nietzsche recognized that free spirits endanger themselves by violating the in-group loyalty expected of them as members of their communities. Nietzsche himself did so by emphatically rejecting nationalism and anti-Semitism and criticizing the reigning philistinic values characteristics of his time and the German people's anti-cultural ethos (BGE 243; TI 'Germans'). In his middle and late works he spurned his culture's elites via his criticism of Wagner and his explicit disdain for the remaining authority of the (mis)ruling aristocracy of his declining age (NCW). All of this is worth noting in terms of the psychological bases of his value judgements and corresponding critique of morality. In proffering these appraisals, Nietzsche undertakes the task of revaluing nineteenth-century Europe's dissipative, anti-human values. The judgements entailed in doing so reflect the application of contending considerations, including the justifiableness of an act – or its prohibition – weighed in terms of the good it fosters or the harm it likely causes. While suffering is no objection to life, seeking the good entails objections to certain kinds of dissatisfaction and anguish. Nietzsche's free spirits aspire to perfect themselves, consistent with a yearning to improve their lives – and the world – born of experiences of pain and suffering. In declining ages this is frequently due to their subjugation to decadence values.

What of the psychological dynamic involved in one's adjudications where potential harms are recognized for what they are and accepted as necessary? As there are no 'victimless' value judgements, Nietzsche 'errs' in favour of cultural flourishing. As strong individuals are the likeliest to facilitate the cultural greatness of society and enhance its prosperity via the higher meanings their creative acts bestow, their good should be privileged over the herd's (BGE 268). The naturalistic inequality this value prioritization and equivalent socio-cultural organization affirms accords with the rank order of difference that applies and is reciprocally enforced by the pathos of distance in a healthy society (BGE 270). The pathos of distance distinguishes the range of types that comprise a society and indicates the values suitable to each, within a range of acceptability determined (in a dynamic agonism) by the community (BGE 257). It is inherently adversative to Judeo-Christian values and the secular, post-Enlightenment liberal-democratic ideals Nietzsche deemed anti-natural and decadent. The psychological motivation of his valuations arises from an assessment of human nature that entailed recognition of the ressentiment inherent in the response of the weak to their condition versus the strong. From that reaction and *ressentiment* it generates, convoluted notions of justice and corresponding ideological programmes were conceived with the aim of weakening the best individuals (GM I, 10).

Nietzsche's hostility to the socialist, democratic and anarchist values of his day (A 57) originates not in a reactionary defence of Europe's then-discredited hereditary aristocracy, but from disgust for the decadence those anti-natural values symptomatize (McNeal 2018: 148–9). Although echoing Nietzsche's language here, his valuations concern *fairmindedness*. While this concern may seem, prima facie, to unduly emphasize the interests of the strongest (and be misread as advancing a crass, regressive elitism), that is a result of *our* egalitarian prejudices and *his* provocative rhetoric. The *natural* values that he advocates conduce the full realization of every person's abilities.

Those values promise to enhance the lives of the community's weaker members – the majority – by abating the decadence that entices them to succumb to nihilism (GM I 12, III 27; A 7).

Nietzsche's thinking (and conclusions) about suffering were prompted in part by his concern with mitigating the numerous harms – distinct from suffering, per se – produced by decadence values. Among these harms is that healthy individuals, whose instincts are likelier to be stymied by anti-natural ascetic values than are those of the weak, suffer disproportionately in relation to the rabble who promote dissipative values. The healthy are hindered and frequently ruined by them. Contrariwise, as the unhealthy are less free, they do not find egalitarian decadence values oppressive; the illusions and corresponding practices compelled by ascetic ideals make life seem more endurable to them. Free spirits suffer for resisting decadence values.

The psychological motivation of Nietzsche's valuations originates in a dual concern for harm reduction and the related development of his unconventional conception of fairness, one distinctly at odds with crude egalitarianism. This is also mixed with disgust for the decadence that propagates those harms, as well as disdain for and distrust of the ascetic-priests promulgating decadence values. Towards the realization of the maximum autonomy of each of society's members, these concerns are central to Nietzsche's effort to revalue all values (BGE 203).

Nietzsche challenged traditional metaphysics and (echoing Hume) sought to demonstrate the metaphysical basis of our need for a 'true world' – which Nietzsche endeavours to show is a fable (TI 'Fable' 1–6) – as well as faith in truth, reason, causal relations, cause and effect and free will. His examination of the underlying psychological needs that metaphysical explanations of existence aim to provide was motivated, in part, by Epicurus' rejection of metaphysical explanations of existence (GS 45). Regarding the problem of humankind's place in the seemingly mechanistic natural world, he concludes that – being 'still undetermined animals'– it straddles the limitations imposed by physical existence and the possibility of transfiguring the world (BGE 62). This insight arose from a complex of interrelated concerns that prompted his emergent ontological will to power hypothesis, specifically on the interrelatedness of our unconscious desires, conscious longings and belief in causality, as well as the faith in free will and insistence upon responsibility (BGE 36). By extension, his distinctions between noble and base types, and master and slave moralities, develop in order to explain corresponding responses to the human condition (suffering) in disparate peoples, their moralities and the forms of social life they engender (BGW 260).

What constitutes noble suffering? In post-Zarathustra works Nietzsche distinguishes

> two types of sufferers: first, those who suffer from a superabundance of life – they want a Dionysian art as well as a tragic outlook and insight into life – then, those who suffer from an impoverishment of life and demand quiet, stillness, calm seas. … Revenge against life itself – the most voluptuous type of intoxication for people who are impoverished in this way! (NCW Antipodes)

Despite his acclamations of Epicurus, the latter assertion seems to exemplify the person whose suffering originates in a dearth of vitality. As one who advanced the cultivation of tranquillity for the avoidance of suffering, Epicurus' concern with preventing pain does not indicate an interest in the tragic outlook on life that Nietzsche identifies in earlier Greek tragedians. Furthermore, this suggests that Hellenistic Epicureans were attracted to their philosophical programme by an inherent need to avoid striving and conflict generative of suffering. Reflecting on the comparable loathing of pain in prosperous modern Europe, Nietzsche observed:

> The general inexperience with ... pain and the relative rarity of the sight of suffering individuals have an important consequence: pain is hated much more now than formerly ... one can hardly endure the presence of pain as a thought and makes it a matter of conscience and a reproach against the whole of existence. (GS 48)

The eschewal of distress by those who are 'inexperienced in great pains of the soul ... or bodily sufferings', in order to protect themselves from the agonies of life, originates in 'excessive sensitivity' and a psychological need for the guarantees of security required by children that grows into an anti-natural rejection of life and blossoms into a desire for revenge against existence – everything strong, self-assured and commanding. What if the people whose instinctive predisposition inclines them towards Epicureanism, those so 'exhausted, and unsure of themselves, were to moralize: what type of moral valuations would they have?' In such circumstances, Nietzsche concludes, 'a pessimistic suspicion of the whole condition of humanity would probably find expression, perhaps a condemnation of humanity along with its condition' (BGE 260). Their pessimism stems from an inability to accept or to contend with pain and suffering, both physiological and psychological. They extol

> qualities that serve to alleviate existence for suffering people ... : pity, the obliging, helpful hand, the warm heart, patience, industriousness, humility, and friendliness receive full honors here –, since these are the most useful qualities and practically the only way of holding up under the pressure of existence. (BGE 260)

In her 'fight against pain' the ascetic priest worked relentlessly to diminish human consciousness (GM III 18). Her aversion to suffering, and the thorough 'dampening of sensibility, of susceptibility to pain' – central aspects of the human condition – she encourages, do nothing to alter that condition, or to assuage misery. Rather, she exacerbates self-contempt and provokes disgust with humanity (GM III: 18). Opposing the ascetic priest's effort, Nietzsche seeks to increase the suffering of the highest spirits:

> To those human beings who are of any concern to me I wish suffering, desolation, sickness, ill-treatment, indignities – I wish that they should not remain unfamiliar with profound self-contempt, the torture of self-mistrust, the wretchedness of the vanquished: I have no pity for them, because I wish them the only thing that can prove today whether one is worth anything or not – that one endures. (KSA 12:10[103])

Suffering inures the exceptional individual who undergoes it and overcomes herself (or 'endures') thereby, but among those who seek to abolish suffering, pity is among the most common psychological/rhetorical stratagems they employ. Thus, the improvers of man promote pity, which inhibits overcoming suffering and increases nihilistic pessimism. Consequently, both parties are frustrated. Nietzsche associates this disease of the will with decadence (BGE 208), and perceives pity for all sufferers as an enticement to nihilism:

> Pity preserves things that are ripe for decline, ... and it gives a depressive and questionable character to life itself by keeping alive an abundance of failures of every type. ... Pity negates life, it makes life worthy of negation, – pity is the *practice* of nihilism [and] wins people over to *nothingness*. (A 7)

The psychological impulse inducing prospective adherents to follow Epicurus' philosophy closely parallels that which, directed towards ressentiment for what succeeds, gives rise to the slave revolt in morals; as Milkowski observed, by conducting that impulse towards sanguinity towards life, Epicureanism may immunize the herd against decadence. Contra Epicurus, Nietzsche takes the inexorableness of suffering to commend the need for practices with which to productively transmute it, albeit not practices such as ataraxia, meant to foster peacefulness, but practices that intensify the agon. His aim of increasing suffering was premised on an acceptance of it as a gift for those with the great health needed to 'receive' it and propel themselves via increased struggles to greater heights of awareness and feeling (GS 382).

Among the most significant distinctions between Nietzsche and Epicurus, is the former's recognition that unconscious needs of philosophers, conditioned by involuntary drives symptomatic of their health, are lenses through which they view and interpret the world (BGE 6; GM III 6-8). Nietzsche's conclusions, namely, the necessity of suffering, impugn key tenets of Epicurus' philosophy and lead him to recognize – despite admiring the ethos of his thought – that the Greek for whom 'the highest good is pleasure' was 'a *typical* decadent' (A 30).

III

It is through intensification of suffering, Nietzsche maintains, that one may heighten one's experience, and corresponding acts of value creation that one may cope with the uncertainty and fear inherent to existence. For Nietzsche, calm self-possession may be nurtured by an embrace of one's fate, and to the extent that it promotes pleasure with the world and oneself, such cultivated equanimity demonstrates one's fragmented state (and its role in one's existential suffering) and place within the whole of existence, the latter insight (that 'the fatality of human existence cannot be extricated from the fatality of everything that was and will be') strengthening one in the attempts to overcome the former condition towards becoming the integrated unity one yearns to be (TI 'Errors' 8).

Knight notes that 'the importance which Epicurus attaches to friendship has an astonishingly close affinity with many significant utterances of Nietzsche' (Knight 1933: 441). Indeed, Nietzsche's interpretation of Epicureanism informed his own emphasis on the crucialness of friendship and the existentially edifying and spiritually elevating pleasures they provide. With Epicurus, who asserts that 'the same conviction which inspires confidence that nothing we have to fear is eternal or even of long duration, also enables us to see that in the limited evils of this life nothing enhances our security so much as friendship' (PD-28), Nietzsche maintains that healthy individuals (free spirits) venerate their friends for having spurred them to overcome themselves (often via the 'good Eris' [HC]), just as each esteems the other's self-squandering. Friends are able to enjoy each other's realization of their more or less shared 'higher ideal' (GS 338) while the productive agon between them incites their efforts to perfect themselves and sustains their mutual affection as 'best enem[ies]' to one another (Z I 14, IV Science). 'The pleasure we take in ourselves tries to preserve itself by time and again changing something new into ourselves – that is simply what possession means' (GS 14). Friends suffer in a process of possession-taking, even as 'they call the lust for new possessions that is awakened in them "love"' (GS: 14).

However, this is not entirely exploitative. It relates to the acquisition of a capacity for deeper suffering and commensurately higher joys, an expanded spiritual capaciousness which fortifies each for the experiments and dangers they will undertake in the future. Their 'joying-with' (*Mitfreude*; GS 338) provides reciprocal support and assists them in affirming life. By extension, joying-with empowers their more radical affirmation of both their own and one another's past, present and future. Embracing their respective fates, intertwined in friendship, they foster courage in themselves and one another, taking pleasure in uncertainty. Each comes to recognize the other *and* their mutual bond as an inextricable part of existence. Epicurus asserts, 'Of all things that wisdom provides for living one's entire life in happiness, the greatest by far is the possession of friendship' (PD 27). His emphasis on friendship consists of, and may have influenced, Nietzsche's own, and thereby anticipates the metaphysical significance of the latter's notion of the eternal return (BGE 56). If, between two friends, the 'shared higher thirst for an ideal above them' (GS 14) should wane, if 'the almighty force of [their] projects drove [them] apart once again, into different seas and sunny zones' they should not 'be ashamed of it'. They may 'rise to [the] thought' that even if they be 'earth enemies' their relationship will remain a 'star friendship' in which each continues to honour the other as a former inspiration (GS 279). As those 'who *know* how to honor' they exalt one another, either as current, amicable collaborators or as former companions in accordance with the ethos of their master morality, which induces recognition of that which is noble in every individual (BGE 260). Caygill asserts that 'Nietzsche's self-proclaimed Epicureanism ... is not part of a religion of love ... but a star friendship, with the sense of risk that for Nietzsche attends such friendship' (2006: 113).

Linking Zarathustra's overflowing spirit to Nietzsche's free spirits (cf. Z P4 to BGE 44 and A 37), he meant to convey that free spirits express the will to power they are (BGE 13) via creative works that manifest their health and strength.[7] They thereby transfigure their suffering into intoxication with life (TI 'Skirmishes', 8–11). Through this bestowing virtue – a conferral of their affirmation of existence – the suffering that facilitated it is forgotten. The passion it exhibits spurs witnesses of their self-expenditure to emulate them through creative experiments of their own. This promulgates the aforementioned forgetting – the dis-remembering of the suffering that originally spurred the free spirits' erotically arousing artistic creation – and, by mitigating the horror of existence, inspires them to pursue their passion and expend/squander themselves. The free spirits' pursuit of increasingly difficult challenges and trials augment the power they are. Attempts at self-overcoming enhance their strength, elevating them whether or not they 'succeed' in attaining their immediate goal – their happiness derives from struggling to enhance themselves (McNeal 2018: 154).

Through creative acts free spirits mediate a world deprived by modern science (a 'cult of the untrue', itself an art) of transcendent meaning. Art particularly 'furnishes us with the eye and hand and above all the good conscience to be able to make such a[n aesthetic] phenomenon [via self-creation, that goddess "we carry across the river of becoming"] of ourselves' (GS 107). It makes possible any philosophy of life. A free spirit's acts of self-creation, from *pathos*, arouse the *erōs* of others and inspire their emulation. This spreads the desire to strive creatively and grow (i.e., suffer) among prospective free spirits and generates further tests of mettle they may undertake and overcome. However, the struggle self-creation entails risks exhausting their humour, necessitating periods of philosophical recuperation:

> At times we need to have a rest from ourselves by looking at and down at ourselves and, from an artistic distance, laughing *at* ourselves or crying *at* ourselves; we have to discover the *hero* no less than the *fool* in our passion for knowledge; we must now and then be pleased about our folly in order to be able to stay pleased about our wisdom! And … nothing does us as much good as the *fool's cap*: we need it against ourselves – we need all exuberant, floating, dancing, mocking, childish, and blissful art lest we lose that *freedom over things* that our ideal demands of us. (GS 107)

Joviality rejuvenates free spirits, serving as a buoy to compensate for the heaviness of their task, which 'transforms things until [things in the world] reflect [their] own power, – until [those things in the world] are the reflexes of [their] perfection. This need to make perfect is – art. He even finds inherent pleasure in things that he himself is not; in art, people enjoy themselves as perfection' (TI 'Skirmishes' 9). This enjoyment sustains them in their seriousness; the latter cannot succeed without the former, and self-overcoming and perfection cannot occur without their dynamic interaction. Cheerfulness enables them to come up for breath after diving for the pearls of wisdom they seek in the depths they explore. Emanating from the deep-down of their 'granite of spiritual *fatum* (BGE 231)' it extends to 'the ultimate pinnacle of [their] spirit' (BGE 75).

In addition to revealing his decadent instincts, Epicurus' condemnation of suffering may render his recommended practices for attaining tranquillity futile, and the happiness they promise imaginary at best – a compensatory psychological strategy employed to re-present their having resigned themselves innumerable times throughout their lives to circumstances they lack the strength to overcome. Weakness masquerading as calm repose, it entices the adherents of his philosophy to deny suffering and leads them to their own immiseration in a 'wretched contentedness' (GS 338), which they are unlikely to recognize as the source of their irresolvable and fruitless suffering, being an outgrowth of their botched existence. Nietzsche's notion has parallels to, but is not synonymous with, the Greek notion of *akrasia*. *Akrasia* (weakness of will) conveys something more akin to Epicurus' idea of choosing coarse sensual pleasures over refined, cerebral ones, whereas Nietzsche conceives of the impulses and drives (*Trieb*) that impel action and striving after certain types of pleasures as involuntary symptoms of a person's instincts.

Nietzsche suggests that the embrace of suffering often indicates great health. As one capable – self-possessing and strong enough – of ignoring stimuli (incitements to react) – such an individual demonstrates the power they are. Such self-control is not analogous to inuring oneself to emotions, or repressing or denying one's feelings, 'for it would be the loss of all losses, for them, to forfeit their subtle sensitivity' (GS 306). Contra Epicurus, free spirits do not do so in an effort to avoid suffering but are driven to overcome themselves in the pursuit of more difficult contests, more *profound* suffering. Towards this, and in favour of an Epicurean temperament, Nietzsche suggests that among those comprising 'the higher ranks' of a people, 'Epicurean philosophy … refreshes, refines, and *makes the most* of suffering' (BGE 61). Moreover, 'it even sanctifies and justifies' their suffering (BGE 61). This suggests that the calm that Epicurean philosophy sustains during breaks in one's suffering enables the assimilation of difficult experiences and rejuvenates one for future trials. However, Nietzsche does not specify how it does so, whether referring to the *ethos* of Epicurean philosophy, or how the benefits he perceives in it accord with Epicurus' central tenet: the need to *avoid* suffering by means of retreating from the world, both of which Nietzsche explicitly rejects throughout his corpus.[8]

Conclusion

Nietzsche's enduring affinity for and evolving response to Epicurus philosophy traced key aspects of the former's philosophical development. Epicurus' opposition to suffering spurred Nietzsche to think through the existential problems raised by suffering and pain. Epicurus' views also informed Nietzsche's responses, by which he provided – via the laughter and forgetting necessary for noble suffering (GS 302; BGE 225; A 8) – a means of attaining intoxication with life that Epicurus' principled advocacy of maximizing serenity to sustain pleasure could not. The suffering of Nietzsche's free spirits is ennobled by the pleasure they take in contests towards the elevation of life (BGE 44). Such pleasure in struggle entails acceptance of the possibility of failure and increased pain, which intimates spiritual pregnancy and the promise of further self-squandering via their striving to become who they are (BGE 41; EH 'Clever' 9).

In a propitiatory moment Nietzsche declares, 'I do not want to wage war against what is ugly. I do not want to accuse; I do not even want to accuse those who accuse. Looking away shall be my only negation' (GS 276). He articulates an active strategy for protecting himself and his fellow free spirits from poisonous ressentiment and the degenerate mob 'well away from all madhouses and hospitals of culture … away from the evil fumes of inner corruption' (GM III 14), while engaging in value creation. Other free spirits contend with their anguish through quasi-Epicurean methods:

> There are free, impudent spirits who would like to hide and deny that they are shattered, proud, incurable hearts; and sometimes even stupidity is the mask for an ill-fated, all-too-certain knowing. (BGE 270)

Cheerfulness deployed as a mask ('One of the most refined forms of disguise is Epicureanism [BGE 270]') combined with periods of rejuvenating solitude are vital conditions for free spirits who cultivate the 'bestowing virtue' through them and gain foresight – a piece of their 'certain knowing' – of the approaching 'great noon', thereby (Z III Evils 2).[9] That 'great noon [occurs when] human beings stand at the midpoint of their course between animal and overman and celebrate their way to evening as their highest hope: for it is the way to a new morning' (Z I 'Bestowing'. 3).

Nietzsche maintained that the suffering we undergo is inextricably connected to our experiences of pleasure and joy in that suffering begets agonic engagements, ergo possibilities for self-overcoming through which joyous experiences arise. Conversely, Epicurus' desire for a 'hypnotic feeling of nothingness' attained through the 'absence of suffering' (GM III 17) – and the values advanced to realize it – denied the need for distress-inducing struggle and fructifying pain, thus rejecting a fundamental feature of human life and prerequisite for happiness. That life-denying project had to give rise to decadence, just as those for whom his ideal was needed – those whose commanding need agreed with his manner of thinking and valuing – had their dissipation exacerbated through it. Epicurus' repudiation of crucial features of human existence put his followers at odds with themselves. Nietzsche saw parallels between the life-denial characteristic of Epicureans and that of the later '"Christian",… a kind of Epicurean who follows the principle of hedonism as far as possible with his "faith makes blessed" – over and above every principle of intellectual integrity' (NCW 'Antipodes'). Although Epicurus opposed the proto-Christian Platonism of his day, 'the subterranean cults, the whole of latent Christianity' (A 58 [cf. D 72]), his philosophy enticed followers to identify pleasure in forms of life-denial.[10] Nietzsche perceived similar aversions to suffering in modern secularism, fostered by the relative ease and security typifying over-ripe cultures such as that of late-nineteenth-century Europe. Such comfortableness deadens peoples' desire for change while increasing their sensitivity and distress.

A middle-period aphorism anticipates Nietzsche's mature turn away from Epicurus. Pondering the modern obsession with eradicating suffering and the means of correcting it, he suggests that 'there is a recipe against pessimistic philosophies and excessive sensitivity […] that] would itself be counted among the signs that lead people to judge, "existence is something evil". Well, the recipe against this "distress" is: *distress*' (GS 48). An increase in sources of meaningful suffering was needed to alleviate the undue sympathy evident in the effeminate tendency to commiserate with all that suffers and preempt the spirit of revenge that results. This consists in his 'calls for the higher affirmation of tragic-joy' (Vincenzo: 384). In an unpublished note Nietzsche rebuffs Epicurus' contention that the avoidance of pain leads to tranquillity-induced pleasure:

'Any "Epicurean delight" [serenity-produced happiness] is out of the question. Only Dionysian joy is sufficient' (KSA 11:25[95]). Towards such joy one does '*not* [seek] to escape horror and pity' but embraces them in order to '*be* the eternal joy in becoming, – the joy that includes even the eternal *joy in negating*' (TI 'Ancients', 5). Dionysian joy is fostered 'as far away as possible from the happiness of weaklings, from "resignation"', and rooted in a clear-headed engagement with the world necessary for intoxication with life (A 1).

Why did Nietzsche then assert that he and his fellow free spirits 'seem to be Epicureans'? The answer lies in the *ethos* he perceived in the extant works and ancient secondary sources from which he created his interpretation of Epicurus. Nietzsche recognized a kindred spirit in Epicurus whose attitude towards life corresponded with his joie de vivre and taste for noble pleasures. Consisting with the Epicurean 'taste' that his Epicurus commends, Nietzsche identifies 'an almost Epicurean bent of knowledge develop[ing] that will not easily let go of the questionable character of things' (GS 375). Here Nietzsche perceived – or oneirically envisaged – the nascent community of free spirits whose creative experiments out of intoxication with life would condition the possible appearance of philosophers of the future (BGE 44).

Notes

1 I am grateful to Marcelo Hoffman, Paul Kirkland and Gabriel Zamosc for providing critical feedback on this chapter.
2 From the inside announcement page of GS, first edition (Kaufmann translation).
3 Swift notes that 'some of the principle tenets of Epicurean philosophy come curiously close to Nietzsche's philosophic moods in their attempt to rule out supernaturalism' (Swift: 16).
4 Power observes that 'Nietzsche's Democritus [is] a strange hybrid of abstract propositions concerning "the nature of things", consciously filtered through the web of 19th-century questions about matter, idealism and knowledge' (123).
5 In *his Letter to Menoeceus* Epicurus specifies that in arguing for pleasure as the chief aim of life, he 'do[es] not mean the pleasures of the prodigal or the pleasures of sensuality, [but that by] pleasure we mean the absence of pain in the body and of trouble in the soul'. What produces the tranquillity that ensures such 'a pleasant life … is sober reasoning, searching out the grounds of every choice and avoidance, and banishing those beliefs through which the greatest tumults take possession of the soul'.
6 Regarding the former, while humanity may have no shared goal, the aim of free spirits is the enhancement of the species, which differs from its preservation. In striving to enhance humanity, free spirits condition the possibility that philosophers of the future may revalue decadent values. That is their particular goal *for* humanity as a whole.
7 Nietzsche created his free spirits (HH I P 2) to advance a practical yet semi-heroic ideal through which the future community he envisaged could be realized. 'A spirit *that has become free*, that has taken hold of itself (EH, HH 1)', enacts 'a formula of the *highest affirmation* born out of fullness, out of overfullness, an unreserved yea-saying even to suffering, even to guilt, even to everything questionable and strange about existence' (HH BT 2).

8 After retreating from society (Z I 'Bestowing', 3) Zarathustra learns this lesson and returns (beginning of Part Two) to teach the *Übermensch* (Z I P 3).
9 On the need to 'shun the multitude' entailed in Epicurus' doctrine of *lathe biōsas*, see Groff (2017).
10 On Nietzsche's views of Epicurus' alleged opposition to the 'mystery-cults' of the late Roman Empire, see Rempel (2012).

14

'The milieu in which he moved as a foreign figure'

Nietzsche's revaluation of Epicurus

Daniel Conway

Nietzsche's generally favourable reception of Epicurus undergoes significant revision in the writings from the post-Zarathustran period of his career. Having grown increasingly sceptical of all expressions of Greek 'cheerfulness', he takes direct aim at Epicurus, whom he suspects of disguising a heretofore undiagnosed 'affliction' (BT 10). Despite having praised Epicurus as 'one of the greatest of men, the inventor of an heroic-idyllic mode of philosophizing' (HH II: 2, 295), he concludes that Epicurus was, in fact, a 'typical décadent' (A 30) whom he proposes to collect (along with Jesus) under the diagnostic umbrella of 'the Redeemer type' (A 29). Like Jesus, Nietzsche concluded, Epicurus promoted a brand of hedonism that could culminate only in a 'religion of love' (A 30).

In this chapter, I account for Nietzsche's volte-face evaluation of Epicurus by placing it in the context of what eventually became his preferred autobiographical narrative, wherein he charts his progression through the successive stages corresponding to decline, near death, recovery and rebirth. What he eventually came to realize, in short, was that his earlier enthusiasm for Epicurus was tinctured by his illness, which prompted him to seek the refreshment promised by an idyllic life predicated on modest pleasures. Upon recovering from this illness, or so he claims, he was finally in a position to solve the riddle of Epicurus, which he accomplished, I offer, by marshalling the insights reaped from his own experience with (and in opposition to) décadence.

I

In the writings from Nietzsche's so-called 'middle' period, Epicurus receives consistently favourable reviews. In *Human, All Too Human* (1878–80), for example, Nietzsche wistfully associates 'the name of Epicurus' with 'wisdom in bodily form' (224). He proceeds to identify Epicurus as one of the select 'shades' from whom he would 'accept judgment' while travelling infernally (HH II: 408), and he praises the 'wonderful insight' that led Epicurus to dispense to posterity the 'pacifying formulae' that are ingredient to the therapies of 'consolation' [*Trost*] that are prescribed in his name (HH II: 2, 7).[1] Finally, Nietzsche hails Epicurus as 'the inventor of an heroic-idyllic mode of philosophizing' (HH II: 2, 295), which he apparently adopted as the model for his own efforts to re-establish philosophy as a viable way of life.[2]

In *Daybreak* (1881), Nietzsche recounts the 'triumph' of Epicurus (via Lucretius) over the 'secret cults' that prospered in the early years of the Roman Empire (D 72). At the same time, however, he laments that this triumph 'came too early' to discredit the teachings of Paul, the apostle to the Gentiles, who 'knew of nothing better that he could say of his Redeemer than that he had *opened* the gates of immortality to everyone' (D 72). In the first edition of *The Gay Science* (1882), Nietzsche commends Epicurus for permitting him 'to enjoy the happiness of the afternoon of antiquity', even as he acknowledges that 'such happiness could be invented only by a man who was suffering continually' (45). The suggestion here, which Nietzsche later would develop into a full-blown diagnosis, is that Epicurus prudently counselled himself and his followers to content themselves with the relatively 'modest' pleasures that were available to them (GS: 45). A kind of happiness remained within their reach, this Epicurus advised, even if it was but a faded, surface-bound version of the happiness to which nobler Greeks formerly knew themselves to be entitled.

In the writings from the post-Zarathustran period of his career, Nietzsche forwards an overtly sceptical evaluation of Epicurus. For the Epicureans, he insists, the ideal achievement of happiness does not involve a positive or peak experience, but a strictly privative experience, namely 'the absence of suffering', which 'sufferers and those profoundly depressed will count ... as the highest good, as the value of values' (GM III:17). He also finds Epicurus guilty by association, linking him to the nihilistic teachings of Indian Buddhism (GM III:17), Jesus (A 58), Christianity (BGE 200), Schopenhauer (GM III:6; GS 370) and, by implication, Wagner (GM III:5; GS 370). Here, too, the concern is that Epicurus found his primary motivation not in the joyful pursuit of pleasure but in a pathologically reactive 'fear of pain' (A 30). If that were the case, of course, Epicurus would hardly count as an *epicure* in the most familiar sense of that term.[3]

Especially intriguing in this respect is the stipulated kinship between Epicureans and Christians (GS 370; cf. BGE 200).[4] The basis of this kinship, Nietzsche discloses, is the common source of their suffering, which arises in them not 'from the *overfullness of life*', which is the distinguishing mark of the Dionysian, but 'from the *impoverishment of life*' (GS 370). Those who 'suffer most and are poorest in life' – here he identifies Epicureans and Christians as fellow *romantics* – 'need above all mildness, peacefulness, and goodness in thought as well as deed' (GS 370). He thus exposes Epicurus as 'the opposite [*Gegensatz*] of a Dionysian pessimist',[5] while also insisting that 'the "Christian" ... is actually only a kind of Epicurean – ' (GS 370).[6] What they share in common, Nietzsche later adds, is their propensity to 'follow the principle of hedonism as far as possible – far beyond any intellectual integrity' (NCW 'We Antipodes').

II

In order to appreciate what motivates Nietzsche's change of heart, let us examine the larger context of his discussion of Epicurus in *The Anti-Christ*. While his primary concern in these sections is to account for the Jesus who appears in the Gospels, he recommends this account as equally illustrative of the teachings of Epicurus.

Nietzsche's bold foray into the thicket of nineteenth-century Christology begins with a summary dismissal of those scholars who '*in the absence of any other documents*', attempt to make sense of the canonical Gospels (A 28).[7] Rather than trafficking in this brand of 'scholarly idleness', Nietzsche sets out, instead, to build a profile of 'the psychological type of the Redeemer', of which he names Jesus and Epicurus as representative tokens (A 29). According to Nietzsche, this 'type' may be understood to be 'contained' in the Gospels, 'transmitted' [*überliefert*] by them, even though the Gospels themselves cannot be accepted as valid or even credible historical sources. Despite themselves, that is, the Gospels may be mined by intrepid scholars for indirect evidence of the Redeemer type.

Refusing Renan's influential interpretation of Jesus as both a *genius* and a *hero*, Nietzsche insists that nothing could be further from the truth:

> What are the 'glad tidings'? True life, eternal life, has been found – it is not promised, it is here, it is *in you*: as a living in love, a love without subtraction and exclusion, without regard for station. (A 29)

Translating this psychological insight into his preferred technical vocabulary, namely, that of the *physiologist*, Nietzsche explains that

> we know a state in which the *sense of touch* is pathologically excitable and shrinks from any contact, from grasping a solid object. One should translate such a physiological habitus into its ultimate consequence – an instinctive hatred of every reality, a flight into 'what cannot be grasped', 'the incomprehensible' ...; a being at home in a world which is no longer in contact with any kind of reality. (A 29)

Nietzsche thus attributes to the Redeemer type a permanent, non-negotiable condition of recoil from anyone or anything that smacks of substantiality. This pathological expression of hypersensitivity consigns would-be redeemers to an extreme and persistent fugue state, wherein they are obliged to dissociate themselves not only from their own identities, but also from any hint of shared worldly perdurance. As a result, the 'redemption' they find within themselves is describable only via indirection, allusion, parable and analogy. Their experience of being 'redeemed' is exclusively subjective and, therefore, impervious to criticism and challenge.

To '*the instinctive hatred of reality*' Nietzsche then adds '*the instinctive exclusion of any antipathy*', which, he insists, eventually must find expression in the fateful embrace of 'love as the only, as the *last* possible, way of life' (A 30). From these two '*physiological realities*' he thus derives what he calls the 'doctrine of redemption', which he proceeds to identify as 'a sublime further development of hedonism on a thoroughly morbid basis' (A 30). This is an important (if grotesque) elaboration of his profile of the Redeemer type, for it confirms his intention to account for (rather than call into question) the standard designation of Epicureanism as an expression of philosophical hedonism. That Epicurus was, in fact, a hedonist is true not with respect to the intensity or the variety of the pleasures he recommended and enjoyed, but with respect to his understanding of himself as guided by his pursuit and possession of those pleasures that he believed to be conducive to (or constitutive of) happiness. Epicurus qualifies as a hedonist, that is, inasmuch as he believed and taught that one need and should not defer those pleasures that will redeem one's mortal existence. That his critics refuse to acknowledge these 'pleasures' as sufficient to render *their* existence meaningful is significant, but not disqualifying.

According to Nietzsche, Epicurus was a '*typical décadent*', whose 'fear of pain, even of infinitely minute pain … can end in no other way than in a *religion of love*' (A 30). In his pursuit of this end, Nietzsche conjectures, Epicurus developed a 'pagan' version of the 'doctrine of redemption' that was promulgated more famously by Jesus (A 30). In both cases, Nietzsche explains, 'redemption' was understood simultaneously as the most pleasurable condition attainable by mortals *and* as a release from pain, suffering, disturbance and discomfort. Despite his reputation for promoting the enjoyment of pleasure, Epicurus, in fact, enrolled his clients in a pain-avoidance programme, which Nietzsche describes as 'most closely related' to the meek hedonism that is more generally characteristic of the 'redeemer type' (A 30). Much like the Jesus whom Nietzsche profiles in *The Anti-Christ*, though blessed with 'a generous admixture of Greek vitality and nervous energy' (A 30), Epicurus offered his followers a 'salvation' that was not only promised but also 'attained' in the here and now, with no metaphysical or eschatological conditions attached (A 33). Again, like Jesus, and with a similar motivation, Epicurus encouraged his followers to adopt 'love as the only, as the *last* possible, way of life' (A 30).

That Epicurus was a 'décadent', and 'typical' to boot, is apparently meant to stand as a solution, long overdue, to the riddle of

> that old schoolmaster from Samos, who sat, hidden away, in his little garden at Athens and wrote three hundred books. (BGE 7)

In Nietzsche's profile of the Redeemer type, however, we find no trace of the 'rage' and 'ambition' that he earlier proffered as the hidden keys to the motivations of Epicurus (BGE 7). In their place, as we have seen, he now postulates an acute hypersensitivity to pain, which would render prohibitive all outbursts of 'rage', 'ambition' and all other intolerably strong affects. As he now understands the type of which Epicurus is supposedly representative, the pursuit of *ataraxia* necessarily must involve a therapeutic effort to liberate oneself from the disturbances associated with the expression of all overpowering affects.

This is also true of the teachings of Jesus, inasmuch as these teachings may be discerned independently of the malign interpretation imposed on them by the apostle Paul. According to Nietzsche, the Jesus of the Gospels promised happiness in real time to all those, independent of profession, station, race, class, caste, nationality or ethnicity, who wished to be redeemed (A 33). All they needed to do was to commit themselves to an ethics of unconditional, indiscriminate love, which the life of Jesus was meant and believed to exemplify (A 34). In both cases, of course, it would be a mistake to classify the hedonism in question as the outcome of a proper *choice*, that is, as one viable option among several (or many), even if that is how its champions and adherents prefer to describe it. According to Nietzsche, the hedonism preached by Epicurus and Jesus (and, presumably, by any other representative of the Redeemer type) was a matter of physiological necessity: the modest pleasures (or 'pleasures') in question were recommended to those unfortunates who lived in permanent, involuntary retreat from even the slightest pains and discomforts. As we are now in a position to understand, in fact, the seemingly perverse insistence that the privation of suffering constitutes a kind of pleasure was (and remains) an important component of the Epicurean therapy: Thinking of oneself as a full-bodied *agent*, actively engaged in the pursuit and enjoyment of pleasure, may contribute to the alleviation of one's suffering.

III

Speaking almost exclusively of Jesus, Nietzsche continues to build his profile of the Redeemer type. 'The glad tidings', we learn, 'are precisely that there are no longer any opposites' (A 32). Rather than risk the suffering that attends conflict and disagreement, the redeemer locates Redemption (e.g. 'the kingdom of heaven') in the here and now, as already (or nearly) within the reach of his childlike disciples (A 33). As a consequence, any and all formulations or descriptions of redemption are welcome; any and all experiences of redemption are immediately confirmed and acknowledged as such. In the case of Epicurus, as we shall see, each individual is affirmed as the final arbiter of his own experience of pleasure, which cannot be meaningfully questioned or discredited by another.

By identifying Epicurus as representative of the Redeemer type, finally, Nietzsche is able to account for (and celebrate) the novelty of his diagnosis. His guiding hermeneutic principle here is that tokens of the Redeemer type will appear in the historical record as the shape-shifting bearers of multiple, conflicting and contradictory interpretations (A 30). Physiologically indisposed towards negations and denials of any kind, taking no sides and all sides simultaneously, these figures cannot help but become omni-affirmative repositories of the ideas, values and teachings projected onto them by their contemporaries. Speaking explicitly of Jesus, though presumably of the Redeemer type more generally, Nietzsche explains that 'he must show traces [*Spuren*] of the milieu in which he moved *as a foreign figure*' (A 31, emphasis added). Although he does not say so explicitly, Nietzsche also appears to mean that the 'foreignness' of the Redeemer type is sufficiently faint and subtle so that it is either difficult to discern, readily forgotten, easily disregarded or resistant to classification in the milieu in which it is encountered. In other words, Nietzsche apparently understands the Redeemer type on the model of the *outsider inside*, who, for the most part, successfully *passes* within 'the milieu in which he moves'.

As Nietzsche readily acknowledges, he helps himself in these sections of *The Anti-Christ* to Dostoyevsky's brilliant profile of *The idiot*, Prince Myshkin, who, simply because he affirms all positions and opinions directed his way, embracing each and every claimant upon his time and attention, finds himself at the centre of the convoluted dramas unfolding around him. Recently arrived in St. Petersburg from a sanatorium in Switzerland, where he received treatment for epilepsy,[8] Prince Myshkin was not entirely at home in the milieu in which he moved.[9] Unwilling (and, according to Nietzsche, unable) to take sides in the various debates swirling around him, he served, involuntarily, as an occasion for the ensuing disruptions in his adopted 'milieu' (and, we might add, in the ever expanding 'milieu' of scholarship and critical response pertaining to *The Idiot*). Nietzsche's point here, to paraphrase Jn 17.16, is that representatives of the Redeemer type are *in* (but not *of*) the milieu in which they move. For his part, Prince Myshkin may be understood to be physically present in the milieu described by Dostoevsky, and discernible as such, but only inasmuch as he withholds himself, ever so slightly, from its defining tenor and characteristic features. If we wish to limn the type he represents, Nietzsche thus suggests, we are obliged to track his eccentric movements through this milieu, as he partakes (albeit from an emotional distance) of the controversies that exercise his contemporaries.

Inasmuch as Nietzsche's interpretation of Jesus also applies to Epicurus, we should be able to discern his character by scouring the historical record for traces of his alien (or eccentric) presence in the milieu in which he moved. Here we may recall Nietzsche's various efforts to portray Epicurus as inauthentic, as out of joint with the milieu in which he moved, and as striving to disguise his extra-Hellenic (and, perhaps, extra-worldly) character and temperament. In particular, we know, Nietzsche questions the character (or intensity) of the pleasures that were prescribed by this timid hedonist. While Epicurus spoke eloquently of his high esteem for pleasure, the pleasures he actually affirmed would not have been recognized as such by Greeks of noble bearing. Where was the feasting, the drinking, the revelling, the wrestling, the spirited contest for honour and glory? Whence the emphasis on alleviating those pains and discomforts that prove a hero?

Hence the provenance of Nietzsche's otherwise curious supposition that the Greeks may not have understood Epicurus at all (BGE 7, 27). Epicurus may have *seemed* Greek, especially in his 'Hellenically cool' display of a typically Greek expression of philosophical optimism (GM III:17), but the depth of his suffering (GS 45, BGE 7), which he was able for the most part to mask from view, led him to attach a positive value to the 'absence of suffering' (GM III:17). If we pursue this line of interpretation, in fact, we may be tempted to entertain the possibility that Epicurus was every bit 'as un-Greek, as anti-Greek', as Plato and Socrates (TI 'Socrates' 1).

As with the Jesus who appears in the Gospels, we may expect to find that Epicurus too 'is preserved for us only in extensive distortion' (A 32). These distortions are produced, Nietzsche suggests, through the (entirely understandable) attempts by denizens of a particular milieu to make sense of the passing outsider in their midst. Unable to behold the Redeemer as such, for example, as the inhabitant of an alternative reality in which redemption is truly 'at hand', they invariably will interpret (and, so, remake) the Redeemer in their image, projecting onto him their defining anxieties and insecurities. In doing so, they will determine that the Redeemer inhabits their shared milieu after all, even if his manner of living and speaking occasionally suggests otherwise. As his eccentricities are noted and accommodated, he will be absorbed into his adopted milieu until such a time as the 'redemption' he provides proves to be unacceptably disjointed from the redemption his contemporaries seek and expect. Like Jesus, Nietzsche might say, Epicurus is available to us as only as an elusive cypher, whose 'doctrine of redemption' was presented for all to interpret as they saw (and see) fit, as the champion of pleasures of various kinds and intensities, *including* the pleasure associated with having no pleasure (or feeling) at all. It is *this* Epicurus whom Nietzsche claims to have been the first to have discovered.

IV

In light of this startling diagnosis, what are we to make of Nietzsche's earlier enthusiasm for Epicurus? How, in short, did Nietzsche shift from a posture of respectful admiration to a position of diagnostic suspicion?

Here we should note that Nietzsche's philosophy is unusually dependent for its urgency on the anthropodicy on which it rests. Rather than seeking or asserting a supernatural justification of the suffering and grief that are incident to our mortal existence, Nietzsche looks, instead, to the creative labours of those 'higher' human beings, whose daring deeds have permanently expanded the horizon of human aspiration. Whether appealing to the signature exploits of the heroes and nobles of Greek antiquity, of the rampaging beasts of prey, of the artists and thinkers responsible for raising the stakes and prospects of European culture or of Zarathustra's dimly envisioned *Übermensch*, Nietzsche assigns a uniquely central cultural role to those 'higher' human beings whose very existence, or so he insists, bodies forth a justification of life itself.[10]

In this respect, Nietzsche's early expressions of admiration for Epicurus should not surprise us. Having lost faith in Wagner, whom he had praised in *The Birth of Tragedy* as a similarly exemplary figure (BT P), capable of fulfilling the promise of a genuinely tragic culture in late-modern Europe (BT 24), Nietzsche turned his attention to Epicurus, whom he revered, as we have seen, for striking a masterful balance between the 'heroic' and the 'idyllic' vocations of philosophy. The Epicurus whom he hailed in *Human, All Too Human* had succeeded, as Nietzsche saw it then, in aligning his teachings of hedonism with his exquisitely curated way of life. As such, this Epicurus was not simply a teacher of this-worldly virtue, but an authentic exemplar of the virtues he promoted. His success in practising what he preached yielded an expression of personal integrity, which, according to Nietzsche, encouraged others to experience their lives to be justified, notwithstanding the pains and hardships they would and did endure. The life that Epicurus was able to justify, moreover, was unapologetically that of ineluctably *mortal* creatures, whose limited and finite existence should not be subjected to the surplus disturbances produced by irrational fears. The Epicurus whom Nietzsche channelled in *Human, All Too Human* was thus celebrated as similarly committed to providing his companions with the anthropodicy they both sought and deserved to receive.[11]

At the time, the Epicurean garden must have struck Nietzsche as a welcome, salutary alternative to the toxic environment he encountered at the rehearsals for the inaugural Bayreuth Festival (EH: 'Human' 2). Writing about Epicurus, imaginatively placing himself in the lineage of an Epicurean tradition of philosophizing, may have served as compensation for the garden idyll he was not in a position to enjoy. As he later realized, of course, the Epicurus in question was but a wishful projection, that is, an *ideal* (in the distinctly pejorative sense favoured by Nietzsche). The *real* Epicurus, as Nietzsche confirms in the writings of 1888, was far more complicated (and interesting) than the idealized companion whom we encounter in the pages of *Human, All Too Human*.

It may be the case, in fact, that the idealized Epicurus who appears in *Human, All Too Human* may have been one of those 'free spirits' whom Nietzsche admits to having '*invented*' in order to buoy his spirits over the course of his illness and recovery (HH P2).[12] Unlike those 'active and audacious fellows' whose tantalizing approach the recovered Nietzsche now dares to herald, the 'free spirits' conjured by the afflicted author of *Human, All Too Human* were but 'phantoms and hermit's phantasmagoria', summoned 'as compensation for the friends [he] lacked' (HH P2). In the case of the Epicurus whom Nietzsche recommended as 'wisdom in bodily form' (HH II: 224), the compensation in question is clear enough: The companionship of this idealized Epicurus would have served as a hedge against resignation, despair and the will to nothingness. The 'heroic-idyllic' example set by this Epicurus, though phantasmic, was both necessary and sufficient to vouchsafe Nietzsche's return to health.

What this means, however, is that the Epicurus who gave succour to the sickly scribbler of *Human, All Too Human* eventually became expendable. As Nietzsche's health rebounded, he no longer needed the tender companionship of the 'garden god' whom his sickness had summoned on his behalf. Having outgrown the idealized Epicurus of *Human, All Too Human*, Nietzsche was free, finally, to engage with the real Epicurus and to take the diagnostic measure of his suspiciously cheerful optimism. As an expression of his newfound freedom from the idols of his youth, Nietzsche forwards an unflattering profile of Epicurus, grouping him with Jesus and other 'typical décadents' under the umbrella designation of the 'Redeemer type'.

As Nietzsche suggests in *Ecce Homo*, his earlier enthusiasm for Epicurus was a mistake born of his own (as yet undiagnosed) décadence. What he saw in Epicurus, though he knew it not at the time, was a spectre of himself: a man obliged by his illness to mistake the lack of feeling for happiness and to associate pleasure with the remission of pain. Inasmuch as Nietzsche at the time was content with a modest menu of 'sensual pleasures', he was naturally impressed by the wisdom of a philosopher who defined happiness in terms of 'a little garden, figs, little cheeses and in addition three or four good friends' (HH II:2, 192). In other words, his praise for Epicurus in *Human, All Too Human* was symptomatic of the illness that gripped him at the time.

This is not to suggest, however, that his praise for Epicurus was either hollow or false. What Nietzsche intuited in *Human, All Too Human* (and then came to understand more clearly as he recovered) was that Epicurus offered *genuine* 'consolation' to 'the unfortunate, ill-doers, hypochondriacs, [and] the dying' (HH II:2, 7). The justification of life he bodied forth was *real*, even if the appeal of its anthropodicy was limited to those for whom a return to health, to a life replete with kinetic pleasures, was unlikely.

Inasmuch as Nietzsche's illness placed him within the ambit of this luckless clientele, he was understandably pleased at the time to receive and transmit the 'pacifying' wisdom of Epicurus. Had he been a 'typical décadent', in fact, he might not have budged from his effusive admiration for the teachings of Epicurus.

As he recovered from this illness, however, Nietzsche outgrew the need (and desire) for 'consolation'. Turning his misfortune to his advantage (EH 'Wise' 2), he took possession of an improved and more intimate understanding of the physiology of décadence. Presenting himself as (what we may call) an *atypical* décadent, he attributes his copious wisdom to the productively dual identity he now manifests (EH 'Wise' 2).[13] In particular, he developed a more sophisticated interpretation of the appeal of Epicurus and his famous garden: the Epicurean philosophy may have promised a life of pleasure and freedom from the fear of death, but what it actually delivered was a life of minor enjoyments and, eventually, freedom from the suffering associated with life itself. The Epicurean garden may have been a place of respite and refreshment for those determined to partake once again of the fullness of life,[14] but it was also, and perhaps more regularly (BGE 61), a quiet place of hospice for those who wished to be relieved of their suffering.

While the appeal of the Epicurean philosophy is real, Nietzsche came to understand, the 'pleasures' it promotes are not especially hedonistic. In particular, or so he apparently believed, the décadents among the clients of Epicurus were encouraged, gradually, to exchange a positive conception of pleasure for the negative (or privative) conception that suited their afflicted condition. After becoming accustomed to the modest pleasures recommended by Epicurus, for example, the décadents among his clients were instructed to seek permanent relief from their suffering. At the gentle urging of Epicurus, pleasure was equated with the loss or derangement of all feeling and, at the limit, with the release from consciousness itself (GM III:17). Hence the genius of the Epicurean philosophy: its most unfortunate adherents take themselves to be pursuing pleasure even as they seek the cure afforded them by death itself.

V

Here we would do well to acknowledge the extent to which Nietzsche's profile of the Redeemer type overlaps with (and draws upon) his influential profile of the ascetic priest. As we know from GM and elsewhere, this latter profile turns on Nietzsche's insistence that the ascetic priest only *appears* to be the physician or healer he claims to be (GM III:17). Able to treat only the symptoms of distress, the ascetic priest prescribes remedies that both (immediately) relieve and (eventually) aggravate the suffering of those to whom he ministers.

Towards this dual end, the priest's signature effort is his creative redirection of the expression of ressentiment: rather than allowing the sufferers entrusted to his care to lash out against the nobles who oppress them, the ascetic priest persuades his charges to seek the cause of their suffering within themselves (GM III:15). This ingenious gambit not only obviates the suicidal outburst which his charges were imprudently spoiling for but also transforms these sufferers into *sinners*, who naturally aggregate themselves, in their company-loving misery, as a docile herd. Later, acting on his improved understanding of the formative power of his ministry, the ascetic priest urges these sinners to find themselves 'guilty' (i.e. as irremediably sinful), precisely so that he may dispatch them against his nemeses among the knightly-aristocratic order of nobles (GM III:19).[15]

At the same time, however, Nietzsche acknowledges that the ascetic priest acts with good intentions, believing all the while that the 'affect-medication' he dispenses actually cures or improves the clientele he serves (GM III:20). (As Nietzsche readily concedes, the ascetic priest 'defends his sick herd well enough', even 'from itself' (GM III:15).) For this reason, there is no point in trying to persuade the ascetic priest (or his clients) of the harm he actually causes. His only experience of 'health' pertains to the short-term improvement in outlook that his 'affect-medication' produces in his docile, self-policing herd. Any other account or determination of 'health', pertaining perhaps to one's long-term prospects for increased strength and resurgent vitality, will strike the ascetic priest either as nonsensical or as a potentially cruel recipe for ruin. Owing to his share in the illness he is pledged to treat (GM III:15), the ascetic priest simply has no knowledge of, or recourse to, the superior 'physiological' perspective the recovered Nietzsche claims to command (GM III: 17; Conway 2008: 123–5). According to Nietzsche, in short, the ascetic priest can neither deliver the healing he promises nor acknowledge his failure to do so.

Marshalling this profile of the ascetic priest, we may attempt to reconstruct the basis for Nietzsche's post-Zarathustran diagnosis of Epicurus. Much like the ascetic priest, or so Nietzsche insists, Epicurus was able to address only the symptoms (or affects) of those whom he treated. Powerless to diagnose (much less cure) the underlying afflictions of his clients, he helped himself to the familiar categories and methods of philosophical hedonism: the best life for mortals is spent in pursuit of those pleasures that are most obviously conducive to (or constitutive of) happiness. Or, as he explains in his letter to Menoeceus:

> And so we speak of pleasure as the starting point and the goal of the happy life because we realize that it is our primary native good, because every act of choice and aversion originates with it, and because we come back to it when we judge every good by using the pleasure feeling as our criterion. (Strodach 1963: 182)

As Nietzsche correctly points out, however, Epicurus was also careful to distinguish himself from the more typical voluptuary hedonists with whom he was so often (and erroneously) linked:

> The pleasant life is not the product of one drinking party after another or of sexual intercourse with women and boys or of the sea food and other delicacies afforded by a luxurious table. On the contrary, it is the result of sober thinking – namely, investigation of the reasons for every act of choice and aversion of those false ideas about the gods and death which are the chief source of mental disturbances. (Strodach 1963: 183–4)

Notwithstanding his declaration of allegiance to hedonism, Epicurus not only preferred the cultivation of temperate pleasures, but also extolled the 'pleasure' associated with the absence or remission of pain. For a trained philologist like Nietzsche, this is precisely the kind of discrepancy that demands further investigation.

The fruits of this investigation include the diagnosis (and deflationary interpretation) in question. As a *faux* physician in his own right, Epicurus perfected the delivery of a 'tranquilizing ... medicine and way of life', which guided his clients towards an understanding of happiness on the model of 'resting, of not being disturbed, of satiety, of finally attained unity, as a "sabbath of Sabbaths"' (BGE 200). He thus encouraged his followers to embrace the idea that the 'absence of suffering' is 'the highest good', 'the value of values', '*the* positive as such' (GM III: 17). As Nietzsche explains, moreover, this teaching is thoroughly nihilistic, for it aims not at a positive experience of voluptuary, self-swelling pleasure, but at 'the hypnotic sense of nothingness, the repose of deepest sleep, in short *absence of suffering*' (GM III).

To his credit, Nietzsche is apparently determined to take Epicurus at his word. As he knows, for example, the term Epicurus prefers, *ataraxia*, is distinctly privative, signifying an elimination or cessation of painful disturbances in the body and soul. Inasmuch as Epicurus identifies *ataraxia* as the highest and most desirable human end, it is not unreasonable to conclude that he meant to place a premium on the cessation of suffering and pain. In his letter to Menoeceus, in fact, Epicurus famously draws a distinction between competing accounts of 'pleasure':

> Thus when I say that pleasure is the goal of living I do not mean the pleasures of libertines or the pleasures inherent in positive enjoyment, as is supposed by certain persons who are ignorant of our doctrine or who are not in agreement with it or who interpret it perversely. I mean, on the contrary, the pleasure that consists in freedom from bodily pain and mental agitation. (Strodach 1963: 183)

Here, too, the emphasis is clearly privative, falling squarely on the absence of pain and the relative modesty of the pleasures to be cultivated in the pursuit of happiness. Indeed, the explicit expression of disdain for 'the pleasures of libertines' would appear to confirm the suspicions of those critics who, like Cicero, found little or no trace of hedonism in the Epicurean philosophy.[16]

Finally, in the third of the *Sovran Maxims* (or *Principal Doctrines*) [*Kuriai Doxai*], as recorded by Diogenes Laertius (1931: 662–4)[17], Epicurus is said to have professed that

> the magnitude of pleasure reaches its limit in the removal of all pain. When pleasure is present, so long as it is uninterrupted, there is no pain either of body or of mind or of both together. (SM: 665)[18]

This maxim has been widely debated and, some would say, widely misunderstood. The dominant concern here is that Epicurus appears to equate pleasure in its peak 'magnitude' with the 'removal of all pain'. This concern has led many critics, including Nietzsche, to suppose or conclude that this maxim trades on an unfortunate (and possibly innocent) equivocation on the word 'pleasure'. For Nietzsche, of course, this equivocation is both telling and decisive, inasmuch as it faithfully reflects (what he has diagnosed as) the décadence of Epicurus. As a 'typical décadent', Epicurus would have had only a very limited experience of pleasure in excess of the removal or remission of pain. Like the ascetic priest, that is, Epicurus would have been confined by his affliction to a cramped perspective and a correspondingly restricted understanding of health, happiness and human welfare more generally. He would have called in good faith for a pursuit of those pleasures that are most likely to secure one's happiness, despite having only an extremely limited experience of (and tolerance for) pleasure itself.[19]

VI

To be sure, Nietzsche is loath to blame Epicurus for this misunderstanding or for the equivocation on which it trades. Like any 'typical décadent', Epicurus was powerless to do or to be otherwise. What he understood (or sensed or intuited) was that his prescribed remedies would suffice in most cases to pacify his followers and companions. Although his clients would embark upon these remedies fully intending to enjoy lives of pleasure, they soon would accept without complaint the remission of pain that Epicurus was, in fact, able to deliver. Some, perhaps many, would go so far as to lay claim to a positive experience of katastematic pleasure, in excess of their experience of the cessation of pain.[20] They would be mistaken in doing so, just as Epicurus was mistaken in promising an experience of pleasure that was simply unattainable by many or most of his clients. In both cases, Nietzsche apparently believes, the mistake was both honest and (mostly) harmless.

In his own gentle, non-coercive way, Epicurus thus achieved something like the result produced by the ascetic priest: his promise of a life of pleasure set in motion the transformation of his death- or god-fearing clients into a pacified, garden-bound collective.[21] Like the ascetic priest, moreover, Epicurus may have perfected this bait-and-switch scheme unwittingly and with a clear conscience. Unaware of (or estranged from) his own share in the décadence he offered to treat, he may not have considered the possibility that his therapeutic remedies would normalize the décadence of his sickest clients. For all we know, he too may have been convinced of the (false) equivalency between the hedonism he promoted and the *ataraxia* he actually delivered. In any event, Nietzsche might say, Epicurus did for his followers all that he could do, holding nothing in reserve, believing to the end in the healing properties of the remedies he devised. Indeed, only an *atypical* décadent, a recovered sufferer like Nietzsche himself (EH 'Wise' 2), would be in a position to expose (and object to) the bait-and-switch scheme developed by Epicurus.

On the strength of Nietzsche's interpretation, we may be tempted to conclude that Epicurus perpetrated the perfect ruse. Despite promising his followers a positive experience of pleasure, he convinced them to pursue the (lesser) good within their reach – namely, to be relieved of their pain and to relax into the ensuing experience of blissful nothingness. They very well may have succeeded in eliminating their pain and suffering, but only by blotting out virtually all feeling and by disowning the selves they initially (and naively) were determined to possess. By whetting their appetite for *ataraxia*, Epicurus unwittingly steered them towards the strictly privative 'happiness' that actually was available to them. If this was the perfect ruse, finally, it was made so by the childlike innocence of the 'healers' responsible for its success. As Nietzsche makes clear in his profile of the Redeemer type, Epicurus would have perpetrated this ruse with no inkling of the bait-and-switch scheme over which he presided. For a 'typical décadent' like Epicurus, there would have been no meaningful distinction to be drawn between the (privative) experience he provided and the (positive) experience he promised.[22]

What is more, this Epicurus left it to his clients to determine if and when they found pleasure in the absence of their pain. As a 'typical décadent', he would have refused to incur or inflict the gratuitous suffering that would result from serving (or intruding) as the arbiter of someone else's pleasure (A 32–3). Here, too, we are reminded of the ascetic priest and his seminal contribution to the 'slave revolt in morality': Epicurus positioned his followers to believe that they had *chosen* a way of life, predicated on a limited menu of modest pleasures, which was, in fact, their non-negotiable lot, dictated to them by the afflictions of their physiology. Although they claimed to prefer the 'sensual pleasures' associated with 'a little garden, figs, little cheeses and in addition three or four good friends' (HH II: 2, 192), they were, in fact, powerless to seek (much less enjoy) more ambitious pleasures. In his unwitting efforts to rebrand necessity as virtue, privation as repletion, Epicurus authorized a *pia fraus* similar to that on which the slave morality was founded.

Conclusion

If we may infer from Nietzsche's general remarks about the Redeemer type, and about Jesus in particular, we may conclude that his final position on Epicurus was likely one of conditional affirmation and wistful, what-might-have-been appreciation.[23]

According to Nietzsche, the timely intervention of the apostle Paul deprived European civilization of 'an entirely original basis for a Buddhistic peace movement, for an actual, *not* merely promised *happiness on Earth*' (A 42). Despite its non-negotiable status as a 'religion of décadence' (A 42), he explains, Indian Buddhism is to be preferred to its European counterpart, precisely because it succeeds, where Christianity does not, in actually relieving the suffering of the afflicted. The suggestion here is that the rise of a Buddhistic 'religion of décadence' in the West, based on the actual teachings of the actual Jesus, would have been a welcome development not only within the Roman Empire but also within the larger unfolding of European civilization.[24] Two envisioned outcomes are noteworthy here: suffering would have been addressed and relieved within the lowest orders of society; and the threat of priestly mischief would have been minimized.

Nietzsche offers a similar appreciation of what Epicurus and his followers might have wrought. In his speculative retelling of the fall of Rome, Nietzsche asserts that the Epicureans offered the empire a pagan philosophy worthy of its pagan aspirations. Despite predating the founding of Christianity by several centuries, Epicurus, in fact, 'waged war' against Christianity, albeit in its 'latent', 'pre-existent form' (A 58). He did so, Nietzsche explains, inasmuch as the *subterranean* cults' he battled promoted a doctrine of immortality that anticipated in important respects the teaching that Paul later developed and disseminated.

Had the conditions of this 'war' persisted, Nietzsche insists, 'Epicurus would have won', which means, or so he supposes, that the empire eventually would have yielded the bountiful 'harvest' that Europe never managed to reap (A 58). The Epicureans prevailed in the early years of the empire not only because they successfully allayed the fear of death but also because the 'subterranean cults' they battled remained relatively insignificant in both size and influence. As the empire prospered and expanded, however, its leaders (and the nobility more generally) became easy targets for the hatred and resentment accumulating throughout its lowest orders (A 51). According to Nietzsche, the 'subterranean cults' over which the Epicureans had prevailed were 'outbid' by the apostle Paul, who, on the strength of an alternative doctrine of immortality, united the various enemies and victims of the empire (A 43). When confronted with this alternative doctrine of immortality, which they had neither anticipated nor imagined, the Epicureans proved to be powerless. Dedicated to the reduction of pain and the elimination of discord, they did not think to develop arguments against, much less design therapies for, a doctrine of immortality that would enjoin sufferers to amplify and dignify their earthly misery.

In the end, these two representatives of the Redeemer type were undone by Paul, the apostle to the Gentiles.[25] Had he not appeared, or had he not staged the particular intervention attributed to him by Nietzsche, the kindred teachings of Jesus and Epicurus might have infused the empire (and Western civilization more broadly) with an occidental version of Buddhism. On Nietzsche's dreamy rendition of this alternative history, the combination of a pacific religion of love (Jesus) and a hedonism keyed to modest pleasures (Epicurus) would have afforded the afflicted the this-worldly redemption they both sought and deserved to receive.

Notes

1. Nietzsche summarizes these 'pacifying formulae' as follows: 'firstly, if that is how things are they do not concern us; secondly, things may be thus but they may also be otherwise' (HH II:2, 7).
2. Here I follow Hadot (1995a), especially 271–5. I am also indebted here to Ansell-Pearson (2014b, 2013, 2018). See also Conway (2016), especially 3–6, from which several sentences in this section are descended.
3. On the relevance of Nietzsche's speculation that Epicurus 'forgot his name', I am indebted to Shearin (2014), especially 76–8.
4. For sceptical appraisals of Nietzsche's diagnosis of Epicurus, see Bett (2005); Ansell-Pearson (2018), especially 148–50; and Porter (2014).
5. This insight was anticipated in a prescient note from Spring 1884, in which Nietzsche contrasts 'Epicurean pleasure [*Vergnügen*]' with 'Dionysian joy [*Lust*]'. He associates the latter with his unprecedented discovery of 'the tragic' and registers his preference for it (KSA 11:25 [95].33).

6 Inasmuch as Nietzsche recognizes 'the Christian' as a species of the 'improvement-morality', we are presumably justified in recognizing 'the Epicurean' as a kindred species as well.
7 Here I follow Jensen (2019), especially 121–6.
8 See Dostoyevsky (1969), especially 26–32.
9 I am indebted here to Shapiro (2019). As Shapiro notes, the Redeemer type profiled by Nietzsche is indebted not only to Dostoevsky's portrayal of Myshkin but also to Tolstoy's interpretation of Jesus in *My Religion* (2010: 240–44).
10 I am indebted here to the interpretation developed by Cavell (1990), especially 46–57; see also Conway (1998).
11 Nietzsche later confirms that an effect of the 'Epicurean philosophy' on 'sufferers of a higher rank' is that it 'makes the most of suffering, and in the end even sanctifies and justifies it' (BGE 261).
12 See Conway (2015), especially 235–9. See also Ansell-Pearson (2018), especially 142–4.
13 He concludes this section by reiterating this claim: 'Well then, I am the *opposite* [*Gegenstück*] of a décadent for I have just described myself' (EH 'Wise' 2).
14 This is true, for example, of 'those sufferers of a higher rank' who come into contact with the Epicurean philosophy (BGE 61).
15 Here I follow Ridley (1998), especially 138–41.
16 For an effective riposte to Cicero, see Cooper (2012), especially 235–41. See also Meyer (2008), especially 97–102.
17 See also Konstan (2008), especially 127–35.
18 See also Conway (2017), especially 85–88.
19 For a sensible reckoning of Nietzsche's seemingly disparate views on the values of happiness, see Bett (2005), especially 48–54.
20 For a charitable account of the distinction between the experience of kinetic pleasure and the experience of katastematic pleasure, see Cooper (2012), especially 229–41; and Meyer (2008), especially 98–9.
21 As Nietzsche explains, 'Human beings of late cultures and refracted lights will on the average be weaker human beings: their most profound desire is that the war they *are* should come to an end. Happiness appears to them, in agreement with a tranquilizing (for example, Epicurean or Christian) medicine and way of thought, pre-eminently as the happiness of resting, of not being disturbed, of satiety, of finally attained unity, as a "Sabbath of Sabbaths", to speak with the holy rhetorician Augustine who was himself such a human being' (BGE 200).
22 By drawing on his profile of the ascetic priest, Nietzsche is able to distinguish meaningfully between the simplicity of the Redeemer type and the simplicity of Wagner's Parsifal, that 'poor devil and country boy', for whom he offers unreserved contempt (GM III:3).
23 Similar conclusions are reached by Bett (2005: 59–61); See also Shearin (2014), especially 76–8; and Porter (2014).
24 Here I follow Panaïoti (2019), especially 55–60.
25 See Conway (2016), especially 8–12. See also Caygill (2006), especially 108–9.

Bibliography

Abbey, Ruth (2000), *Nietzsche's Middle Period*, Oxford: Oxford University Press.
Acharya, Vinod (2014), *Nietzsche's Meta-Existentialism*, Berlin and Boston: De Gruyter.
Alberti, Antonina (1990), 'Paura della morte e identità personale nell'epicureismo', in *Logica, mente, persona: Studi sulla filosofia antica*, 151–206, Florence: Olschki.
Allen, James Sloan (1991), 'The State of Letters: The Existential Reader: Or Reading, Rumination, and the Classics', *The Sewanee Review*, 99 (1): 86–100.
Allison, David B. (2001), *Reading the New Nietzsche*, Lanham: Rowman & Littlefield.
Allison, David B., Prado de Oliveira, Mark S. Roberts and Allen S. Weiss, eds (1988), *Psychosis and Sexual Identity: Toward a Post-Analytic View of the Schreber Case: Towards a Post-Analytic View of the Schreber Case*, Albany: State University of New York Press.
Amicus, Cassius (2010), *Lion of Epicurus: Lucian and His Epicurean Passages*, Smashwords.
Annas, Julia (1987), 'Epicurus on Pleasure and Happiness', *Philosophical Topics. Ancient Greek Philosophy*, 15 (2): 5–21.
Annas, Julia (1993), *The Morality of Happiness*, Oxford: Oxford University Press.
Annas, Julia (1994), *Hellenistic Philosophy of Mind*, Berkeley: University of California Press.
Annas, Julia (2011), *Intelligent Virtue*, Oxford: Oxford University Press.
Ansell-Pearson, Keith (2010), 'For Mortal Souls: Philosophy and Therapeia in Nietzsche's Dawn', *Royal Institute of Philosophy Supplement*, 66: 137–63.
Ansell-Pearson, Keith (2013), 'True to the Earth: Nietzsche's Epicurean Care of Self and World', in Horst Hutter and Eli Friedland (eds), *Nietzsche's Therapeutic Teaching for Individuals and Culture*, 97–116, London: Bloomsbury.
Ansell-Pearson, Keith (2014a), 'Care of Self in Dawn: On Nietzsche's Resistance to Bio-political Modernity', in Barry Stocker and Manuel Knoll (eds), *Nietzsche as Political Philosopher*, 269–86, Berlin and Boston: De Gruyter.
Ansell-Pearson, Keith (2014b), 'Heroic-Idyllic Philosophizing: Nietzsche and the Epicurean Tradition', *Royal Institute of Philosophy Supplement*, 74: 237–64.
Ansell-Pearson, Keith (2015a), 'A Melancholy Science? On Bergson's Appreciation of Lucretius', *Pli: The Warwick Journal of Philosophy*, 27: 83–101.
Ansell-Pearson, Keith (2015b), 'Beyond Selfishness: Epicurean Ethics in Nietzsche and Guyau', in Rebecca Bamford (ed.), *Nietzsche's Free Spirit Philosophy*, 49–68, New York: Rowman and Littlefield.
Ansell-Pearson, Keith (2015c), 'The Need for Small Doses: Nietzsche, Fanaticism, and Epicureanism', in Celine Denat and Patrick Wotling (eds), *Aurore, tournant dans l'œuvre de Nietzsche?*, 193–227, Reims: ÉPURE.
Ansell-Pearson, Keith (2015d), '"We Are Experiments": Nietzsche on Morality and Authenticity', in Vanessa Lemm (ed.), *Nietzsche and the Becoming of Life*, 280–302, New York: Fordham University Press.
Ansell-Pearson, Keith (2018), *Nietzsche's Search for Philosophy: On the Middle Writings*, London: Bloomsbury.

Arendt, Hannah (1958), *The Human Condition*, Chicago: University of Chicago Press.
Aristotle (1984), *Complete Works*, Volumes 1 and 2, ed. Jonathan Barnes, Princeton, NJ: Princeton University Press.
Aristotle (2009), *The Nicomachean Ethics*, ed. Lesley Brown, trans. David Ross, Oxford: Oxford University Press.
Aristotle (2016), *Metaphysics*, trans. C. D. C. Reeve, Indianapolis: Hackett.
Asmis, Elizabeth (1970), *The Epicurean Theory of Free Will and Its Origins in Aristotle*, New Haven: Yale University Press.
Asmis, Elizabeth (1984), 'Motion', in *Epicurus' Scientific Method*, 277–81, Ithaca: Cornell University Press.
Asmis, Elizabeth (2003), 'Epicurean Economics', in John T. Fitzgerald, Glenn Holland and Dirk Obbink (eds), *Philodemus and the New Testament World*, 131–76, Leiden: E. J. Brill.
Attwood, Janet Bray and Chris Attwood (2006), *The Passion Test*, Iowa: First World Publishing.
Augustine (1984), *City of God Against the Pagans*, trans. H. Bettenson, Harmondsworth: Penguin.
Aurelius, Marcus (2011), *Meditations*, trans. R. Hard, Oxford: Oxford University Press.
Babich, Babette (1994), *Nietzsche's Philosophy of Science*, Albany: State University of New York Press.
Babich, Babette (2003), 'Nietzsche's Imperative as a Friend's Encomium: On Becoming the One You Are, Ethics, and Blessing', *Nietzsche-Studien*, 33: 29–58.
Babich, Babette (2004), 'Nietzsche's göttliche Eidechse: "Divine Lizards", "Greene Lyons" and Music', in Christa Davis Acampora and Ralph A. Acampora (eds), *Nietzsche's Bestiary*, 264–83, Lanham: Rowman & Littlefield.
Babich, Babette (2007), 'Greek Bronze: Holding a Mirror to Life', *Yearbook of the Irish Philosophical Society*, 7: 1–30.
Babich, Babette (2009a), 'Nietzsche's Philology and Nietzsche's Science: On the "Problem of Science" and "fröhliche Wissenschaft"', in Pascale Hummel (ed.), *Metaphilology: Histories and Languages of Philology*, 155–201, Paris: Philologicum.
Babich, Babette (2009b), '"Une promesse de bonheur"— Von Plastik zu Poesie', in Stefan Wilke (ed.), *Die Glücklichen sind neugierig*, 7–43, Weimar: Bauhaus Universitätsverlag.
Babich, Babette (2015), 'Genius Loci: Nietzsche, Lou, and the "New Jerusalem"', *New Nietzsche Studies*, 9 (3, 4): 137–67.
Babich, Babette (2018), 'Spirit and Grace, Letters and Voice', *Journal of the Philosophy of Education*, III: 1–27.
Babich, Babette (2020), 'Nietzsches Lebensontologie: Negative Ontologie', in Jan Urbich and Jörg Zimmer (eds), *Handbuch Ontologie*, Frankfurt am Main: Metzler.
Bacon, Francis (2000), *The New Organon*, eds. Lisa Jardine and Michael Silverthorne, Cambridge: Cambridge University Press.
Bamford, Rebecca (2016), 'The Ethos of Inquiry: Nietzsche on Experience, Naturalism and Experimentalism', *The Journal of Nietzsche Studies*, 47 (1): 9–29.
Barber, Dan (2014), *The Third Plate*, New York: Penguin Books.
Bartlett, A. W. (2002), 'The Swerve of Desire: Epicurus, Economics and Violence', *Revista Portuguesa de Filosofia*, 58 (2): 319–32.
Bayertz, Kurt Otto (2017), 'On German Materialism', *3:AM Magazine*. Available online: https://316am.site123.me/articles/on-german-materialism?c=end-times-archive.
Benjamin, Walter (1999), *The Arcades Project*, trans. Howard Eiland and Kevin McLaughlin Cambridge: Belknap Press.

Benne, Christian (2012), *Nietzsche und die historisch-kritische Philologie*, Berlin: De Gruyter.
Bennett, Jane (2010), *Vibrant Matter: A Political Ecology of Things*, Durham and London: Duke University Press.
Bennett, Michael James (2013), 'Deleuze and Epicurean Philosophy: Atomic Speed and Swerve Speed', *Journal of French and Francophone Philosophy, Revue de la philosophie française et de langue française*, 21 (2): 131–57.
Berchoux, Joseph (1819), *La Gastronomie, Suivi des Poésies Fugitives de l'Auteur*, 5th edn, Rue de Cléry no. 15: L.G. Michaud.
Bergmann, Peter (1987), *Nietzsche, 'The Last Antipolitical German'*, Bloomington: Indiana University Press.
Bertino, Andrea Christian (2007), 'Nietzsche und die hellenistische Philosophie: Der Übermensch und der Weise', *Nietzsche-Studien*, 36 (1): 95–131.
Bett, Richard (2005), 'Nietzsche, the Greeks, and Happiness (with Special Reference to Aristotle and Epicurus)', *Philosophical Topics*, 33 (2): 45–70.
Bishop, Paul (2017), *On the Blissful Islands with Nietzsche and Jung*, London: Routledge.
Bishop, Paul (2019), *German Political Thought and the Discourse of Platonism: Finding a Way out of the Cave*, New York: Palgrave Macmillan.
Bloch, Olivier (2009), 'Epicureanism – Yesterday and Today', *Iris*, 1 (2): 483–95.
Blondel, Eric (1991), *Nietzsche: The Body and Culture*, trans. Seán Hand, Stanford: Stanford University Press.
Borchardt, Rudolf ([1937–1938] 2016), *Der leidenschaftliche Gärtner*, Berlin: Mathes & Seitz.
Bornmann, Fritz (1984), 'Nietzsches Epikur', *Nietzsche-Studien*, 13 (1): 177–88.
Branham, Bracht (1984), 'The Comic as Critic: Revenging Epicurus: A Study of Lucian's Art of Comic Narrative', *Classical Antiquity*, 3 (2): 143–63.
Brobjer, Thomas H. (1995), *Nietzsche's Ethics of Character: A Study of Nietzsche's Ethics and Its Place in the History of Moral Thinking*, Ph.D. diss., Uppsala University.
Brobjer, Thomas H. (2000), 'Nietzsche's Forgotten Book', *New Nietzsche Studies*, 4 (1, 2): 157–61.
Brobjer, Thomas H. (2008), *Nietzsche's Philosophical Context: An Intellectual Biography*, Urbana and Chicago: University of Chicago Press.
Brod, Max (1922), 'Der Dichter Franz Kafka von Max Brod', in Gustav Krojanker (ed.), *Juden in der deutschen Literatur. Essays über zeitgenössische Schriftsteller*, 55–62, Berlin: Welt-Verlag.
Brown, Eric (2009), 'Politics and Society', in James Warren (ed.), *The Cambridge Companion to Epicureanism*, 179–96, Cambridge: Cambridge University Press.
Brown, Kristen (2006), *Nietzsche and Embodiment: Discerning Bodies and Non-dualism*, Albany, NY: State University of New York Press.
Brown, Thomas and Eric Miller (2006), 'Epicurean Gardens in William Temple and John Wilmot', *The Dalhousie Review*, 86 (3): 229–344.
Brun, Jean (1993), *Épicure et les épicuriens*, Paris: Presses Universitaires de France.
Brusotti, Marco (1997), *Die Leidenschaft der Erkenntnis. Philosophie und ästhetische Lebensgestaltung bei Nietzsche von Morgenröthe bis Also sprach Zarathustra*, Berlin and New York: De Gruyter.
Burkert, Walter ([1962] 1972), *Lore and Science in Ancient Pythagoreanism*, trans. Edward L. Minar, Cambridge: Harvard University Press.
Burkert, Walter ([1972] 1983), *Homo Necans: The Anthropology of Ancient Greek Sacrificial Ritual and Myth*, Berkeley: University of California Press.

Burton, R. W. (1962), *Pindar's Pythian Odes: Essays in Interpretation*, Oxford: Oxford University Press.
Carter, L. B. (1986), *The Quiet Athenian*, Oxford: Oxford University Press.
Casey, John (1990), *Pagan Virtue: An Essay in Ethics*, Oxford: Clarendon Press.
Cavell, Stanley (1990), *Conditions Handsome and Unhandsome: The Constitution of Emersonian Perfectionism*, 46–57, Chicago: University of Chicago Press.
Caygill, Howard (1994), 'The Consolation of Philosophy, or "Neither Dionysus nor the Crucified"', *Journal of Nietzsche Studies*, 7: 131–50.
Caygill, Howard (2006), 'Under Epicurean Skies', *Angelaki: Journal of the Theoretical Humanities*, 11 (3): 107–15.
Chappell, Vere, ed. (1999), *Hobbes and Bramhall on Liberty and Necessity*, Cambridge: Cambridge University Press.
Chroust, Anton-Hermann (1973), *Aristotle: New Light on His Life and on Some of His Lost Works Volume 1*, London: Routledge.
Cicero, Marcus Tulius (1927), *Tusculan Disputations*, trans. J. E. King, Cambridge: Harvard University Press.
Cicero, Marcus Tulius (2010), *De Finibus Bonorum et Malorum: Libri Quinque*, ed. Johan Nicolai Madvig, Cambridge: Cambridge University Press.
Cilliers, Louise and François Retief (2009), 'Horticulture in Antiquity, with Emphasis on the Graeco-Roman Era', *Akroterion*, 54: 1–10.
Clark, Maudemarie (1990), *Nietzsche on Truth and Philosophy*, Cambridge: Cambridge University Press.
Clay, Diskin (1972), 'Epicurus' Κυρία Δοξά XVII', *Greek, Roman, and Byzantine Studies*, 13 (1): 59–66.
Clay, Diskin (1983), *Lucretius and Epicurus*, Ithaca: Cornell University Press.
Clay, Diskin (1989), 'A Lost Epicurean Community', *Greek, Roman, and Byzantine Studies*, 30 (2): 313–35.
Clucas, Stephen (1994), 'The Atomism of the Cavendish Circle: A Reappraisal', *The Seventeenth Century*, 9 (2): 247–73.
Cohen, Jonathan R. (2009), *Science, Culture and Free Spirits: A Study of Nietzsche's Human, All-Too-Human*, New York: Humanity Books.
Conway, Daniel (1998), 'Love's Labour's Lost: The Philosopher's Versucherkunst', in Salim Kemal, Ivan Gaskell and Daniel Conway (eds), *Nietzsche, Philosophy, and the Arts*, 287–309, Cambridge: Cambridge University Press.
Conway, Daniel (2008), *Nietzsche's On the Genealogy of Morals: A Reader's Guide*, London and New York: Continuum Books.
Conway, Daniel (2015), 'Almost Everything Is Permitted: Nietzsche's Not-So-Free Spirits', in Rebecca Bamford (ed.), *Nietzsche's Free Spirit Philosophy*, 233–52, London: Rowman & Littlefield International.
Conway, Daniel (2016), 'Epicurus Avenged?', *Pli: The Warwick Journal of Philosophy*, Special Volume (Self-Cultivation: Ancient and Modern): 3–24.
Conway, Daniel (2017), 'Why Nietzsche Is a Destiny: Epicurean Themes in *Ecce Homo*', *The Agonist,* 10 (2): 75–93.
Cooper, John (1998), 'Pleasure and Desire in Epicurus', in *Reason and Emotion: Essays on Ancient Moral Psychology and Ethical Theory*, 485–514, Princeton: Princeton University Press.
Cooper, John (2012), *Pursuits of Wisdom: Six Ways of Life in Ancient Philosophy from Socrates to Plotinus*, Princeton, NJ: Princeton University Press.

Cragg, Gerald R. (1964), *Reason and Authority in the Eighteenth Century*, Cambridge: Cambridge University Press.
Crisp, Roger (1998), *How Should One Live: Essays on the Virtues*, Oxford: Oxford University Press.
Crisp, Roger and Michael Slote (1997), *Virtue Ethics*, Oxford: Oxford University Press.
D'Agostino, Fred, Gerald Gaus and John Thrasher (2017), 'Contemporary Approaches to the Social Contract', in Edward N. Zalta (ed.), *The Stanford Encyclopedia of Philosophy*. Available online: https://plato.stanford.edu/archives/win2017/entries/contractarianism-contemporary.
Danziger, Shai, Jonathan Levav and Liora Avnaim-Pesso (2011), 'Extraneous Factors in Judicial Decisions', *Proceedings of the National Academy of Sciences of the United States of America*, 108 (17). Available online: https://doi.org/10.1073/pnas.1018033108.
Danziger, Shai, Jonathan Levav and Liora Avnaim-Pesso (2011), 'Extraneous Factors in Judicial Decisions', *PNAS*, 108 (17) (26 April): 6889–92.
De Lacy, Phillip (1969), 'Limit and Variation in Epicurean Philosophy', *Phoenix*, 23 (1): 104–13.
Delattre, Daniel and Pigeaud Jackie (2010), *Les Épicuriens*, Paris: Gallimard, coll. Bibliothèque de la Pléiade.
Deleuze, Gilles (1983), *La Cours de Gilles Deleuze*, 11 February. Available online: http://www2.univ-paris8.fr/deleuze/article.php3?id_article=124.
Deleuze, Gilles (2017), 'Lucretius and Naturalism', in Abraham Jacob Greenstine and Ryan J. Johnson (trans.) and Jared C. Bly (eds), *Contemporary Encounters with Ancient Metaphysics*, 245–53, Edinburgh: Edinburgh University Press.
Denat, Céline and Patrick Wotling (2013), *Dictionnaire Nietzsche*, Paris: Ellipses.
Dennis, Matthew James and Federico Testa (2017), 'Pleasure and Self-Cultivation in Guyau and Nietzsche', *The Agonist: A Nietzsche Circle Journal*, 10 (2): 94–117.
Derrida, Jacques (1974), 'White Mythology: Metaphor in the Text of Philosophy', *New Literary History*, 6 (1): 5–74.
Descartes, Rene (1984), 'Objections and Replies', in John Cottingham, Robert Stoothoff and Dugald Murdoch (trans.), *The Philosophical Writings of Descartes*, 2: 63–397, Cambridge: Cambridge University Press.
DeWitt, Norman Wentworth (1954), *Epicurus and His Philosophy*, Minneapolis: University of Minnesota Press.
Diels, Hermann (1879), *Doxographi Graeci*, Berlin: Wiedemann.
Diels, Hermann (1903), *Die Fragmente der Vorsokratiker*, Berlin: Weidmann.
D'Iorio, Paolo (2000), 'Nietzsche et l'éternel retour. Genèse et interprétation, in Nietzsche', *Cahiers de l'Herne*, 361–89, Paris: l'Hern.
D'Iorio, Paolo (2012), *Le voyage de Nietzsche à Sorrente. Genèse de la philosophie de l'esprit libre*, Paris: CNRS Éditions.
D'Iorio, Paolo (2016), *Nietzsche's Journey to Sorrento: Genesis of the Philosophy of the Free Spirit*, trans. Sylvia Mae Gorelick, Chicago: University of Chicago Press.
Dirk Obbink (1989), 'The Atheism of Epicurus', *Greek, Roman and Byzantine Studies*, 30 (2): 187–223.
Donner, Wendy (2010), 'Morality, Virtue and Aesthetics in Mill's Art of Life', in Ben Eggleston, Dale E. Miller and David Weinstein (eds), *John Stuart Mill and the Art of Life*, 146–65, Oxford: Oxford University Press.
Dostoyevsky, Fyodor (1969), *The Idiot*, trans. Henry and Olga Carlisle. New York: Signet/NAL.
Drochon, Hugo (2016), *Nietzsche's Great Politics*, Princeton: Princeton University Press.

Duckworth, Angela (2016), *Grit: The Power of Passion and Perseverance*, New York: Scribner.
Duncan, Stewart (2005), 'Hobbes's Materialism in the Early 1640s', *British Journal for the History of Philosophy*, 13 (3): 437–48.
Duncan, Stewart (2013), 'Materialism', in S. A. Lloyd (ed.), *Bloomsbury Companion to Hobbes*, 55–7, London: Bloomsbury.
Ebersbach, Volker (2014), 'Nietzsche im Garten Epikurs', *Nietzsche Forschung*, 8: 43–62.
Eggleston, Ben, Dale E. Miller and David Weinstein, eds (2010), *John Stuart Mill and the Art of Life*, Oxford: Oxford University Press.
Eliot, George (1972), *Middlemarch*, Harmondsworth, UK: Penguin.
Epicurus (1963), *The Philosophy of Epicurus: Letters, Doctrines, and Parallel Passages from Lucretius*, trans. George K. Strodach, Evanston, IL: Northwestern University Press.
Epicurus (1994), *The Epicurus Reader: Selected Writings and Testimonia*, eds and trans. Brad Inwood and L. P. Gerson, Indianapolis: Hackett.
Erler, Michael (2009), 'Epicureanism in the Roman Empire', in James Warren (ed.), *The Cambridge Companion to Epicureanism*, 46–64, Cambridge: Cambridge University Press.
Ewin, R. E. (1991), *Virtue and Rights: The Moral Philosophy of Thomas Hobbes*, Boulder, CO: Westview.
Farneti, Roberto (2007) 'Hobbes on Salvation', in Springborg (ed.), *Cambridge Companion to Hobbes's 'Leviathan'*, 291–308, Cambridge: Cambridge University Press.
Festugière, André-Jean (1946), *Épicure et ses dieux*, Paris: Presses Universitaires de France.
Festugière, André-Jean (1956), *Epicurus and His Gods*, trans. C. W. Chilton, Cambridge: Harvard University Press.
Feuerbach, Ludwig (1989), *The Essence of Christianity*, trans. George Eliot, New York: Prometheus Books.
Feuerbach, Ludwig (1992), *Thoughts on Death and Immortality*, ed. and trans. James A. Massey, Berkeley: University of California Press.
Flacelière, Robert (1954), 'Les Épicuriens et l'amour', *Revue des Etudes Grecques*, 67: 69–81.
Foot, Philippa ([1991] 2002a), 'Nietzsche's Immoralism', in *Moral Dilemmas and Other Topics in Moral Philosophy*, 144–58. Oxford: Oxford University Press.
Foot, Philippa ([1977] 2002b), 'Virtues and Vices', in *Virtues and Vices*, 1–18, Oxford: Oxford University Press.
Forrer, Thomas (2017), 'Philologische Dichtung: Friedrich Nietzsche Lied eines theokritischen Ziegenhirten', in Katharina Grätz and Sebastian Kaufmann (eds), *Nietzsche Als Dichter: Lyrik – Poetologie – Rezeption*, 154–78, Berlin and Boston: De Gruyter.
Förster-Nietzsche, E. and Schöll, F., eds (1923), *Friedrich Nietzsche's Briefwechsel mit Erwin Rohde*, Leipzig: Leipzig University Press.
Foucault, Michel (1978), *History of Sexuality I: Introduction*, trans. R. Hurley, London: Penguin Books.
Foucault, Michel (1985), *History of Sexuality II: The Use of Pleasure*, trans. R. Hurley, London: Penguin Books.
Foucault, Michel (1986), *History of Sexuality III: The Care of the Self*, trans. R. Hurley, London: Penguin Books
Foucault, Michel (1997), 'Course Summary: The Hermeneutic of the Subject', in Paul Rabinow (ed.), Robert Hurley (trans.), *Ethics: Subjectivity and Truth*, 93–106, London: Penguin Books.
Fouillée, Alfred (1902a), *Nietzsche et l'immoralisme*, Paris: Félix Alcan.

Fouillée, Alfred (1902b), 'The Ethics of Nietzsche and Guyau', *International Journal of Ethics*, 13 (1): 13–27.
Franco, Paul (2011), *Nietzsche's Enlightenment: The Free-Spirit Trilogy of the Middle Period*, Chicago: University of Chicago Press
Frank, Thomas (2014), 'He Posed as a Progressive and Turned Out to Be Counterfeit. We Ended Up with a Wall Street Presidency, a Drone Presidency', *Salon*, 24 August. Available online: https://www.salon.com/2014/08/24/cornel_west_he_posed_as_a_progressive_and_turned_out_to_be_counterfeit_we_ended_up_with_a_wall_street_presidency_a_drone_presidency/
Freud, Sigmund (2003), *The Schreber Case*, trans. Andrew Webber, New York: Penguin Classics.
Frischer, Bernard (1982), *The Sculpted Word: Epicureanism and Philosophical Recruitment in Ancient Greece*, Berkeley: University of California.
Frost, Samantha (2008), *Lessons from a Materialist Thinker: Hobbesian Reflections on Ethics and Politics*, Stanford: Stanford University Press.
Frost, Samantha (2013), 'Body', in S. A. Lloyd (ed.), *Bloomsbury Companion to Hobbes*, 29–31, London: Bloomsbury.
Gaasterland, Hedwig (2016), 'Anti-Stoic Lessons for the Concept of *Amor Fati* in *The Gay Science* IV', *Pli: The Warwick Journal of Philosophy*, Special Volume (Self-Cultivation: Ancient and Modern): 70–89.
Gaskin, John (1995). *The Epicurean Philosophers*, London: Everyman.
Gassendi, Pierre (2006), *Vie et mœurs d'Épicure*, ed. and trans. Sylvie Taussig, Paris: Les Belles Lettres.
Gaus, Gerald F. (2013), 'Hobbesian Contractarianism - Orthodox and Revisionist', in S. A. Lloyd (ed.), *Bloomsbury Companion to Hobbes*, 263–78, London: Bloomsbury.
Ghedini, Francesco (1999), *Il Platone di Nietzsche*, Napoli: Edizioni Scientifiche Italiane.
Giesecke, Annette Lucia (2001), 'Beyond the Garden of Epicurus: The Utopics of the Ideal Roman Villa', *Utopian Studies*, 12 (2): 13–32.
Gigandet, Alain and Morel Pierre-Marie, eds (2007), *Lire Épicure et les épicuriens*, Paris: Presses Universitaires de France.
Gill, Christopher (2006), *The Structured Self in Hellenistic and Roman Thought*, Oxford: Oxford University Press.
Glöckner, Andreas (2016), 'The Irrational Hungry Judge Effect Revisited: Simulations Reveal That the Magnitude of the Effect Is Overestimated', *Judgment and Decision Making*, 11 (6): 601–10.
Goldschmidt, Victor (2006), *Le système stoïcien et l'idée de temps*, Paris: Vrin.
Goldsmith, M. M. (1996), 'Hobbes on Law', in Tom Sorell (ed.), *Cambridge Companion to Hobbes*, 274–304, Cambridge: Cambridge University Press.
Gordon, Pamela (2012), *The Invention and Gendering of Epicurus*, Ann Arbor: University of Michigan Press.
Graham, Allison (2016), 'Epicureanism and Cynicism in Lucian', *Pseudo-Dionysius*, 18: 41–8.
Greenblatt, Steven (2011), *The Swerve: How the World Became Modern*, New York: W. W. & Norton Company.
Gregory, Fredrick (1977), *Scientific Materialism in Nineteenth Century Germany*, Dordrecht: D. Reidel Publishing Company.
Groff, Peter S. (2006), 'Wisdom and Violence: The Legacy of Platonic Political Philosophy in al-Fārābī and Nietzsche', in Douglas Allen (ed.), *Comparative Philosophy in Times of Terror*, 65–81, Lanham: Lexington Books.

Groff, Peter S. (2014), 'Leaving the Garden: Al-Rāzī and Nietzsche as Wayward Epicureans', *Philosophy East and West*, 64 (4): 983–1017.
Groff, Peter S. (2016), 'Cultivating Weeds: The Place of Solitude in the Political Philosophies of Ibn Bājja and Nietzsche', Paper presented at the 11th East-West Philosophers' Conference, University of Hawai'i at Mānoa, May.
Groff, Peter S. (2017), 'Great Politics and the Unnoticed Life: Nietzsche and Epicurus on the Boundaries of Cultivation', *The Agonist*, 10 (2): 59–74.
Groff, Peter S. (2018), 'Zarathustra's Blessed Isles', Paper presented at the 24th International Conference of the Friedrich Nietzsche Society: Nietzsche and the Politics of Difference, Newcastle University, Newcastle on Tyne, September.
Groff, Peter S. (forthcoming), 'The Return of the Epicurean Gods', in Russell Re Manning, Carlotta Santini and Isabelle Wienand (eds), *Nietzsche's Gods: Critical and Constructive Perspectives*.
Gunzel, Stephan (2003), 'Nietzsche's Geophilosophy', *Journal of Nietzsche Studies*, 25 (1): 78–91.
Guyau, Jean-Marie ([1878] 1927), *La morale d'Épicure et ses rapports avec les doctrines contemporaines*, Paris: Librairie Félix Alcan.
Guyau, Jean-Marie (2002), *La morale d'Épicure et ses rapports avec les doctrines contemporaines*, eds. Gilbert Romeyer Dherbey and Jean-Baptiste Gourinat, Paris: encre marine.
Guyau, Jean-Marie (2008), *Esquisse d'une morale sans obligation ni sanction*, ed. Philippe Saltel, Paris: encre marine.
Haas, Albert (1896), 'Über den Einfluss der epikureischen Staats- und Rechtsphilosophie auf die Philosophie des 16. and 17. Jahrhunderts', Ph.D. diss., University of Berlin, Berlin.
Hadot, Pierre ([1987] 1995a), *Philosophy as a Way of Life: Spiritual Exercises from Socrates to Foucault*, ed. Arnold I. Davidson, trans. Michael Chase, Oxford: Blackwell.
Hadot, Pierre (1995b), *Qu'est-ce que la philosophie antique?*, Paris: Gallimard.
Hadot, Pierre ([1995] 2002), *What Is Ancient Philosophy?*, trans. Michael Chase, Cambridge: Harvard University Press.
Hadot, Pierre (2011), *The Present Alone Is Our Happiness: Conversations with Jeannie Carlier and Arnold Davidson*, 2nd edn, trans. Marc Djaballah and Michael Chase, Stanford: Stanford University Press.
Hamilton, J. (2004), 'Ecce Philogus: Nietzsche and Pindar's Second Pythian Ode', in Paul Bishop (ed.), *Nietzsche and Antiquity: His Reaction and Response to the Classical Tradition*, 54–69, New York: Boydell and Brewer.
Hammerstaedt, Jürgen, Pierre-Marie Morel and Refik Güremen, eds. (2017), *Diogenes of Oinoanda · Diogène d'Œnoanda: Epicureanism and Philosophical Debates · Épicurisme et controversies*, Leuven: Leuven University Press.
Harrison, Charles T. (1933), 'Bacon, Hobbes, Boyle, and the Ancient Atomists', *Harvard Studies and Notes in Philology and Literature*, 15 (1): 191–218.
Harrison, Charles T. (1934), 'The Ancient Atomists and English Literature in the Seventeenth Century', *Harvard Studies in Classical Philology*, 45: 1–80.
Harrison, Robert (2008), *Gardens: An Essay on the Human Condition*, Chicago: The University of Chicago Press.
Havelock, Eric (1981), *The Literate Revolution in Greece and Its Cultural Consequences*, Princeton, NJ: Princeton University Press.
Havelock, Eric, (1986), *The Muse Learns to Write: Reflections on Orality and Literacy from Antiquity to the Present*, New Haven: Yale University Press.

Hayes, Peter (1999), 'Hobbes's Silent Fool: A Response to Hoekstra', *Political Theory*, 27 (2): 225-29.
Heberdey, R. and Kalinka, E. (1897), 'Die philosophische Inschrift von Oinoanda', *Bulletin de Correspondance Hellénique*, 21: 346-443.
Hegel, G. W. F. (1969), *Science of Logic*, trans. A. V. Miller, London: Humanities International Press.
Hegel, G. W. F. (1976), *Science of Logic*, London: Humanities International Press.
Heidegger, Martin ([1950] 1975), 'The Anaximander Fragment', in David Krell and Frank Capuzzi (trans.), *Early Greek Thinking*, New York: Harper & Row.
Heidegger, Martin (1991), *Nietzsche*, Volumes 1 and 2, trans. David Farrell Krell, San Francisco: HarperCollins.
Helmer, Étienne (2011), 'Les Épicuriens ou la sagesse de l'économie', *Revue du MAUSS*, 38: 445-65
Hicks, R. D. (1910), 'Epicurus and Hedonism', in *Stoic and Epicurean*, London: Longmans Green.
Hobbes, Thomas (1839-1845), *The English Works of Thomas Hobbes*, 11 volumes, ed. Sir William Molesworth, London: Longman, Brown, Green and Longmans.
Hobbes, Thomas (1844), *The English Works*, Volume 10, ed. Sir William Molesworth, London: Longman, Brown, Green and Longmans.
Hobbes, Thomas (1976), *Thomeas White's 'De Mundo' Examined*, trans. Harold Whitmore Jones, London: Bradford University Press.
Hobbes, Thomas (1983), *De Cive*, ed. Howard Warrender, Oxford: Clarendon Press.
Hobbes, Thomas (1969), *The Elements of Law, Natural and Politic*, ed. Ferdinand Tönnies, London: Cass.
Hobbes, Thomas (1996), *Leviathan* [Revised Student Edition], ed. Richard Tuck, Cambridge: Cambridge University Press.
Hoekstra, Kinch (1997), 'Hobbes and the Foole', *Political Theory*, 25 (5): 620-54.
Hoekstra, Kinch (1999), 'Nothing to Declare? Hobbes and the Advocate of Injustice', *Political Theory*, 27 (2): 230-5.
Hoekstra, Kinch (2007), 'Hobbes on the Natural Condition of Mankind', in Patricia Springborg (ed.), *Cambridge Companion to Hobbes's 'Leviathan'*, 109-27, Cambridge: Cambridge University Press.
Homer (1993), *The Odyssey: A Verse Translation, Backgrounds, Criticism*, ed. and trans. Albert Cook, 2nd edn, New York and London: W. W. & Norton Company.
Horace (2011), *Satires and Epistles*, trans. John Davie, Oxford: Oxford University Press.
Hume, David (1983), *An Enquiry Concerning the Principles of Morals*, ed. J. B. Schneewind, Indianapolis: Hackett.
Hume, David (1987), *Essays: Moral, Political and Literary*, ed. Eugene F. Miller, Indianapolis: Liberty Fund Inc.
Hume, David (1998), *Dialogues Concerning Natural Religion*, ed. Richard H. Popkin, Indianapolis: Hackett.
Hume, David (2007), *An Enquiry Concerning Human Understanding*, ed. Peter Millican, New York: Oxford University Press.
Husserl, Edmund (1970), *The Crisis of European Sciences and Transcendental Phenomenology: An Introduction to Phenomenological Philosophy*, trans. David Carr, Evanston: Northwestern University Press.
Hutter, Horst (2005), *Shaping the Future: Nietzsche's New Regime of the Soul and Its Ascetic Practices*, Lanham: Lexington Books.

Hutton, Sarah (1997), 'In Dialogue with Thomas Hobbes: Margaret Cavendish's Natural Philosophy', *Women's Writings*, 4 (3): 421–32.
Hymers, John (2006), 'Verteidigung von Feuerbachs Moleschott Rezeption: Feuerbachs offene Dialektik [In defence of Feuerbach's Moleschott reception: Feuerbach's open dialectic]', in U. Reitemeyer, T. Shibata and F. Tomasoni (eds), *Identität und Pluralismus in der globalen Gesellschaft. Ludwig Feuerbach zum 200. Geburtstag*, Muenster and New York: Waxmann Verlag.
Inwood, Brad. and L. P. Gerson, eds and trans. (1994), *The Epicurus Reader: Selected Writings and Testimonia*, Indianapolis: Hackett.
Inwood, Brad and L. P. Gerson, trans. (1997), *Hellenistic Philosophy: Introductory Readings*. Indianapolis: Hackett.
Inwood, Brad and L. P. Gerson (2008), *The Stoics Reader: Selected Writings and Testimonia*, Indianapolis: Hackett.
Inwood, Brad and L. P. Gerson ([2001] 2010), *Natural Goodness*, Oxford: Oxford University Press.
Inwood, Christine Sourvinou (2006), 'Elysium', in *Brill's New Pauly Encyclopedia of the Ancient World: Antiquity*, Leiden: E. J. Brill.
Jesseph, Douglas (1996), 'Hobbes and the Method of Natural Science', in Tom Sorell (ed.), *Cambridge Companion to Hobbes*, 86–107, Cambridge: Cambridge University Press.
Jensen, Anthony K. (2019), 'Nietzsche's Quest for the Historical Jesus', in Daniel Conway (ed.), *Nietzsche and The Antichrist: Religion, Politics, and Culture in Late Modernity*, 117–39, London: Bloomsbury.
Johnson, Ryan J. (2017), *The Deleuze-Lucretius Encounter*, Edinburgh: Edinburgh University Press.
Jones, Howard (1992), *The Epicurean Tradition*, New York: Routledge.
Jungkuntz, Richard P. (1962), 'Christian Approval of Epicureanism', *Church History*, 31 (3): 279–93.
Junttila, Henri (2013), *Find Your Passion: 25 Questions You Must Ask Yourself*, New York: CreateSpace.
Kant, Immanuel (1974), *Gesammelte Schriften*, 1–22 hrsg. von der Preussischen Akademie der Wissenschaften, Bd 23 von der Deutschen Akademie der Wissenschaften zu Berlin, ab Bd 24 von der Akademie der Wissenschaften zu Göttingen.
Kaufmann, Walter (1974), *Nietzsche: Philosopher, Psychologist, Antichrist*, Princeton: Princeton University Press.
Kirkland, Paul (2010), 'Nietzsche's Tragic Realism', *The Review of Politics*, 72 (1): 55–78.
Klosko, George (2012), *History of Political Theory: An Introduction*, 2nd edn, 2 vols, Oxford: Oxford University Press.
Knight, A. H. J. (1933), 'Nietzsche and Epicurean Philosophy', *Philosophy*, 8 (32): 431–45.
Kofman, Sarah (1972), *Nietzsche et la métaphore*, Paris: Payot.
Kofman, Sarah (1994), *Nietzsche and Metaphor*, Stanford: Stanford University Press.
Konstan, David (2008), *A Life Worthy of the Gods: The Materialist Psychology of Epicurus*, Las Vegas: Parmenides Publishing.
Konstan, David (2011), 'Epicurus on the Gods', in Jeffrey Fish and Kirk R. Sanders (eds), *Epicurus and the Epicurean Tradition*, 53–71, Cambridge: Cambridge University Press.
Korsmeyer, Carolyn (2002), *Making Sense of Taste*, Ithaca, NY: Cornell University Press.
Kostka, Alexandre and Irving Wohlfarth, eds (1999), *Nietzsche and the Architecture of Our Minds*, Los Angeles: Getty.

Krell, David Farell and Donald Bates (1997), *The Good European: Nietzsche's Work Sites in Word and Image*, Chicago: University of Chicago Press.

Krom, Michael P. (2013), in S. A. Lloyd (ed.), *Bloomsbury Companion to Hobbes*, 65–8, London: Bloomsbury.

Kudrass, Tiffany (2017), *When a Dream Turns into a Nightmare: Die Dekonstruktion des amerikanischen Traumes*, Munich: Herbert Utz Verlag.

Laertius, Diogenes (1931), *Lives of Eminent Philosophers*, Vol. II, trans. R. D. Hicks, Cambridge: Harvard University Press.

Laertius, Diogenes ([1925, 1931] 1958), *Lives of Eminent Philosophers*, Vol. II, trans. R. D. Hicks, Cambridge: Harvard University Press.

Laertius, Diogenes (2018), *Lives of the Eminent Philosophers*, ed. James Miller, trans. Pamela Mensch, New York: Oxford University Press.

Lahiji, Nadir, ed. (2014), *The Missed Encounter of Radical Philosophy with Architecture*, London: A & C Black.

Lakens, Daniël (2017), 'Impossibly Hungry Judges', *Nautilus*, 5 July. Available online: http://nautil.us/blog/impossibly-hungry-judges.

Laks, André (2018), *The Concept of Presocratic Philosophy*, Princeton: Princeton University Press.

La Mettrie, Julien Offray (1996), 'System of Epicurus', in *Machine Man and Other Writings*, trans. Ann Thomson, 89–116, Cambridge: Cambridge University Press.

Lampert, Laurence (1986), *Nietzsche's Teaching: An Interpretation of 'Thus Spoke Zarathustra'*, New Haven and London: Yale University Press.

Lampert, Laurence (2001), *Nietzsche's Task: An Interpretation of Beyond Good and Evil*, New Haven: Yale University Press.

Lampert, Laurence (2004), 'Nietzsche on Plato', in Paul Bishop (ed.), *Nietzsche and Antiquity: His Reaction and Response to the Classical Tradition*, 205–19, Suffolk: Camden House.

Lampert, Laurence (2017), *What a Philosopher Is: Becoming Nietzsche*, Chicago: University of Chicago Press.

Lange, Friedrich Albert ([1866] 2018), *Geschichte des Materialismus und Kritik seiner Bedeutung in der Gegenwart*, Vollständige Ausgabe: 1 & 2: e-artnow.

Langer, Monika (2010), *Nietzsche's Gay Science: Dancing Coherence*, Basingstoke: Palgrave Macmillan.

LeBuffe, Michael (2007), 'Hobbes's Reply to the Fool', *Philosophy Compass*, 2 (1): 31–45

Leddy, Neven and Avi S. Lifschitz, eds (2009), *Epicurus in the Enlightenment*, Oxford: Voltaire Foundation, University of Oxford.

Lemetti, Juhana (2013), 'History and Historical Knowledge', in S. A. Lloyd (ed.), *The Bloomsbury Companion to Hobbes*, 88–91, London: Bloomsbury.

Lessay, Franck (2007), 'Hobbes's Covenant Theology and Its Political Implications', in Patricia Springborg (ed.), *Cambridge Companion to Hobbes's 'Leviathan'*, 243–70, Cambridge: Cambridge University Press.

Lloyd, S. A., ed. (2013), *Bloomsbury Companion to Hobbes*, London: Bloomsbury.

Locke, John (1988), *Two Treatises of Government*, ed. Peter Laslett, Cambridge: Cambridge University Press.

Loeb, Paul S. (2010), *The Death of Nietzsche's Zarathustra*, Cambridge: Cambridge University Press.

Loeb, Paul S. (2017), 'The Colossal Moment in Nietzsche's *Gay* Science 341', in Paul Katsafanas (ed.), *The Nietzschean Mind*, London: Routledge.

Long, A. A. (1977), 'Chance and Natural Law in Epicureanism', *Phronesis*, 22 (1): 63–88.

Long, A. A. (2006), *From Epicurus to Epictetus: Studies in Hellenistic and Roman Philosophy*. Oxford: Oxford University Press.
Lord, Albert (1960), *The Singer of Tales*, Cambridge, MA, Harvard University Press.
Lucretius (1992), *On the Nature of Things*, trans. W. H. D. Rouse, Cambridge: Harvard University Press.
Lucretius (2001), *On the Nature of Things*, trans. Martin Fergusson Smith, Indianapolis: Hackett.
Ludwig, Bernd (1998), *Die Wiederentdeckung des Epikureischen Naturrechts: Zu Thomas Hobbes' philosopher Entwicklung von 'De Cive' zum 'Leviathan' im Pariser Exil 1640–1651*, Frankfurt am Main: Klostermann.
L'Yvonnet, F. (2008), 'Préface', in Jean-Marie Guyau (ed.), *Contre l'idée de sanction*, Paris: Éditions de L'Hermes.
Macfarlane, Robert (2013), *The Old Ways*, London: Penguin.
MacIntyre, Alasdair (2007), *After Virtue: A Study in Moral Theory*, Notre Dame, Indiana: University of Notre Dame Press.
Magnus, Bernd (1978), *Nietzsche's Existential Imperative*, Bloomington: Indiana University Press.
Malcolm, Noel (2004), '*Leviathan*, the Pentateuch, and the Origins of Modern Biblical Criticism', in Tom Sorell and Luc Foisneau (eds), *'Leviathan' after 350 Years*, 241–64, Oxford: Clarendon Press.
Mann, Joel E. and Getty L. Lustila (2011), 'A Model Sophist: Nietzsche on Protagoras and Thucydides', *Journal of Nietzsche Studies*, 42 (1): 51–72.
Mansfeld, Jaap and David Runia (1997), *Aetiana: The Method and Intellectual Context of a Doxographer: The Sources (Philosophia Antiqua 73)*, Leiden: E. J. Brill.
Marder, Michael and Adrian del Caro (2004), *Grounding the Nietzsche Rhetoric of Earth*, Berlin and Boston: De Gruyter.
Martinich, A. P. (2013), 'Scripture', in S. A. Lloyd (ed.), *Bloomsbury Companion to Hobbes*, 255–60, London: Bloomsbury.
Martinich, A. P. (2007), 'The Bible and Protestantism in *Leviathan*', in Patricia Springborg (ed.), *The Cambridge Companion to Hobbes's 'Leviathan'*, 375–91, Cambridge: Cambridge University Press.
Marx, Karl (1841), *Difference Between the Democritean and the Epicurean Philosophy of Nature*, Ph.D. diss., University of Jena.
McNeal, Michael J. (2018), 'Nietzsche on the Pleasure of the Agon and Enticements to War', in Herman Siemens and James Pearson (eds), *Conflict and Contest in Nietzsche's Philosophy*, 147–65, London: Bloomsbury.
Merleau-Ponty, Maurice (2002), *Phenomenology of Perception*, trans. Colin Smith, London and New York: Routledge
Mérimée, Prosper (1874), *Lettres à une inconnue*, Paris: Librairie Nouvelle.
Meyer, Susan Sauvé (2008), *Ancient Ethics: A Critical Introduction*, London: Routledge.
Michalski, Krzysztof (2011), *The Flame of Eternity: An Interpretation of Nietzsche's Thought*, trans. Benjamin Paloff, Princeton: Princeton University Press.
Milkowski, Marcin (1998), 'Idyllic Heroism: Nietzsche's View of Epicurus', *Journal of Nietzsche Studies*, 15: 70–9.
Mill, John Stuart ([1859] 2003), *On Liberty, Utilitarianism, and Other Essays*, Oxford: Oxford University Press.
Miller, Ted H. (2013), 'Opinion', in S. A. Lloyd (ed.), *Bloomsbury Companion to Hobbes*, 105–8, London: Bloomsbury.
Moleschott, Jacob (1850), *Die Lehre der Nahrungsmittel*, Erlangen: Ferdinand Enke.

Moleschott, Jacob (1852), *Der Kreislaufdes Lebens*, Mainz: v. Zabern.
Morel, Pierre-Marie (2000), *Atome et nécessité. Démocrite, Épicure, Lucrèce*, Paris: Presses Universitaires de France.
Morel, Pierre-Marie (2010), *Épicure*, Paris: Vrin.
Most, Glenn W. (1985), *The Measures of Praise: Structure and Function in Pindar's Second Pythian and Seventh Nemean Odes*, Göttingen: Vandenhoeck and Ruprecht.
Nail, Thomas (2018), *Lucretius I: An Ontology of Motion*, Edinburgh: Edinburgh University Press.
Nehamas, Alexander (2016), *On Friendship*, New York: Basic Books.
Németh, Attila (2017), *Epicurus on the Self*, New York: Routledge.
Nietzsche, Friedrich (1868), 'Beiträge zur Kritik der griechischen Lyriker', *Rheinisches Museum für Philologie, Neue Folge* 23, Frankfurt am Main: Sauerländer: 480–9.
Nietzsche, Friedrich (1868–1869), 'De Laertii Diogenis fontibus', *Rheinisches Museum für Philologie. Neue Folge*, Volumes 23 and 24 Jahrgang, 181–228, 632–53, Frankfurt am Main: Verlag von Johann David Sauerländer.
Nietzsche, Friedrich (1870), 'Analecta Laertiana', *Rheinisches Museum für Philologie. Neue Folge*, 25: 217–31.
Nietzsche, Friedrich (1870–1873), 'Der Florentinische Tractat über Homer und Hesiod, ihr Geschlecht und ihren Wettkampf', *Rhenisches Museum für Philologie. Neue Folge*, Volumes 25 and 28, Frankfurt am Main: Verlag von Johann David Sauerländer.
Nietzsche, Friedrich (1887), *Die fröhliche Wissenschaft*, Leipzig: E.W. Fritzsch.
Nietzsche, Friedrich (1896), *Philosophie im tragischen Zeitalter der Griechen*, in *Nietzsches Werke*. 2. Abteilung, Vol. X, 1–132, Leipzig: C. G. Naumann.
Nietzsche, Friedrich (1913), *Nietzsche's Werke. Philologica. Unveröffentliehtes zur antiken Religion und Philosophie*, eds. Otto Crusius and Wilhelm Nestle, Leipzig: Alfred Kroner Verlag.
Nietzsche, Friedrich, (1921), *Gesammelte Werke. Vierter Band, Vorträge, Schriften und Vorlesungen* 1871–1876, Munich: Musarion.
Nietzsche, Friedrich (1933), *Werke und Briefe: Historisch-kritische Gesamtausgabe*, eds. Karl Schlechta, Hans Joachim Mette and Carl August Emge, München: C.H. Beck.
Nietzsche, Friedrich (1954), *Thus Spoke Zarathustra*, trans. Walter Kaufmann, Viking Penguin.
Nietzsche, Friedrich (1962), *Philosophy in the Tragic Age of the Greeks*, trans. Marianne Cowan, Washington, DC: Regnery.
Nietzsche, Friedrich (1967a), *Basic Writings*, ed. and trans. Walter Kaufmann, New York: Modern Library.
Nietzsche, Friedrich (1967b), *The Birth of Tragedy* and *The Case of Wagner*, trans. Walter Kaufmann, New York: Random House.
Nietzsche, Friedrich (1967c), *Werke: Kritische Gesamtausgabe*, eds. Giorgio Colli and Mazzino Montinari, Berlin: De Gruyter.
Nietzsche, Friedrich (1968a), *Twilight of the Idols* and *The Anti-Christ*, trans. R. J. Hollingdale, England: Penguin.
Nietzsche, Friedrich (1968b), *The Will to Power*, ed. Walter Kaufmann and trans. Walter Kaufmann and R. J. Hollingdale, New York: Random House/ Vintage Books.
Nietzsche, Friedrich (1969), *Thus Spoke Zarathustra*, trans. R. J. Hollingdale, England: Penguin.
Nietzsche, Friedrich (1974), *The Gay Science*, ed. and trans. Walter Kaufmann, New York: Random House.

Nietzsche, Friedrich (1980), *Sämtliche Werke: Kritische Studienausgabe in 15 Bänden*, eds. Giorgio Colli and Mazzino Montinari, Berlin: dtv, De Gruyter.
Nietzsche, Friedrich (1982), *The Antichrist, Nietzsche Contra Wagner, Thus Spoke Zarathustra* and *Twilight of the Idols*, ed. and trans. Walter Kaufmann, *The Portable Nietzsche*, New York: The Viking Press.
Nietzsche, Friedrich (1986), *Sämtliche Briefe: Kritische Studienausgabe in 8 Bänden*, eds. Giorgio Colli and Mazzino Montinari, Berlin: De Gruyter.
Nietzsche, Friedrich (1989a), *Beyond Good and Evil: Prelude to a Philosophy of the Future*, trans. Walter Kaufmann, New York: Random House/ Vintage Books.
Nietzsche, Friedrich (1989b), *On the Genealogy of Morals*, trans. Walter Kaufmann and R. J. Hollingdale and *Ecce Homo*, trans. Walter Kaufmann, New York: Random House/ Vintage Books.
Nietzsche, Friedrich ([1986] 1996a), *Human, All Too Human: A Book for Free Spirits*, Volumes I and II, trans. R. J. Hollingdale, Cambridge: Cambridge University Press.
Nietzsche, Friedrich (1996b), *Selected Letters of Friedrich Nietzsche*, ed. and trans. Christopher Middleton, Indianapolis: Hacket.
Nietzsche, Friedrich ([1982] 1997a), *Daybreak: Thoughts on the Prejudices of Morality*, trans. R. J. Hollingdale, Cambridge: Cambridge University Press
Nietzsche, Friedrich (1997b), *Untimely Meditations*, trans. R. J. Hollingdale, Cambridge: Cambridge University Press.
Nietzsche, Friedrich (2005a), *The Anti-Christ, Ecce Homo, Twilight of the Idols and other writings*, trans. Judith Norman, eds. Aaron Ridley and Judith Norman, Cambridge: Cambridge University Press.
Nietzsche, Friedrich (2005b), *Thus Spoke Zarathustra*, trans. Graham Parkes, New York: Oxford University Press.
Nietzsche, Friedrich (2006), 'On Truth and Lies in a Nonmoral Sense', in Keith Ansell-Pearson and Duncan Large (eds), *The Nietzsche Reader*, Malden: Blackwell.
Nietzsche, Friedrich (2007), *Ecce Homo*, trans. Duncan Large, Oxford: Oxford University Press.
Nietzsche, Friedrich (2012), *Human, All Too Human II* and *Unpublished Fragments from the Period of Human, All Too Human II (Spring 1878–Fall 1879)*, trans. Gary Handwerk, Stanford: Stanford University Press.
Nikolsky, Boris (2001), 'Epicurus on Pleasure', *Phronesis*, 46: 440–65.
Nizan, Paul ([1931] 1960), *Aden Arabie*, Paris: Éditions Maspero.
Nizan, Paul ([1936] 1982), *Les Matérialistes de l'Antiquité: Démocrite, Epicure, Lucrèce*, Paris: Maspero.
Nuffelen, Peter van (2011), *Rethinking the Gods: Philosophical Readings of Religion in the Post-Hellenistic Period*, Cambridge: Cambridge University Press.
Nuovo, Victor (2017), 'Epicurus, Lucretius, and the Crisis of Atheism', in *John Locke: The Philosopher as Christian Virtuoso*, Oxford: Oxford University Press.
Nussbaum, Martha C. (1994), *The Therapy of Desire: Theory and Practice in Hellenistic Ethics*, Princeton: Princeton University Press.
Nussbaum, Martha C. ([1986] 2001a), *The Fragility of Goodness: Luck and Ethics in Greek Tragedy and Philosophy*, Cambridge: Cambridge University Press.
Nussbaum, Martha C. (2001b), *Upheavals of Thought: The Intelligence of Emotions*, Cambridge: Cambridge University Press.
O'Keefe, Tim (forthcoming), 'The Normativity of Nature in Epicurean Ethics and Politics', in Peter Adamson and Christof Rapp (eds), *State and Nature: Essays in Ancient Political Philosophy*, Berlin and Boston: De Gruyter.

Olivier, Abraham (2002), 'When Pain Becomes Unreal', *Philosophy Today*, 46 (2): 115–30.
Olshausen, Eckart (2006), 'Makarōn Nēsoi', in *Brill's New Pauly Encyclopedia of the Ancient World: Antiquity*, Leiden: E. J. Brill.
Onfray, Michel (2001), 'À ceux qui ne veulent pas jouir: Comment peut-on ne pas être hédoniste?', in *L'Archipel des comètes: Journal hédoniste III*, 267–82, Paris: Grasset.
Onfray, Michel (2013), *Les consciences réfractaires* (*Contre-histoire de la philosophie*, Vol. 9), Paris: Grasset.
Onfray, Michel (2017), *Décadence: Vie et mort du judéo-christianisme* (*Brève encyclopédie du monde*, 2), Paris: Flammarion.
Ong, Walter J. (1982), *Orality and Literacy: The Technologizing of the Word*, London: Methuen & Co.
Osborn, Ronald E. (2017), *Humanism and the Death of God: Searching for the Good After Darwin, Marx, and Nietzsche*, Oxford: Oxford University Press.
Overhoff, Jürgen (2000), *Hobbes's Theory of the Will: Ideological Reasons and Historical Circumstances*, Lanham: Rowman & Littlefield.
Overhoff, Jürgen (2013), 'Deliberation and the Will', in S. A. Lloyd (ed.), *Bloomsbury Companion to Hobbes*, 119–24, London: Bloomsbury.
Pacchi, Arrigo (1978), 'Hobbes e l'epicureismo', *Rivista Critica di Storia della Filosofia*, 33 (1): 54–71.
Paganini, Gianni (2001), 'Hobbes, Gassendi and the Tradition of Political Epicureanism', *Hobbes Studies*, 14 (1): 3–24.
Paganini, Gianni (2010), 'Hobbes and Renaissance Philosophy', *Hobbes Studies*, 23 (1): 1–5.
Paganini, Gianni (2013), 'How Did Hobbes Think of the Existence and Nature of God? *De motu, loco et tempore* as a Turning Point in Hobbes's Philosophical Career', in S. A. Lloyd (ed.), *Bloomsbury Companion to Hobbes*, 286–303, London: Bloomsbury.
Paganini, Gianni (2015), 'Art of Writing or Art of Rewriting? Reading Hobbes's De Motu Against the Background of Strauss' Interpretation', in Winfried Schroeder (ed.), *Reading Between the Lines – Leo Strauss and the History of Early Modern Philosophy*, 99–128, Berlin and Boston: De Gruyter.
Panaïoti, Antoine (2019), '*Comparative Religion in The Antichrist*: Pastiche, Subversion, Cultural Intervention', in Daniel Conway (ed.), *Nietzsche and The Antichrist: Religion, Politics, and Culture in Late Modernity*, 55–60, London: Bloomsbury.
Parkes, Graham (1994), *Composing the Soul: Reaches of Nietzsche's Psychology*, Chicago: University of Chicago.
Patton, Paul (1993), 'Politics and the Concept of Power in Hobbes and Nietzsche', in Paul Patton (ed.), *Nietzsche, Feminism and Political Theory*, 144–61, London and New York: Routledge.
Patton, Paul (2001), 'Nietzsche and Hobbes', *International Studies in Philosophy*, 33 (3): 99–116.
Pelz, Joachim (1996), *Und übrig bleibt das Nichts: Ein kritisch ironischer Streifzug durch Philosophie und Physik, von Parmenides über Kant und Heidegger zu Hawking*, Baden-Baden: Ergon.
Pfeiffer, Rudolf (1949), *Callimachus—Volumen I fragmenta*, Oxford: Oxford University Press.
Pfeiffer, Rudolf (1968), *History of Classical Scholarship: From the Beginnings to the End of the Hellenistic Age*, Oxford: Oxford University Press.
Pindar (1997), *Olympian Odes; Pythian Odes*, ed. and trans. W. H. Race, Cambridge: Harvard University Press.

Plato (1913), *Euthyphro, Apology, Crito, Phaedo, Phaedrus*, trans. Harold North Flower, London: Heinemann.
Plato (2005), *The Republic*, trans. C. D. C. Reeve, Indianapolis: Hackett.
Plato (2016), *The Laws*, ed. Malcolm Schofield, Cambridge: Cambridge University Press.
Plutarch (1967), *Moralia, Volume XIV, That Epicurus Actually Makes a Pleasant Life Impossible. Reply to Colotes in Defence of the Other Philosophers. Is 'Live Unknown' a Wise Precept? On Music*, trans. Benedict Einarson and Phillip De Lacy, Cambridge: Harvard University Press.
Polansky, David (2015), 'Nietzsche on Thucydidean Realism', *The Review of Politics*, 77 (3): 425–48.
Pollan, Michael (2007), *The Omnivore's Dilemma: A Natural History of Four Foods*, New York: Penguin Books.
Porter, James (forthcoming), 'Epicurus in Nineteenth-Century Germany: Hegel, Marx, Nietzsche', in P. Mitsis (ed.), *The Oxford Handbook of Epicureanism*, New York: Oxford University Press.
Powell, Eric A. (2015), 'In Search of a Philosopher's Stone: At a Remote Site in Turkey, Archaeologists Have Found Fragments of the Ancient World's Most Massive Inscription', *Archaeology*, July–August.
Powell, John Undershell and Eric Arthur Barber (1921), *New Chapters in the History of Greek Literature: Recent Discoveries in Greek Poetry and Prose of the Fourth and Following Centuries BC*, Oxford: Clarendon Press.
Power, Nina (2001), 'On the Nature of Things: Nietzsche and Democritus', *Pli: The Warwick Journal of Philosophy*, 12: 118–30.
Purinton, Jeffrey (1999), 'Epicurus on "Free Volition" and the Atomic Swerve', *Phronesis*, 44 (4): 253–99.
Rempel, Morgan (2012), '*Daybreak* 72: Nietzsche, Epicurus and the After Death', *Journal of Nietzsche Studies*, 43 (2): 49–68.
Reginster, Bernard, (2006), *The Affirmation of Life: Nietzsche on Overcoming Nihilism*, Cambridge: Harvard University Press.
Rhodes, Rosamond (1992), 'Hobbes's Unreasonable Fool', *The Southern Journal of Philosophy*, 30 (2): 93–102.
Rider, Benjamin (2019), 'The Ethical Significance of Gratitude in Epicureanism', *British Journal for the History of Philosophy*, 27 (6): 1092–112.
Ridley, Aaron (1998), *Nietzsche's Conscience: Six Character Studies from the Genealogy*, Ithaca: Cornell University Press.
Riedel, Manfred (1998), *Freilichtgedanken. Nietzsches dichterische Welterfahrung*, Stuttgart: Reclam.
Robinson, Ken (2009), *The Element: How Finding Your Passion Changes Everything*, London: Penguin Books.
Rogers, G. A. J. (2007), 'Hobbes and His Contemporaries', in Patricia Springborg (ed.), *The Cambridge Companion to Hobbes's 'Leviathan'*, 413–40, New York: Cambridge University Press.
Roos, Richard (1980), 'Nietzsche et Epicure: l'idylle héroïque', *Revue d'Allemagne et des pays de langue allemande*, 12 (4): 497–546.
Roos, Richard (2000), 'Nietzsche et Epicure: l'idylle héroïque', in J. F. Balaudé and P. Wotling (eds), *Lectures de Nietzsche*, Paris: Livre de epoche.
Rose, Valentin (1863), *Aristoteles pseudepigraphus*, Volume 1, Leipzig: Teubner.
Rose, Valentin (1868), *Anacreontis Teii quae vocantur Συμποσιακὰ ἡμιάμβια per il Literarisches Centralblatt für Deutschland*, Leipzig: Teubner.

Rosen, Frederick (2003), *Classical Utilitarianism from Hume to Mill*, New York: Routledge.
Rosen, Stanley (1995), *The Mask of Enlightenment: Nietzsche's Zarathustra*, Cambridge: Cambridge Unity Press.
Rosenbaum, Stephen E. (1996), 'Epicurean Moral Theory', *History of Philosophy Quarterly*, 13 (4): 389–410.
Roskam, Geert (2007), *'Live Unnoticed': On the Vicissitudes of an Epicurean Doctrine*, Leiden: Brill.
Roskam, Geert (2017), 'Diogenes' Polemical Approach, or How to Refute a Philosophical Opponent in an Epigraphic Context', in Jürgen Hammerstaedt, Pierre-Marie Morel and Refik Güremen (eds), *Diogenes of Oinoanda/Diogène d'Œnoanda: Epicureanism and Philosophical Debates/Épicurisme et controverses*, 241–70, Leuven: Leuven University Press.
Roy, Parama (2010), *Alimentary Tracts: Appetites, Aversions, and the Postcolonial*, Durham: Duke University Press.
Ryan, Alan (1996), 'Hobbes's Political Philosophy', in Tom Sorell (ed.), *The Cambridge Companion to Hobbes*, 208–45, Cambridge: Cambridge University Press.
Santner, Eric L. (1997), *My Own Private Germany: Daniel Paul Schreber's Secret History of Modernity*, Princeton: Princeton University Press.
Scarre, Geoffrey (1994), 'Epicurus as a Forerunner of Utilitarianism', *Utilitas*, 6 (2): 219–31.
Schacht, Richard (1985), *Nietzsche*, London: Routledge and Kegan Paul.
Schacht, Richard (1994), 'The Nietzsche-Spinoza Problem: Spinoza as Precursor?', in *Making Sense of Nietzsche*, Urbana: University of Illinois Press.
Schofield, Malcolm (2000), 'Epicurean and Stoic Political Thought', in Christopher Rowe and Malcolm Schofield (eds), *The Cambridge History of Greek and Roman Political Thought*, 436–7, Cambridge: Cambridge University Press.
Schofield, Malcolm (2007), 'Epicureanism and Politics', *The Classical Review New Series*, 57 (1): 179–81.
Schrift, Alan D. (1990), *Nietzsche and the Question of Interpretation: Between Hermeneutics and Deconstruction*, New York and London: Routledge.
Sedgwick, Peter R. (2013), 'Nietzsche, Illness and the Body's Quest for Narrative', *Health Care Analysis*, 21 (4): 306–22.
Sedley, David (1983), 'Epicurus' Refutation of Determinism', in *SUZHTHSIS: Studi sull'epicureismo greco e romano offerti a Marcello Gigante*, 11–51, Naples: Biblioteca della Parola del Passato.
Sedley, David (1999), 'Lucretius' Use and Avoidance of Greek', *Proceedings of the British Academy*, 93: 227–46.
Sellars, John (forthcoming), 'Self or Cosmos: Foucault *versus* Hadot', in Marta Faustino and Gianfranco Ferraro (eds), *The Late Foucualt: Ethical and Political Questions*, London: Bloomsbury.
Seneca (1917), *Epistles, Volume I: Epistles*, trans. Richard M. Gummere, 1–65, Loeb Classical Library 75, Cambridge, MA: Harvard University Press.
Seneca (1920), *Epistles, Volume II: Epistles*, trans. Richard M. Gummere, 66–92, Loeb Classical Library 76. Cambridge, MA: Harvard University Press.
Seneca (1925), *Epistles, Volume III: Epistles*, trans. Richard M. Gummere, 93–124, Loeb Classical Library 77, Cambridge, MA: Harvard University Press.
Serres, Michel (2018), *The Birth of Physics*, trans. David Webb and William Ross, London: Rowman & Littlefield Press.

Shapiro, Gary (2013), 'Earth's Garden-Happiness: Nietzsche's Geoaesthetics of the Anthropocene', *Nietzsche-Studien*, 42 (1): 67–84.

Shapiro, Gary (2016), *Nietzsche's Earth: Great Events, Great Politics*, Chicago: University of Chicago Press.

Shapiro, Gary (2019), 'Reading Dostoevsky in Turin: The Antichrist's Accelerationism', in Daniel Conway (ed.), *Nietzsche and The Antichrist: Religion, Politics, and Culture in Late Modernity*, 229–52, London: Bloomsbury.

Shearin, Wilson H. (2014), 'Misunderstanding Epicurus? A Nietzschean Identification', *Journal of Nietzsche Studies*, 45 (1): 68–83.

Slatin, Patricia (2014a), 'Epicurean Eternal Recurrence: No Reason to Doubt the Mortality of the Soul?', 24 June. Available online: http://www.carmentablog.com/2014/06/24/epicurean-eternal-recurrence-no-reason-to-doubt-the-mortality-of-the-soul/

Slatin, Patricia (2014b), 'Eternal Recurrence: Nietzsche and the Stoics', 12 June. Available online: http://www.carmentablog.com/2014/06/12/eternal-recurrence-nietzsche-and-the-stoics/

Small, Alastair and Carola Small (1997), 'John Evelyn and the Garden of Epicurus', *Journal of the Warburg and Courtauld Institutes*, 60: 194–214.

Small, Robin (2010), *Time and Becoming in Nietzsche's Thought*, London: Continuum.

Smith, Martin Ferguson (1996), *The Philosophical Inscription of Diogenes of Oinoanda*, Vienna: Österreichische Akademie der Wissenschaften.

Snell, B. and H. Maehler (1978), *Pindari carmina cum fragmentis*, Leipzig: Teuber.

Soll, Ivan (1973), 'Reflections on Recurrence: A Re-examination of Nietzsche's Doctrine, die ewige Wiederkehr des Gleichen', in R. C. Solomon (ed.), *Nietzsche: A Collection of Critical Essays*, 339–42, Garden City: Anchor Press.

Sommerville, Johann (2007), '*Leviathan* and Its Anglican Context', in Patricia Springborg (ed.), *Cambridge Companion to Hobbes's 'Leviathan'*, 358–74, Cambridge: Cambridge University Press.

Sommerville, Johann (2013), 'Works', in S. A. Lloyd (ed.), *The Bloomsbury Companion to Hobbes*, 24–8, London: Bloomsbury.

Sor Juana Inés de la Cruz (2009), *The Answer*, trans. Electa Arenal and Amanda Powell, New York: The Feminist Press at CUNY.

Sorell, Tom (2007), 'Hobbes's Moral Philosophy', in Patricia Springborg (ed.), *Cambridge Companion to Hobbes's 'Leviathan'*, 128–53, Cambridge: Cambridge University Press.

Springborg, Patricia (1996), 'Hobbes on Religion', in Tom Sorell (ed.), *Cambridge Companion to Hobbes*, 356–80, Cambridge: Cambridge University Press.

Springborg, Patricia (2010), 'Hobbes's Fool the *Stultus*, Grotius, and the Epicurean Tradition', *Hobbes Studies*, 23: 29–53.

Sreedhar, Susanne (2013), 'State of Nature', in S. A. Lloyd (ed.), *Bloomsbury Companion to Hobbes*, 219–22, London: Bloomsbury.

Stack, Gregory J. (1983), *Lange and Nietzsche*, Berlin and Boston: De Gruyter.

Stirner, Max (1995), *The Ego and Its Own*, ed. D. Leopold, Cambridge: Cambridge University Press.

Strauss, Leo (1983), 'Note on the Plan of Nietzsche's *Beyond Good and Evil*', in *Studies in Platonic Political Philosophy*, 174–91, Chicago: University of Chicago Press.

Strauss, Leo (2017), *On Nietzsche's Thus Spoke Zarathustra*, ed. Richard L. Velkley, Chicago: Chicago University Press.

Strodach, George K. (1963), *The Philosophy of Epicurus*, Evanston, IL: Northwestern University Press.

Swift, Paul A. (2005), *Becoming Nietzsche: Early Reflections on Democritus, Schopenhauer and Kant*, Lanham: Lexington Books.
Taylor, Charles (1992), *Ethics of Authenticity*, Cambridge: Harvard University Press.
Temple, William (1908), *Sir William Temple Upon the Gardens of Epicurus, with Other XVIIth Century Garden Essays*, London: Chatto and Windus.
Testa, Federico and Michael Ure (2018), 'Foucault and Nietzsche: Sisyphus & Dionysus', in Alan Rosenberg and Joseph Westfall (eds), *Foucault and Nietzsche: A Critical Encounter*, 127–49, London: Bloomsbury.
Thrasher, John (2013), 'Reconciling Justice and Pleasure in Epicurean Contractarianism', *Ethical Theory and Moral Practice*, 16 (2): 423–36.
Tolstoy, Leo (2010), *My Religion*, Guildford: White Crow Books.
Tongeren, Paul van (2018), *Friedrich Nietzsche and European Nihilism*, Newcastle upon Tyne: Cambridge Scholars Publishing.
Treiber, Heribert (1992), 'Wahlverwandtschafte zwischen Nietzsches Idee eines ‚Klosters für freiere Geister' und Webers Idealtypus der puritanische Sekte. Mit einem Streifzug durch Nietzsches Ideale-Bibliothek', *Nietzsche-Studien*, 21: 326–62.
Tsouna, Voula (2009), 'Epicurean Therapeutic Strategies', in James Warren (ed.), *The Cambridge Companion to Epicureanism*, 249–65, Cambridge: Cambridge University Press.
Tuck, Richard (1993), 'The Civil Religion of Thomas Hobbes', in Nicholas Philippson and Quentin Skinner (eds), *Political Discourse in Early Modern Britain*, 120–38, Cambridge: Cambridge University Press.
Tuck, Richard (1996), 'Hobbes's Moral Philosophy', in Tom Sorell (ed.), *Cambridge Companion to Hobbes*, 175–207, Cambridge: Cambridge University Press.
Ure, Michael (2008), *Nietzsche's Therapy: Self-Cultivation in the Middle Works*, Lanham: Lexington Books.
Ure, Michael (2009), 'Nietzsche's Free Spirit Trilogy and Stoic Therapy', *Journal of Nietzsche Studies*, 38: 60–84.
Ure, Michael (2018), 'Nietzsche's Ethics of Self-Cultivation and Eternity', in Matthew Dennis and Sander Werkhoven (eds), *Ethics and Self-Cultivation: Historical and Contemporary Perspectives*, 84–103, London: Routledge.
Usener, Hermann (1887), *Epicurea*, Leipzig: Teubner.
Usener, Hermann (1892) 'Epikureische Schriften auf Stein', *Rheinisches Museum* 47: 414–56.
Usener, Hermann (1977), *Glossarium Epicureum edendum curaverunt*, Roma: M. Gigante et W. Schmid.
Usener, Hermann (2010), *Epicurea*, Cambridge: Cambridge University Press.
Vercelloni, Matteo and Virgilio Vercelloni (2010), *The Invention of the Western Garden: The History of an Idea*, Lanark: Waverly Books.
Verkerk, Willow (2017), 'Nietzsche's Joyful Friendship: Epicurean Elements in the Middle Works', *The Agonist*, 10 (2): 25–40.
Vincenzo, Joseph P. (1994), 'Nietzsche and Epicurus', *Man and World*, 27 (4): 383–97.
Walther-Dulk, Ilse (2008), *De Guyau à Proust: Essai sur l'actualité d'un philosophe oublié*, trans. M. Dautrey, Weimar: VDG.
Walther-Dulk, Ilse (2014), 'Regard sur la réception de Guyau par Nietzsche à la lumière de ses annotations sur L'Irréligion de l'avenir', in J. Riba (ed.), *L'effet Guyau: De Nietzsche aux anarchistes*, Paris: L'Harmattan.
Warren, J. (2001), 'Lucretian Palingenesis Recycled', *The Classical Quarterly*, 51 (2): 499–508.

Wasserstein, A. (1978), 'Epicurean Science', *Hermes*, 106 (3): 484–94.
Webb, Mark (1985), 'Cicero's Paradoxica Stoicorum: A New Translation with Philosophical Commentary', MA diss., Texas Tech University.
West, Cornell (2017), 'Pity the Sad Legacy of Barack Obama', *The Guardian*.
Westfall, R. S. (1958), *Science and Religion in Seventeenth Century England*, New Haven: Yale University Press.
Wicks, R. (2018), 'Nietzsche's Life and Works', in E. N. Zalta (ed.), *The Stanford Encyclopedia of Philosophy*. Available Online: https://plato.stanford.edu/archives/fall 2018/entries/nietzsche-life-works
Winiarczyk, Marek (1984), 'Wer galt im Altertum as Atheist?', *Philologus*, 128 (2): 157–83.
Young, Damon (2012), *Philosophy in the Garden*, Melbourne: Melbourne University Publishing.
Young, Julian (2010), *Friedrich Nietzsche: A Philosophical Biography*, Cambridge: Cambridge University Press.
Zanker, Andreas T. (2016), *Greek and Latin Expressions of Meaning*, Munich: Beck.
Zick, Michael (2008), 'Platon-Schelte in Stein. In den Ruinen von Oinoanda fanden Archäologen eine Schmähung des Philosophen. Sie gehört zur größten Inschrift der Antike', *Die Zeit, ZEITmagazin*, 37 (4).
Zizek, Slavoj (2011), 'Hegel and Shitting', in Slavoj Zizek, Clayton Crockett, Creston Davis and Jeffrey W. Robbins (eds), *Hegel and the Infinite: Religion, Politics, and Dialectic*, New York: Columbia University Press.

Index

Abraham 116, 192
Academy, the 55
Acharya, Vinod 191
Achilles 120
akrasia 201
Alexander the Great 120, 173
Allison, David 58
amor fati 5, 39, 45, 48
Anaximander 16, 17
animals 2–4, 27, 29, 39, 49, 57, 93, 100, 114, 121–2, 134, 145–6, 196
anonymity 143, 152–4; *see also lathe biōsas*
Ansell-Pearson, Keith 1, 42, 98–9, 135, 190–1
The Anti-Christ 22, 72, 99, 111, 168, 207–8, 210
Apollo 59, 61, 111
Apollodorus 12
Archilochus 17
Aristippus 101–2, 104; *see also* Cyrenaics
Aristophanes 14
Aristotle 3, 7, 11, 12, 15–16, 18, 20, 26, 28, 53, 55, 76, 113, 126–7, 166, 173
asceticism 110–11, 159
ascetic priest 196–7, 213–14, 216–17
Asclepius 49
Assorted Opinions and Maxims/ Mixed Opinions and Maxims 47, 70, 131–2, 160
ataraxia 7, 42, 44, 48, 58, 60, 100, 112, 150, 161, 173, 190, 198, 208, 215–17; *see also* tranquillity
Athenaeus 32
atomism 3, 19, 32, 54, 114, 159
Aurelius, Marcus 61
autarkeia 150; *see also* self-sufficiency

Bacon, Francis 2, 118
Barber, Dan 33
Bayle, Pierre 159

beauty 3, 13, 20, 45, 47, 61, 103, 116, 155–6
becoming what one is 43, 130–3, 136, 138
Bentham, Jeremy 54, 161
Berchoux, Joseph de 32
Bergson, Henri 54
Berry, Jessica 135
Bett, Richard 75
Beyle, Marie-Henri (Stendhal) 162–3, 167, 169
Beyond Good and Evil 27, 59, 74–5, 99, 111, 118, 161–2, 176
Bible 116
body 44, 68–73, 76–7, 117–19, 144, 150, 152
 and earth 35, 39, 43–4
 embodiment 5, 33, 46–8, 72, 75–6, 96, 99, 145, 156, 162
 and mind 28, 36, 89, 94, 117–19, 192, 215
boredom 151, 155
Bornmann, Fritz 54
Brenner, Albert 178
Brobjer, Thomas 55, 139
Brod, Max 61
Brown, Kristen 74
Browne, Sir Thomas 58
Buddhism 7, 206, 217–18
Burkert, Walter 60

Callimachus 12, 52
Casanova, Giacomo 54
causality 196
Cavell, Stanley 53
Cavendish Circle, the 115
Caygill, Howard 57, 60, 101, 191, 199
chance 45, 104, 121, 143, 148–9, 156
cheerfulness 70–1, 152, 166, 169, 190, 200, 202, 205
Chinese, the 59, 161

Christ, Jesus 7, 55, 116, 205–12, 217–18; *see also* redeemer type
Christianity 59, 69, 74–5, 99, 110, 114, 121–2, 133, 143–6, 154, 161, 172, 202, 206, 217–18
Chrysippus 12, 14, 53
Cicero, Marcus Tullius 14, 34, 54–5, 106, 136, 215
Clay, Diskin 53
climate 39–44, 47, 69–70, 128, 176
commercial society 147, 152
conscience 30, 90–2, 120, 131, 152, 163–4, 197, 200, 216
   bad conscience 91, 122
   intellectual conscience 131, 168
contest 53, 119–20, 189, 201, 210
convalescence 49, 69–71; *see also* health
cosmology 28, 54, 57, 60, 81–3, 88–90, 119, 150
courage 7, 76, 82, 87, 89, 118, 143, 148, 152, 155–6, 162, 192, 199
customs 128–9, 133–4, 144–6, 149; *see also* morality, of custom
Cynics, the 28–9, 38, 60, 163, 173, 176
Cyrenaics, the 101–2, 104, 107

Darwin, Charles 161
Daybreak/Dawn 7, 30, 40–1, 43, 70–1, 75, 99, 120, 133, 143–4, 149, 155, 166, 177, 206
death 22, 49–50, 55, 58, 84–6, 106, 112, 120, 137, 144–5, 156, 172–3, 189–92; *see also* fear, of death
decadence 2, 7, 16, 36, 69, 99–101, 110, 191–8, 202, 205, 212–13, 216–17
Deleuze, Gilles 27, 54
Democritus 3–4, 17–19, 52–3, 55, 59, 190
demon 43, 90–1, 105
Descartes, Rene 2, 46, 71, 114–19
desires 1, 34, 41, 102, 110, 127–8, 137, 155, 173, 190–2, 196
   Epicurean classification of 27, 73–6, 149–51
determinism 43, 117, 149
Diels, Hermann 54–5
diet 29–32, 40, 56, 69, 75
Diocles 13

Diogenes of Oinoanda 53–4, 56, 62
Dionysius of Halicarnassus 15
Dionysus 59, 101
   Dionysian 12, 17, 22, 58–9, 99, 190, 194, 196
   Dionysian joy 1, 98–9, 111, 203
   Dionysian pessimism 61, 169
D'Iorio, Paolo 58
Donner, Wendy 135
Dostoyevsky, Fyodor 210

earth 4–5, 35, 39, 41–4, 48–9, 119–22, 145, 147, 174, 180, 217–18
eating as philosophy 5, 26–8, 31, 34–6; *see also* diet
   abomassum 27
   appetite 27, 118–19, 217
   autonomy 32
   kanṓn 32
   moral effects of food 5, 26, 30
   rumination 14, 27–8
Ebersbach, Volker 54
Ecce Homo 22, 30, 32, 40, 43, 45, 48, 69–71, 77, 132, 212
education 14–18, 21, 42, 72–6, 131–3, 138, 151
Egyptians 17–18, 27, 120
Empedocles 17, 55
Empiricus, Sextus 136
English, the 30, 193
Enlightenment 155, 195
ephexis 168
Epictetus 47, 59, 136
Epicureans, the 12, 14, 81–4, 86, 88–90, 122, 137, 159–69, 194, 197, 202–3, 206, 217–18
Epicurean sage 6, 14, 101, 103–4, 136
Eris 119–20, 199
errors 71, 147, 156
eternal recurrence/ return 5–6, 39, 43–5, 48–9, 57–8, 81–94, 104–7, 131, 191, 199
   continuity of memory 82–5, 94
   as a spiritual exercise 6, 81, 89, 92, 94, 104–5, 107
Euripides 14, 18
Evelyn, John 58
Ewin, R. E. 119

exaltation   146–7, 154, 156
existence   22, 39, 45, 76–7, 82–90, 97, 100–7, 136–7, 149–50, 156, 167, 189–93, 196–8
  of god(s)   60, 99, 111, 116–17
  justification of   145–7, 169, 199–200, 208, 211
  non-existence   82–3, 85, 87–8
experimentalism   148–50, 153, 155–6
Ezra   116

fanaticism   165–9
fear   3, 99, 112, 143–4, 146–8, 152, 154, 156, 160, 173, 198–9, 206, 208
  of death   77, 81–3, 87–9, 94, 101, 110, 113, 148–51, 155, 169, 213, 218
  of the gods   55, 60, 73, 164, 169, 216
  of the individual   145, 147–8, 151
  of recurrence   83–6, 94
feeling of power   147, 154
feelings   22, 74, 129–30, 145–7, 154–5, 194, 201
Feuerbach, Ludwig   28–9, 106–8
Foucault, Michel   54, 61, 137–8
Fouillée, Alfred   96–9
freedom   4, 44–5, 71–4, 83, 104, 112, 118, 120, 122, 146–55, 200, 213, 215
free spirit   49, 62, 70, 131, 163, 175–8, 189–96, 199–203, 212
free will   118, 196
Freud, Sigmund   58, 127
friendship   30, 45, 60, 113, 127, 178–9, 189, 194, 198–9

Galileo   2, 115
garden   1, 4–6, 26, 33–4, 39, 42, 44–7, 55–9, 111, 122, 136, 143, 149–54, 173, 176–80, 212–13
  philosopher of the   96, 99, 194
Gassendi, Pierre   53, 113–18, 159
Gaus, Gerald F.   116
The Gay Science   1, 30, 39–40, 43, 45–9, 57, 60, 62–3, 70–2, 75, 82, 90, 99, 111, 119, 131, 162, 167–8, 177, 206
genius   70, 120, 207
Genoa   39, 40, 46
geography (place/ location)   4–5, 39–48, 69–70, 213

gods   41, 45, 55, 58, 110–11, 117, 120, 146–8, 164, 189, 214; *see also under* existence, of god(s); fear, of the gods
  Epicurean   54, 58, 122, 136–7, 166
Goethe, Johann Wolfgang von   14, 111, 131
Goldschmidt, Victor   107
good (flourishing) life, the   4, 32, 75–6, 83, 125–9, 133–9, 149–51, 190, 193
gratitude   7, 45, 48–9, 143, 145, 153, 156, 177–8
greatness   3, 41, 43, 48, 86, 148, 195
Günzel, Stefan   58
Guyau, Jean-Marie   96–107

habit   21, 32, 44–5, 47–9, 76, 133, 146–7, 151, 161–2, 190
Hades   58, 164
Hadot, Pierre   45, 54, 60, 81, 86, 92–3, 99–104, 136–9, 155
happiness   34, 39, 42, 45, 49, 55–7, 61–3, 72–6, 96, 100, 111, 144–7, 153–5, 166, 172, 189–94, 199–203, 206–8, 212–17; *see also* pleasure
Harrison, Charles T.   114
Harrison, Robert   42
health   4–6, 27, 33–5, 43, 49–50, 62, 68–77, 100, 128, 133, 167, 189, 195–201, 212–16
  will to health   69, 72–3
Hecato   13
hedonism   73, 101, 107, 168–9, 202, 205–11, 214–18
Hegel, Georg Wilhelm Friedrich   27–8, 71, 159
Heidegger, Martin   1, 111, 135
Hellenistic period (late antiquity)   16, 139, 143–4, 164
Heraclitus   11, 55, 59, 119, 132
Hermarchus   50
hermeneutics   5, 62, 132, 209
Hermes   58
Herodotus   17, 110
heroic-idyllic   6, 47–8, 96, 111, 162, 172, 194, 205–6, 212
Hesiod   119–20, 179
Hieron of Syracuse   130

Hippocrates   17
Hobbes, Thomas   110–22
Hoffman, E.   45
Hölderlin, Friedrich   56
Homer   17, 55, 57, 106, 118
honesty   7, 143–4, 153–6, 167
Human, All Too Human   20, 34, 38, 49, 55–8, 60, 62, 70, 99, 111, 120, 131, 133, 161, 163, 166–8, 205, 211–12
Hume, David   54, 118, 159, 196
Husserl, Edmund   71

illness/sickness   7, 32–5, 38, 49, 68–77, 133, 192, 197–8, 205, 212–14
incorporation (*Einverleibung*)   27
individual, the   3, 43, 69, 92–3, 97, 114, 144–8, 151–2, 173, 191–9
individuality/individuation of character   3, 6, 29, 91–2, 97, 122, 125–40, 144
intellect   34, 60, 74, 144–5, 147, 154
intellectual conscience   131, 168, 202
internalization   121
Ionian region, the   16–17
Ionic dialect, the   17
Italian Riviera   39–40

Jahn, Otto   62
Jehovah   116
joy   1, 5, 39–41, 44–50, 71, 76, 90, 94, 97–107, 152–3, 169, 193, 199–203
justice   34, 99, 112–13, 116, 119

Kafka, Franz   61
Kant, Immanuel   3, 35, 71, 91, 115, 133, 161
Kaufmann, Walter   99
Knight, A.H.J.   98–9, 198
knowledge   2, 4, 13–15, 18–20, 27, 43–5, 57, 62, 81–6, 111, 127, 132, 143–56, 163–9
   passion for   3, 5, 7, 146, 153–4, 166, 169, 200
Kofman, Sarah   27–8
Köselitz, Heinrich (Peter Gast)   11–12, 15, 19, 22, 40, 42, 50, 56, 99, 179

Laertius, Diogenes   12–15, 52–6, 215
La Fontaine, Jean de   54

La Mettrie, Julien Offray de   159
Lampert, Laurence   120
landscape   39, 41, 44–9, 54
Lange, Friedrich Albert   114
Langer, Monika   71–2
lathe biōsas   40, 45, 172, 176, 178; *see also* anonymity
Leibniz, Gottfried Wilhelm   20
Lessing, Gotthold Ephraim   58
Letter to Herodotus   110
Letter to Menoeceus   110, 214–15
Letter to Pythocles   14, 110, 164
Leucippus   53
life-affirmation   39, 43–4, 49, 189–90; *see also amor fati*; eternal recurrence
limits   4, 33–5, 93, 127–8, 149–51, 172
Locke, John   54, 115, 118
Long, A. A.   93
Lorraine, Claude   47, 58
love   7, 35, 45, 48–9, 86–90, 125–8, 138–9, 145, 153, 163, 177–8, 199, 205–9, 218
Lucretius   6, 12, 54, 81–90, 94, 115
Ludwig, Bernd   113–15
Lyceum, the   42

Macfarlane, Robert   47
MacIntyre, Alisdair   120
madman, the   119
madness   145
magnanimity   7, 143, 148, 152–3
Magnus, Bernd   92
Marx, Karl   28–9, 54, 159
materialism   26, 28–30, 74, 118
memory   13, 72, 82–6, 94, 103
Merleau-Ponty, Maurice   77
metaphysics   2–3, 28–30, 32–3, 41, 60, 71, 84–6, 114, 118–19, 144–7, 154, 196, 199, 208
meteorology   41, 57, 60, 165
Meysenbug, Malwida von   178
Michalski, Krzysztof   101, 103–5
middle period writings (Nietzsche's)   1–2, 4–6, 38–40, 43–4, 70, 72–3, 96, 98–9, 127, 130–5, 143, 172, 177, 179–80, 189–92, 205
Milkowski, Marcin   101, 103–5
Mill, Harriet Taylor   134

Mill, John Stuart   6, 54, 126–30, 133–9, 161
Miller, Alice   58
Mimnermus   17
modernity   2–4, 19, 27, 122, 143–8, 159–60, 172, 174, 202
modesty   42, 45, 56–7, 59, 172, 215
Moleschott, Jacob   29–31
Molière   54
Montaigne, Michel de   54, 111
morality   2–3, 30–1, 35, 69, 71, 91, 110, 112, 115, 119, 122, 143, 146–9, 156, 173, 177, 193, 195, 199, 217
  of custom   133–4, 144–5
  individual-centric   144
Moses   116
multiplicity of hypotheses   41, 156, 164

naturalism   21, 54, 179–80
nature   2–4, 20–1, 29, 32–5, 42, 44, 81–2, 86–9, 92–3, 97, 112–19, 143–56, 180, 189
nearest (or closest) things   2, 39–49, 52, 148, 152
neighbour   44–6, 147–8, 153, 177
Newton, Isaac   2
nihilism   3, 105, 120, 193–8, 206, 215
Nizan, Paul   122
noble suffering   189, 196, 201; *see also* suffering

Obama, Barack   59
Odysseus   111
Okeanos   179
Onfray, Michel   110–12
ontology   74, 117, 119, 196
originality   12, 53, 122, 127, 130, 133–8
other-worldly   3, 45, 145, 147, 150; *see also* this-worldly
Overbeck, Franz   40
Overhoff, Jürgen   117

Pacchi, Arrigo   114
Paganini, Gianni   116
pain   1, 22, 33–4, 50, 73, 82–7, 99–105, 149–51, 160, 162, 173, 189–97, 201–2, 206–12, 215–18
Parmenides   17, 32

passions   99, 102–4, 116–19, 125–9, 135–9
perspectivism   76; *see also* multiplicity of hypotheses
pessimism   22, 61, 70, 111, 168, 197–8; *see also under* Dionysus, Dionysian pessimism
Philodemus   55
philology   12, 19–20, 52–5, 62, 116, 130, 167–8
philosophy
  as the art of living   34–5, 40, 73, 92, 101, 166, 172, 180, 194
  philosophical therapy   86, 173 (*see also* therapy)
  philosophizing as an activity   68–76
  as quest for knowledge   164–6
Phoenicians   17–19
phronēsis   7, 126, 143, 148–51, 176
physician   71, 213, 215
physics   4, 18, 32, 52, 81–6, 117, 150, 165
physiology   31, 75, 97, 128, 154, 207, 209, 213–14, 217
Pindar   54, 130–1, 179
pity   147–9, 153, 177–9, 190, 197–8, 203
Plato   3–4, 11–20, 26–8, 52, 55, 59, 77, 111–13, 118, 166, 173–9, 210
Platonism   2, 43, 45–6, 49, 202
pleasure
  Epicurean conception of   33–4, 48–9, 73, 100–3, 106, 150–1, 160–2, 173, 192–3, 214–17
  katastematic   34, 216
  kinetic   34, 212–13
  Nietzsche's critique of   190–3, 202–3, 205–13, 216–17
Plutarch   34
politics   33, 41, 59, 110–13, 118, 143, 151, 155, 172–5, 179–80
  great politics   1, 7, 172–4, 179–80
  petty politics   174
Portofino   63
Poussin, Nicolas   48, 58
present moment, the   43, 101–3, 107, 150
Presocratics, the   52, 54, 99, 106
pride   18, 145–7, 150, 153, 163
Prometheus   29

Protagoras   121
punishment   30, 106, 110, 113, 120–2, 143–5, 150–1
Pythagoras of Samos   17–18, 29

Queneau, Raymond   54

Raphael   12
redeemer type   205–13, 217–18; *see also* decadence
Rée, Paul   56, 160–1, 178
Reformation   46
Reginster, Bernard   84, 193
Reid, Thomas   54
Renaissance   46, 192
Renan, Ernest   207
ressentiment   48, 121, 193, 195, 198, 201, 213
revaluation of values   6, 35, 69, 174
rhetoric   5, 15–7, 20–1, 155, 198
Ritschl, Friedrich Wilhelm   52
Rohde, Erwin   54, 130
Roos, Richard   160
Rose, Valentin   15
Rosenbaum, Stephen   151
Roskam, Geert   173
Rousseau, Jean Jacques   21, 111
Rowling, J. K.   57

St. Moritz   40, 47–8
salvation   32, 116, 144, 146, 155, 168, 208
The School of the Educators   178
Schreber, Daniel Paul   58
Schreber, Mortiz   58
science   17–19, 29, 31, 53, 71, 113, 115–16, 143, 161, 191
 Epicurean science   1, 4, 59–60, 83–6
 gay science (as a concept)   7, 70–2, 166–9, 190
 modern science   2–3, 145, 154, 200
scientific spirit   5, 19–20, 146, 168
security   112–15, 143, 147, 151–2, 172–3, 195–9, 202
Sedgwick, Peter   72
self-alienation   3, 49, 152
self-cultivation   2, 4–5, 91–3, 129–30, 135–9, 144, 148–56, 177–80
self-knowledge   43, 93, 127, 138–9, 150

self-overcoming   189–91, 200–2; *see also* free spirit
self-sufficiency   7, 56, 143, 148–53, 190
Seneca   6, 12, 54, 57, 81–2, 86–90, 93–4, 136
Serres, Michel   54
Seydlitz, Reinhart von   38
Shapiro, Gary   58
Shearin, Wilson   190
Sils Maria   39, 47
Silvaplana   47
simplicity   21, 34, 41, 56, 152
Skeptics, the   135–6
Slatin, Patricia   84
Small, Robin   100, 102
social contract, the   5–6, 110, 113–16, 118–21
Socrates/Socratic philosophy   6, 11, 13, 16–18, 29, 52, 125–7, 144, 154, 173, 210
 the dying Socrates   49, 173
solitude   40–1, 70, 98, 112, 150–5, 176–8, 189, 194, 202
Sophists, the   13
soul   30, 42–50, 58–62, 73–5, 138, 163–4, 168, 180
 and body   28, 76, 118–19, 144, 148, 150, 215
 immortal/eternal   32, 41, 155
 mortal/finite   82, 86, 155–6, 172–3
Spencer, Herbert   161
Spinoza, Baruch   111, 169, 176
spirit   27, 29–30, 36, 41, 70–2, 117, 146–7, 149, 151–4, 168, 174; *see also* free spirit; scientific spirit
spiritual exercise   6, 81, 89, 92, 94, 100, 104–7, 136–9
Stirner, Max   97
Stoicism   5, 29, 45, 75, 82, 114
Stoics, the   12, 14, 21, 28–9, 59, 75, 81–2, 86–90, 107, 115, 161, 173
Strauss, David   58, 118
Strodach, George   113, 151
style (literary)   5, 11–16, 20–2, 38
 aphoristic   5, 27, 38, 56
 poetry *vs.* prose   15–20
 principle of clarity   14–15, 20–1
style (thinking)   4, 20–1, 154
 physical or material   4–5, 39–50

subjectivity   2–4, 44, 93, 143, 149
suffering   30, 39–40, 43, 49–50, 68–77, 82–9, 100–2, 111, 143–7, 153–4, 176–7, 189–202, 206–18
superstition   75, 101, 143, 167
swerve   4, 33, 54

taste   26, 30–6, 56, 74, 145, 155, 166, 168, 192, 203; *see also* eating as philosophy
telos   103, 145, 150, 193
temperance   76, 99, 144
Temple, Sir William   58
temporality   5–6, 96–108
Tennyson, Alfred Lord   54
tetrapharmakos   55–6, 73
Thales of Miletus   16–18
Theophrastus   12
therapy   75, 81–7, 96, 144, 154, 172–3, 175–80, 206, 208–9, 216
this-worldly   45, 145–7, 155, 211, 218; *see also* other-worldly
Thracians   17–19
Thucydides   18, 118
Thus Spoke Zarathustra   55, 57, 61, 68, 75, 104, 119, 131, 179, 191
timidity   147, 155, 210
tradition   15–19, 26, 125–9, 133–4, 144–6
tranquillity or serenity   4, 38, 41, 45, 48, 53, 82, 84, 101, 103, 106, 150–1, 155, 189–97, 200–3; *see also* ataraxia
transfiguration   72, 174–5
travel   4–6, 38–40, 46–8, 175
truth   1–7, 27–8, 41, 72, 118, 147, 154–6, 165–9, 176, 194
  of recurrence   82, 84–5, 90
  will to truth   2, 174

Twilight of the Idols   63, 74, 118
Tyrrell, James   115

Untimely Meditations   55, 58, 118, 131
Ure, Michael   105–6, 135
Usener, Hermann   54–5, 62
utilitarianism   107, 112–13, 122, 127

Villa of the Papyri   3, 22
Vincenzo, Joseph P.   48, 190
virtues   35, 63, 76, 82, 120, 125–7, 145–56, 176, 193, 199, 202
  Epicurean   5, 7, 41, 143, 148–56, 166, 168, 176, 211

Wagner, Richard   21, 56, 73, 131, 195, 206, 211
walking   38, 40, 44, 47
Walther-Dulk, Ilse   97–8
The Wanderer and his Shadow   41, 44, 47, 55–7, 70–3, 111, 120, 162, 164, 167
waste   32–3, 35
West, Cornel   59
White, Thomas   116–17
Wilkins, Bishop John   114
The Will to Power   74, 99, 111
will to power   1, 72, 101, 121, 199; *see also* feeling of power

Xenocrates   53

Young, Julian   73

Zarathustra   1, 45, 49, 58, 111, 131–2, 174–5, 179–80, 190, 211
Zeno   53
Zeus   122
Zizek, Slavoj   27

www.ingramcontent.com/pod-product-compliance
Lightning Source LLC
Chambersburg PA
CBHW050324020526
44117CB00031B/1769